TERRORIST REHABILITATION

The U.S. Experience in Iraq

TERRORIST REHABILITATION

The U.S. Experience in Iraq

Ami Angell
Rohan Gunaratna

CRC Press
Taylor & Francis Group
Boca Raton   London   New York

CRC Press is an imprint of the
Taylor & Francis Group, an **informa** business

CRC Press
Taylor & Francis Group
6000 Broken Sound Parkway NW, Suite 300
Boca Raton, FL 33487-2742

© 2012 by Taylor and Francis Group, LLC
CRC Press is an imprint of Taylor & Francis Group, an Informa business

No claim to original U.S. Government works

Printed in the United States of America on acid-free paper
10 9 8 7 6 5 4 3 2 1

International Standard Book Number: 978-1-4398-5249-1 (Hardback)

Library of Congress Cataloging-in-Publication Data

Angell, Ami M.
  Terrorist rehabilitation : the U.S. experience in Iraq / Ami M. Angell and Rohan Gunaratna.
      p. cm.
  Includes bibliographical references and index.
  ISBN 978-1-4398-5249-1
  1. Terrorists--Rehabilitation. 2. Terrorism--Prevention. I. Gunaratna, Rohan, 1961-
II. Title.

HV6431.A5394 2011
363.325'18--dc22   2011000172

Visit the Taylor & Francis Web site at
http://www.taylorandfrancis.com

and the CRC Press Web site at
http://www.crcpress.com

Contents

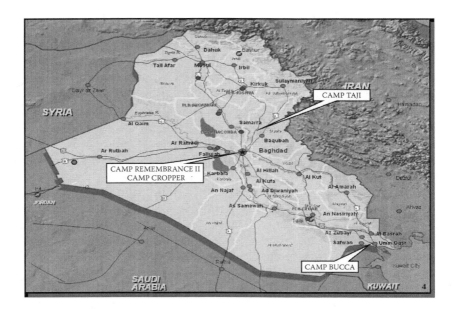

FIGURE ITO.1 Multinational Forces Iraq Theater Internment Facilities in Iraq where detainee rehabilitation programs took place from June 2007 through to the turnover to the Government of Iraq in 2010. (Slide courtesy of the U.S. Department of Defense.)

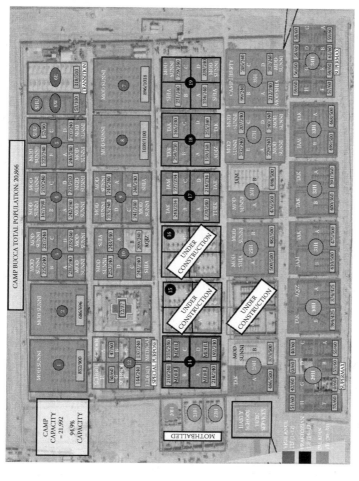

FIGURE ITO.2 The layout and population capacity of the Camp Bucca Theatre Internment Facility for Detainees as of January 1, 2008. Camp Bucca ceased operations on September 12, 2009, and subsequently has been deconstructed. Due to Camp Cropper and Camp Taji still existing under the Government of Iraq's control, it is not permissible to show their layout and populations. (Slide courtesy of the U. S. Department of Defense.)

Previous Detention Process
(Before July 2007)

1. An individual is captured under suspicion of being a security threat to the United States.

2. The individual's case is reviewed and if he is determined to pose a security threat to the United States, he is in-processed as a detainee.

5. Pending the Officer's decision and approval of the Commanding General the detainee is released.

4. After a varying period of time, a general officer reviews the detainee's file.

3. The individual is given detainment clothing and a Qur'an and assigned to a theater internment facility.

FIGURE ITO.3 The usual United States Detention Operations Procedure in Iraq from 2003 to 2006. (Slide adapted to explain process in more depth from original; courtesy of the U.S. Department of Defense.)

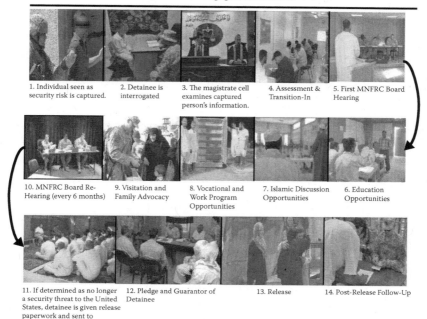

After 2007 Engagement Process

1. Individual seen as security risk is captured.
2. Detainee is interrogated
3. The magistrate cell examines captured person's information.
4. Assessment & Transition-In
5. First MNFRC Board Hearing

10. MNFRC Board Re-Hearing (every 6 months)
9. Visitation and Family Advocacy
8. Vocational and Work Program Opportunities
7. Islamic Discussion Opportunities
6. Education Opportunities

11. If determined as no longer a security threat to the United States, detainee is given release paperwork and sent to Transition-Out Class
12. Pledge and Guarantor of Detainee
13. Release
14. Post-Release Follow-Up

FIGURE ITO.4 The improved United States Detention Operations Procedure in Iraq from 2007 to 2010. (Slide adapted to explain process in more depth from original; courtesy of the U.S. Department of Defense.)

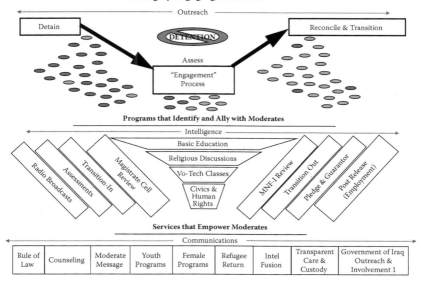

Winning by Engaging Moderates

FIGURE ITO.5 We will always be in a better position to win the fight against terrorism if we actively engage with moderate-minded ideological individuals. By encouraging and providing personal development programs, we can decrease the appeal of extremism while empowering individuals to become a voice of reason. (Slide courtesy of Maj. Gen. Douglas Stone, U.S. Marine Forces Reserve, Ret.)

Acknowledgments

The authors wish to thank all those who made this book possible. Through research and practical application of several countries' terrorist rehabilitation programs, both Dr. Angell and Dr. Gunaratna have arrived at the conclusion that the best and most humanitarian way of combating terrorism is to make terrorist rehabilitation programs an integral element in the global war on terrorism (GWOT). Although Dr. Angell worked for Operational Support and Services in the Iraq rehabilitation programs during 2007 and 2008, it was hardly enough time to span the many changes in the programs as they evolved quickly through trial and error, and under different leadership styles. Likewise, although Dr. Gunaratna contributed to the onset of the rehabilitation programs in Iraq (while head of the International Centre for Political Violence and Terrorism Research in Singapore and without significant field work in Iraq), it was difficult to understand the full complexities of running detainee rehabilitation programs in an active war zone. Consequently, in order to ensure the most accurate portrayal of the programs in Iraq, we felt it was necessary to interview a wide variety of people, including contractors, local Iraqi nationals (LNs), military personnel (officers and enlisted), and detainees directly engaged in the effort. The book is a reflection of the outcome of those copious interviews as well as numerous PowerPoint® presentations, notes, lectures, and documents gathered during Dr. Angell's 44 months working in Iraq and since her departure in September 2008. During 2010, Dr. Angell and Dr. Gunaratna also visited Saudi Arabia, Libya, Afghanistan, Sri Lanka, and Singapore to review the efforts being taken in extremist rehabilitation and to complement the research in Iraq. All of these visits had impact on the writing of this book.

First, we wish to thank Task Force 134, in particular Maj. Gen. Douglas Stone and Gen. David Quantock, who provided invaluable assistance in making available copious information (most of these conversations took place over long periods of time in multiple locations) and ensuring access to relevant documents and individuals. Gen. David Quantock also provided both of us the opportunity to revisit Iraq during

January–February 2010, which proved instrumental in personally under-standing the evolution of the rehabilitation programs. During our 7-day visit, we had the opportunity to visit the two remaining theater intern-ment facilities in Iraq at the time—Camp Cropper and Camp Taji—from which many of our interviews were taken.

We interviewed many people for this book, all of whom are listed in the back of the book under Interviews Cited. There are a few, however, who deserve special recognition for putting up with our countless que-ries when we were fact checking: Maj. Kevin Comfort: We couldn't have done it without your lengthy explanations. Lt. Gen. John Gardner: Your candor was needed and appreciated. Sgt. (Ret.) Brian Emmert: Thank you for always being willing to answer every question we threw at you.

Besides those mentioned above, Dr. Angell had the fortunate expe-rience of working with a dedicated team while a part of Operational Support and Services, the contracting company responsible in part for oversight, operation, and management of the rehabilitation programs in Iraq. Greg Guiney: Thank you for believing in me and giving me an opportunity to be a part of something so important. Ken Reidy: You were and will always remain an important part of the development of the rehabilitation process of detainees in Iraq. Your critical analysis of the programs and information-gathering techniques in addition to your thoughtful insights added a dimension to the rehabilitation process, which otherwise might have been neglected. Feras Khatib: Your con-tinued passion and loyalty to the programs and the local Iraqi nationals did not go without notice. Sheikh Abdul Sattar: You are and will always remain a key element in the success of Iraq's rehabilitation programs.

On the military side of the house, besides the obvious commitment of Maj. Gen. (Ret.) Stone and Maj. Gen. Quantock, there were a number of other individuals who made their mark in the rehabilitation programs. Col. James Brown and Col. Jim Williams were critical in that they car-ried out the concept of rehabilitation at Camp Bucca and made it work, while convincing the soldiers that it was a positive thing. Col. Carol Haas embraced the true meaning of acceptance and tolerance of released and reformed Iraqi detainees by excitedly giving Picasso* (a pseudonym for a previous detainee who was captured by the U.S. military and sub-sequently went through the rehabilitation programs and was released) a chance when none of the other commanders at Camp Bucca at the time was comfortable doing so.* Maj. (Ret.) Guy Jester, your 24/7 work atti-tude for the programs to get up and running went a long way in setting the path to their success. And, finally, the dependable and trustworthy

* An asterisk (*) is used throughout this book to protect the security and confidentiality of certain individuals whose lives might be threatened otherwise.

Task Force 134 liaisons, Dr. Angell and others at Operational Support and Services could not have done it without your support.

We also would like to give special thanks to those whom Dr. Angell worked with in the past who asked not to be mentioned in order to protect their security and confidentiality. You know who you are. Your thoughtful input and advice for the manuscript are invaluable.

Additionally, to Dr. Angell's colleagues (Andrea Holm, Brian Emmert, Daniel Marvin, David Butler Jr., Feras Khatib, Frank Ditchon, Gerald House, Jeffrey Folkertsma, Joseph Rodela, Matthew Sugars, Sonia Herrera, Timothy Linza, Paul Hunt, Guy Jester, and General (Jerry) Nelson Cannon who took the extra effort to dig through Iraq photos and send them to her, we thank you.

We are also appreciative of the cover photo by Andrea Holm and the author photos taken by Akanksha Mehta (www.akankshamehta.com).

Within the International Centre for Political Violence and Terrorism Research, we are indebted to Ava Patricia Avila, associate research fellow, and Ustazah Nur Irfani Binti Saripi, research analysts who spent tens of hours transcribing oral interviews so that we could extract quotes to enrich the text. In addition, we would like to thank Ustaz Mahfuh Bin Haji Halimi, also an associate research fellow, who was invaluable with helping us dissect terminology and references from the Qur'an appropriate to the manuscript.

We also are grateful to Mark Listewnik, our editor from Taylor & Francis Group, for his valuable advice, comments, and suggestions in the ordering and composition of the manuscript.

Finally, Dr. Angell would like to acknowledge that there are a significant number of other individuals who helped with this manuscript, one of whom includes Paul Hunt, her beau, whom she met in Iraq 5 years ago. There are not enough words to express my heartfelt appreciation for your love and support of my hectic 7 days a week and 12 hours a day work schedule over the past year in order to get this book completed.

In closing, we would both just like to say that our highest appreciation goes to those who are willing to put their lives on the line in order to work on making their country a better and safer place, free of terrorism. There were a core group of LNs (you know who you are) and the programs would not have succeeded without your passion and dedication. And, also to the many soldiers of the armed services of the United States who helped make the authors' commitment that much easier, this book is dedicated to all of you.

About the Authors

Ami M. Angell, PhD, LLM, is currently a research fellow at the International Centre for Political Violence and Terrorism Research in Singapore. She has spent a substantial amount of time working in the Middle East, including 44 months in Iraq (2005–2008) and 24 months in the Occupied Palestinian Territories and Israel. She also has worked and lived in Lebanon, Jordan, Qatar, Italy, Switzerland, and England. While in Iraq, Angell's primary focus was working alongside the U.S. military in detainee operations. She resided primarily at Camp Bucca, then considered the largest detainee facility in the world with over 20,000 detainees. As program lead for Operational Support and Services (OSS), she was responsible for the direct supervision and implementation of detainee rehabilitation programs to include religious discussion, education, vocational training, creative arts, and civics. This included daily active interaction with the extremist detainee population in addition to the hire and oversight of 150 local Iraqi professionals who lived on base and directly administered the programs.

In 2010 she was invited to Libya, Afghanistan, Pakistan, and (back to) Iraq to evaluate and advise on the emerging and evolving extremist rehabilitation programs and assess their quality. In addition to detainee rehabilitation, Dr. Angell is passionate about programs in capacity building, the right to education, human trafficking, and protection from torture.

Angell has a PhD in Public International Law from American University of London, an LLM in Human Rights Law from the University of Essex, an MA in the Theory and Practice of Human Rights from the University of Essex, and a BA in Theology, Philosophy, and Sociology from Newman University in Wichita, Kansas. She is originally from Oregon, U.S.A.

Rohan Gunaratna, PhD, is a specialist of the global threat environment, with expertise in threat groups in Asia, the Middle East, and Africa. He is head of Singapore's International Centre for Political Violence and Terrorism Research (ICPVTR), one of the largest specialist counter terrorism research and training centers in the world. He is also a professor of Security Studies at the S. Rajaratnam School of International Studies, Nanyang Technological University, Singapore.

A member of the steering committee of George Washington University's Homeland Security Policy Institute, Dr. Gunaratna is also senior fellow both at Fletcher School for Law and Diplomacy's Jebsen Centre for Counter Terrorism Studies and the Memorial Institute for the Prevention of Terrorism, Oklahoma City, Oklahoma. A former senior fellow at the U.S. Military Academy's Combating Terrorism Center at West Point, he holds a master's in international peace studies from the University of Notre Dame, South Bend, Indiana, and a doctorate in international relations from the University of St. Andrews in Scotland.

Invited to testify before the 9-11 Commission on the structure of al Qaeda, Dr. Gunaratna led the specialist team that built the U.N. database on al Qaeda, Taliban, and their entities. He was a debriefer of detainees in the United States, Asia, and the Middle East, including high-value al Qaeda detainees in Iraq. Author and editor of 12 books including *Inside Al Qaeda: Global Network of Terror* (Columbia University Press, 2002), an international bestseller, Dr. Gunaratna is also the lead author of *Jane's Counter Terrorism*, a handbook for counterterrorism practitioners. His latest book with Chandler, former chairman of the UN Monitoring Group into the Mobility, Weapons, and Finance, is *Countering Terrorism: Can We Meet the Threat of Global Violence?*

A litigation consultant to the U.S. Department of Justice, Dr. Gunaratna was a United States expert in the trial of Jose Padilla, a U.S. citizen engaged in terrorism.

Foreword

Throughout history there have been no shortage of movements meant to influence the thinking and behavior of large populations; today's battle for the Ummah's mind by violent Islamists is no exception. Understandably, not all of those whom the Islamists want to influence desire to adopt the radical perspectives being forced upon them. This conflict, this "battle for the mind," is being lodged by strong-willed, committed, often genuine believers who have self-radicalized on an extreme interpretation of Islam's most sacred texts. It is this radicalization process that should draw the attention of those who do not want to lose in this fight for recruits to fill the ranks of the forces committed to violent Islamist interpretations and behaviors. This book is a story and a study of one effort to understand the depth and complexity of the challenge that such radicalization processes can create, and to, in a very elementary manner, launch a counterinitiative with and for the less extreme members that make up the vast majority of the Ummah's mind set. This is a story of an effort to address the very fundamental challenge in this conflict, de-radicalization, both in large mass populations, in small cells, in cliques, and, ultimately, into the individual's own thought process. The Islamic and non-Islamic world alike, and any of those who care for our global humanity will want to read this book, consider its challenges in the full context of history, and ponder on its findings. The reader will want to consider the situational components of this historical challenge and, we hope, engage in support of the view that a global need exists for institutional programs, in every nation, that focus on de-radicalization and rehabilitation efforts, tuned to the unique needs of their own culture and challenge. The hope, in this age and in this movement, is that the true body of Islamic believers, joined by nation of supporters, will, with the de-radicalization tools now in place and being built on pioneering efforts discussed in this book, reach out to every corner of our globe and confront violent Islamists' behavior, and do so via a process of rehabilitation with de-radicalization as a central element.

In closing, it needs to be said that without question our efforts would not have been possible without the actions of very brave, very committed Iraqis and a grand host of contractors from many nations, including our own United States, who grasped the rehabilitation and reintegration concept, engaged the rigors of life in a combat zone, and brought change to a system, the detainees, and their families, and by doing so helped to ensure our mission's success. Likewise, in both Iraq and Afghanistan where the principles that we pioneered have now taken root in U.S. detention operations, it has to be made clear that the individual soldiers, marines, sailors, airmen and Coast Guard personnel from the U.S. Joint Forces are the real heroes of this effort (often from National Guard and reserve units joined by regular forces). However, it was and remains these committed and honorable men and women more often operating well outside their military occupational specialty, who see the changes needed, initiate those changes, evaluate the progress, suffer the hardships, and continue to serve their country in ways that only those who have had the privilege to serve with them can fully appreciate and admire. With these great patriots there is nothing our country cannot do in defense of the Constitution they so admirably serve, nor any innovation and solution they cannot find if allowed the opportunity and freedom of action coupled with a leader's support.

Maj. Gen. Douglas Stone was detention operations commander TF-134 in Iraq during 2007–2008, and was responsible in large part for the success of the detainee rehabilitation programs. He retired from the U.S. Marine Force Reserve in 2010 after 37 years of service. However, he continues to be actively involved in advocating the necessity of rehabilitation and deradicalization programs in detention centers and prisons worldwide.

Maj. Gen. Douglas Stone (Ret.)

Introduction

We are participants, supporters, and advocates of global rehabilitation of insurgents, terrorists, and extremists. Collectively and individually, we have invested our time and energy to make rehabilitation work wherever there are detainees and inmates. Our vision is to seed and strengthen rehabilitation and community engagement programs wherever insurgents, terrorists, and extremists are incarcerated or wherever those with militant views operate.

I, Ami Angell, began this journey in 2000 while working in the West Bank as a humanitarian worker with Defense for Children International/Palestine, a national section of an international child rights organization and movement. As an American, I was encouraged to travel to the West Bank after reading an article about human rights violations occurring there daily; I wanted to see if the accusations were true. From my experience of interviewing many Palestinian men, women, and children who had been detained by Israeli forces, I witnessed the limits of military power by Israel to change a mindset. Physical incarceration only will be a temporary solution to containing violence. Violence begets and ends in the minds of men, women, and children. No one is born a terrorist. A terrorist is made. And, I found that some Palestinians had actually become more ideologically extreme after their experience of being detained by Israeli forces. Not long after my experience in the West Bank, after completing an MA and LLM in Human Rights Law at the University of Essex in England in 2005, I had an opportunity to go to Iraq and work for a public relations firm in Baghdad. What I discovered while gathering information from Iraqi citizens was that those individuals who had been detained by U.S. forces were full of anger about the invasion and were more determined than ever to share their anger, whether that be through acts of violence against U.S. troops or even through just convincing family members that Americans are untrustworthy. Just as in the West Bank, in some cases, being detained had caused Iraqis to turn more ideologically extreme. I have no doubt that the United States unknowingly had a hand in the encouragement of religious extremism by methods of improper classification and separation of extremist detainees from those who were moderate in detention during the early years of the war.

Fortunately, I was offered a unique position to impact this theory when Operational Support and Services (OSS), a private company with a history of supporting the Department of Defense and other U.S. government agencies, hired me in the summer of 2007. As "program lead" of the detainee rehabilitation programs at Camp Bucca, Iraq (once considered the world's largest detention site with over 20,000 detainees), I experienced first hand the difference the correct classification separation and rehabilitation programs for detainees makes in detention operations. No longer were detainees trying to escape, hurting one another, and hurting the guard force. After introduction of the programs, detention center violence decreased by more than 50 percent. At the same time, intelligence gathered from the detainee population increased three times what it was previously. The rehabilitation programs were empowering to the detainee population. These programs effectively gave detainees a way to become better informed and better prepared for life after release. During my 44 total months in Iraq, I was fortunate to witness a complete turnaround of detention operations, in large part due to the introduction and growth of the rehabilitation programs, first by Maj. Gen. Douglas Stone and then by Maj. Gen. David Quantock, both Americans. In 2007, the U.S. military in Iraq was unsure of how the programs would be received by detainees, so we were authorized to permit only 20 local Iraqi nationals to teach the program curricula. However, the programs proved to be successful so quickly that, by 2008, I was supervisor to more than 150 local Iraqi nationals, including clerics, teachers, and social workers who directly implemented the programs. Some of these individuals had previously been detainees who had gone through the programs themselves. As a result of my experience, people have asked me how I know that the programs work. Well, the bottom line is that I don't. When you are dealing with hearts and minds, there is no black and white answer to that question. Instead, I have to go by what I see, hear, and experience. And, what I have witnessed, as this book will go into great detail about, has been the end result of: I don't *think* they work, I *know* they work. Based on my field work and academic studies, I am convinced that rehabilitation and deradicalization programs have the potential to positively impact thousands of detainees and inmates globally if utilized to their full capacity.

I, Rohan Gunaratna began my journey to Iraq with Ustaz Mohammed Bin Ali in late November 2006, with the invitation of Lt. Gen. John D. Gardner, who was then Task Force 134 commander of detention operations. As advisors to TF-134, both Ustaz Mohammed and I drew from our experience of terrorist rehabilitation to seed a rehabilitation program in Iraq. As staff of the International Centre for Political Violence and Terrorism Research (ICPVTR), a specialist center of the S. Rajaratnam School of International Studies (RSIS) in Singapore, which focuses on reducing the threat of politically motivated violence and at mitigating its effects on the international system, we have been fortunate to build capacity in rehabilitating terrorists. While terrorist rehabilitation has been probed previously in other countries with little success, Singapore has led the effort in successful terrorist rehabilitation since January 2002, when a group of Singapore Muslims were arrested and found to be members of Southeast Asia's terror network, the Jemaah Islamiyah (JI). The revelation shocked the public, as most Singaporeans never thought that such a threat could happen. In 2003, the Singapore government approached a small group of religious leaders to ask if they could counsel the detained members of the JI. Recognizing the national security implications of the JI's actions, the Ulama—led by Ustaz Ali Mohammed and Ustaz Mohamad Hasbi Hessan—formed the Religious Rehabilitation Group (RRG) to counsel these misguided Muslims. The RRG has since then developed an ideological counter to extremist ideology, which is used to educate the wider community against the dangers of extremism. The RRG is a group trained in religious counseling and counterideology in the hope that one day after years of religious counseling, the detained JI members will be released as mainstream and productive citizens. ICPVTR's special relationship with RRG enabled us to devise new strategies and evolved methods of addressing extremism and its vicious by-product—terrorism. After our visit to Iraq, I served as a consultant to OSS and its successor, The Line Group, LLC, on terrorist rehabilitation. At the request of Maj. Gen. Stone, I offered advice on improving and extending the ongoing efforts to rehabilitate detainees in Iraq. Our efforts to support rehabilitation programs in Iraq and elsewhere created the impetus for Singapore to host the inaugural International Conference on Terrorist Rehabilitation (ICTR) from February 24 to 26, 2009. Organized by ICPVTR and the RRG in Singapore, the conference attended by hundreds of delegates from around the world introduced several important avenues in envisioning terrorist rehabilitation as a global imperative.

Fortunately, both of us had the opportunity to test the longevity and continued impact of the programs in Iraq when we were invited to revisit Iraq in January 2010 by Maj. Gen. David Quantock. What we found was completely revamped detention operations, where rehabilitation programs played an increasingly important role. For their efforts, 2009 experienced no detainee escapes, only minor detainee-on-detainee violence, and a detainee recidivism rate of less than 1 percent. There is no doubt that the introduction and carrying out of the rehabilitation programs into the detention centers in Iraq altered the war effort. During 2010, we also visited Saudi Arabia, Yemen, Libya, Pakistan,

Afghanistan, Sri Lanka, and Singapore to review the efforts being taken in rehabilitation and to complement the research in Iraq. All of these visits also had an impact on the writing of this book.

In the complexity of today's global landscape, we feel it is increasingly more relevant to devise smart methods of addressing the terrorist threat. When we embarked on this project, our object was two-fold: (1) to highlight the success of a rehabilitation programs curriculum by the U.S. military to detention operations in Iraq, and (2) to encourage individuals and governments to embrace rehabilitation programs as the next most logical step in fighting terrorism. *Terrorist Rehabilitation: The U.S. Experience in Iraq* attempts to shed light on the terrorist threat in Iraq by first going into the recent history of threat groups in Iraq before briefly highlighting where the United States went awry in its war effort. Fortunately, the United States recognized what operations could be improved and took necessary steps to correct the situation, which Chapter 3 and Chapter 4 detail. When Maj. Gen. Douglas Stone arrived in the summer of 2007, the stage was ripe for changes. Through his efforts, rehabilitation programs to include the religious program, vocational training program, education program, creative expressions program, and Tanweer (Arabic word for enlightenment) program were introduced into the detainee population, all of which have a chapter devoted to understanding each program in detail. The final chapters discuss the best way forward based on lessons learned in current rehabilitation programs. For years, governments have been focused on detaining and imprisoning radical populations only, but we now know that if we do not address the ideological mindset during prolonged incarceration, the individual will only become more extreme. It is time to stop adding fuel to the fire. It is time to even the playing field.

CHAPTER 1

A Recent History of Iraq

THE EXTREMIST THREAT

While terrorism has been with us for centuries, the destructive power and global reach of modern terrorism are unprecedented. The potential for radicalization of desperate persons caught in a conflict they did not choose or understand poses a threat of unknown magnitude to the national security of the United States and the global arena. Foreign occupations of distant lands have long been places where extremist ideology and calls to violence could find a willing ear, and where conditions are often conducive to radicalization. If the post-September 11th world has taught us anything, it is that the tools for conducting serious terrorist attacks are becoming easier to acquire. The emergence of amorphous and largely unknown terrorist individuals and groups operating independently (freelancers) and the new recruitment patterns of some groups, such as recruiting suicide commandos, female and child terrorists, and scientists capable of developing weapons of mass destruction, provide a measure of urgency to increasing our understanding of the psychological and sociological dynamics of terrorist groups and individuals. Therefore, a background analysis of the extremist threat in Iraq—past and present—is essential, as intention and purpose remain an important factor in the continued evolution and challenge of rehabilitating extremists and terrorists as well as those in danger of becoming one.

INTRODUCTION

A controversial invasion, the U.S.-led coalition occupation of Iraq, which began on March 20, 2003, dramatically transformed the global, regional, and national threat landscape. No invasion in contemporary times, including the Soviet invasion of Afghanistan on Christmas Day in 1979, has had the profound national security impact as the invasion of Iraq. For Iraq, the invasion had multiple outcomes. The civil conflict produced human suffering, virulent ideologies, sectarian violence, internal displacement, refugee flows, and extremists and terrorists. The most enduring outcomes included (1) the origin and development of national and regional threat groups, (2) reorientation of groups to develop ideological and operational links with Al Qaeda, and (3) the relocation to Iraq of foreign threat groups, notably Al Qaeda. Today, these indigenous and foreign threat groups with extremist and insurgent capabilities pose a threat to Iraq, the region, and the world. Even after U.S. disengagement, Iraq presents a suitable climate and a fertile environment for the continuing presence of a diverse range of threat groups. A fountain of poisonous ideology and lethal technology, these groups continue to mount both domestic and international terrorist operations. An understanding of the complexities of the creation and execution of these operations is absolutely crucial in proceeding with a plan of action to counter the threat.

The Iranian Revolution (1979), the Soviet invasion of Afghanistan (1979–1989), the Persian Gulf War (1990–1991), the Bosnian War (1992–1995), and the U.S. invasion of Afghanistan (among others) all helped to radicalize a generation of Muslim youth. Still, the U.S.-led invasion and co-occupation of Iraq (2003–2010) radicalized an even wider segment of the Muslim community. Since the Iraqi invasion and occupation, Al Qaeda, its associated groups, and affiliated cells have utilized new media technologies to reach and radicalize a larger audience than was previously possible. Notably, the Internet was the medium for reaching a broader audience, but it was the use of media for advertising and promotion to recruit that was revolutionary. For example, Al Qaeda produced propaganda compact discs (CDs) professionally tailored to combine footage of real terrorist attacks with religious excerpts from the Qur'an to justify such actions. These CDs also contained real footage of Iraqi casualties combined with the images of Abu Ghraib prisoners, which were intended to inflame Muslim sensitivities (M. Alexander,* personal interview, November 4, 2009).* It is this proliferation of ideas, technology, and tactics in Iraq—both on the ground and in cyberspace—that will continue to sustain the global terrorist and extremist threat in the foreseeable future. In terms of the sustained and uncontrolled violence in Iraq, the suffering of Iraqis and their Muslim brethren worldwide, the spawning and reinforcement of virulent ideologies, and the global impact, there is no comparable conflict to the Iraq war and its aftermath.

---

* An asterisk (*) is used throughout this book to protect the security and confidentiality of certain individuals whose lives might be threatened otherwise.

THE CASE AGAINST IRAQ

Even before September 11, 2001, the political leadership of the United States appeared keen to invade Iraq. The U.S. intelligence community actively looked for links between Al Qaeda and Saddam as well as between Saddam and weapons of mass destruction (WMD). They could find none that were credible (Curveball, 2007, p. 19; Gunaratna, 2003). Meanwhile Saddam's security services sent Iraqi intelligence officers to join Islamist groups in order to report back the groups' plans and preparations. As the United States lacked comprehensive understanding of the threat groups, it misconstrued the presence of former and serving intelligence operatives—even within Al Qaeda-linked Kurdish Islamist groups—as Saddam's links to Al Qaeda. Perhaps worse, to continue to justify the invasion of Iraq, the White House then influenced the assessment(s) of the U.S. intelligence community. In fact, at least a segment of the international intelligence community still believes that Saddam worked with Al Qaeda and its associate groups in Iraq. Many years after the invasion, when the intelligence archives of Saddam have been meticulously examined, it will show that there is a small group of people who still believe that Saddam directed Osama bin Laden. Yet, these remain unsubstantiated comments based on misinterpretation of information derived during harsh interrogation or other unreliable sources, and which have not been corrected.

On February 5, 2003, when addressing the U.N. Security Council on the U.S. case against Iraq, U.S. Secretary of State Colin Powell, asserted:

> ... But what I want to bring to your attention today is the potentially much more sinister nexus between Iraq and the Al Qaeda terrorist network, a nexus that combines classic terrorist organizations and modern methods of murder. Iraq today harbors a deadly terrorist network headed by Abu Musab Zarqawi, an associate and collaborator of Osama bin Laden and his Al Qaeda lieutenants. ... We are not surprised that Iraq is harboring Zarqawi and his subordinates. This understanding builds on decade's long experience with respect to ties between Iraq and Al Qaeda (Powell, 2003).

Misinterpretation of intelligence, such as this, and the apparent lack of understanding of the Middle East led the Bush administration to invade Iraq, an event that would eventually compound the global threat.

Immediately after Powell, while at the U.N., referred to a facility allegedly manufacturing poisons and explosives at Khurmal, Ansar al Islam fi Kurdistan (Supporters of Islam in Kurdistan, more commonly referred to as "Ansar") invited journalists to visit and inspect the camp. This occurred on February 5, 2003 (Daragahi, 2003). And, in fact, it is very likely that the facility was used to experiment and train in the use of cyanide, ricin, and other poisons (McElroy, 2003). However, it is also known that this Al Qaeda-supported Kurdish Salafi group operated against both Kurdish secular groups *and* Saddam's regime. Even the International Crisis Group (ICG) report noted that there is little independent evidence of links between Ansar al Islam (a radical Islamic group in the Iraqi part of Kurdistan) and Baghdad (International Crisis Group, 2003). ICG also judged that it would be very hard for people or military supplies to pass between Baghdad and the Ansar enclave because a secular Kurdish group hostile to both of them controlled all the routes between the two.

The United States believed Ansar al Islam played a key role in linking Osama bin Laden's Al Qaeda network with the Iraqi government. This does not appear to be true. When the U.S. forces invaded Iraq, they were under the impression that Ansar was working with Saddam, thus chemical, biological, radiological, and nuclear (CBRN) means could be used against U.S. forces. In an attempt to build the case for the invasion of Iraq, the U.S. political leadership used counterterrorism intelligence that was apparently questionable and uncorroborated. This included the debriefing of Abd al-Hamid al-Fakhiri (alias Ibn al-Shaykh al-Libi, more commonly referred to as "al-Libi"), the Internal Emir of Khalden Camp in Afghanistan, who was captured by the Pakistani government in early 2002. Although al-Libi was not an Al Qaeda member, together with Abu Zubaidah, the External Emir of Khalden Camp, he worked with Al Qaeda after its camp was shut down in 1999. Because the Central Intelligence Agency (CIA) believed him to be uncooperative, it flew him to Egypt. The revelations by al-Libi contributed appreciably, *if not totally*, to the justifications that led to the U.S. decision to invade Iraq.

In September 2002, the CIA reported that al-Libi declared that Iraq had "provided" chemical and biological weapons training for two Al Qaeda associates in 2000, but "did not know the results of the training." Then, while still under CIA interrogation, in January 2003, al-Libi elaborated further: "Iraq, acting on the request of Al Qaeda militant Abu Abdullah, who was Muhammad Atif's emissary, agreed to provide unspecified chemical or biological weapons training for two Al Qaeda associates beginning in December 2000." The two individuals departed for Iraq, but did not return, so al-Libi was not in a position to know if any training had taken place.

A month before the CIA assessed these revelations as unreliable (Turner, 2005), Powell told the U.N.:

> Al Qaeda continues to have a deep interest in acquiring weapons of mass destruction. As with the story of Zarqawi and his network, I can trace the story of another senior extremist operative telling how

Iraq provided training in these weapons to Al Qaeda. Fortunately, this operative is now detained, and he has told his story (Powell, 2003).

The statement was repeated, both before and after the U.N. address, on several occasions. In a major Cincinnati speech in October 2002, Bush informed the public: "Iraq has trained Al Qaeda members in bomb making and poisons and gases" (Jehl, 2005).

After the U.S. invasion, al-Libi recanted claims of contact between Al Qaeda, Saddam's government, and the Iraqi training in WMD having been provided to Al Qaeda (Priest, 2004). On November 22, 2003, Egyptian service returned al-Libi to the CIA. In January 2004, after U.S. interrogators presented al-Libi with new conflicting evidence from other detainees, he acknowledged that while he was under interrogation in Egypt, he had deliberately misled interrogators. Al-Libi indicated that his interrogators did not like his responses and then "placed him in a small box approximately 50 cm × 50 cm (20 in. × 20 in.)." He claimed he was held in the box for approximately 17 hours. When he was let out of the box, al-Libi claims that he was told it was his last opportunity to "tell the truth." When al-Libi did not satisfy the interrogator, al-Libi claimed that "he was knocked over with an arm thrust across his chest and he fell on his back." Al-Libi told CIA debriefers that he then "was punched for 15 minutes." It was after all this that al-Libi told his interrogators that Iraq had trained Al Qaeda operatives in chemical and biological weapons, information that was later used in Colin Powell's speech to the U.N. Security Council to justify war with Iraq. A bipartisan report by the Senate Select Committee on Intelligence found that al-Libi "lied (about the link) to avoid torture" (HRW, 2009; also sourced to CIA Operational Cable on February 5, 2004).

The Defense Intelligence Agency (DIA) was aware of the possibility that al-Libi was misleading interrogators as early as February 2002, according to DIA declassified documents that emerged in November of 2005. They illustrate that, at the same time the administration was making its case for Iraq, the DIA did not believe the source of the U.S. government's repeated assertions that Iraq had provided Al Qaeda with chemical and biological weapons training. Moreover, the report asserted that it could no longer be sure there was a strong link between Saddam and Al Qaeda.

This is the first report from Ibn al-Shaykh in which he claims Iraq assisted Al Qaeda's CBRN efforts. However, he lacks specific details on the Iraqi's involved [sic], the CBRN materials associated with the assistance, and the location where training occurred. It is possible he does not know any further details; it is more likely this individual is intentionally misleading the debriefers. Ibn al-Shaykh has been undergoing debriefs for several weeks and may describing [sic] scenarios to the debriefers that he knows will retain their interest. ... Saddam's regime is intensely secular and is wary of Islamic revolutionary movements. Moreover, Baghdad is unlikely to provide assistance to a group it cannot control (Levin, 2005).

Interestingly, while the above information was known as early as February 2002, it would remain classified until November 2005. And instead, politicians would continue to repeat assertions that Iraq had provided Al Qaeda with chemical and biological weapons training, using it as a justification for the invasion and continued occupation of Iraq. On January 27, 2005, President Bush said, "Torture is never acceptable, nor do we hand over people to countries that do torture" (Mayer, 2005). Yet, what happened to al-Libi was far from the U.S. government's stated policy. Regrettably, it was the impact of the false information al-Libi gave interrogators (while under torture) that became one of the primary factors for the United States' decision to invade Iraq. It has been proved time and again that while being tortured, detainees and inmates will say whatever interrogators want/need them to say, and al-Libi was no exception.

THE CONTEXT

The United States-led coalition invasion of Iraq on March 20, 2003, created an uncertain global security climate, especially in the Muslim world. An unintended consequence of invasion was the emergence of Iraq as one of the most important global epicenters for insurgent, terrorist, and extremist activity. Another consequence was the overflow effect of the insurgency and extremist campaign into neighboring countries, threatening and destabilizing the region around and in the vicinity of Iraq. Yet another enduring outcome was the politicization, radicalization, and mobilization of a segment of Muslims worldwide, and their local and regional threat groups. The U.S. invasion of Iraq created an anti-Western Muslim transnational support base that helped to facilitate the transformation of Al Qaeda into a global movement. As the Al Qaeda family of groups seeks to identify its struggle as a jihad, it can be referred to as the global jihad movement. For informatics, the root of the word *jihad* is *juhd* which means *effort*. Another related word is *ijtihad* which means *working hard or diligently*. Jihad is simply the process of "exerting the best efforts," involving some sort of "struggle" and "resistance," to achieve a particular goal. In other words, jihad is a struggle against, or resistance to, something for the sake of a goal. However, some modern Islamic leaders, many of whom now have World Wide Web sites, have twisted and oversimplified this definition to take it a step farther, suggesting that it is the call of *Allah* to wage jihad against all oppressors. This has since evolved to a seemingly interchangeable definition of *jihad* with *holy war*,* a term which is more commonly referred to, referenced, and utilized by Al Qaeda operatives.

Interestingly, contrary to public opinion, Al Qaeda, the most hunted terrorist group in history, had established a presence in Iraq long before the U.S. invasion of Iraq in 2003. A few threat groups located in the north of Iraq, notably the Islamic Movement of Kurdistan (IMK) developed links with Al Qaeda in the 1990s. The Al-Ikhwan Al-Muslium (a.k.a. Muslim Brotherhood), a group that was born from and continues to have a strong and controversial presence in Egypt, has arguably been a contributing force behind IMK's strong link with Al Qaeda. After the terrorist training and operational infrastructure in Afghanistan was dismantled by the United States-led coalition intervention in Afghanistan in 2001, Al Qaeda and several other threat groups selected northern Iraq, a no-fly zone protected by the West, to establish a large-scale and enduring presence in Iraq. The Kurdish Islamists played a decisive role in planting the seeds, providing a platform, and launching a renewed campaign of insurgency. After the U.S. invasion, the threat from the Kurdish areas of Iraq percolated to the middle of Iraq, and then to the rest of the country. From Iraq, the threat from Sunni groups spread through the region and beyond. As the Sunni groups were the best organized, militarily and structurally, many Baathists (a.k.a. Arab Socialist Baathist Party, which identifies as a secular Arab nationalist movement opposed to Western imperialism in the Arab World, and continually seeks to unify all Arab countries in one state), especially former regime elements, and nationalists joined them. Both the Baathists and the nationalists organized and formed their own threat groups. The threat from Shia groups, including those sponsored by Iran, spread from the south to the center of Iraq. The IMK, the oldest threat group formed to fight Saddam Hussein (the secular and brutal dictator of Iraq), then splintered into multiple groups. These groups included Kata'ib al Tawhid (Brigades of Faith), Komala Islami Kurdistan (Islamic Society of Kurdistan), and Ansar al Islam fi Kurdistan (Supporters of Islam in Kurdistan). The latter worked with foreign fighters including foreign threat groups, such al Tawhid wal-Jihad (The Group for the Oneness of God and Jihad), which later renamed itself Al Qaeda in Iraq.

---

* According to Mahfuh bin Haji Halimi, holy war is not an Islamic term, but instead is a westernized explanation of jihad. Jihad is the phrase most commonly used to incite Muslim populations into action, usually violent, against non-Muslims (Mahfuh Bin Haji Halimi, personal interview, July 15, 2010).

The threat groups in Iraq can be divided into four classes: the Baathists (pro-Saddam Hussein), the Sunni nationalists, the Sunni Islamists (pro-Al Qaeda), and the Shia Islamists (pro-Iran). The Sunni insurgency is not a monolithic threat.* Iraq's most powerful Sunni insurgent group, Al-Jaish Al-Islamy (the Islamic Army), was founded in February 2004 (*Agence France-Presse*, 2008). The Al Qaeda-led Islamic State of Iraq (Dawlat al-'Iraq al-Islamiyya) was established on October 15, 2006.† Within the Islamic State of Iraq (ISI), Al Qaeda in Iraq was the largest (Kazimi, 2006). (*Al Qaeda claimed its strength to be 12,000 fighters, when in reality its hardcore was but a few thousand fighters.*) In October 2007, 23 groups came together to form the Supreme Command for Jihad and Liberation, led by former Iraqi vice president and deputy chairman of the Iraqi Revolutionary Command Council, Izzat Ibrahim ad-Douri.‡ The Sunni nationalists and Islamists feared the Shia-dominated government of Iraq. The threat groups, including offshoots of the Baath Party, such as Al Fatih Army (Jaysh al Fatih), assumed an outward

---

* The most prominent Sunni groups in Iraq were Salahudeen al-Ayyubi Brigades (JAAMI), Al-Fatihin Army, 1920s Revolution Brigades, Al-Qassas Brigade, Iraqi Jihad Union, Army of al-Mustafa, Dera Islam Brigade, Saad bin abi Waqqas Brigades, The Kurdistan Brigades, Al Qaeda in Iraq, Army of the Victorious Sect, Army of Ahlus Sunnah wal Jamaah, Ansar al-Islam, Islamic Army in Iraq, Mujahideen Army, Hamas of Iraq, and Al-Rashideen Army.

† The most prominent Sunni groups in Iraq were Salahudeen al-Ayyubi Brigades (JAAMI), Al-Fatihin Army, 1920s Revolution Brigades, Al-Qassas Brigade, Iraqi Jihad Union, Army of al-Mustafa, Dera Islam Brigade, Saad bin abi Waqqas Brigades, The Kurdistan Brigades, Al Qaeda in Iraq, Army of the Victorious Sect, Army of Ahlus Sunnah wal Jamaah, Ansar al-Islam, Islamic Army in Iraq, Mujahideen Army, Hamas of Iraq, and Al-Rashideen Army. Katbiyan Ansar Al-Tawhid wal Sunnah (Brigades of Monotheism and Religious Conservatism), Jeish al-Taiifa al-Mansoura (Army of the Victorious Sect), Monotheism Supporters Brigades, Saray al-Jihad Group, al-Ghuraba Brigades, al-Ahwal Brigades, Jamaat Ansar al-Sunna (formerly Jaish Ansar al-Sunna, Ansar al-Islam), ar-Rayat as-Sawda (Black Banner Organization), Asaeb Ahl el-Iraq (Factions of the People of Iraq), Wakefulness and Holy War, Abu Theeb's group, and Jaish Abi Baker's group.

‡ The Command consisted of the Army of the Men of the Naqshbandi Order, The Army of the Prophet's Companions, The Army of the Murabiteen, The Army of al-Hamzah, The Army of the Message, The Army of Ibn al-Walid, The United Command of the Mujahideen in Iraq, The Liberation Brigades, The Army of al-Mustafa, The Army of the Liberation of Iraq, Squadrons of the Martyrs, The Army of the Sabireen, The Brigades of the Jihad in the Land of the Two Rivers, The Army of the Knight for the Liberation of the Self-Rule Area, Squadrons of the Jihad in Basra, Jihadist Squadrons of Fallujah, The Patriotic Popular Front for the Liberation of Iraq, The Squadrons of the Husayni Revolution of at-Taff, Squadrons of the Liberation of the South, Army of Haneen, Squadrons of Diyala for Jihad and Liberation, The Squadrons of Glory for the Liberation of Iraq, and Kurdistan Liberation Army.

Islamic character.* The Shia groups fought both the Sunni groups and the U.S.-led coalition.† Two dozen well-structured groups worked with nearly 100 smaller groups to make Iraq the most violent conflict in the world. The insurgency peaked in 2006 and 2007, but has declined since. While at its peak, U.S. military estimates of the insurgency ranged from 8,000 to 20,000, although Iraqi intelligence officials have issued figures as high as 40,000 fighters plus another 160,000 supporters (*BBC News*, August 2006). At this time, the most lethal threat groups in Iraq were Al Qaeda, which reported 2,000 to 3,500 fighters and Ansar al Islam with 3,000 to 4,000 fighters. Of the nearly 100 threat groups, Al Qaeda and Al Ansar belong to the strain of groups that are ideologically resilient, experienced, and networked. Therefore, they are likely to last long after the other groups have been dismantled and/or have abandoned violence. This chapter outlines the origins, development, and international linkages of these two most significant threat groups in Iraq during the Saddam and the post-Saddam periods, and assesses their likely continued impact as the country struggles with the slow withdrawal of U.S. forces.

BACKGROUND

Kurdish Islamism emerged not only from a mix of global Islamist movements supported by the Muslim Brotherhood and the efforts of Saddam to quash them, but also largely as a response to Saddam's dictatorship that discriminated against and persecuted the Kurds. During the anti-Soviet, multinational Afghan mujahidin (*mujahidin* is the plural form of *mujahid*, which literally translates as *struggler, justice-fighter* or *freedom-fighter*; basically, it is a person who is fighting for freedom) campaign from 1979 to 1989, the Kurdish Islamists from Iraq established links with foreign fighters in Afghanistan. Their natural points of contact and interface were Afghan and Pakistani groups as well as with the Arab groups. The Kurdish Islamists worked with Abdul Rabi Rasul Sayyaf's Ittehad-e Islami that formed in 1981 and Abdullah Azzam's Maktab-il-khidamat (MaK, a.k.a. Afghan Service Bureau)

---

* The Baathist groups include Fedayeen Saddam (Saddam's Men of Sacrifice), al-Awda (The Return), General Command of the Armed Forces, Resistance and Liberation in Iraq, Iraqi Popular Army, New Return, Patriotic Front, Jihaz al-Iilam al-Siasi lil hizb al-Baath (Political Media Organ of the Ba'ath Party), Popular Resistance for the Liberation of Iraq, and Al-Abud Network.
† The Shia groups were Mahdi Army (Jaish al-Mahdi aka JAM); its faction, Abu Deraa; Badr Organization (Badr Brigade/Bader Corps), the armed wing of the Supreme Council for the Islamic Revolution in Iraq (SCIRI); Jund As-Samaa (Soldiers of Heaven/Supporters of the Mahdi); Asaeb Ahl Al-Haq (League of the Righteous People); and other special groups backed by Iran.

that formed in 1984 (A. Paghman, personal interview, 2008). Unlike the other Afghan commanders, Sayyaf was educated in the Middle East and worked closely with the Arabs and other foreign fighters, including Kurds. One Arab he worked closely with was Nashwan Abdulrazaq Abdulbaqi (alias Abdal Hadi al Iraqi) from Mosul, a former major of Saddam's army who claimed responsibility for downing an American fighter jet in Afghanistan in 2005 (Baier, 2005). Abdal Hadi gave up his Baathist leanings and joined the mujahidin fighting the Soviet army in Afghanistan during the late 1980s. He then served as an instructor in Sayyaf's Sadda camp in Pakistan. He was described as one of Osama Bin Laden's top global deputies. While many mujahid remained to serve the cause in Afghanistan, others returned to serve the Islamist movements in their own countries; Sa'adoon Mohammed Abdul Latif (alias Abu Wa'il), an Iraqi intelligence officer, was another example of intelligentsia who abandoned Saddam's service and instead turned to Ansar Al Islam. Najmeddin Faraj Ahmad (alias Mullah Krekar) was a Kurd from the Iraqi province of Al Sulaymaniyah and studied jurisprudence under Azzam. As MaK evolved into Al Qaeda, Azzam's deputy and successor, Osama bin Laden, took over the leadership.* Although the leadership of Al Qaeda was Arab during the formative years, as it grew it established links with both Arab and non-Arab Muslim groups in fighting both Muslim and non-Muslim regimes worldwide.

After the Soviets withdrew in February 1989, a few thousand foreigners remained on the Afghanistan–Pakistan border. Those remaining in this area included some "5,000 Saudis, 3,000 Yemenis, 2,000 Egyptians, 2,800 Algerians, 400 Tunisians, 370 Iraqis, 200 Libyans, and scores of Jordanians" (Bruce, 1995, p. 175). Among the Iraqis, only a few had joined Al Qaeda. After serving with Sayyaf to fight the Soviets, Abdal Hadi al Iraqi joined Al Qaeda in training and in dispatching fighters (including dispatches to Chechnya), and contributed to the *Encyclopedia of Jihad.*† As a commander and accountant for Al Qaeda,

---

* According to the Al Qaeda founding documents recovered from Bosnia, since the creation of Al Qaeda (The Base) in Peshawar, Pakistan on August 18, 1988, Al Qaeda was led by Osama bin Laden, a former citizen of Saudi Arabia. (International Centre for Political Violence and Terrorism Research (ICPVTR) database, Singapore (www.pvtr. org)).

† The Encyclopedia of Jihad, a manual of 10 or 11 volumes, is a lengthy textbook for jihadists-in-training allegedly compiled by Osama Bin Laden and his operatives. The encyclopedia details how to make explosives, fire guns, target areas with maximum casualties, conduct assassinations, and stage ambushes, among many others. A copy was discovered in May of 2004 at the London residence of Islamic Sheikh Abu Hamza al-Masri, who subsequently was convicted in 2006 on several charges including "one count of possessing an item of potential use in an act of terrorism," referring to the encyclopedia. The original had reputedly been stolen from the headquarters of Osama Bin Laden's fighters in Kandahar, also the home base of Afghanistan's Taliban rulers.

Abdal Hadi ran both the Al Qaeda army and maintained an office in the Ashara guest house in Kart-E-Parwan Province in Kabul, Afghanistan. He rose rapidly inside Al Qaeda's hierarchy to later become the head of Al Qaeda's military forces in the Kabul area (*United States of America v. Abdul Zahir*, 2006). With determination, he then rose to join Al Qaeda's Majlis Shura (consultative council), its highest decision-making body. As a Kurd, he was the only non-Arab to serve on Al Qaeda's apex council. After marrying a local woman and fathering a son, Abdal Hadi settled down in Peshawar and later in Kabul, where he maintained links with both the Iraqi Sunnis and Iraqi Kurds.

A multinational group, Al Qaeda historically resided in non-Arab lands, and operated both in Arab and non-Arab lands (to include Iraq, Chechnya, Algeria, Somalia, Saudi Arabia, Yemen, and a dozen others). After Al Qaeda relocated to Khartoum, Sudan, in 1991, an Al Qaeda instructor visited northern Iraq and trained those in the IMK. The training course conducted in 1992 was the first known formal contact between Al Qaeda and IMK. These links between Al Qaeda and IMK persisted throughout the 1990s. Intermittently, both Iraqi Sunnis and Kurds traveled to Pakistan to either train or join Al Qaeda and Taliban to fight against the Northern Alliance. As one of the commanders in the frontline, Abdal Hadi al Iraqi, commanded 200 Afghans, Arabs, and other foreigners, including Iraqi Sunnis and Iraqi Kurds (Mazzetti and Cloud, 2007; U.S. Defense Department, 2007). Contact between northern Iraq and Al Qaeda took many facets. Through delegations and individuals that visited with Osama bin Laden, IMK dispatched videos of the atrocities committed by Saddam in the north of Iraq and the suffering of the Kurds. Of the 250 videotapes recovered by CNN in Afghanistan, at least two tapes were IMK or pro-IMK (Robertson and Boettcher, 2002; *BBC News*, August 2002).

After Al Qaeda's September 11, 2001 most symbolic attacks on America's landmarks, the ideological and operational links between the Kurdish Islamists and Al Qaeda intensified. Thereafter, following the U.S. coalition response in October 2001, a segment of the Al Qaeda leadership moved to tribal Pakistan and to Iran (Shrader, 2007). There, under international pressure, Iran began to crack down on the Al Qaeda presence in its country. Because of this, a few hundred foreign fighters (including Al Qaeda members) moved through Iran and settled in northern Iraq, a safe haven from Saddam Hussein's atrocities. Although the global footprint of Al Qaeda included Iraq, the Kurdish Islamist groups were opposed to Saddam. If not for that safe haven, established north of Iraq's 36th parallel after the 1991 Gulf War, Saddam's military would very probably have dismantled the Islamist groups (Hedges, 1996).

ORIGINS AND DEVELOPMENT OF THREAT GROUPS

Poor governance led to the emergence of Kurdist separatist and subsequently Islamist groups in the 1980s. During the Iran–Iraq war from September 1980 to August 1988, a segment of the Kurds in the north of Iraq did not support Saddam Hussein, the then-ruler of Iraq. In response to the rebellion in Kurdistan, Saddam Hussein launched al Anfal, a campaign in Iraqi Kurdistan beginning in 1986. Kurdish Islamists from Iraq gathered in Dizly, Iran, to form the IMK in 1987. Together with his brothers (Ali, Osman, Sadik, and Omar), Osman Abdul Aziz founded it. An imposing person, Osman was also joined by Ahmed Kaka Mohamed, Sheikh Mohamed Barzinjy, Ali Papier, and other leaders. Iran's Ministry of Intelligence and National Security (known as Etelaat) supported IMK at its formation. Saddam responded by campaigning against the Kurds in Iraq's Kurdish north, resulting in the death of 30,000 Kurds between the years of 1986 and 1989. His campaign of terror included the use of chemical agents—the worst incident occurring in March 1988 in Halabja, a town in the Sulaymaniyah Governorate, located about 10 miles from the Iranian border. The attack instantly killed thousands of people (3,000–5,000) and injured between 7,000 and 10,000 more. Thousands more died of complications, diseases, and birth defects in the years after the attack, which occurred right as the Iraq–Iran war drew to a close. As of this writing, it was the largest chemical weapons attack directed against a civilian populated area in history.

Kurdish Islamists not only benefited from Iran, but also from the developments in Afghanistan. Several dozen Kurds traveled to Pakistan and fought against the Soviets throughout the 1980s. Since 1988, both leaders and members of the IMK have traveled to Peshawar. Initially, they were with the Arabs, but then they formed Darul Akrad (House of Kurds). The most prominent leaders were Mullah Krekar, Abu Abdallah al Shafi'i (alias Warba Holiri al-Kurdi), Azo Hawleri, Ayyub Afghani, and Omar Baziany, all of whom can be seen in several photographs hanging in various political offices in Afghanistan (according to representatives from the Security Service of Kurdistan, 2009).

Without exception, they all became significant leaders in Kurdish Islamist movements over the next decade. Together with the Afghan veterans, IMK members were determined and motivated to fight the Saddam regime. Supported by Etelaat, IMK entered Iraq in 1989 and relocated itself in Halabja. IMK leaders exercised their influence by preaching jihad; showing photos and screening videos of their experience in Afghanistan; and recruiting members, supporters, and sympathizers to their movement. According to an interview with the Head of Islamic Groups in the Security Service of Kurdistan, the IMK leaders proclaimed, "Allah succeeded us" and trained followers to fight the way they learned in Afghanistan (Security Service of Kurdistan, 2009). In 1990, after recruiting several hundred Kurds in mosques, they began to fight against Saddam's rule. In 1991, in hopes of a stronger uprising against Saddam, IMK joined Patriotic Union of Kurdistan (PUK), Kurdistan Democratic Party (KDP), and other Kurdish secular groups. However, the unity among these rival groups was short lived. With the Kurdish returnees from Afghanistan and Pakistan joining IMK, a faction of the IMK adopted the ideology of jihad as a strategy. Consequently, as the IMK Afghan veterans began to exercise their new practice(s) and ideology on the population, tensions emerged between the secular KDP and PUK with IMK.

Between 1993 and 1994, IMK's extremists started to spread their influence in Irbil, Halabja, and Sulaimaniyah. One of their first violent acts included bombing a barbershop and throwing acid on the legs of a lady who had gotten a haircut. Consequentially, IMK's extremists came into increased conflict with PUK and KDP. In 1994, tensions rose to a new level between PUK and IMK, which resulted in PUK (with the help of KDP), killing a few hundred members of IMK. This bloodshed, combined with many elevating disagreements over the new practices, caused IMK to be split into several factions. Mullah Krekar, who was closest to Osama bin Laden, formed Salafia. Ali Abdul Aziz, who had the loyalty of many tribes, formed Jihadiya. Omar Baziany and Mohamed Sofi formed Kurdish Hamas.* At the same time, as the new factions took their followers and set up operations, Ali Papier sought to be the new leader of the IMK.

Meanwhile, on February 5, 1999, the U.S. administration, after consultations with Congress, designated in Presidential Determination 99-13 the IMK as eligible to receive U.S. military assistance. So now, alongside other Kurdish groups opposed to Saddam, IMK also received U.S. assistance (Katzman, 2000). Not long after the U.S. monetary assistance began, IMK suffered splits under the leadership of Shaykh Ali Abd-Aziz, the brother of the movement's founder. The year 2001 was decisive for threat groups globally, and Kurdistan was no different. In July 2001, IMK splinters—Kurdish Hamas and al Tawhid—joined forces to form the Islamic Unity Front (IUF). In August, Second Soran Forces (another IMK splinter) also joined with them. Yet, the union did not last long, and IUF was dissolved in early September 2001. Meanwhile, Jund al-Islam (Soldiers of Islam) was founded on September 1, 2001, under the Kurdish leadership of Abdullah al-Shafi'i (alias Mullah Wuria Hawleri) and Abu

---

* While Mohamed Sofi was killed 3 weeks after the formation of Kurdish Hamas, Abu Musab al Zarqawi, the leader of Tawhid Wal Jihad (later Al Qaeda in Iraq) appointed Omar Baziany as the Wali (chief Amir) of Baghdad.

Abdul Rahman (who had links to Al Qaeda). Abu Abdul Rahman was an Afghan-trained explosives expert, and was responsible for training a number of fighters (including Kurds) before he was killed during warfare in October 2001. Mullah Krekar joined Jund al-Islam shortly after 9/11 occurred, replacing Abdullah al-Shafi'I as leader. Mullah Krekar merged Jund al-Islam with a splinter group of the Islamic Movement in Kurdistan to form the infamous "Ansar al-Islam," which would in time be credited with past attacks of Jund al-Islam (Gregory, 2008). And the previous leader of Jund al-Islam-Shafi'i, who had also trained in Afghanistan, became Ansar's deputy leader (Ram, 2003). Assad Mohammad Hassan (alias Hawleri), formerly the leader of the Second Soran Unit, became Shafi's deputy. The chief of Ansar's Media Bureau—Ayyub Afghani—was an explosives expert who fought in Afghanistan.

Both IMK and its many splinters were operating between Halabja and Hawraman on the border of Iran and Iraq. However, in the wake of 9/11, Ansar al-Islam took hold of a swath of territory in northeastern Iraq along the Iranian border. Ansar established itself in an enclave in northeastern Iraq on the strategic Shinirwe Mountain, overlooking the town of Halabja, near the porous border with Iran. "Ansar barred women from education and employment, confiscated musical instruments, and banned music both in public and private, banned televisions, and threatened the use of Islamic punishments of amputation, flogging, and stoning to death for offenses, such as theft, the consumption of alcohol, and adultery" (Gregory, 2008). This location was chosen strategically as it was outside of Saddam Hussein's control. The group also seized the border town of Tawella as well as the villages of Mila Chinara, Khak Kelan, Kharpan, Zardalhala, Hanadi, Dargashikhan, Balkha, Mishla, and Palyanaw.

Over time, Ansar expanded its influence to engage the PUK, which was considered the most established power in the region. It was near the villages of Biyara and Tawela, in the Hawraman region of Sulaymaniyah Province that Ansar fought the PUK. At the beginning, Ansar controlled "a string of villages in the plains and mountains between the town of Halabja and the mountain ridge that marks Iraq's border with Iran. ... dubbed 'Iraq's Tora Bora' by some locals after the Al Qaeda stronghold in Afghanistan" (Muir, 2002). It was here that, in September 2001, Ansar committed a terrible atrocity. In the village of Khela Hama, near Halabja, Ansar captured and massacred 42 members of the PUK, which controlled the eastern half of Iraqi Kurdistan. In the carnage, Ansar killed leaders, bombed restaurants, and desecrated Sufi shrines. The carnage continued into December when Ansar killed 103 and injured 117 members of PUK who were returning home to celebrate the end of Ramadan. The pictures of the killings were placed on the Internet (Schanzer, 2004).

But, Ansar had just gotten started. It was sometime in early 2002 that Al Qaeda members (including Abu Musab Zarqawi, who relocated from Afghanistan) started influencing both the modus operandi and targeting strategy of Ansar. In April 2002, Ansar attempted to assassinate Prime Minister Burham Salih, the head of the PUK-led Iraqi Kurdistan regional government. The attack, in which five of Salih's bodyguards were killed, was ordered most probably by Abu Musab al Zarqawi (a.k.a. Ahmed Fadil Nazal al-Khalayleh). Then in July 2002, Ansar desecrated tombs of The Army of the Men of the Naqshbandi (Sufi) order. A usually tolerant Kurdish society condemned this act, but Ansar was on a roll. On February 10, 2003, Ansar assassinated Shawkat Hajji Mushir, a founding member of PUK and a member of the Kurdish parliament, along with two other Kurdish officials. They were negotiating with Ansar members in the belief that a substantial number of them wanted to defect. However, it was a trap, which resulted in the officials' deaths. Kurdistan then suffered its first suicide bomb attack on February 26, 2003, when an Ansar suicide bomber used a Land Rover taxi (that regularly plies the route between Halabja and the town of Sayyid Sadiq) to cross from Ansar-held territory into the zone controlled by government forces (Ware, 2003). When confronted by government troops at a roadside checkpoint, the taxi passenger killed two soldiers, the taxi driver, and himself. The attack purposely coincided with a conference of Iraqi opposition organizations on a post-Saddam political order, attended by Zalmay Khalilzad, President Bush's special envoy to the Iraqi opposition (Ware, 2003). It is very likely that the attacker wanted to target the meeting, but, when confronted by the guards, he felt he had no choice but early detonation. This was the attack that would illuminate Ansar al-Islam as the most threatening extremist group to the multinational forces in Iraq.

THE THREAT LANDSCAPE

An estimated 300 to 400 Iraqi Kurds were joined by 200 to 300 Arab and other fighters who fled Afghanistan after United States-led coalition intervention in Afghanistan. Their leader, Mullah Krekar, was the host to a few hundred Arabs, including Abu Musab al Zarqawi, who ran a training camp in Herat, Afghanistan, near the Iranian border. With financial support from Al Qaeda, al-Zarqawi established links with groups and individuals in the Levant while visiting Zarqa, Jordan. Most of the recruits of al-Zarqawi's group (Tawhid Wal Jihad) were from the Levant (countries bordering on the eastern Mediterranean Sea), although some were living in Europe. Al-Zarqawi, who was close to Al Qaeda leadership, especially to Osama bin Laden and Dr. Ayman al Zawahiri, fled to Iran in late 2001. After the Iranians detained al-Zarqawi briefly, he relocated to Iraq in the late summer of 2002. Al-Zarqawi's host—Mullah Krekar—opposed unity moves by IMK to join the PUK, and so worked with the United States in order to create an autonomous Kurdish state in the north of Iraq. However, what the United States did not realize was that Mullah Kreker, driven by the ideology of Al Qaeda, was not intending to create just a Kurdish state in the north of Iraq, but rather intended to create an Islamic state in the north of Iraq, and then subsequently in the rest of Iraq.

With the help of Ansar, al-Zarqawi settled in Halabjah and established training facilities in the northern Kurdish areas outside the Saddam-controlled Iraq. Benefiting from the protection of the U.S. northern No-Fly Zone, al-Zarqawi replicated the camp in Herat where training was imparted in poison (especially ricin) and explosives (his favored weapon). Al-Zarqawi had already built a vast network of followers in the Levant and Europe, and utilized these to carry out his cause. One Palestinian–Jordanian, Adnan Muhammad Sadik (alias Abu Atia), a graduate of Zarqawi's camp in Afghanistan, served in Pankisi Valley in Georgia against the Russians in Chechnya. He was arrested in Azerbaijan and handed over to the CIA. Based on Abu Atia's interrogation, it was discovered that at least nine North Africans were dispatched in 2001 to France, Britain, Spain, Italy, Germany, Russia, and elsewhere in Europe to conduct poison and explosive attacks. As of early 2003, 116 operatives were arrested, including the North African operatives, many of them believed to have been trained by al-Zarqawi himself (Powell, 2003; McGregor, 2005).

From his new operating base in Halabjah, al-Zarqawi conducted operations in Iraq, Saudi Arabia, Syria, Lebanon, and Jordan (his own country of birth). An executive officer of the U.S. Agency for International Development (USAID), Laurence Michael Foley, 62, was shot several times in the chest and head while he walked from his house to his car in Amman, Jordan, on October 28, 2003 (*BBC News*, October 2002; Brisard and Martinez, 2005). Al-Zarqawi was tried and sentenced to death in absentia for his role in the murder (Associated Press, 2006). A regional terrorist, al-Zarqawi enjoyed personally working newly established networks, including a chemical attack in Jordan that would have killed several thousands of people had it been successful. From Iraq, al-Zarqawi visited Syria in 2002, where he organized finance, weapons, and training for his cell members in Syria, and arranged for their departure to Jordan with instructions for the chemical attack. Fortunately, the information was intercepted before any destruction took place, and 11 terror suspects were charged in Jordan. For his role in the operation and planning, al-Zarqawi earned yet another death sentence in absentia (Halaby, 2004; Associated Press, 2006).

In May 2002, al-Zarqawi arrived in Baghdad for medical treatment and remained in the capital of Iraq for two months (Scarborough, 2002). Western intelligence services tracked him to Baghdad, but did not take any action. They assumed that Saddam must have collaborated in order to bring al-Zarqawi for treatment; however, at least one intelligence officer interviewed declared that Saddam had no knowledge of it, stating that otherwise al-Zarqawi's outcome might have been very different.

By the time of the United States-led coalition intervention in Iraq in March 2003, there were multiple threat groups. Iraq's north had emerged as an important safe haven for a few threat groups, both domestic and foreign. Ansar al-Islam (with its links to Al Qaeda and other Arab threat groups from Afghanistan) remained the most structured extremist group. Ansar controlled Beriya, a tiny pocket of territory between Halabja and the Iranian border, an area around 80 km southeast of the PUK's administrative center of Suleimaniya (Rubin, 2003). As an associate group of Al Qaeda, Ansar was the host to Tawhid Wal Jihad (led by Abu Musab al-Zarqawi). Tawhid Wal Jihad relocated from Afghanistan to Iraq in 2001 after the U.S. intervention in Afghanistan. Al-Zarqawi brought volunteers he had been training since 1999 (from Lebanon, Syria, Jordan, and Palestine) with him. These volunteers worked closely with Ansar, which modeled itself on the Afghan Taliban.

When the United States first entered Iraq, the initial series of extremist camps targeted belonged to Ansar. At that time, the United States believed that the camps were trying to develop crude chemical weapons and had links to both Osama bin Laden's Al Qaeda and Saddam Hussein's regime. U.S. Special Forces and air strikes supported by the PUK (a U.S. ally) attacked Ansar hideouts. From the Red Sea, U.S. Tomahawk cruise missiles and warplanes devastated Khurmal and six mountain villages in northern Iraq on March 21, 2003 (Skelton, 2003). With the exception of Abu Taisir al Urdani, a specialist on poisons, and al-Zarqawi's representative in northern Iraq, the air strike failed to kill any of the targeted leaders. Instead, more than 100 other Ansar al-Islam members perished. However, the attack was still deemed successful as significant documents, including foreign passports and training manuals, were recovered from the aftermath. According to a news report, one of the manuals discovered was a copy of one of the chapters from the *Encyclopedia of Jihad*, which directly linked the group to the Al Qaeda network in Afghanistan (Chivers, 2003). In a message "to the Muslims of Kurdistan, Iraq, and the world," Ansar al-Islam leader Abu Abdullah al Shafi'i threatened "martyrdom operations (suicide attacks) against the American and British Crusader forces." It claimed that "more than 300 martyrdom fighters have renewed their devotion to God" by the means of suicide attacks. "We will make Iraq a cemetery for the Crusaders and their servile agents," it said (AFP, 2003). During the attack, most of their fighters dispersed to Iran and regrouped on the border. Some Ansar al-Islam leaders, such as Abu Abdullah al-Shafi'i, Ayyub Afghani, and Sa'adoon Mohammed Abdul Latif (alias Abu Wa'il), were seen in the Iranian border city of Sanandaj in June and July 2003, regrouping their fighters and recruiting new men.

The United States also targeted a lesser-known group—Komala—also in Khurmal. Leaders of Komala—Sheikh Mohamed Barzinjy and Ali Papier (first leader of Komala)—had good relations with Iran. They also had representation in the PUK-led Kurdish administration. The simultaneous attacks by the United States targeted the political head-quarters of Komala, killed 60, and injured another 50 members, over several days of aerial bombardment and 12 hours of fighting. A few days after the attack(s) had ceased, "I asked him ['Lucky' a translator who survived the attack] if the moderate Komala is any different from Ansar." He replied, "After the American missile attacks, I assure you the number of fundamentalists in Komala increased from anger." Although Komala was a moderate Islamic political group and part of the coali-tion Kurdish regional government, it had friendly relations with Ansar (Rubin, 2003). So, when the U.S. decision to target Komala was ques-tioned, the United States defended its position by pointing out these links of "friendly relations of Komala with Ansar," although these links were not accepted by all.

Ansar al-Islam fi Kurdistan (Ansar al-Islam)

Since its very inception, Ansar al-Islam has been operated by experi-enced Kurdish and foreign fighters. With the overall aim of creating an Islamic state, Ansar responded to the U.S. invasion by mounting attacks against Western, Iraqi, and Kurdish government targets, includ-ing foreign contractors working in Kurdish areas. On March 22, 2003, at the crossroads checkpoint outside the village of Khurmal, a suicide car bomb detonated, killing Australian journalist Paul Moran and four Kurds, and injuring dozens of other Kurdish peshmerga (Armed Forces of Kurdistan fighters) and civilians, including ABC correspondent Eric Campbell (Rubin, 2003). The bomber's name was Abu Hur and his attack was declared justified by then Ansar leader Mullah Krekar, who lived in Norway at the time (*BBC News*, 2003). Then on September 9, 2003, three people were killed during Ansar's attempt to bomb a U.S. Department of Defense office in Irbil.

As a group of Kurds operating with foreigners, Ansar's opera-tions were initially limited only to northern Iraq. However, Ansar desired to spread its operations all over Iraq, so on September 20, 2003, it changed its official name (Ansar al Islam fi Kurdistan) to Ansar al-Sunnah (supporters of the Tradition). To support the name change, Ansar recruited Sunni Arabs in central Iraq to join the mostly Kurdish group from the north. Then, influenced by the Arabs who fought in Afghanistan, particularly Tawhid wal Jihad, Ansar al-Sunnah conducted graphic beheadings. In October 2004, Ansar al-Sunnah released a video beheading of a Turkish truck driver on its Web site. The kidnappers on the video identified themselves as members of Tawhid wal Jihad, the Al Qaeda affiliate group led by al-Zarqawi. Ansar's other tactics included vehicle and human-borne suicide attacks, abductions, assassinations, improvised explosive device attacks, rocket and mortar attacks, and roadside bombings. In October 2003, the Pentagon declared that Ansar al-Sunnah had become the principal "terrorist adversary" of U.S. forces in Iraq. When Ansar started operations in central Iraq, including Baghdad, Ansar fighters were divided into six battalions: Nasr, Fat'h, Badr, Quds, Fida'iyun, and Salahuddin. Ansar fought most actively in the "Sunni Triangle," north and west of Baghdad, which was the main battleground between U.S. troops and insurgents.

Tawhid wal Jihad, operationally close to Al Qaeda, influenced Ansar's operational outlook. Ansar focused on conducting high-profile attacks on symbolic and strategic targets, inflicting mass casualties and fatalities. In November 2003, Italian intelligence reported that an Ansar member helped to organize the truck bombing(s) of the Italian military contingent headquarters in Nasariyah, southern Iraq. On February 1, 2004, Ansar's suicide bombers hit PUK and KDP Eid celebrations in Irbil, killing 109 and wounding over 200. Ansar al-Sunnah stated that the attack was in support of "our brothers in Ansar al-Islam." Both Ansar and Tawhid wal Jihad vied for recognition by Al Qaeda. However, it was Tawhid wal Jihad who received the most recognition from Al Qaeda, prompting al-Zarqawi to change the name of "Tawhid wal Jihad" to "Al Qaeda in Iraq" in October 2004.

Due to disagreements about the daily escalating killings of Shiite Iraqis by Al Qaeda in Iraq during September 2005, Al Qaeda in Iraq and Ansar al-Sunnah split their alliance. However, although split, both factions continued to maintain direct communication channels with Al Qaeda. It is known that an Ansar leader, Abbas bin Farnas bin Qafqas (alias Ali Wali), communicated directly with Al Qaeda leaders in Pakistan several times during 2005. However, this communication channel was short-lived; Ali Wali was killed during a counterterrorism raid in Baghdad in May 2006 (American Forces Press Service, 2006). Probably this led to Ansar being instrumental in forming an alliance of seven Sunni groups in July 2007 to prepare for the withdrawal of American and allied forces. In December 2007, Ansar al-Sunnah formally acknowledged being derived from Ansar al Islam.

Although over a hundred large-to-small threat groups emerged in Iraq during the U.S. invasion, Ansar and Al Qaeda in Iraq were the two groups that posed the biggest threat. Both under the influence of Al Qaeda, the threat groups favored suicide attacks against high profile, strategic, and symbolic targets. As most of their attacks were spectacular, they influenced the tempo of battle in Iraq and even inspired threat groups in the region and beyond.

Tanzim Qaedat fi Bilad al-Rafidayn (Al Qaeda in Iraq)

In October 2004, Tawhid wal Jihad renamed itself Tanzim Qaedat fi Bilad al-Rafidayn (Al Qaeda Organization in the Land of the Two Rivers, or more commonly known as Al Qaeda in Iraq) (Brisard and Martinez, 2005). After Al Qaeda in Iraq severed its ties with Ansar, the group came under the greater influence of Osama bin Laden's Al Qaeda. Led by al-Zarqawi, Al Qaeda in Iraq emerged as the most violent terrorist group in the world. In fact, for information leading to al-Zarqawi's death or capture, the United States offered a reward of US $25 million, the highest reward ever offered for an extremist. The key strength of Al Qaeda in Iraq was the Majlis al-Shurra Mujahidin fi al-Iraq (the Mujahidin Shura Council of Iraq [MSC]), an umbrella organization of eight groups with "Al Qaeda in Iraq" at its core (Kavkaz Center, 2006). MSC came under criticism by Al Qaeda in Iraq because they had to seek permission from other members before they could conduct certain operations. This criticism later led to the MSC (created in January 2006) being replaced by the Hilf al-Mutayyabin (The Alliance of the Scented Ones)* (*The Jihadism and Terrorism Threat Monitor*, 2006; Hisham, 1994, p. 168).

Al Qaeda in Iraq is responsible for the most suicide attacks and generally the most spectacular attacks in Iraq. In addition to coalition forces and foreign diplomats, Al Qaeda in Iraq targeted national and provincial government officials, especially military and police personnel; professionals, and academics. Although 90 percent of the group was Iraqi by 2006, foreigners constituted about 90 percent of its suicide bombers. The scandal of Abu Ghraib, with the images of Iraqis being tortured, dramatically enhanced Al Qaeda's ability to recruit foreign fighters. Abu Ghraib helped all the Sunni insurgent groups in Iraq not

---

* According to classical Islamic sources, Hilf al-Mutayyabin was an oath of allegiance taken in pre-Islamic times by several clans of the Quraysh tribe, which they undertook to protect the oppressed and the wronged. The name "oath of the scented ones" apparently derives from the fact that the participants sealed the oath by dipping their hands in perfume and then rubbed them over the Ka'ba. It is widely believe that this practice was then later adopted by the Prophet Muhammad and incorporated into Islam.

only with recruitment, but also by greatly enhancing their motivations for picking up arms and, hence, strengthening their morale. One such example was a video entitled "Abu Musab al-Zarqawi shown slaughtering an American." The video was released on May 11, 2004, and showcased the beheading of Nick Berg, a U.S. civilian who went to Iraq seeking work repairing antennas. The executioners in the video claim the beheading was "in response to the abuse in the Abu Ghraib prison," and "urge all Iraqis to unite to seek revenge" (*USA Today*, 2004).

At its peak, in 2006, the total number of Al Qaeda in Iraq combatants ranged between 2,000 and 3,500. This increase was likely due to the fact that a great number of Sunni Iraqis joined Al Qaeda in Iraq because they desired protection from Shia militias. In the words of one detainee, "It was a marriage of convenience." Further, "Sunnis had no lost love for Al Qaeda, but Al Qaeda had money and weapons that the Sunnis needed desperately" (M. Alexander,* Interview, November 4, 2009).

Aside from attacking coalition and Iraqi security forces, Al Qaeda in Iraq has a confrontational policy against civilian Shiites and Iraqi nationalist resistance groups. Al Qaeda's leadership discouraged al-Zarqawi's actions, but he refused to change his course. Although the orientation has now changed, the organization is still executing the same massacres as it did during al-Zarqawi's tenure, and it remains generally disliked among other militant groups in Iraq. These other militant groups have on many occasions appealed to Osama bin Laden for him to reel in Al Qaeda in Iraq. However, the only response from Al Qaeda's leadership was instead support of the unpopular establishment of Dawlat al-Iraq al-Islamiyah (The Islamic State of Iraq), which has tried to entice and coerce other militant groups to join. The ISI was calibrated by Al Qaeda to serve the best interest of Al Qaeda in Iraq. Twelve smaller militant groups and Al Qaeda in Iraq operated within the structure of the ISI, which received a great deal of praise from Al Qaeda's leadership in Pakistan.

Al Qaeda in Iraq focused on vehicle and human-borne suicide attacks. The group also improvised explosive device attacks, car bombings, and roadside bombings. However, this steep scale of violence by Al Qaeda in Iraq did not go down well with other Iraqis. With the public providing intelligence to the Iraqi government and to the United States, the group suffered the loss of its key leadership, leading to an eventual dilapidation of the organization. Starting with the capture of al-Zarqawi's deputy, Hassan Mahmud Abu Nabha (alias Milad al-Lubnani), in Lebanon during January 2006, key arrests led intelligence to al-Zarqawi. This culminated in two 500-lb bombs being dropped on his "safe house" in Baquba, Iraq, thereby causing al-Zarqawi's death on June 7, 2006 (*BBC News*, June 2006). At the time of his death, the insurgency in Iraq was at its peak and continued at that pace for another year. His successor, Abd-al Munim Izzidine Ali Ismail (alias Abu Ayyub al-Masri, alias Abu Hamza al-Muhajir) was from the Egyptian Islamic Jihad, a group led by Dr. Ayman al Zawahiri that had merged with Al Qaeda. A former instructor at the al-Faruq camp in Kandahar from 1999 to 2000, al-Muhajir fled Afghanistan, relocated to Iran, and was in Baghdad before the U.S. invasion in 2003 (*Gulf Times*, 2006). A founding member of Tawhid wal Jihad, he also became an instructor on the manufacture of improvised weapons and facilitating the travel of foreign fighters to Baghdad.

After al-Zarqawi's death, al-Muhajir pledged allegiance to Abu Umar al-Baghdadi, who had just been declared Amir al-Mu'minin (Leader of the Faithful) of ISI (Ridolfo, 2007). Al-Muhajir then followed al-Zarqawi's tradition of extensive use of multimedia communication; his messages aimed to galvanize the Iraqis and terrorize the United States by encouraging the population to use "dirty bombs" (radioactive material combined with conventional explosives) against U.S. bases in Iraq and even went so far as to directly threaten the United States and Europe in online Web broadcasts. But, despite al-Muhajir reaching out to the Iraqis (and their groups) fighting the coalition and Iraqi forces, Al Qaeda in Iraq faced insurmountable challenges. The backlash against the actions that al-Zarqawi had caused when he was alive had done its damage to general Iraqi support. So, although al-Muhajir tried to appeal to the wider Iraqi population, even going so far as to call on every follower to "kill an American in 15 days" in speeches and Web sites worldwide, the previous massacres of tribal leaders and civilians already had led to a steep deterioration of public support.

The beginning of the decimation of Al Qaeda in Iraq was the unity among Anbar's 25 tribes over the high civilian casualties caused by attacks executed by Al Qaeda in Iraq. After being questioned about the authority and legitimacy of tribes in al-Anbar, one Al Qaeda in Iraq member said, "This tribal system is un-Islamic; we are proud to kill tribal leaders who are helping the Americans" (*BBC News*, September 2006). The tribal formations included Hamzah Brigade, created in 2004 and mainly made up of the Albu-Mahal tribe from the al-Qaim area of al-Anbar province. The group has since been officially sanctioned by the Iraqi government, under the name of Desert Protection Corps. Another tribal formation sprang forth in 2005 and was known as the Tribal Council. This council was led by the powerful Abu-Fahad tribe, from Al Ramadi. Unfortunately this council was severely weakened when Al Qaeda in Iraq killed the leader, Sheikh Nasser Abdulkarim al-Miklaf, in January 2006. All of the 25 tribal formations were either based on one single tribe or the tribes around one town or city. Although quite fragmented, they were all united with the same vow of stopping Al Qaeda in Iraq's violence against the civilian population. "We just want to live like everyone else. We're sick of all this bloodshed," said one Ramadi resident, voicing anger at Al Qaeda. Unfortunately, due to their small and fragmented powerbase, these tribal formations were often defeated and their leaders frequently killed. Fortunately, this changed during the summer of 2006, when Majlis al-Shurra Inqath fi al-Anbar (The al-Anbar Salvation Council, more commonly known as the Awakening Council) was formed. The council was formed by 11 tribes who took part in "The Awakening of al-Anbar Conference." Each of the 11 tribes then created its own armed formations. Combined, the Awakening Council allegedly had a military force of 30,000 tribal fighters (*BBC News*, September 2006). In September 2006, 51 tribal leaders from the Awakening Council, led by Al-Shaykh Abd-al-Sattar Buzay Abu-Rishah, met with Iraqi Prime Minister Nuri al-Maliki. The Awakening Council asked the Iraqi government for help in combating the extremists (Al Qaeda in Iraq/MSC) in al-Anbar; to which al-Maliki pledged Iraqi security forces to help establish security in Al-Anbar in addition to committing to undertake projects to restore the governorates infrastructure (Ridolfo, 2006).

Pledges were soon put to the test when, in November 2006, forces from the Awakening Council battled ISI forces near the town of Sofia in al-Anbar. Keeping their word, the coalition forces assisted the tribal force with air and artillery strikes, providing what backup they could. According to the leader of the Awakening Council, Al-Shaykh Abd-al-Sattar Buzay al-Rishawi, forces from the Awakening Council had raided an Al Qaeda in Iraq stronghold and killed 55 members, while losing only nine of their own (Reuters, 2006). By mid-February 2007, the tribes of al-Anbar had contributed 2,400 individuals to the local police forces, and 1,600 members to a new tribal force called the Emergency Response Unit (later transformed to the Concerned Local Citizens (CLC) and then most recently to the Sons of Iraq program). The Emergency Response Unit received training from U.S. forces in Iraq. By February 2007, the United States was cooperating with 12 tribes, up from 3 in June 2006 (*Washington Times*, 2007).

By the beginning of February 2007, the Awakening Council had become such a threat to the forces of ISI (led by Al Qaeda in Iraq), that ISI started a large terror campaign against the leaders, members, and families of the Al-Anbar Awakening Council. In the middle of February 2007, more than 20 mourners traveling from a funeral in Fallujah were pulled from their bus and massacred by ISI, due to their alleged family ties with members of the Awakening Council. During the same period, two suicide bombers struck, respectively, the blast wall outside and the house of tribal leader Al-Shaykh Abd-al-Sattar Buzay al-Rishawi, who leads the al-Anbar Awakening Council. Five police officers and six civilians were killed in the attack, but the main target escaped. In late February 2007, a suicide bomber detonated his truck outside a Sunni mosque in the town of Habbaniyah in al-Anbar province, killing at least 39 people. The mosque was targeted because the Imam (prayer leader) of the mosque had spoken out against "extremists," and was believed to support the Awakening Council (Murphy, 2007).

The opponents of Al Qaeda in Iraq argued that it is guilty of fratricide, and that its transnational goals in Iraq endangered the Iraqi people. On September 14, 2007, Al Qaeda in Iraq claimed that Hamas in Iraq (a former faction of the 1920 Revolutionary Brigades) "worked hard to uncover the weapons of the mujahedeen and stood side-by-side with the [U.S.] occupiers and fought us" (Nefa Foundation, September 2007). However, Hamas in Iraq claimed that it "did not participate in any fight against the Al Qaeda network and will never, ever cooperate with the occupiers." On October 27, 2007, the Islamic Army of Iraq claimed that Al Qaeda in Iraq "waged an insidious attack in al-Shakhat (a part of al-Latifiyah), which resulted in the death of four unarmed citizens (as well as) an element of the Islamic Army, and which destroyed 14 houses (Nefa Foundation, October 2007). The accusations and bickering continued into 2008; on January 4, 2008, Hamas asserted:

> Al Qaeda's fight against the resistance and mujahedeen units are to be considered toward the benefit of the U.S. occupiers ..., [and this has] put a drain on our youth and weaponry. The occupying forces were unable to enter Diyala, until Al Qaeda paved the way for them by killing Sunnis and demolishing their homes, mosques, and hospitals. ... Several individuals from the ISI are responsible for killing commanders and fighters from our brigades in the Diyala province ... killing them and mutilating them ... killing our men's wives and children (Nefa Foundation, January 2008).

After the United States reached out to the Iraqi Sunni groups, the Al Qaeda in Iraq's ISI started to fight the rival Sunni insurgent groups. Groups argued that Al Qaeda in Iraq had started to "terrorize the mjuahidin" under the pretext that their banners were agent banners. And, further, that it turned on leaders of the Muslim Movement of the Mujahidin of Iraq, of whom even if one disagrees with one of them, he should not be killed. The main argument made by the rival Sunni groups was that Al Qaeda in Iraq had distorted the resistance by fomenting sectarian conflict. On April 15, 2008, the Army of al-Mustafa, a breakaway faction of ISI, claimed:

> ISI threatened one of our field commanders with death for no apparent reason. ... We see no justification for the acts carried out by the brothers from the ISI—they have blackmailed us, threatened us, and seized the assets of the Army of al-Mustafa (Nefa Foundation, April 2008).

After al-Zarqawi's death, ISI lost its strongholds in Kirkuk and the Diyala and Salahadin provinces. However, fighting continued in Nineveh, particularly in Mosul, between coalition forces and the ISI. The attacks in Mosul during 2009 included operations that targeted U.S. and Iraqi forces in addition to militiamen from an Awakening Council in Latifiyah (Babil province) as they waited to receive their salaries. The emergence of the Kurdistan Brigades demonstrated Al Qaeda in Iraq's ambition to establish a foothold in the Kurdish areas. Pledging their allegiance to al-Baghdadi (the leader of the Al Qaeda in Iraq-led ISI), a representative of the brigades declared:

> We are your brothers in the Kurdistan Brigades and we pledge our allegiance to the Islamic State of Iraq ... [and] to the two Kurdish puppets, Jalal Talabani and Masud Barzani. ... I swear by God that we have no mercy or sympathy towards the traitors who sold themselves to the enemies of God. Your throats will be slit (*CBS News*, October 2008).

The orientation of (Al Qaeda in Iraq-led) ISI attacks shifted from coalition and Iraqi forces to attacks against the awakening movement. This caused fear, opposition, and revenge against the Al Qaeda in Iraq-led ISI. Due to declining support as well as increasing confrontations with the tribes of al-Anbar, the ISI moved most of its operations into the Baghdad and Diyala provinces. Especially in Diyala province, the ISI had received some positive responses to al-Muhajir's outreach and reconciliation efforts. On October 4, 2006, a statement from the Bubaz tribes referred directly to Abu Hamza's call for reconciliation between the tribes of Iraq and Muslim groups, by declaring, "Permanent reconciliation between the warring groups ... [such] opens the field for the sons of the tribe to follow any faction or Jihadi brigade they wish to join, in the quest for reward from Allah and destruction of the Crusader invade" (MEMRI, 2006).

In Diyala and Baghdad provinces, Al Qaeda in Iraq, and especially the Iraqi Salafiyah groups, such as Jaish al-Islami, managed to draw some support from local Sunni Arabs. Local Sunni Arabs perceive these groups as their only guardians against the Shiite death squads, who have killed thousands (by the Shiite's very confession). However, despite these developments in Diyala and Baghdad, it can be assessed that al-Muhajir's outreach program has been a miserable failure. The outreach program has not been able to entice major Iraqi-resistance or the militant Salafiyah movement into the ISI. Instead, the actions on the ground by members of Al Qaeda in Iraq have only further alienated these actors.

Although ISI remains the umbrella group of Sunni militant factions dominated by Al Qaeda in Iraq, on April 23, 2009, Iraqi security officials claimed to have captured the leader of ISI—al-Baghdadi. Yet, widely the capture of al-Baghdadi is still unconfirmed and reports vary on whether he was a fabrication or a real person, in addition to whether or not he has been captured or is still at large. Meanwhile, despite his speeches and efforts at networking, al-Muhajir has generally been unable to change the dynamics on the ground, and, thus, Al-Qaeda in Iraq remains a fringe group, far removed from the mainstream Sunni–Iraq militant groups. On the ground, al-Zarqawi's ideologically uncompromising legacy and the tit-for-tat cycle of revenge are still guiding the local Al Qaeda in Iraq leaders, members, and supporters. While Al Qaeda in Iraq may find a significant base in Iraq since the (arguably) rapid U.S. withdrawal, it still faces mounting opposition from most Iraqi groups. Nevertheless, Al Qaeda in Iraq remains one of the largest and best-funded militant organizations in Iraq. The group remains at the center of the ISI and remains the single most influential Sunni militant group in Iraq.

U.S. IMPACT ON THREAT GROUPS IN IRAQ

Since the United States-led coalition invasion of Iraq in March 2003, the national, regional, and global threat landscape altered dramatically. In late 2003, when the United States-led coalition forces failed to provide the basic necessities to the public, the Iraqi insurgency took off. As U.S. administrators failed to understand how best to manage Iraq and its people, many of the general public turned against the occupation force. The United States failed to provide basic services from water to electricity to the people. Furthermore, the United States arguably made a long-range strategic error by dismantling the Iraqi military. Public support for trained Iraqi persons led to a sustained insurgency. Beginning in late 2003, three clusters of threat groups emerged: pro-Al Qaeda groups, pro-Baathist groups, and pro-Iran groups. With the flow of foreign fighters, Iraq emerged as the most violent theater in 2004.

By error, the United States perceived the biggest threat to Iraq coming from the Baathists and not from the militant Islamists. L. Paul Bremer (then head of the Coalition Provisional Authority), who dismantled the Iraqi army, and (then Secretary of State) Condoleezza Rice failed to understand that the core threat stemmed from (Al Qaeda in Iraq-led) ISI. While the White House and the State Department blamed Syria, the U.S. military and the CIA knew the threat, but lacked support to focus on the real enemy. Sheikh Talal al-Gaood, a Sunni businessman who had close ties to Anbar's leaders, was enraged by the "endless mistakes" of the U.S. leadership (Perry, 2009). He said: "You [Americans] face a Wahhabi threat that you cannot even begin to fathom," and he derided White House "propaganda" about the role of Syria in fueling the insurgency (Perry, 2009). When the U.S. military wanted to co-opt the tribal leaders, the White House and State Department blocked it. The first round of talks started in August 2003, when tribal leaders met with U.S. military officials in Jordan. A second round of talks took place in Anbar province in November 2004. Had the U.S. politicians understood the importance of co-opting the tribal leaders in 2003 or 2004, arguably the insurgency would not have escalated to such a level, nor caused such a colossal loss of life and property.

The turning point of the insurgency occurred when Sunni tribal groups, led by tribal sheikhs, formed unified clusters in order to protect their tribes from ISI. With the steadfast increase in violence in Iraq and no assistance from the Shia-dominated Baghdad government or Washington, the Sunni tribes reached out to the U.S. Marines for help. Although initially reluctant, U.S. Colonel (Col.) John Coleman, the Chief of Staff for the First Marine Expeditionary Force, disregarded Washington's advice and went to Fallujah, a city in the heart of the Sunni triangle. He went there with intent to assist the call of the tribal leaders to fight Al Qaeda in Iraq, after the vicious killing of four U.S. contractors in April 2004. The U.S. security contractors had been part of a convoy when they were viciously attacked. Their corpses were burned and mutilated by an angry mob in Fallujah, who then hung two of the bodies from a bridge overlooking the Euphrates river. The insurgents made a video of the attack and images were broadcast around the world. Former Iraqi military personnel and a Saddam-lookalike former general also turned up to help the coalition forces in Fallujah with promises to bring more men to the fight.

> From studying the enemy, the Marines realized the insurgents can be separated into five disparate groups with widely varying goals: foreign fighters (some of whom are very skilled bomb makers), religious extremists, violent criminals released from prison by Saddam and willing to kill for money, Saddam loyalists (those Col. Coleman described as "bloody up to their elbows" in the old regime), and former military personnel (Miniter, 2004).

Incredibly, keeping his earlier promise, the former Iraqi general assembled hundreds of former Iraqi soldiers willing to fight the insurgency. Col. Coleman realized that there were "so many former Iraq soldiers willing to fight insurgents that the 'Fallujah Brigade' could easily grow to several thousand if the Marines would let it" (Miniter, 2004). Although the resistance from Washington to the U.S. military cooperating with tribal leaders remained, the collaboration between the United States and Iraqi tribes was supported by Marine Lieutenant General

(Lt. Gen.) James T. Conway, General (Gen.) David Petraeus, and Robert Gates (then U.S. Secretary of Defense).

As U.S. understanding of Iraqi nationalism grew, the United States worked together with Iraqi Sunni groups in its quest to defeat the (Al Qaeda in Iraq-led) ISI. The tipping point arrived when tribes started to receive long-overdue financial support, political guidance, and military advice from the United States. The U.S. politico–military strategy paid dividends when the United States started to work with Iraqi Sunni groups, dividing the potential and actual support base of ISI. After Fallujah, similar efforts sprang up among army units patrolling in Tel Afar and Ramadi, where, five months after Col. Coleman's Fallujah initiative, American military officers began tentative approaches to the Rishawi tribe (Perry, 2009). Starting early in 2007, the U.S. alliance with Babil's leaders (who were former enemies) grew and, by May 2007, the Babil tribes received U.S. funding, including "$370 for each provincial policeman hired by Babil's Janabi tribe," which was quite a large and influential amount for southern and western Iraq (Perry, 2009).

Things were looking up, relations between tribal leaders and the coalition forces were getting stronger, when tragedy struck. When the Americans called for a meeting of the Awakening Council with the Shia-dominated Iraqi government (which was skeptical of the U.S. tribes' strategy officials) on June 25, 2007, a suicide bomber penetrated three levels of security and killed 12 Iraqis, including six key members of the Awakening Council (Perry, 2008). Not long after, in September 2007, Ramadi's Sheikh Abdul Sattar Abu Risha was killed in a car bomb attack. According to the Ministry of Interior, over 100 members of the Awakening Council have been killed by Al Qaeda in Iraq, and many more have been injured.

But, still the Awakening Council had been conceptualized and it was determined. The tribes' strategy continued to spread, and even took root in Babil province's "Triangle of Death," the heavily fought-over area south of Baghdad (Perry, 2009). Although Al Qaeda's objective has been to try to break apart the Awakening Movement by targeting several tribe leaders and their families, the Awakening movements in Iraq continue to thrive and make a difference. This is evident by the fact that the group's number has grown between 65,000 and 80,000 members (Rubin and Cave, 2007; Lanchin and Mahmoud, 2008) since its inception. A large number of members are Sunni groups that had previously worked with Al Qaeda in Iraq before realizing that "they [Al Qaeda in Iraq] did not have the best interests of Iraq in their hearts." In fact, although sometimes fraught with tensions, these groups have made such a positive impact on reducing Al Qaeda-sponsored violence that, beginning in 2007, Baghdad started taking an active role in recruiting Awakening movement members (now more popularly called the Sons of Iraq) into the police and army. So, although the U.S. surge of forces definitely helped in lowering violence, the Awakening movement that began in Anbar Province and continues to promulgate throughout Iraq, can arguably be said to be the "most significant reason for the decline" (Rubin and Cave, 2007; Lanchin and Mahmoud, 2008).

CONCLUSION

While this chapter primarily addresses the background and origin of recent threat groups in Iraq to the United States—the majority of which were Sunni-led with ties to Al Qaeda—it should not be assumed that the United States did not have problems with the Shiite population. After the fall of Saddam, Muqtada al-Sadr, a charismatic Iraqi cleric from a powerful clerical dynasty, emerged as a leader of the Shiite population. He had powerful influence over the Shiite reactions to the U.S. invasion. Al-Sadr publicly decried the United States an enemy, insisting that U.S. troops leave the country immediately. In reaction, this spurred many acts of violence against U.S. troops by the Shiite population. However, perhaps based on the unique circumstances of the Sunni population under Saddam Hussein's rule (advanced positions in society, higher education possibilities, etc.), it was the Sunni that were overwhelmingly the most resistant to the invasion of the United States. Meanwhile, although the Shiite felt their ties with Iran threatened during the U.S. invasion, there were few other reasons to be distraught as many Shi'a were quickly hired into government, police force, and military positions while the country was restructured. Perhaps in part due to this, the majority of captured persons in theater internment facilities across Iraq were Sunni.

The country of Iraq is a continual work in progress. Based on the complex and multilayered history of terrorist groups within Iraq, the U.S. military had their hands full throughout the occupation of Iraq. The road has been long and wrought with difficulties with many varying threat groups coming and going. But, fortunately, there was a group of dedicated and determined leaders (both Iraqi and American) that were committed to seeing Iraq and its citizens evolve into a democratic and more peaceful nation in one part due to the encouragement of the Awakening Movement and the introduction of rehabilitation programs into the theater internment facilities throughout Iraq (as this book details in the following chapters). However, the process wasn't easy; it was painful and wrought with emotion as mistakes were made, risks were taken, hard lessons learned, and compromises made. But, ask anyone who was involved with the ups as well as the downs and they are bound to agree that the United States might have made a lot of mistakes, but they also did a lot of good for the Iraqi people. Through their efforts, the terrain of terrorist threat groups in Iraq has been forever altered, and "liberty" once seemingly so out of grasp for the everyday Iraqi, is finally within reach. And, while there is still much more to learn and bound to be more mistakes, with the official end of U.S. combat operations in Iraq in 2010, the path is set. The United States provided a plethora of lessons over the past 7 years, and it is now up to the Government of Iraq to decide which of the those lessons to take with them.

CHAPTER 2

State of Affairs of Detainment and Detainees

THE PREDICAMENT

In a town not far from Baghdad, a heavily armed convoy of U.S. armored army Humvees passes quickly through the streets. They are on their way to deliver some much needed school supplies to a group of Iraqi children whose school has been destroyed by the fighting. As the convoy rounds a corner, a roadside bomb blast comes out of seemingly nowhere. The improvised explosive device (IED), strategically planted to hit its mark, flips the third Humvee in the convoy into the air. The others react instinctively and surround and protect the destroyed Humvee. Commands and instructions are shouted into radios. Some soldiers leap out of their vehicles to pull their comrades from the wreckage and check the wounded for injuries. The rest of the soldiers set up their weapons, scan the horizon, and prepare to shoot down any visible threat. After a moment, no threat has emerged, so the soldiers set out on foot to search for those who set off the IED and might still be in the area. As they search the surrounding area, the soldiers round up and detain any adult Iraqi male they can find within a half-mile radius of the blast. When the military holding truck arrives, the Iraqis are forced into the vehicle and the truck rushes off for the nearest U.S. internment facility. At a later date, investigations reveal that many of the detained persons are merely honest Iraqis who just happened by chance to be in the area when the attack occurred. They are released back into society; but from that point on, they hold resentful feelings against the United States and its military.

The above situation describes what can easily happen in warfare. Warfare, as we are well aware, inevitably generates detainees: enemy combatants, opportunists, troublemakers, saboteurs, common criminals, former regime officials, and some innocents as well. These people must be carefully, but humanely, processed to sort out those who remain dangerous or possess militarily valuable intelligence from those who do not (Schlesinger, Brown, Fowler, Homer, & Blackwell, 2004). But determining which individuals are innocent and which individuals are security threats is often a hard distinction to make. Add in the complexities of war, language barrier, and heightened emotions, mistakes are bound to be made. Similar situations like the one above have occurred in multiple theaters of operation since 9/11. In many cases, detainees express bewilderment as to why they were detained. Mohammed,* a detainee from Camp Bucca, was one such detainee. "I was buying milk and eggs with my 5-year old daughter when the blast occurred. And they took me! The soldiers forced me to leave my daughter and groceries and go with them. My wife had no idea what happened to me" (Mohammed,* personal interview, 2007). Even Col. Austin Schmidt, a U.S. commander at Camp Bucca in 2005, estimated that one in four prisoners "perhaps was just snagged in a dragnet-type operation" or were victims of personal vendettas (Fainaru & Shadid, 2005, p. 2). The International Committee of the Red Cross (ICRC) supported these claims in its 2004 leaked report, stating that coalition military intelligence officers estimate between 70 to 90 percent of persons detained have been arrested by mistake (ICRC, 2004).

Given that many individuals are locked up when they should not be, with respect to the fact that prisons have traditionally been breeding grounds for some of the world's most violent and organized criminal organizations, anyone can see the predicament at hand. Prison environments often inspire the creation of well-organized gangs and networks that thrive behind prison walls. In the United States alone, organized gangs, such as the Black Guerilla Family, the Aryan Brotherhood, and the Mexican Mafia, have formed in an effort to promote ethnic and racial solidarity and compete for power and influence inside and outside the penal system. In many cases, these networks are comprised of effective leadership councils, chains of command, and strict codes of conduct for members. Members of prison gangs are forced to join and/or often include those who are psychologically vulnerable inmates seeking the physical protection that gang members appear to provide. Often, these individuals are indoctrinated in what they perceive as a worthy cause or a sense of belonging.

Given this common background, a number of prominent Islamist radicals, including Ayman al-Zawahiri and Abu Musab al-Zarqawi, spent years in Egypt and Jordan prisons. The Egyptian and Jordanian prison systems are known to have harsh conditions that include systematic abuse and torture (Zamelis, 2006). Assumptions, therefore, can be made that these experiences were contributors to their radicalization.

---

* An asterisk (*) is used throughout this book to protect the security and confidentiality of certain individuals whose lives might be threatened otherwise.

These two Al Qaeda leaders were notorious in both Afghanistan and Iraq. Similarly, in Spain, Jose Emilio Suarez Trashorras, a Spanish mineworker, was jailed in 2001 for a drug offense. Trashorras was incarcerated with Jamal Ahmidan who was also convicted of a petty crime. Both Trashorras and Ahmidan were not religious or politically motivated; it was while in custody that they embraced radical Islamic fundamentalist beliefs and were recruited into an Al Qaeda-linked Moroccan terrorist group. This group was responsible for the Madrid train bombings in Spain, which influenced the 2004 Spanish presidential elections (Cuthbertson, 2004).

U.S. DETAINEE OPERATIONS

The U.S. military has been conducting some form of detainee operations since the Revolutionary War. The formalization of the treatment of detainees was finalized in 1947 with the Geneva Hague Protocols under the Laws of Land Warfare. Historically, the U.S. military's detainee operations' doctrine is founded on the principles of release or repatriation of prisoners of war or retained persons upon completion of the conflict, and/or they are handed over to another entity, organization, or host nation authority. This trend has been consistent throughout every conflict the U.S. military has been involved in since the Korean War and through to Desert Storm. In Korea, transfer authority was given to the South Koreans; in Vietnam, it was the noncommunist Republic of Vietnam forces; in Grenada, custody of detainees was transferred to a Caribbean peacekeeping force; in Panama, the host nation control transitioned as quickly as feasible; and finally, in Desert Storm, the Kingdom of Saudi Arabia assumed control of the detention and repatriation mission. Historical evidence illustrates that the detainee operations' mission is one that the U.S. military has tried to avoid burdening tactical commanders with throughout the majority of its conflicts. The significant fact of this is that not much emphasis is placed on this task, yet, as a detaining power, the United States is ultimately responsible for the conduct of its soldiers and for the overall treatment of detainees with the U.S. coalition.

In accordance with the Department of the Army *FM 3-19.40* U.S. Military Police Internment/Resettlement Manual, detainees fall within four categories: enemy prisoner of war (EPW), retained person (RP), civilian internee (CI), or other detainee. These four fall in one of two categories under the Military Commissions Act of 2006: unlawful enemy combatant or lawful enemy combatant. Unlawful enemy combatant has a subcategory of cobelligerent. An EPW is a lawful enemy combatant and is a member of an enemy's armed forces, a militia, or a volunteer corps forming part of an enemy's armed forces. An RP is a person who is a member of the medical service or a chaplain attached to an enemy's armed forces. An RP is similar to an EPW in that he/she is afforded additional privileges due to his/her profession. The next classification is a CI, which is considered a belligerent person who is interned under U.S. custody because he/she has committed an offense that makes him/her a security risk to coalition forces, is an insurgent, or has committed a criminal act against coalition forces. The final classification is the "other detainee." This category is the catchall for detainees who have not been classified. The other detainee will maintain the status of an EPW until a legal competent authority can determine legal status.

U.S. policy states that the U.S. military will treat all detainees under the principles of the Geneva Convention, relative to the treatment of Prisoners of War (GPW) (Department of the Army FM 3-19.40, 2001). Yet, under the contemporary operating environment, the prisoner of war concept has become minimized and so might require a modified approach to handle an enemy who is categorized as an unlawful enemy combatant or cobelligerent under the Military Commissions Act of 2006. These new enemies are often insurgents (ideological and/or radicals) and/or common criminals. Meanwhile, U.S. policy states that all detainees will be treated in accordance with the principles of GPW, regardless of status (Rumsfeld, 2002).*

The term *detainee* became the common language with U.S. operations in the Balkans. In Kosovo, the United States was not at war and was acting under International Mandate, so the United States did not have EPWs. Under this mandate, the United States had authority to retain or detain persons in order to enable and ensure a "safe and secure" environment, which is a broad criterion for operational commanders. In Kosovo, war tribunals were not used to determine detainee status, but rather were the result of a combined effort between military police, military intelligence, staff judge advocates, and tactical commanders. Kosovo became the turning point on how the United States conducts

---

* The 109th U.S. Congress of the United States, Military Commissions Act of 2006, defines an "unlawful enemy combatant" and "co-belligerent" as:
(A) Unlawful Enemy Combatant: (i) A person who has engaged in hostilities or who has purposefully and materially supported hostilities against the United States or its co-belligerents who is not a lawful enemy combatant (including a person who is part of the Taliban, Al Qaeda, or associated forces); or (ii) a person who, before, on, or after the date of the enactment of the Military Commissions Act of 2006, has been determined to be an unlawful enemy combatant by a Combatant Status Review Tribunal or another competent tribunal established under the authority of the President or the Secretary of Defence. (B) Co-Belligerent: In this paragraph, the term "co-belligerent," with respect to the United States, means any state or armed force joining and directly engaged with the United States in hostilities or directly supporting hostilities against a common enemy.

detainee operations. Due to the success and the methods used there, it became the basis of how detention operations are executed today.

The current objectives of internment and resettlement operations are to "process, handle, care for, account for, and secure … [Detainees]" (Department of the Army *FM 3-19.40*, 2001, pp. 1–13). However, without programs in place, these objectives imply that the U.S. detainee operations program serves as a punitive system of incarceration rather than the more effective corrections system of rehabilitation. Missing is the purpose to prevent combatants from continuing the fight, especially upon release or repatriation. Perhaps that is because what is not effectively understood at the higher level is that the United States is fighting a *war of ideologies*, and, in order to fight this effectively, we must commit to addressing the root causes. In 2006, then-president George W. Bush confirmed in his National Security Strategy that this war on ideologies was going to be a "long war" (White House, 2006). Many experts couldn't agree more, and while steps have most certainly been taken to look at the root causes of the problem, there is debate on how effective or involved our approach has been (given our lack of understanding historically).

Between the end of 2003 and August 2010, U.S. detention facilities in Iraq had anywhere between 5,500 and 26,000 Iraqi detainees at any given time. With such large populations, there are significant risks of creating radical extremists of those who may not have previously held any radical ideologies. Especially at risk were those who might have just been in the "wrong place at the wrong time" and who because of it, now harbor a resentment of the United States not only for the shame of being detained for a crime he/she didn't commit, but also for the shame of leaving behind a family unable to fend for itself. These are the individuals who are most susceptible to extremist propaganda encouraging violence against those who are now seen as the perpetrators—the U.S. military. Therefore, the U.S. military needs to take preventive measures to ensure that further radicalization of these individuals does not occur. To accomplish this, the U.S. detainee operations program requires modification. Logical lines of operation should include not only the obvious, e.g., *operations phase* (training, going operational, preparation of plans, terrorist operations, capture, interrogation, and resistance), but also the *entry phase* (proselytization and selection, indoctrination and radicalization, calibrating commitment, and recruitment), and *exit phase* (detention [and further radicalization], tribunal or trial, release [or imprisonment], return to jihad) (Jenkins, 2006, p. 123).

Unfortunately, in most global theaters only the obvious, i.e., the *operations phase,* is being addressed when dealing with extremism. But, if we really want to have a long-lasting effect, detainee operations are going to need to reach farther. The objective of detainee operations should be to detain enemy combatants and to prevent combatants from continuing the fight against the United States and its allies. It also should include a process to identify enemy combatants' threat and intelligence value. Finally, it should address, and find alternatives to, eliminating radicalization while under detention with whatever means are most effective. In order to have the greatest impact, detainee operations need to address what is not obvious: the *entry phase* and *exit phase*. Only then will the program meet its potential. By addressing the root causes of the issue, it will effectively become a shaping effort for current and future operations on winning the global war on terrorism.

PROCESS IN DETAINEE OPERATIONS

Today, there are more than 2.3 million people serving time in American correctional facilities at home and overseas. An estimated one third of them claim some form of religious affiliation. Research suggests that many of these prisoners began their incarceration with little or no religious calling, but adopted a faith during their imprisonment (Hamm, 2009, pp. 667–685). That number has shown to significantly increase while on foreign soil. U.S. detainee operations in Iraq have had an unparalleled impact on how the world views Islam and extremism. Through the evolution of the detainee process—from the point of capture, through the detention, to the release or transfer to host nation authorities—the overall aim of the United States is to detain unfriendly and unlawful enemy combatants from continuing the fight against the United States and its allies. Therefore, correctly recognizing and identifying who the enemy is, is critical. The local populaces are those who are looking for a better life, and their purpose for living is to support themselves and their families. The foreign fighters have similar goals, but their ways of achieving these goals are often extreme. Supporters are those who do not necessarily care for U.S. forces, but see a need to cooperate with them for security and economic reasons. The center of gravity for both the insurgents (extremist) and counterinsurgents (U.S. coalition forces) are the fence sitters. The fence sitter is the majority of the population and is waiting to decide whom they will support (Chiarelli & Michaelis, 2006). While not all fence sitters are ideological extreme, they can easily be manipulated to support the one who provides the most, and this becomes a target audience for the insurgents and counterinsurgents. Therefore, there must be a clear and logical line of operations and intent in order to achieve the overall goals of release or transfer of detainees and preventing further radicalization of detained persons. The first significant logical line to defeat an insurgency within the wire begins with this process.

Upon capture, security forces process detainees within the principles of: search, tag, report, evacuation, segregation, and safeguarding; detainees must be treated in accordance with the GPW Convention during this process. Processing a detainee into U.S. custody remains a critical task, as it can have a significant impact on how an individual responds to the rest of his detention under U.S. custody. If a detained person is not given food or water (especially in the sweltering heat of Iraq), he is less likely to be coherent enough to cooperate. If a person is flexi-cuffed so tightly his wrists bleed and/or if he is shamed, kicked, and/or hit when arrested, this also will have a lasting effect. Similarly, if an individual's home is destroyed in the arrest and/or if he is not permitted to retrieve his eyeglasses or medicine during arrest, this can greatly impact future detainee relations as well. As part of the initial process, everything on a detainee—to include clothing, money, jewelry, etc.—is seized, bagged, and tagged by the U.S. military. The detainee is given a list of the items taken from him and then fingerprints and signs the list if it is accurate. If the detainee feels the list is not complete, he can file a complaint on the missing items as well. The items are then inaccessible until the detainee is released, after which they will be returned. The only types of things seized from detainees that are generally not returned include items such as computers, thumb drives, and hard drives. At one point, the United States had more than $1 million cash in custody from detainees. (During Saddam's era, many banks in Iraq were known to be corrupt, causing most Iraqis to keep their money hidden in their houses or on their person.) Because of the enormity of this sum, the United States started permitting detainees to sign back their money during visitation to give to their families, which helped ease the burden of responsibility, according to Maj. Gen. Douglas Stone (personal interview, October 25, 2009).

Administrative accountability begins with the establishment of the detainee record. Within detainee operations, some of the "enabling technology" and databases are the Detainee Registration System and the Biometrics Automated Toolset (BAT). While the Detainee Registration System assigns an internment serial number (ISN) and creates a detainee file, BAT captures the identity of the detainee. The ISN is similar to a U.S. Social Security Number; this number is imprinted on a bracelet that the detainee is required to have on his person at all times. It tracks all activities of the detainee, participation in rehabilitation classes, and movement. This is found to be particularly important and relevant in a place like Iraq, where there are many differing ways to translate an Arabic name into English; it significantly reduces mistaken identity and ensures accountability of each detainee. In addition, these tools enable further classification of the detainee, which enables personnel to make better decisions for segregation prior to movement within the compound. For example, this could help label a detainee as Shi'a, therefore placing him in a compatible compound. If he has been particularly violent toward multinational forces, it also can highlight that and, therefore, make sure he is put in a compound with a tighter confinement area.

The BAT is a key "enabling technology" that captures individual biometrics. Biometrics is measurable physiological and behavioral characteristics that establish and verify an individual's identity. It is a multimodal biometric system that collects and compares fingerprints, iris images, and facial photos and is effectively used to enroll as well as build digital dossiers on individuals (Lasso, 2009). The significance of BAT is that not only does it help with compound placement, it allows the United States to discern between individuals. It creates a psychological effect that creates a sense of accountability in the identity of an individual. No longer can a detainee claim a different alias. While this is an effective tool within detainee operations, its full utility is not yet maximized as it has yet to be properly integrated into missions in the field, especially when conducting counterinsurgency operations. The BAT, when used both in the field and within detainee operations, will certainly enable commanders to produce clearer measures of effectiveness and performance when dealing with enemy combatants, in addition to reducing the number of innocents who may otherwise be detained by mistake.

Initial detainee classification is based on evidence collected upon capture and on unsupported statements or documentation provided by the detained individual. Once basic classification is established, the more difficult task of segregating detainees is attempted. U.S. doctrine clearly identifies the requirement to classify and segregate detainees to "meet the needs of the detaining power." However, it does not make it a training task to fully comprehend and understand the ideological, cultural, tribal, and clan differences, which if not fully understood can create radicalization and insurgents of the detainee population. The U.S. military is attempting to address this deficiency with cultural awareness classes prior to mobilization and deployment in foreign countries; however, much is still left to be desired.

In Iraq, after the initial classification, detainees are further separated by their ideological threat. The *red detainees* are known to have the most radical ideologies and are considered the greatest threat to security within the internment facility. These individuals are often put in the smallest and most controlled compounds and only let outside for a few hours a day in a diminutive and well-protected courtyard. The *yellow detainees* are those who still pose a significant threat, but may be swayable. They are put in compounds a bit larger than the *red detainees*, and given more benefits and hours of sunlight. Finally, what is referred to as the *green detainees* are those individuals who are generally caught up in sweeps and who might—or might *not*—actively practice Islam. This group is the overwhelming majority of detainees in Iraq, and includes copious fence sitters as well as Christians, and other foreign workers. These detainees are given the most privileges, live in the largest compounds, and generally can walk around their courtyard most hours of the day.

Essential services (food, water, shelter, and protection), in addition to medical services, are a requirement in accordance with the GPW for all detainees. And, in general, the United States has been shown to go above and beyond to ensure that these standards are exceeded. However, two medical services that have not yet been addressed nor properly resourced within U.S. detainee operation manuals are rehabilitative and mental treatment services. So, unfortunately, the number of detainees in U.S. custody who have mental disorders that require treatment or have chemical dependencies that may have contributed to their actions against the United States and its allies is unknown. Yet multiple outside studies have been conducted on the importance of this subject. One such study conducted by the Developing Justice Coalition in their published report, "Current Strategies for Reducing Recidivism," found that corrections programs with rehabilitative and treatment services have a lower recidivism rate than those that do not offer any services (McKean & Ransford, 2004). Likewise, if we want to change a detainee's thought and behavior characteristics to a favorable outcome, we may first need to address physical aspects that possibly could be impeding the change.

Due process within detainee operations is similar to what it means in any society. It is the idea that laws and legal proceedings must be fair and in accordance with the law. Within detainee operations, due process must be administered in accordance with applicable law and under legally constituted authority per the GPW, the Geneva Conventions, the Uniform Code of Military Justice, and the Manual for Court Martial (Department of the Army *AR 190-8*, 1997). Due process becomes an effective and logical line of operation to reach the overall objective of detainee behavior modification, in that it enforces the rule of law and creates a psychological effect on the detainee. The due process model, which highlights the Multinational Force Review Committee (MNFRC) in Iraq (to be elaborated on in Chapter 4) should be expanded on and explained in detail to each detainee in order to give the detainee a sense of predictability and assurance that he will be afforded appropriate due process in accordance with the rule of law. While great steps have been taken in this direction, there remains a large amount of research that could be examined in order to make the process even more effective.

As happens in warfare, the No. 1 priority of detainee operations is to establish security. Justice Sandra Day O'Connor, writing for the majority of the Supreme Court of the United States in *Hamdi v. Rumsfeld* on June 28, 2004, pointed out, "The purpose of detention is to prevent captured individuals from returning to the field of battle and taking up arms once again." But, detention operations also serve the key purpose of intelligence gathering in order to capture or prevent other individuals—both in and out of detention—from being or becoming a security threat. In Iraq's internment facility environment, it is the military police commander's responsibility to establish and oversee security in order to effectively control detainees. Besides protecting security force personnel from detainees, detainees also must be protected from external and internal threats. Security is one of the essential logical lines of operations that tie the other lines of operations together; without effective security, the objective can never be achieved. As such, the establishment, practice, and enforcement of the rules for the use of force within detainee operations enforce both security and due process. The rules for the use of force must be strictly enforced and explained to both the detainees and the security staff in order to prevent unnecessary death and injury. Obviously, something should be done in situations where detainees might hurt themselves, each other, or soldiers. In such situations. the use of "less lethal" and "nonlethal" force (referred to as *enabling technologies*) may be justifiable. However, the real intent should be in controlling situations before they ever get to the level where enabling technologies are necessary. Otherwise, abuse of these enabling technologies could easily turn a moderate detainee into a radical extremist, completely undermining the mission.

The physical construction and location of the internment facility have just as much of an effect on security as do the security personnel. Site selection is perhaps one of the most significant factors that influence all the lines of operations. In accordance with the GPW, the detaining power must not set up places of internment in areas particularly exposed to the dangers of war. It is no small secret that when Abu Ghraib was operating, most of its detainees were housed in canvas tents that held 25 each. The detainees slept on mats on the ground and only a short stack of sandbags protected detainees from incoming mortars, which at times was a nightly occurrence (Michaels, 2004). This had its consequences. In July 2003, the commander of Abu Ghraib internment facility reported 25 attacks of shelling by mortars and other weapons, which on several occasions resulted in death or injury of detainees. In August 2003, at least five detainees were killed and 67 were injured in a mortar attack. And, in April 2004, a mortar attack killed 22 detainees and injured 91 (Schlesinger et al., 2004, p. 11). It is very easy for a detainee to turn to radical extremism when the detaining power should be providing safety and security, yet fails to even accomplish this fundamental task.

IMPACT OF THE ABU GHRAIB ABUSE

Overwhelmingly, the hugest backlash and longest-lasting impact on U.S. detainee operations in Iraq has been from what occurred primarily during a 3-month period at Abu Ghraib from October to December of 2003. The impact that U.S. soldiers mistreating detainees at Abu Ghraib had (and continues to have) on detainee operations cannot be overemphasized. The story first emerged globally in the spring of 2004 when photographs of naked, humiliated Iraqi detainees and smiling U.S. soldiers first flashed around the world. As the highest levels of command and leadership in the Department of Defense reportedly did not know about the pictures' existence, they were not adequately informed nor prepared to respond to Congress and the American public when copies were released by the press, thus adding fuel to the fire.

Of the 17 detention and holding facilities in Iraq at the time, the largest, Abu Ghraib, housed up to 7,000 detainees in October 2003, with a guard force of only about 90 personnel from the 800th Military Police Brigade. Abu Ghraib was seriously overcrowded, under resourced, and under continual attack. Of course, it did not help that in the era of Saddam Hussein, Abu Ghraib was one of the world's most notorious prisons, with torture, weekly executions, and vile living conditions. During the Saddam regime, as many as 50,000 men and women—no accurate count is possible—were jammed into Abu Ghraib at one time, in 12 × 12-ft cells that were little more than human holding pits. With this stigma attached, Iraqis could only assume the worst about how the United States was using the detention center.

Abu Ghraib highlighted the lack of standardization and lack of skills necessary to control and impart impartiality in detainee operations. So, to some, it came as little surprise when on January 13, 2004, a soldier stepped forward with tales of abuse. Army Specialist Joseph Darby anonymously gave the army Criminal Investigation Division (CID) a copy of a CD containing a collection of Iraqi detainee abuse photos that he had been given from the computer of Army Spc. Charles A. Graner, Jr., who was in charge of a group of Tier 1 detainees in Abu Ghraib. The next day, the army launched a criminal investigation. Soon after, albeit in the face of promises of retaliation by fellow Americans, Spc. Darby stepped forward to admit that he had been the one to deliver the shocking images. In his sworn testimony, Spc. Darby divulged, "I was scared ...." but "I knew I had to do something. I didn't want to see any more prisoners being abused because I knew it was wrong" (Zernike, 2004).

On January 31, 2004, Major General (Maj. Gen.) Antonio M. Taguba was appointed to write an internal report on findings of detainee abuse in U.S. detainee internment facilities in Iraq. Together with a team, he conducted over 50 interviews of witnesses, potential criminal suspects, and detainees. What they uncovered was disturbing. They discovered copious photos and videos portraying in graphic detail detainee abuse by military police personnel on numerous occasions from October to December 2003 (Taguba, 2004, p. 11). Based on time signatures from the digital cameras used, all the photographs and videos were taken between October 18, 2003, and December 30, 2003 (Benjamin, 2006). The report was meant to be internal, but was leaked in the spring of 2004 along with many of the now-famous photographs that accompanied it. It recounted that, during this period in 2003, frequent incidents of "sadistic, blatant, and wanton criminal abuses were inflicted on several detainees" (Taguba, 2004, p. 11). Abuses occurred such as:

(a) Punching, slapping, and kicking detainees; jumping on their naked feet; (b) videotaping and photographing naked male and female detainees; (c) forcibly arranging detainees in various sexually explicit positions for photographing; (d) forcing detainees to remove their clothing and keeping them naked for several days at a time; (e) forcing naked male detainees to wear women's underwear; (f) forcing groups of male detainees to masturbate themselves while being photographed and videotaped; (g) arranging naked male detainees in a pile and then jumping on them; (h) positioning a naked detainee on an MRE [meal, ready-to-eat] box, with a sandbag on his head, and attaching wires to his fingers, toes, and penis to simulate electric torture; (i) writing "I am a Rapest" [sic] on the leg of a detainee alleged to have forcibly raped a 15-year-old fellow detainee, and then photographing him naked; (j) placing a dog chain or strap around a naked detainee's neck and having a female soldier pose for a picture; (k) a male MP [Military Police] guard having sex with a female detainee; (l) using military working dogs (without muzzles) to intimidate and frighten detainees, and, in at least one case, biting and severely injuring a detainee; (s) taking photographs of dead Iraqi detainees (Taguba, 2004, p. 12).

In addition to the abuses highlighted above, several reliable detainees also collaborated by describing other forms of abuse to include:

(a) Breaking chemical lights and pouring the phosphoric liquid on detainees; (b) threatening detainees with a charged 9-mm pistol; (c) pouring cold water on naked detainees; (d) beating detainees with a broom handle and a chair; (e) threatening male detainees with rape; (f) allowing a military police guard to stitch the wound of a detainee who was injured after being slammed against the wall in his cell; (g) sodomizing a detainee with a chemical light and perhaps a broom stick; (h) using military working dogs to frighten and intimidate detainees with threats of attack, and, in one instance, actually biting a detainee (Taguba, 2004, p.12).

What might even be more appalling about the abuses that occurred at Abu Ghraib is that many of those detained held little information of intelligence value. In an investigative report into the abuses at Abu Ghraib, Maj. Gen. George R. Fay wrote:

> Sgt. Jose Garcia, assigned to the Abu Ghraib Detainee Assessment Board, estimated that 85 to 90 percent of the detainees were of no intelligence value. … Large quantities of detainees with little or no intelligence value swelled Abu Ghraib's population and led to a variety of overcrowding difficulties. … Complicated and unresponsive release procedures ensured that these detainees stayed at Abu Ghraib—even though most had no value (Danner, 2009).

In addition to detainees being held who little to no intelligence value, it also came to the forefront that many of those being held posed little to no threat to the United States. This realization, that many detainees were humiliated and tortured only for the pleasure of the soldiers, undermines America's mission in Iraq. Abu Ahmad discussed his time at Abu Ghraib as being one he would rather not remember. He talked about "being made to walk naked in front of all the other prisoners and soldiers, including females," and then elaborated. "For 32 days, I was without clothes, even if we wanted to pray, we had to pray naked." He also said that he witnessed other abuses from his cell. "One day, they brought three or four detainees, maybe more, they were about 40 years old or older. They took off their clothes, forced them to climb on top of each other and started taking photos. … I saw it with my own eyes," he said. Abu Ahmad spent a total of 20 months in U.S. custody between Abu Ghraib and Camp Bucca and endured emotional and physical abuse, and yet he was never charged with a single crime (Perry, 2009).

What the released 279 pictures and 19 videos of Abu Ghraib detainees left in their aftermath, as detainees were either released or transferred to other institutions, such as Camp Bucca and Camp Cropper, was a lot of fear and anger. The pictures hit the media in full force and shocked Iraqis and other Arabs because the images seemed to confirm so vividly and precisely a reality that many had suspected and feared, but tried not to believe. To these individuals, Americans had continued the policy of torture and humiliation for which Abu Ghraib was known. In some cases, women who had been detained while in U.S. custody were released to find their families, and husbands wanted nothing more to do with them. A good Iraqi woman is considered virtuous and pure, so family members had to consider what might have or had been done to their loved ones: forced nakedness, pictures being taken of them, rape. For some, it was too much to bear. Detainees who were transferred to other internment facilities took their horrific stories of abuse with them. They took the opportunity to tell detainees who were not at Abu Ghraib the appalling details of what it was like. Or, in some cases, their refusal to discuss their time at Abu Ghraib was all that was needed to incite hatred against Americans. Sheik Mohammed Bashir summoned up the nation's feelings at Friday prayers at Um al-Oura in Baghdad on June 11, 2004:

> It was discovered that the freedom in this land is not ours. It is the freedom of the occupying soldiers in doing what they like, such as arresting, carrying out raids, killing at random, or stealing money. No *one* can ask them what they are doing because they are protected by their freedom. No *one* can punish them, whether in our country or their country. The worst thing is what was discovered in the course of time: abusing women, children, men, and the old men and women whom they arrested randomly and without any guilt. They expressed the freedom of rape, the freedom of nudity, and the freedom of humiliation* (Cody, 2004).

Sheik Bashir did not need to show pictures to illustrate his point. People across the globe nodded their heads in agreement.

REACTION TO ABU GHRAIB

Too little was done too late as a response to Abu Ghraib. Although other instances might be even more widespread than we—as Americans—would care to acknowledge, the pictures of the smiling soldiers next to the tortured detainees are what captured the hearts of the world. Few know about other criminalized instances of detainee abuse, such as what occurred preceding (and subsequent) to Abu Ghraib. One example is the four soldiers from the 320th MP Battalion who were formally charged under the Uniform Code of Military Justice (UCMJ) with detainee abuse in relation to their actions in May 2003 at Camp Bucca (Taguba, 2004, p. 29). But, without media representation, the event received little publicity and virtually no backlash. We have all heard the phrase, "A picture is worth a thousand words." Well, in this case, one might veer to add, not only a thousand words, but perhaps "a thousand lives were lost because of those pictures." Matthew Alexander,* an outspoken opponent of the use of torture in interrogations and the leader

---

* The Washington Post, 2004. Reprinted with permission.

of a team in Iraq responsible for the capture of Abu Musab al-Zarqawi, elaborates further:

> I learned in Iraq that the no. 1 reason foreign fighters flocked there to fight were the abuses carried out at Abu Ghraib and Guantanamo. Our policy of torture was directly and swiftly recruiting fighters for Al Qaeda in Iraq. The large majority of suicide bombings in Iraq are still carried out by these foreigners. They are also involved in most of the attacks on U.S. and coalition forces in Iraq. It's no exaggeration to say that at least half of our losses and casualties in that country have come at the hands of foreigners who joined the fray because of our program of detainee abuse. The number of U.S. soldiers who have died because of our torture policy will never be definitively known, but it is fair to say that it is close to the number of lives lost on Sept. 11, 2001. How anyone can say that torture keeps Americans safe is beyond me—unless you don't count American soldiers as Americans (Alexander, 2009).

The United States realizes that it can never again afford to tolerate such unethical behavior or lack of discipline as occurred at Abu Ghraib. Although the circumstances of Abu Ghraib and the military chain of command responsible are a bit convoluted and controversial, we can be sure that it was a wake-up call for America. The United States has taken positive steps in the right direction of rebuilding global trust. One of the first responses, once the pictures landed on the desk of CID, was to start investigations. In light of what happened at Abu Ghraib, a series of comprehensive investigations has been conducted by various components of the Department of Defense. In Iraq during 2004, this first included the leaked Taguba Report, and then there was the Fay/Jones Report (Fay & Jones, 2004), the Schlesinger Report, the classified Provost Marshal General Donald Ryder Report, and the classified Except-for-the-Executive-Summary Church Report. It also prompted the United States to action regarding its detainee internment facilities elsewhere. Since Abu Ghraib, the U.S. military and security operations have apprehended over 50,000 individuals. From this number, over 300 allegations of abuse in Afghanistan, Iraq, or Guantanamo have arisen. From the substantiated cases, approximately one third occurred at the point of capture or tactical collection point, frequently under uncertain, dangerous, and violent circumstances (Schlesinger et al., 2004, p. 5). In 2004, then-U.S. President George W. Bush tried to demolish Abu Ghraib by sending a message to the world that America was going to take action on the abuses that occurred there, but the Iraqi interim president, Ghazi Mashal Ajil Al-Yawer, opposed that decision. The matter remained undecided for a couple of weeks until on June 21, U.S. military judge Col. James Pohl ruled that the prison was a crime scene, and, therefore, could not be demolished. To most who had been there during the scandalous operations, this only delayed the desirable and inevitable.

Abu Ghraib had always been a questionable facility from the standpoint of conducting operations. It had none of the typical morale incentives for troops: any gym, barbershop, mess hall, or even shopping store for basic necessities. In addition, its location next to an urban area and its large size in relation to the small MP unit tasked to provide a law enforcement presence, made it impossible to achieve the necessary degree of security. The detainee population of approximately 7,000 outmanned the 93 MPs by approximately a 75:1 ratio in 2003 and the beginning of 2004 (Schlesinger et al., 2004, p. 60). These were all factors that key leadership knew needed to change if they were going to keep operations running at Abu Ghraib. They also realized that the previous method of operation was going to need to undergo a drastic overhaul in order to make it work. The commander of the 18th Military Police Brigade, Col. James Brown, used a personal experience to shape the thinking of leaders of the 306th Military Police Battalion, who were preparing for mobilization to Abu Ghraib in late 2004. He told of a meeting he once had with a German landlord who had spent time as a prisoner of war (POW). Col. Brown extended his sympathies, but the landlord said it was the best thing that could have happened to him. He was removed from the fighting and treated well by the Americans. This former German soldier's treatment forever changed his view toward Americans. This simple story highlighted the fact that any military police force deploying to a detention facility following the Abu Ghraib scandal would have to be on its best behavior.

However, with many American military members being prejudiced against Muslims (M. Alexander,* personal interview, November 4, 2009), this view by some Americans—that Iraqis (or even Arabs, more generally) as less than them—would have to undergo a major overhaul. Every move they made would be watched not only by the detainees who interacted daily with them, but also by the world. In this sense, the 2003 Abu Ghraib abuses caused the requirement of preparation, training, involvement, and discipline to attain a higher level than ever before. This elevated level of detainee interaction and discipline worked to establish a better reputation among detainees and units alike, commencing with Abu Ghraib's smooth transfer of authority between the U.S. and Iraqi forces in March 2006.

Other prevention and preparation methods of operandum included opening up training centers. Mock detention facility training centers were opened up in the United States for soldiers preparing to deploy. The detention centers equipped soldiers with the necessary skills and mindset to be most effective for running detention centers overseas. On June 2, 2006, the army opened an Iraqi-based detention center training facility at Fort Leonard Wood, Missouri, called Camp Charlie (Choike, 2006).

This new facility was designed to model after the detainee internment facility at Camp Bucca. A similar facility was opened at Fort Leavenworth in August 2006 (Thompson, 2006). These mock detention training centers went hand-in-hand with a manual published by The Department of Defense Detainee Program (DODD 2310.01E) on September 5, 2006. The manual was published to address shortfalls of the U.S. detainee operations program. It directed all personnel dealing with detainees to "receive instruction and complete training, commensurate with their duties, in laws, regulations, policies, and other issuances applicable to detainee operations" (Department of Defense, 2006). Soldiers would never again have a reason to be unfamiliar with the Geneva Convention and other international laws applicable in warfare situations.

Abu Ghraib was a mess, training was deficient, and the chain of command was dysfunctional. But, it is simply not credible that military intelligence soldiers would have no idea what was being done to prisoners whom they spent hours and hours each day interrogating. The Pentagon's own probes acknowledged that military commanders, civilian contractors, the Central Intelligence Agency (CIA), and the government policymakers all bear some responsibility for the abuses. Everyone realized someone needed to pay. And, they did. Nine enlisted soldiers have been prosecuted for their crimes at Abu Ghraib with sentences ranging from only a few months in prison to a 10-year prison sentence. An additional four soldiers and eight officers, including Col. Thomas Pappas (former head of military intelligence at Abu Ghraib), Lieutenant Colonel (Lt. Col.) Steven L. Jordan (former director of the Joint Interrogation Debriefing Center at Abu Ghraib), and Army Reserve (then Brigadier General) Janis Karpinski,* who was in charge of military police at Abu Ghraib, also have been reprimanded. (Pappas and Karpinski were also relieved of their posts.) However, to date, no high-level U.S. officials have been brought to justice in a court of law for what went on at Abu Ghraib (Walsh, 2006).

Colonel Karpinski discussed a letter apparently signed by Donald Rumsfeld, which allowed civilian contractors to use enhanced interrogation techniques during interrogation. "The methods consisted of making prisoners stand for long periods, sleep deprivation ..., playing music at full volume, having to sit uncomfortably. ... Rumsfeld authorized these techniques," she said. According to Col. Karpinski, the handwritten signature was above his printed name and in the same handwriting in the margin, it was written: "Make sure this is accomplished." According to

---

* Brigadier General Janis Karpinski retired as a U.S. Army Colonel in the 800th Military Brigade. She was demoted from Brigadier General following the Abu Ghraib scandal for dereliction of duty, making a material misrepresentation to investigators, and failure to obey a lawful order.

the February 16, 2008, edition of *The Economist*, Rumsfeld also wrote in a 2002 memo: "I stand for 8 to 10 hours a day. Why is standing [by prisoners] limited to 4 hours?" There has been no comment from either the Pentagon or U.S. Army spokespeople in Iraq on Col. Karpinski's charges. Other soldiers suggest that not only did Donald Rumsfeld approve sleep deprivation, he also approved sensory deprivation, water boarding, exposure to heat and cold, stress positions, threats of death to family members, and the use of dogs (M. Alexander,* personal interview, November 4, 2009). Some view as scandalous the fact that he was not held accountable for any of his direct indications to utilize enhanced interrogation techniques. Dr. Stjepan Mestrovic, a sociologist from Texas who testified as an expert witness at several Abu Ghraib trials, calls the Pentagon's attempt to blame the scandal on a few low-ranking "bad apples" little more than "magical thinking." "It doesn't make any sense," he says. "There is no way that a handful of low-ranking soldiers could have invented techniques—all by themselves—that curiously enough were used [at the naval detention facility] Guantanamo and at other places in Iraq and Afghanistan" (Zagorin, 2007).

It is important to recognize that Abu Ghraib is only one snapshot of tactics the United States has used since 2001 in the global war on terror. There have been many other allegations of abuse, torture, and other practices that violate international law, from holding prisoners without charging them at Guantanamo Bay and other secretive U.S. military bases and prison facilities around the world to the practice of "rendition," or the transporting of detainees to foreign countries whose regimes use torture, to ongoing human rights violations inside detention facilities in Iraq. The Fay/Jones report highlighted this by making it plain that the U.S. forces had begun torturing detainees in Afghanistan in 2001, that barbarism was routinized in 2002 at Guantanamo, and that the techniques for breaking prisoners had migrated from one theater to the next until they became standard procedure at Abu Ghraib. General Fay attributed much of the cruelty to "confusion" on the part of the interrogators who just couldn't be sure anymore what "techniques" could be used at what time on which detainees (Wypijewski, 2008).

The ICRC also was aware of what was going on in Iraq and voiced these concerns to the U.S. military in its compiled report of October 2003, even before the infamous photos were shot. The report clearly refers to what was going on at Abu Ghraib as "tantamount to torture."

> In early July [2003] the ICRC sent the U.S. military a working paper detailing approximately 50 allegations of ill treatment in the military intelligence section of Camp Cropper, at Baghdad International Airport. ... In one illustrative case, a person deprived of his liberty arrested at home by the CF [Coalition Forces] on suspicion of

involvement in an attack against the CF was allegedly beaten during interrogation in a location in the vicinity of Camp Cropper. He alleged that he had been hooded and cuffed with flexi-cuffs; threatened to be tortured or killed; urinated on; kicked in the head, lower back, and groin; force-fed a baseball, which was tied to his mouth using a scarf; and deprived of sleep for four consecutive days. Interrogators would allegedly take turns ill-treating him. When he said he would complain to the ICRC, he was allegedly beaten some more. An ICRC medical examination revealed hematoma in the lower back, blood in urine, sensory loss in the right hand due to tight handcuffing with flexi-cuffs, and a broken rib (ICRC, 2004, p. 3.4: 34).

However, the ICRC's concerns went unheeded. A leaked 2004 ICRC report intended only for the military gave the American public a glimpse of what the ICRC had witnessed first hand. Covering the span of March to November 2003, the ICRC had conducted 29 visits in 14 internment and holding facilities throughout Iraq, and detailed the fact that several international laws had been consistently broken, to include:

- Brutality against protected persons upon capture and initial custody, sometimes causing death or serious injury.
- Absence of notification of arrest of persons deprived of their liberty to their families causing distress among persons deprived of their liberty and their families.
- Physical or psychological coercion during interrogation to secure information.
- Prolonged solitary confinement in cells devoid of daylight.
- Excessive and disproportionate use of force against persons deprived of their liberty resulting in death or injury during their period of internment.

The report also detailed that "ill treatment during capture was frequent." And, that allegations and accounts of ill treatment occurred primarily in a few key areas (Baghdad, Basrah, Ramadi, and Tikrit), which further indicated a consistent pattern with respect to times and places of brutal behavior during arrest. Additionally, the ICRC indicated that the repetition of such behavior by the military appeared to go beyond "reasonable, legitimate, and proportional use of force required to apprehend suspects or restrain persons resisting arrest or capture, and seemed to reflect a usual modus operandi by certain CF battle group units" (ICRC, 2004, Exec. Summ.).

The August 2009 partially declassified report by President Obama's administration describes the early implementation of the agency's interrogation program in 2002 and 2003 as ad hoc and poorly supervised, leading to the use of "unauthorized, improvised, inhumane, and undocumented" techniques. The Obama administration was forced to release the CIA documents because of a wide-ranging Freedom of Information Act lawsuit the American Civil Liberties Union (ACLU) filed in 2003. Inside the report were facts such as the CIA's first high-value detainee—Zayn al-Abidin Muhammed Hussein, better known as Abu Zubaida—was waterboarded 83 times in August 2002. Mohammed was ultimately waterboarded 183 times, according to Justice Department memos. Although he provided more information after the technique was applied to him, "it is not possible to say definitively that the waterboard is the reason" for his increased cooperation or if other factors, "such as the length of detention, was a catalyst," the inspector general's report concluded. Interestingly, the 2004 report by the then-Inspector General John L. Helgerson noted that "the agency faces potentially serious long-term political and legal challenges as a result of the ... program, particularly its use of [enhanced interrogation techniques] and the inability of the U.S. government to decide what it will ultimately do with terrorists detained by the agency." The report said CIA personnel "are concerned that public revelation" of the program will "seriously damage" personal reputations as well as "the reputation and effectiveness of the agency itself." One officer said he could imagine CIA agents ending up before the World Court on war crimes charges. "Ten years from now, we're going to be sorry we're doing this," said the CIA officer. But "it has to be done" (Finn, Warrick, & Tate, 2009).

CONCLUSION

The rule of law has many definitions. Its foundational definition as applied within detainee operations is based on the principle that every member of the facility, to include the detaining power, must follow the rules and laws established. It is a belief that there is a universal standard of justice, equality, and impartiality. Applying and enforcing the rule of law within detainee operations establishes a framework for a detainee to operate in and reassures the safety and security for both the detainees and internment staff. Without the rule of law, a radical extremist can easily capitalize and take advantage of the system by promoting and developing radical extremist ideologies. Much, many might argue, like what became the outcome of Abu Ghraib.

Abu Ghraib might have been its own particular hell, but the variations of individual abuse perpetrated appear to be exceptional in only one way: they were photographed and filmed. So, 7 years on, the backlash of Abu Ghraib is still with us today. The Hooded Man has taken its place among the symbols calling forth, in some parts of the world, a certain image of the United States and what it stands for. Because of it, people across the globe still flinch in fear with the thought of being taken into U.S. custody. Movies and books have been written about the events and circumstances at Abu Ghraib. Lives have been shattered, torn apart, and, in some cases, forever changed. Still the questions, "Where does this leave us?" and "What have we learned?" loom large. In his book, *Unconquerable Nation* (2006), Brian Jenkins states: "American efforts understandably have focused almost exclusively on thwarting operations and capturing terrorists—the visible tip of the iceberg. We now have to expand the strategy to impede recruiting and encourage rehabilitation." And, in that, many might argue, our answer lies.

CHAPTER 3

Setting the Stage for Terrorist Rehabilitation

DETAINEES (RE)ACT

As the United States searched for answers, radical teachings inside compounds were motivating detainees to react to the injustice of detention. From 2004 to 2006, most detainees felt there was no hope. There were no legal proceedings, compounds were overcrowded, most did not know why they were detained, few were getting family visits, there was nothing to do, and no hope for release. Meanwhile, religious extremists within compounds filled heads with stories of retribution and revenge against the kafir in exchange for everlasting bliss. Nothing unites a group more strongly than a feeling of persecution and injustice. Detainees wanted a reason to retaliate—in some cases against a lifetime of repression—and any reason would do. So, coming together as a whole, in some cases for the first time, detainees lashed out at the people who held them captive (Figure 3.1). They were angry, they were bitter, they were filled with rage, and they were determined to let the American forces know just how much, even if that meant from within detention.

Therefore, when the Abu Ghraib scandal flooded the world with cries of outrage in 2004, detainees joyfully shared in the uproar. Although things were being done on the outside about Abu Ghraib—reports were being written, soldiers were being held accountable, and the American public was knee-jerking an outcry—this meant little to the Iraqis who increasingly had little reason to care. Abu Ghraib provided justification for the anger and resentment many Iraqis secretly felt, but, in most cases, had no reason to express. Abu Ghraib gave them that reason. It brought Muslims around the world together in their rage at injustice and plans for retaliation. Jihadists were given renewed purpose and focus for making the journey to Iraq. Mortars, improvised explosive devices (IEDs), and threats against American

FIGURE 3.1   Detainees riot: Camp Bucca, Iraq, 2007. (Photo courtesy of U.S. Department of Defense.)

troops escalated to new levels. More than ever, troops were risking their lives in trying to maintain a deteriorating security situation. Inside detention centers, riots, hunger strikes, and disobedience increased in intensity and occurrence (Figure 3.2 through Figure 3.5). The number of detainee escapes also steadily increased.

Detainees became more creative in their escape routes, including using fog as a cover, cutting through fences, and digging elaborate tunnels. One of the largest and most impressive tunnels ever discovered in detainee operations was late in the afternoon on March 24, 2005. Hours before a planned prison break for hundreds, an informant tipped off the Americans. What they found was mind-blowing. Hidden beneath the wooden floorboards of a detainee tent was a fully completed tunnel that stretched 357 feet and whose walls were smooth and strong as concrete. An estimated 600 detainees had worked in rotating 5-minute, 10-man shifts in the early hours of morning, ingeniously carting bags of dirt up to their soccer field, which was then churned during daily soccer matches. The detainees had dug with makeshift tent poles and had used

FIGURE 3.2   Detainees set their caravans on fire in protest of being detained: Camp Bucca, Iraq, 2007. (Photo by Andrea Holm.)

water and their daily chai tea* to make the walls strong and resilient. "It was a military operation. It was very organized, and it was very disciplined," said Mohammed Touman, a detainee who was released from the compound where the tunnel was dug. "If only 200 people would have escaped, it would have been a blow to the Americans," he laughed (Fainaru & Shadid, 2005). Col. James B. Brown, who was the commander in charge, said the escape would have been one of the largest from any U.S.-run facility in history.

There were also many other attempted—and, in some cases, successful—escapes from Camp Bucca before and after what is now commonly referred to as "the great escape" tunnel of March 2005. Such as on January 7, 2004, when investigating officers concluded that a detainee was able to escape through an undetected weakness in the wire. He has not been recaptured. On January 12, 2004, seven detainees

---

* The detainee's daily chai tea (served with every meal) was made with brown sugar, thus containing a higher than average amount of cholesterol, which binds sand together firmly. Ken Reidy, while an OSS contractor, suggested that sweetener be substituted in place of the brown sugar. Tunnel walls would not be strong enough to hold a shape and chai rocks would crumble upon impact. However, the major at the time wouldn't allow it. The military was afraid that the detainees wouldn't drink the chai tea if sweetener was used instead of brown sugar (K. Reidy, personal interview, December 18, 2010).

FIGURE 3.3   Pressurized water is sprayed into a compound to put out fires and help put an end to the riot: Camp Bucca, Iraq, 2007. (Photo courtesy of U.S. Department of Defense.)

FIGURE 3.4   Detainees riot: Camp Bucca, Iraq, 2007. (Photo courtesy of U.S. Department of Defense.)

FIGURE 3.5   Detainees riot: Camp Bucca, Iraq, 2007. (Photo courtesy of U.S. Department of Defense.)

escaped through the wire. Only five were recaptured. Then on January 26, 2004, three detainees escaped at night by crawling under a fence during a period of intense fog when visibility was only 10 to 15 meters (GlobalSecurity.org, 2006). On April 16, 2005, 11 detainees escaped Camp Bucca by cutting through the facility's exterior fence and crawling through the unfilled portion of the previously discovered 357-foot escape tunnel. All 11 were recaptured and returned (*CNN News*, 2005). Then on January 1, 2006, three detainees escaped Camp Bucca by cutting through the facility's exterior fence. Two of the detainees were captured by the Iraqi police and returned to Camp Bucca. On December 24, 2006, two detainees escaped from Camp Bucca again during the dense seasonal fog. One of the detainees was allegedly an IED maker and neither has been recaptured. Likewise, throughout the Iraq war, there have been many other examples of creativity and innovation resulting in a successful escape, such as in 2007 when two detainees somehow managed to crawl into the back of a trash truck when it came in to make its rounds. Neither detainee has been recaptured.

Meanwhile, riots and outbursts also increased in frequency and violence as detainees demanded that their voice be heard. Any detainees who did not join with the others faced possible attack and mutilation. On January 31, 2005, a riot broke out in which angry detainees threw rocks and fashioned weapons out of tent poles, causing the death of four and injury of six detainees. The American military, not having enough non-lethal ammunition, felt compelled to use lethal force to quench the riot (Moss & Medkhennet, 2007). Not long after, a significant 4-day riot, resulting in two Iraqis and four soldiers being injured, proved consequential in revamping detainee riot tactics. The riot began on April 1, 2005, in compound 3 at Camp Bucca, where the Shiites were held. It was instigated by the detainee accusation that the U.S. military used unnecessary force when coming into the compound to transfer 10 of the detainees, 4 of which were clerics. Lt. Col. T. Paul Houser, hearing the commotion, jumped in the back of a covered cargo truck to make his way over. But as he traveled, suddenly a chunk of cinderblock flew through the back of the truck unfortunately hitting him in the left eye, fracturing his cheek in three places, and breaking three teeth. The cinderblock had been chiseled from the concrete base of a tent pole; hundreds of pieces had been stored inside a tent the inmates used as a mosque that the military designated off limits to the guards. The detainees used floorboards as shields. They hurled socks filled with a cocktail of feces, dirt, and flammable, slow-burning hand sanitizer, the Americans said. One of the crude devices even ignited a Polaris all-terrain vehicle. But enough was enough, and on the fourth day of the riots, a Black Hawk helicopter flew low over the compound, leveling all the remaining tents and causing detainees to scramble for cover. Bulldozers and 200 heavily armed soldiers encircled the compound, inviting a continued protest. Having not had food for 4 days and little sleep, the detainees surrendered, complying with a list of demands that included handing over their weapons, the remaining floor-boards, and the cinderblock rubble (Fainaru & Shadid, 2005).

These riots were complemented by other continuous sporadic disturbances, such as on April 15, 2005, when a dispute broke out between two groups of detainees causing one detainee's death, and, on March 26, 2006, when a 25-year-old detainee died as the result of injuries suffered in a detainee-on-detainee fight (Task Force 134, 2006). But, quite possibly, the largest riot to ever occur in Iraq happened on August 11, 2006, at Camp Bucca, when detainees initiated a multiple compound riot that included the burning of their living quarters, burning a Humvee, and assaults on other detainees. The reported cause of the riot was detainees being unhappy that their housing areas were searched. (Housing areas and compounds are searched on a regular basis to find and confiscate manufactured weapons similar to stateside jails.) Multiple weapons were found during initial searches (Figure 3.6). Based on the detainees' use of weapons against the guard force, multiple weapons were confiscated in additional searches initiated because of the riot. However, what is notable about this particular riot is that it was not confined to one compound. But rather, one compound was able to successfully provoke and encourage

FIGURE 3.6   Confiscated weapons found in detainee compounds: Camp Bucca, Iraq, 2007. (Photo courtesy of a U.S. soldier.*)

other compounds by an elaborate messaging system to join in the fighting and rioting with them. It illustrates just how little control the military had over the elaborate communication and bonding efforts between compounds.

INSIDE THE WIRE

Detainees throughout Iraq have always been encouraged to take an active interest in what is going on outside the theater internment facility (TIF) in the way of change. As such, entitlements, like voting in the Iraqi Constitutional Referendum, are encouraged. On October 13, 2005, eligible detainees at Camp Bucca, Abu Ghraib prison, and Camp Cropper were allowed to vote in the Iraqi Constitutional Referendum. The rest of the country voted on October 15, 2005. Likewise, when there was a contest for a new Iraqi flag design during 2008, detainees' creative drawings were collected, and after security verification were submitted to the judging committee in Baghdad for consideration.

But, still there is the fact that each compound in each detention center has a self-contained legal process. Tribal law is still powerful and is something not easily changed, nor forgotten. Perhaps tribal law applies particularly in a situation where there is little incentive or motivation to change age-old customs. While most Sunni and Shiite detainees are kept in separate compounds, at Camp Bucca in the Shiite area alone, there were about 20 clerics who were in charge. In most compounds, detainees elect a leader (also known as *chief* or *compound chief*) from

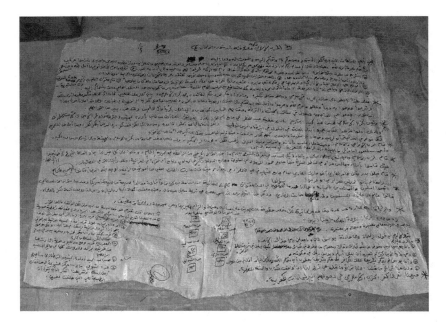

FIGURE 3.7   Found in one of the compounds was a document entitled "The Islamic Party and its relationship to the Constitution and Parliament," which outlines why the new Iraqi constitution is "kafir." In the document, the detainee writer(s) wishes to warn other detainees of the element of unbelief (kufr) that is in the constitution. Following that, those who accept, judge, and call for its institution are deemed as "they who do not judge in accordance with what God has bestowed from on high are, indeed, deniers of the truth!" The writer also questions: "Is it that they [who care for no more than this world] believe in forces supposed to have a share in God's divinity, which enjoin upon them as a moral law that God has never allowed?" Camp Bucca, Iraq, 2007. (Photo courtesy of a U.S. soldier.*)

their ranks. Once in power, detainees said, his decisions are unquestioned (Fainaru & Shadid, 2005). Decrees written by detainees for other detainees, (Figure 3.7) and even drawings and poems inciting violence (Figure 3.8) were not uncommon to find strategically placed around compounds. Those in charge often hand down stern justice. For breaking rules, detainees are denied food or beaten on the soles of their feet with poles, leaving no visible marks. Some tribunals within compounds have carried out punishments to include locking the accused in an outhouse for hours or attacking him with punches on his body not visible to guards. Other punishments have included not permitting him to speak

FIGURE 3.8   Handdrawn note purposely left for guards to discover: Camp Bucca, Iraq, 2007. (Photo courtesy of a U.S. soldier.*)

or forbidding everyone else in the compound from talking to him for a certain length of time. In the most severe cases, a leader's decisions have resulted in the mutilation or death of the accused. Camp Bucca provided some horrific examples. In 2007 alone, there were 6 detainee-caused-by-detainee deaths and 25 severe detainee-caused-by-detainee mutilations. Dr. Angell (coauthor) can recall one particular case in 2008 where a detainee was beaten to death by oranges. His crime was speaking English with the U.S. military guards, a language the *compound chief* did not speak. Naturally, those within the compound decided that he must be giving "Intel" to the soldiers, since they could not understand what he was saying. The compound chief explained that he had warned this detainee to stop his chatter with the soldiers, but, since he would not, there was no other choice but to make an example of him. Other detainees snuck up on him while he slept. Then with socks, sheets, shirts, and other materials that they could stuff with oranges, they beat him unconscious, and eventually to his death. The military did not hear anything or find out about the homicide until roll call several hours later. At that point, when the military asked where this particular detainee was, the chief said, "Oh, I don't think he is ever going to come out again."

Similar instances like the aforementioned have occurred across the theater in Iraq, varying only in their creativity and degree of violence. Of course, ultimately we have no way of knowing if even some of the causes of "natural death" reported also might have been the result of detainee-on-detainee violence. Examples include death resulting from "a heart attack" (30-year-old on May 14, 2005, 43-year-old on October 5, 2005); "natural causes" (31-year-old on January 5, 2005, 36-year-old on March 7, 2006); and "unknown causes" (26-year-old on October 19, 2004). Notably, most public records listing the ages and circumstances of detainee deaths became unavailable after mid-2006.

However, in general, there are two main camps of influence inside the detention centers. There is the infamous Al Qaeda in Iraq (AQI), which with monetary backing is able to recruit more rapidly in detention centers by promising familial support after release in exchange for commitment to the cause. The majority of AQI members are overwhelmingly Iraqis—often thugs and misfits recruited or dragooned into the organization (along with some clerics and more educated leaders)—to carry out "dirty work" and, once in detention, recruitment. While they seldom engage in jihad, they are more easily swayed by radical teachings to commit to Al Qaeda's cause and use this leverage to get others to join with them. This camp also consists of the majority of foreign fighters, who incidentally are 90 percent of all suicide bombers in Iraq. Most foreign fighters initially come to Iraq to join up with this local Al Qaeda chapter through its safe houses, the majority of which are along the Iraq/Syrian border. It is either crossing the border in Iraq, attempting to carry out a mission, or conducting operations elsewhere that usually gets them detained by U.S. forces. Their primary motivation is to wage jihad and to that end they work to recruit other detainees within the facility. However, while these foreign fighters of Al Qaeda do influence in terms of financial backing and upper echelon direction of strategy, they are still viewed as "foreign" by most detainees and often blamed for the violence against people in Iraq.

Wahhabism is a strict sect of Islam attributed to Muhammad ibn Abd-al-Wahhab, an 18th-century scholar from what is today Saudi Arabia, and is the other camp of influence inside Iraq's detention centers. Wahhabists seek to restore the pristine Islam of the Qur'an and the Prophet by a total ban of all bid'a (innovation). Generally, they observe a strict code of the perceived "original" Islam, and those who do not agree are considered Kafir (infidel). As such, most Wahhabists are also takfiri (meaning *excommunicate*). It has been suggested that one of the most important intellectual figures in Al Qaeda, Ayman al-Zawahiri, was a member of the first group of "takfiri" Salafis who disengaged themselves from the surrounding society and planned insurrections. The group was called *Takfir wal-Hijra* (TwH, Excommunication and Holy

Flight/Emigration) and was founded in Egypt in 1971 by Shukri Mustafa (Kepel, 1985, p. 105). There is a bit of murkiness surrounding TwH, but it is suggested that Al Qaeda was responsible for turning the otherwise clumsy and unworkable concept of TwH and its ideological antithesis al-Jihad into a synthesized, sophisticated, and workable revolutionary system. With Al Qaeda's support, al-Jihad then evolved into the Egyptian Islamic Jihad, which al-Zawahiri has led since 1991. Practicing takfir is complex and very sect specific. But in Iraq, a Takfiri is a Muslim who practices takfir, which is to accuse other Muslims of apostasy. According to Islamic (or Sharia) law, a Muslim declared impure can no longer benefit from the protection of the law, and is condemned to death. This generally follows a strict set of rules and guidelines formulated under Orthodox Islam to determine whether or not the accused party is guilty of apostasy or not. In mainstream Sunni Islam, it is considered wrong to engage in takfir. Sunni Islam has a general reluctance to spread *fitna* (sow dissension) or "backbite." Furthermore, to declare takfir is to pre-empt Allah's judgment (Stanley, 2005). The Muslim who considers another's action to be wrong may say so, but will stop far short of declaring that person an apostate from the faith. In principle, the only group authorized to declare a Muslim kafir is the ulema, and this only once all the prescribed legal precautions have been taken. However, in Iraq's detention centers, radical groups have taken on this role. What makes Takfiris sometimes even more difficult to spot is that some Takfiris are not bound by the usual religious constraints regarding wearing a beard, drinking alcohol, or eating pork when such restrictions would interfere with waging effective Jihad. To Takfiris, strict adherence to those laws precludes necessary covert action in defense of Islam. Because Takfiris "blend in," they can organize, plan, and take action necessitated by the overriding duty of Jihad with less risk of identification, interference, or interception. In Iraq's detention centers, Takfiris have been known to recruit though physical threat and mind control. They are the most extreme and are generally disliked by the majority of the detainee population. Anyone unlucky enough to find himself in a Takfiri-controlled compound must generally strictly observe their interpretation of Islam, stealthily try to get a transfer from the U.S. military, or face almost certain persecution. Takfiris are responsible for the overwhelming majority of deaths and mutilations inside the TIFs.

In spite of the two main camps of influence inside Iraq's detention centers, there are many other types of detainees in the various compounds. Among them are veterans of Sadr's Shiite militia, the Mahdi Army, which had organized two armed uprisings against U.S. troops. The Mahdi Army, also known as Jaish Al Mahdi (JAM), is an Iraqi paramilitary force created by the Iraqi Shiite cleric Muqtada al-Sadr in June 2003. It gained notoriety as the group responsible for spearheading one of the first major armed confrontations against the U.S.-led occupation forces in April 2004. There are also Sunni followers of Abu Musab Zarqawi, a Jordanian-born insurgent leader blamed for some of Iraq's worst carnage; other Sunni insurgents loyal to tribes or the former ruling Baath party; and a handful of religious fighters from other Arab countries (Fainaru & Shadid, 2005). Yet, still the overwhelming majority of all detainees in Iraq's detention centers consist of Iraqis with little to no knowledge of Islam who can be swung in any direction, depending on the compound they end up in. There is also a small number of Christians, homosexuals, and what the military refers to as Third Country Nationals (TCNs), many of whom are seemingly uninterested in the politics of Iraq. All of these individuals must be carefully screened as well and put in the correct compound lest they face persecution for their difference.

MAJOR THEATER INTERNMENT FACILITIES (TIFS) IN IRAQ

Aside from the infamous Abu Ghraib, which would eventually close operations, detainees were kept primarily in two detention centers throughout the course of the Iraq war. The majority of years these were Camp Cropper and Camp Bucca. When Camp Bucca shut down its detention operations in 2009, Camp Taji replaced it as the largest U.S. detention operation facility in Iraq. Although the detainee populations fluctuated with the demands/desires of the war, the population was generally kept between 10,000 and 20,000 detainees at any given time. Albeit, according to Maj. Gen. Douglas M. Stone,* "The highest number of Iraqi detainees we had at any one given time was 26,000 during September of 2007" (Maj. Gen. D. Stone, personal interview, October 25, 2009). This was likely due in large part to the surge of 30,000+ U.S. troops that arrived in late 2006 through early 2007, who with their increased numbers intensified sweeps across villages and towns rounding up and detaining security risks. The smallest number of detainees at any given time was around 5,000 in October 2004, according to Maj. Gen, David E. Quantock who was the last TF-134 detention operations commander of Iraq.

Camp Cropper was a theater internment facility operated by the U.S. Army near Baghdad International Airport. It is also referred to as "Camp Remembrance II," which was technically just one component of Camp Cropper. Camp Cropper was split into three different sections:

---

* Maj. Gen. Douglas M. Stone retired from the U.S. Marine Forces Reserve in 2010 after 37 years of service.

females, juveniles under the age of 18, and adult males. At one point, there were 912 juveniles in detention here. But, by late 2009, there only remained two juveniles and no females (Maj. Gen. D. Quantock, personal interview, January 26, 2010). According to Maj. Gen. Stone, "There really is no difference between Camp Cropper and Camp Remembrance II. They were both in the same area, and Remembrance was always generally grouped with Cropper." The facility was initially opened and operated as a high-value detention (HVD) site in April 2003, and was intended to serve as a "central booking" for U.S. forces operating in Baghdad and central Iraq (although detainees from northern Iraq were brought there as well). All the former Baathists after the regime fell were kept here. "Most of the adult males had ongoing medical issues, were part of an Intel gathering, had criminal–legal cases processing in court, or had just arrived and were waiting for processing and moving," Maj. Gen. Stone remarked, "I don't think we ever had more than 5,000 detainees there total." Notably large considering the original concept for Camp Cropper called for a temporary camp that would hold up to 300 detainees for no more than 72 hours. Conceptually, after being processed at Camp Cropper, it was intended that detainees would be shipped to other detention facilities in Baghdad and throughout Iraq. However, in practice, this proved unworkable because most other prisons in Baghdad were badly damaged by looting after the fall of the Baath regime. Early on, this caused overcrowding, and Camp Cropper was forced to expand its capacity of 163 to over 2,000 detainees—numbers that it still maintains today, albeit under Iraqi authority. It was also at this very facility that former Iraqi President Saddam Hussein fed birds and tended to his meager garden prior to his public execution (Saddam a caring Man-Nurse, 2007).

Camp Bucca was a detention facility maintained predominantly by the U.S. military in the vicinity of Um Qasr, Iraq (southern Iraq on the Kuwait border). The facility was initially called Camp Freddy by the British Forces who used it to hold Iraqi prisoners of war. However, it was renamed Camp Bucca after Ronald Bucca, a soldier of the 800th Military Police Brigade and a New York City fire marshal who died in the September 11, 2001, attacks, when the United States took it over in April 2003. After the Abu Ghraib abuse, many detainees from Abu Ghraib were transferred to Camp Bucca. Camp Bucca housed only adult males, and is known to have housed some of the "worst of the worst" detainees, including many Al Qaeda and Al-Mahdi Army members. It also housed some detainees who had been sentenced to death by the Iraqi court, but which the Iraqi forces did not have the room to house. This particular set of detainees wore identifying uniforms of lime green as they awaited the final turnover of power and, thus, their execution date. For a significant period of time during 2007 and 2008, Camp Bucca was known as the largest detention facility in the world. In August 2007, Camp Bucca's population stood at approximately 20,000. When Dr. Angell (coauthor) was there in October 2007, it had been announced that Camp Bucca would be expanded once again to increase its capacity from 20,000 to 30,000 detainees.

There was a successful family visitation allowance program at Camp Bucca initially set up and supported by the International Committee of the Red Cross (ICRC) in October 2005. The ICRC set up operations to help provide monetary assistance to families of detainees held at Camp Bucca to help cover part of the traveling and hotel costs required to visit the facility. The benefits were calculated based on the distance between their home and the city of Um Qasr. Although there were periods of time since the outset that the ICRC was forced to halt the program (extreme unrest, etc.), generally the program was considered a success and was highly supported by the U.S. military, which built a family visitation welcome center staffed by military and civilian volunteers handing out stuffed animals, clothes, and hygiene kits to visiting families. The military also built a gondola, a playground for the children, and painted and decorated the inside of the visitation center in an attempt to make it more warm and welcoming to those who came to visit.

Nevertheless, on September 17, 2009, Camp Bucca sent its last 180 detainees on a plane bound for Camp Cropper, and shut down operations. With the closure of detainee operations in Camp Bucca, the ICRC also ended its family-visit program. During the 4 years that the ICRC program ran, almost 30,000 detained people received 146,000 visits from their relatives with ICRC support. Instead, the newest U.S.-operated detention facility in Iraq, Camp Taji, near Al Taji, Iraq, replaced Camp Bucca. The camp is located in a rural region approximately 16 miles north of the city of Baghdad in the Baghdad Governorate. While under U.S. control, Camp Taji housed adult males from its opening in late 2008 through its closure in early 2010. Many of the same facilities that existed at Camp Bucca also existed at Camp Taji, albeit in a smaller and more temporary measure. The purpose and focus all along was the transfer of Camp Taji to the Government of Iraq (GoI), which finally took place on March 15, 2010.

USCENTCOM

The U.S. Central Command (USCENTCOM) was established on January 1, 1983, and is directly responsible for the events and repercussions of actions taken by the U.S. military in Iraq, to include oversight of the detained population. According to the official Web site, the mission of USCENTCOM is:

With national and international partners, U.S. Central Command promotes cooperation among nations, responds to crises, and deters or defeats state and nonstate aggression, and supports development and, when necessary, reconstruction in order to establish the conditions for regional security, stability, and prosperity.

As its name implies, USCENTCOM covers the "central" area of the globe, located between the European and Pacific Commands. The countries covered include Afghanistan, Bahrain, Egypt, Iran, Iraq, Jordan, Kazakhstan, Kuwait, Kyrgyzstan, Lebanon, Oman, Pakistan, Qatar, Saudi Arabia, Syria, Tajikistan, Turkmenistan, United Arab Emirates, Uzbekistan, and Yemen. The presidential-appointed USCENTCOM Commander is directly responsible for oversight for each area of operation. Country commanders (such as in both Iraq and Afghanistan) report directly to the USCENTCOM Commander.

General John Philip Abazaid, USCENTCOM commander from July 7, 2003, to March 16, 2007, is the most senior U.S. military officer of direct Arab descent and the longest running USCENTCOM commander. He had intended to leave the region and retire earlier, but stayed in the position at the request of Donald Rumsfeld. He perhaps best articulated the then-current nature of combat in testimony before the U.S. Senate Armed Services Committee on May 19, 2004:

> Our enemies are in a unique position, and they are a unique brand of ideological extremists whose vision of the world is best summoned up by how the Taliban ran Afghanistan. If they can outlast us in Afghanistan and undermine the legitimate government there, they'll once again fill up the seats at the soccer stadium and force people to watch executions. If, in Iraq, the culture of intimidation practiced by our enemies is allowed to win, the mass graves will fill again. Our enemies kill without remorse; they challenge our will through the careful manipulations of propaganda and information; they seek safe havens in order to develop weapons of mass destruction that they will use against us when they are ready. Their targets are not Kabul and Baghdad, but places like Madrid, London, and New York. While we can't be defeated militarily, we're not going to win this thing militarily alone. ... As we fight the most unconventional war of this new century, we must be patient and courageous (Senate Armed Services Committee, 2004).

Yet, interestingly, by 2006, Gen. Abazaid's view of the Iraq war had changed, and he adamantly opposed the proposed surge of U.S. troops in Iraq. In November 2006, at a Senate Armed Services Committee hearing, Gen. Abazaid (then-USCENTCOM commander) rejected then-U.S. Senator John McCain's calls for increased U.S. troop levels in Iraq, saying that he "met with every divisional commander, Gen. Casey, the core commander, Gen. Dempsey" and asked them if "bringing in more American troops now, [would] add considerably to our ability to achieve success in Iraq and they all said 'no.'" Further, Gen. Abazaid argued, bringing in a surge of troops would just lead to Iraqis depending on the United States more, and that he (along with all the other commanders) felt that they (the Iraqis) needed to grow more independent if they were to proceed with taking control of their country's security. Yet McCain was unconvinced and was determined to get his way. Some argue that it was this event that led to Gen Abazaid's resignation and a different approach to the war; others suggest that a new fresh approach to the war was not only needed, but long overdue.

Gen. Abazaid was succeeded by Admiral (Adm.) William Fallon as USCENTCOM commander on March 16, 2007, allegedly in preparation for Gen. Abazaid's retirement from the military, which officially took place on May 1, 2007, after 34 years of service. Then on March 11, 2008, just as the surge had evened out and operations began to run increasingly smooth, Adm. Fallon also announced his resignation as USCENTCOM commander and retirement from active duty. He cited administrative complications arising in part from an article in *Esquire Magazine,* which described him as the only thing standing between the Bush administration and war with Iran (Barnett, 2008). The *Esquire* article also hinted at the possibility of Adm. Fallon being replaced (even earlier than the 1 year he lasted) by an individual more pliable with respect to George W. Bush's intentions. Thus, interestingly enough, there was speculation that Adm. Fallon's resignation had been "heavily encouraged" by those higher up in the chain of command. On April 23, 2008, Gen. Petraeus—then-commanding general of Multinational Force-Iraq (MNF-I)—and a natural favorite of then-President George W. Bush, was given a promotion as Adm. Fallon's predecessor. He was confirmed by the U.S. Senate on July 10, 2008, and assumed position as USCENTCOM commander on October 31, 2008 (*CNN Politics,* 2008). As new USCENTCOM commander, it almost seemed fitting that Gen. Petraeus was replaced in his previous MNF-I commanding general position by another individual who had shown increasing innovation and creativity in his approach to the war—General Raymond Odierno. In an official ceremony, Gen. Odierno became (the last) MNF-I general commander on September 16, 2008, a post he held until September 1, 2010.*

Throughout his tenure as commanding general of MNF-I and then USCENTCOM commander, Gen. Petraeus provided candid comments regarding his view of the Iraq war and his thoughts about what he considers "victory." In an interview with *BBC News*, he stated that he did not think using the term "victory" is appropriate when describing Iraq,

---

* MNF-I Iraq officially became United States Forces–Iraq (USF–I) on January 1, 2010.

saying, "This is not the sort of struggle where you take a hill, plant a flag, and go home to a victory parade. ... It's not war with a simple slogan" (*BBC News*, 2008). But then, in March 2008, he clarified his definition of "victory" as being "an Iraq that is at peace with itself, at peace with its neighbors, that has a government that is representative of—and responsive to—its citizenry and is a contributing member of the global community" could arguably be called "victory" (*NPR News*, 2008). However, the term still mystifies. On the eve of Gen. Petraeus's change of command to USCENTCOM commander, in September 2008, Petraeus stated, "I don't use terms like victory or defeat. ... I'm a realist, not an optimist or a pessimist. And the reality is that there has been significant progress, but there are still serious challenges" (Shanker & Farrell, 2008).

GENERAL DAVID H. PETRAEUS

Gen. David H. Petraeus, born on Nov. 7, 1952, commanded the 101st Airborne Division during the 2003 invasion of Iraq—his first combat assignment and one in which he came under fire on several occasions. Early in the occupation, his division operated in and around Mosul, where he was generally regarded as an innovative and effective leader (Spanner, 2008). Then, from late 2005 through February 2007, Petraeus served as commanding general of Fort Leavenworth, Kansas, and the U.S. Army Combined Arms Center (CAC) located there. In this post, he led the military's effort to rewrite its counterinsurgency doctrine, also encouraging the changes in class lectures and drills. Not long after the publication of Field Manual 3-24, *Counterinsurgency,* the body of which was written by an extraordinarily diverse group of military officers, academics, human rights advocates, and journalists who had been assembled by Gen. Petraeus and Marine Lt. Gen. James N. Mattis (who jointly oversaw the publication), Gen. Petraeus was called to test it on the battlefield. (Interestingly, the doctrine calls for protecting the population from violence even at the risk of taking additional military casualties.)

Meantime, while Gen. Petraeus was commanding general of Fort Leavenworth, Gen. Raymond T. Odierno was commanding general of III Corps in Iraq. Gen. Odierno had previously served as commanding general, 4th Infantry Division, from 2001 to 2004 (which was deployed to Iraq) and then was brought back for his second deployment as commanding general of the III Corps from May 2006 to May 2008. As the day-to-day commander of III Corps, he was the operational overseer of the Iraq War troop surge of 2007 and is credited with implementing the counterinsurgency strategy that, along with the earlier rise of the Sunni Awakening militia movement, led to the decrease in violence during his tenure in Iraq from late 2006 to 2008. Frederick Kagan and Kimberly Kagan (2008), writing in the *Weekly Standard*, have argued that his deployment of forces to quell violence across Iraq "adapted the Petraeus doctrine into a successful operational art." Likewise, in an interview with Amazon.com (Tom, 2009) about his book *The Gamble*, Thomas E. Ricks discusses his impression of Gen. Odierno:

> What he did was astonishing: He went around his bosses and basically cooked up the surge. He was the only officer in the chain of command who was for it. (Petraeus also was for it, but he hadn't arrived yet to Iraq.) I think this showed genuine moral courage in what he did. It was a huge risk, going against all of his bosses. As I say in the book, he was the natural father of the surge, and Petraeus was the adoptive father. I have no problem saying that Gen. Odierno is one of the heroes of this book.

Then in February 2007, when Gen. Petraeus took over command of the MNF-I from Gen. George Casey just as then-President Bush revamped his war strategy and ordered what the administration described as the "surge" of forces, a buildup that would peak in summer 2007, the stage was already set. The strategy, in line with what Petraeus had created at Fort Leavenworth (commonly referred to as the *Petraeus doctrine)* on counterinsurgency, was meant to thwart, or at least contain, the multifaceted insurgency, stabilizing Iraq at least enough that a new political consensus could take hold, paving the way for Iraqi forces to take over more responsibility, and ultimately allowing the Americans to begin to withdraw (Spanner, 2008). While the surge predictably went well, what is often neglected is the public's understanding of just how difficult on the military the surge was. According to Ricks in his Amazon.com interview:

> The surge was "more about how to use the troops than it was about the number of them." There were two key aspects to the different use of troops. First, they had a new top priority: protect Iraqis. (Until February 2007, the top priority of U.S. forces in Iraq was to transition to Iraqi control.) Second, to do that, they had to move out into the population. Before this point, they were doing a lot of patrols from big bases, usually in Humvees. They would be in a neighborhood maybe one hour a day, and the other 23 hours of the day belonged to the insurgents. Now, they were living in the neighborhoods, and constantly going out on short foot patrols. They got a lot more familiar with the people, often visiting every single family, and conducting a census. In military terms, they were mapping the sea in which the insurgents swam. Familiarity made them far more effective, and also constrained the movements of insurgents.

Ricks then continues on:

I think there are two big misunderstandings about the surge. The first is that the surge worked. Yes, it did, in that it improved security. But, it was meant to do more than that. It was supposed to create a breathing space in which Iraqi political leaders could move forward. In fact, as Gen. Odierno says in the book, some used the elbow room to move backward. The bottom line is that none of the basic problems facing Iraq have been addressed—the relationship between Shia, Sunni, and Kurds, or who leads the Shias, or the status of the disputed city of Kirkuk, or the sharing of oil revenue. The second misunderstanding is just how difficult the surge was. People back here seem to think that 30,000 troops were added and everything calmed down. In fact, the first six months of the surge, from January through early July 2007, were the toughest months of the war. When troops moved out of their big bases and into little outposts across Baghdad, they got hammered by bombs and rockets. It took some time before being among the people began to lead to improved security, and during that time, a lot of top American officials in Iraq weren't sure the new approach was working. General Petraeus says in the book that he looks back on that time as a "horrific nightmare" (Tom, 2009).

TASK FORCE 134

Task Force 134 (TF-134) was established on April 15, 2004, to "oversee all aspects of the conduct of detainee operations within theater and to serve as the executive agent for execution of theater policy as well as military doctrine." Their mission was care and custody with dignity and respect (Koladish & Briere, 2010). Established after the dismissal of Col. Karpiniski from duties following the Abu Ghraib scandal, TF-134 has been responsible for all detainee operations across the Iraq theater. Maj. Gen. Geoffrey Miller*, amidst controversy and speculation (particularly in light of his encouragement of "improved interrogation techniques") was the first TF-134 commander. However, he only served as commanding general for 8 months before being replaced by Maj. Gen. William Brandenburg.[†] Maj. Gen. Brandenburg served without incident as TF134 commander from November 29, 2004, until December 1, 2005, before being succeeded by Lt. Gen. John D. Gardner.

---

* Maj. Gen. Geoffrey Miller retired from the Army on July 31, 2006, after 34 years of service.
[†] Maj. Gen. William Brandenburg retired on March 1, 2008, after 35 years of service.

When Gen. Petraeus was promoted to MNF-I commander, he became the immediate supervisor to the deputy commander for detention operations/TF-134, which at the date of his deployment in January 2007 was Lt. Gen. Gardner. Lt. Gen. Gardner's direct oversight included all detainee operations at Camp Bucca, Camp Cropper, Fort Suse, and Abu Ghraib prison. A major accomplishment during Lt. Gen. Gardner's command of TF-134 detention operations from 2005 to 2007 was that both Fort Suse and Abu Ghraib prison were returned to the GoI (Roberts, 2006). During his tenure as TF-134 commander, he appeared well-liked by fellow military colleagues, who spoke highly of him. In fact, Lt. Gen. Gardner is highlighted as the first general in Iraq to take direct action in examining the feasibility of the introduction of rehabilitation programs into the Iraq detainee population by bringing in outside specialists.

Detainee Rehabilitation Program Is Put Forth for Consideration

Notably, as TF-134 commander, Lt. Gen. Gardner invited representatives from the International Centre for Political Violence and Terrorism Research (ICPVTR) and the Religious Rehabilitation Group (RRG) from Singapore to come out for a visit and evaluation of the detainee population in Iraq. The ICPVTR, a terrorism think tank, has been involved with profiling and analyzing terrorists and their tendencies since 2002. Likewise, the RRG was arguably one of the first long-term successful examples of terrorist rehabilitation efforts. The RRG has been involved in the religious rehabilitation of terrorist detainees since 2003.

Thus, on November, 29, 2006, a two-member delegation, newly contracted with TF-134 as "advisors," comprised of Dr. Rohan Gunaratna and Ustaz Mohammad Bin Ali, traveled from Singapore to Iraq for an intensive and comprehensive 5-day assessment of the U.S. detainee operations in Iraq and their ability and capability of providing successful rehabilitation programs to Iraqis in detention. Dr. Gunaratna is a specialist on terrorism (and coauthor of this book), and is also the head of ICPVTR, a division of the S. Rajaratnam School of International Studies (RSIS) in Singapore. Ustaz Mohamed Bin Ali is not only a research analyst at ICPVTR, but also a secretariat and counselor of the RRG. Once they arrived in Baghdad, they teamed up with another invited advisor of TF-134: Dr. Anne Speckhard. Dr. Speckhard is a psychologist and adjunct associate professor at Georgetown University Medical Center. Through her previous connections with TF-134, she had voiced interest in analyzing the extremists and thereby adding a psychological profiling element to the equation of rehabilitation. During the 5-day exchange between the three civilians and the military, there were a number of presentations and discussions that took place. Dr. Gunaratna lectured

FIGURE 3.9   Ustaz Mohammed Bin Ali leads a discussion with the U.S. military on how to understand terrorist terminology; Camp Cropper, Iraq, 2006. (Photo by Rohan Gunaratna.)

on the "global threat of terrorism," while Ustaz Bin Ali discussed "understanding terrorists' ideology" (Figure 3.9). Representing the military side of the house, Lt. Col. Karen D. Himmelheber,* the information operations officer for TF-134 under Lt. Gen. Gardner, conducted a presentation outlining a proposed "Counter Extremism Education Program," the outcome of which she credits as a conglomeration of Lt. Gen. Gardner's concept, along with input and recommendations from the visiting delegation (Lt. Col. K. Himmelheber, personal interview, January 14, 2010).

According to TF-134, the intention of the ICPVTR and RRG delegation meeting with the military was to form a working group of manageable expectations and follow-through. The end state would be that TF-134 staff would be more knowledgeable about countering extremism, and the shortcomings in the proposed program could be identified and mitigated and/or removed. In addition, staff organization could be examined in greater detail and a preferential makeup could better be identified. This would then hopefully set the stage for designing a pilot

---

* During her deployment in Iraq from February 2006 to February 2007, Lt. Col. Karen Himmelheber was a major in rank.

program that would be executable given TF-134's desired end state and within operational restraints (M. Bin Ali, personal interview, November 16, 2009).

According to Lt. Col. Himmelheber, the (2006) proposed program was to focus only on confirmed extremists who were not pending trial. An expected 500 to 800 extremists would go through the program, local Imams and scholars would be utilized for it, and the program life expectancy would be 12 to 18 months. The intended effects were:

- Hardcore detainees would begin to doubt or denounce extremist ideologies.
- Detainees would help identify extremist individuals in compounds.
- There would be an increase in actionable intelligence against AGI and other terrorist groups.
- It would present possibilities for newly released detainee dependability and loyalty for future missions.
- Dissemination of counterideological messages to friends, families, and peers would occur.

All of this would result in the desired end state of approximately 10 to 15 percent of graduating detainees completely denouncing extremist ideologies, and deeply established doubt in the minds of the rest. To this end, the initial program concept suggested:

- Two groups of 15 (each) adults and juveniles in separate isolated areas.
- Program 6 weeks in length.
- Program supporters consisting of:
  - Religious scholar mentors
  - Small group facilitators with religious credibility
  - Analysts
  - Psychologist
  - Review board members
- Moderate sermons and other program products serving as base course material.
- Weekly sessions consist of small group and individual sessions, writing assignments (which will drive discussion and debate), supplemental guest speakers, and audio/visual product viewing.
- Incentive for supportive participation will be consideration for early release (during mass release or standard Coalition Committee Review Board (CCRB) review.
- End state is every juvenile and hundreds of confirmed extremist adults have successfully completed the program.

There were also a number of criteria factors for *participant selection* that were discussed. For the adult program, it was decided that participants should be AQI, Takfiri, or Wahhabi; they should be literate; they should be prior military, police, or militia; they should be recent converts; they should be confirmed extremists; they should be compliant with compound rules; and they should have family in the Baghdad area. For the juvenile program, it was decided that participants should be literate; recent converts; have strong extremist type opinions; compliant with compound rules; and have family in the Baghdad area.

Lt. Col. Himmelheber also discussed a proposal on the "way forward." The first suggestions included collecting and compiling a list of local clerics and counselors willing to support the programs once they began. Moderate sermon topics as a basis of the program material also needed to be collected. Other extremist rehabilitation efforts worldwide should be examined and looked at for more resources, and, potentially, some of the individuals going through the first program could be recycled to the second group to add momentum and encourage discussion through the learning process. The long-term plans included being granted a contract for permanent program staff in addition to having a professional staff develop course material designed for Iraqi detainees.

The proposed staff organization included a *full-time analyst* who would be the program lead, work directly for the Task Force Information Operations (TFIO) officer to oversee daily execution of the program, facilitate review and assessment board with the TFIO officer, and have a secret clearance. Then there would also be a *full-time psychologist* who would work directly for the TFIO officer in providing psychological oversight of the program, support refinement of the program, provide progress feedback, conduct participant overviews, direct psychological effort of the program, and be a member of the review and assessment board in addition to having a secret clearance. The *Iraqi national program advisor* would be responsible for working with the program lead to provide language skill sets, have religious studies or counseling background with knowledge of Islam and Al Qaeda ideology, be a contact person with group leaders and guest speakers, and be an Iraqi national (although not necessarily local). The *small group senior mentor* would be a religious scholar with credentials to the level of Mufti with knowledge of Al Qaeda ideology, be the primary group leader and counselor, conduct small group and individual mentoring sessions, and also be an Iraqi national (not necessarily local). Lastly, the *small group facilitator* would be a religious scholar with knowledge of Al Qaeda ideology, a supporting group facilitator and counselor, primarily leader of small group discussion/debate sessions, reviews assignments, and also be an Iraqi national (although not necessarily local), according to M. Bin Ali.

In addition to the tours, presentations, and working group discussions, Dr. Gunaratna, Ustaz Bin Ali, and Dr. Speckhard were given the opportunity to interview 12 detainees from five different compounds within Camp Cropper. Under the pretense of casual conversation, the three met with the detainees and then through active dialogue tried to gauge their ideological mindset. The majority of detainee interviews lasted approximately 30 minutes; however, 3 of the 12 were affiliated to Abu Musab Al-Zarqawi, and the delegation spent almost 4 hours interviewing them. Ustaz Bin Ali, a PhD candidate doing a dissertation on analyzing religious terminology (particularly the concept of loyalty and allegiance), utilized his Qur'anic knowledge and word terminology to best evaluate where the detainees were coming from. In an interview with Dr. Angell on September 14, 2009, Ustaz Bin Ali clarified his intent and approach in questioning the detainees. "In order to win the fight we must be able to work through definitions and recognize terms and their usage for what the real intent is."

The three hard-line detainees admitted to studying under Sheikh Abdul Rahman, the spiritual advisor of Al Qaeda in Iraq. He was killed in a U.S. air strike on June 7, 2006, in Baqubah, Iraq. (*As detailed in Chapter 1, the U.S. forces tracked Sheikh Abdul al-Rahman until he met with Abu Musab al-Zarqawi. They were both killed in a subsequent air strike.*) According to one of the detainees, who previously studied at Mustansiriyah University, there are about 16 Islamic sciences or disciplines taught by Sheikh Abdul Rahman, including: Interpretation of the Holy Qur'an, Hadith (Traditions of Prophet Mohammed), Tauhid (Islamic Theology), Fiqh (Islamic Rulings and Jurisprudence), Sirah Nabawiyah (Life History of Prophet Muhammad), Arabic language, Arabic literature, Arabic rhetoric, Tasawwuf (Islamic Sufism), and Mantiq (Science of Logic). After discussing the detainees' teachings, the delegation then discussed some other topics with the detainees to include:

- Understanding of Jihad (its rulings and interpretation)
- Establishment of Daulah Islamiyah (Islamic State)
- Martyrdom and suicide operations
- Effects and justification of September 11 attacks
- The old and new traditions of Islam, Salafism, Wahhabism, and Takfiris
- Act of Bai'ah (Pledge of allegiance) in radical and extremist groups
- Al Qaeda organization and Al Qaeda in Iraq
- Abu Musab Al-Zarqawi
- Response to Islamic militancy and radical ideology

- U.S. invasion of Iraq
- The future of Iraq

What was discovered by the delegation through the detainee interviews was that while the detainees maintained good rapport and engagement throughout, and appeared sincere and spoke with conviction, there was still a missing element. Their religious knowledge for the most part was impressive, yet it still only scratched the surface, according to Ustaz Bin Ali. The three extremists exhibited quite strong inclinations toward the teachings and ideological concepts propagated by the late Sheikh Abdul Rahman, yet were noticeably reciting the teachings rather than participating with in-depth dialogue about their meaning. Although the three denounced violence and voiced objection against atrocities like September 11, there were grounds to believe that they had not given up their radical ideological orientation completely, and that they might just have been putting on a show in the hopes of early release or good favor of the military. And this, the delegation suggested, might be the biggest challenge in deradicalizing a radical population: that in some cases, despite having rejected tendencies toward violence, extremists like the ones interviewed continue to hold on to radical ideologies in varying degrees and/or might force a change of heart in hopes of gaining military favor. It was determined as well during one of the interviews that the extremist was conducting religious classes for other detainees on a regular basis, which directly undermined what the military was trying to accomplish.

The overall conclusion of the delegation was that, in general, the detainees held by U.S. forces had a high level of religious knowledge coupled with a deep, strong conviction to their beliefs. This level of conviction suggested that rehabilitation processes were expected to be long and challenging. It also meant that a careful selection of experienced and higher-learned Iraqi Muslim scholars and clerics are essential to the program's success. An in-depth study on the history, teachings, and influence of individuals like the late Sheikh Abdul Rahman (as he obviously had a profound impact on some detainees) was also suggested. In addition, detainees, like those who volunteered to be interviewed, should be viewed as valuable assets to potential counterideological programs due to their knowledge and past affiliations with those who propagate extremist ideology; their high level of cooperation and willingness to share information were also positive indicators of their value to any counterideological program.

Before departing Iraq, the delegation met with Lt. Gen. Gardner to discuss their findings and share their assessment of the situation. Dr. Gunaratna generally felt that "Lt. Gen. Gardner took my advice to heart," but, yet, "while he agreed to the principle of rehabilitation, he needed more convincing." According to Dr. Gunaratna, he suggested three things that should urgently be changed in order to effectively conduct detainee operations where terrorists are involved. The first was that "detainees need to be separated by belief; the principle driver of militant jihadism is ideological fascination." And, because it is communal living, radicalizing other individuals is quite easy. The second thing he told Lt. Gen. Gardner was that "soldiers detaining individuals need to be taught to better distinguish between a civilian and a terrorist." According to Dr. Gunaratna, Lt. Gen. Gardner supported this, saying, "Eighty percent of the detainees in Camp Cropper were arrested without intelligence or evidence" (R. Gunaratna, personal interview, December 22, 2009). The third thing that Dr. Gunaratna highlighted to Lt. Gen. Gardner was about vision. He emphasized that "different components of rehabilitation are necessary for reintegration," and that it is important to have vision to ensure that these components are integrated into the detainee operations program.

According to Ustaz Bin Ali, "Initially, TF-134 did not have the confidence, but eventually, through talking and working with them, they were able to see the importance of rehabilitation and desired to adopt and evolve the program to fit their detainee population" (M. Bin Ali, personal interview, November 16, 2009). Likewise, according to Dr. Gunaratna:

Camp Cropper was undergoing a process. First there was suffering, then there was resentment. This would turn to anger, which would open the door to extremist ideologies. They had to do something to stop this.

Dr. Gunaratna also introduced "security screening based on religious orientation." This proved quite controversial and many military did not support it, saying, "We cannot do this!" "The Americans will lobby!" However, he then explained how it is necessary in the global fight on terrorism to do this screening while in detention. Dr. Gunaratna elaborated, "I explained to them how to identify a Takfiri based on his beard and tears in his clothes. And, then they started to understand how necessary it was." Further, Ustaz Bin Ali stated, "We let the military know that we could not do it for them. We would be willing to help in whatever way we could, we could give resources and information, but ultimately it would be up to them to make it happen." According to Ustaz Bin Ali, "It was a short trip, but significant because we introduced the concept." Thankfully, "the military was very welcoming and receptive of it."

LT. GEN. GARDNER ACTS

After the delegation left Iraq, Lt. Gen. Gardner worked on implementing lessons learned during the interaction and from his experiences with detention operations in Iraq—the first of which was a program for juveniles who were detained. According to Lt. Col. Himmelheber, "Just as in the rest of the country, a rift between Shiites and Sunnis had developed within our adult compounds, but thanks to the efforts of two U.S.–Iraqi contractor teachers, the youth were beginning to rise above the rhetoric and asked to study, play together, and live together."

In late 2006, in an effort to mainstream efforts for detainee programs, all education, information operations, and reintegration programs were wrapped under one colonel. According to Lt. Gen. Gardner (personal interview, 2010):

> These included the juvenile school at Cropper, the basic skills education effort at Bucca, the political/history classes at Bucca, and the IO (information operations) effort with films/television/programs/radio/newspapers. It also included the contract effort resulting from the interaction with folks from Singapore.

According to Lt. Gen. Gardner, all the programs had evolved over time and were growing at a pace where a colonel was needed in order to manage them plus have better access to external organizations. While the details were being worked out, Col. Michael Callaghan* arrived in Iraq and filled the position for oversight of all the "reintegration" programs. However, the intention did not go as smoothly as hoped. Personalities and ideals clashed and Col. Callaghan and Lt. Gen. Gardner's relationship, "to put it simply, was difficult for the brief period we worked together." According to Lt. Gen. Gardner:

> Col. Callaghan arrived at the point where we had recently ceased the effort to transfer the facilities to the Iraqis, were expanding the facilities significantly, and were expanding the education/IO/reintegration effort … , and I'm not sure that he had that context. He, along with some of the folks who came in with Maj. Gen. Stone, seemed to feel that nothing of significance had occurred prior to their arrival and didn't understand how the program had evolved over time.

Consequently, it was frustrating for Lt. Gen. Gardner as he prepared to redeploy back to the states.

---

* Colonel Michael Callaghan retired from the U.S. Marine Forces on May 1, 2010, after 28 years of service.

We spent much of early to mid-2006 establishing methods on how to identify who someone really was—to include separating the real foreign fighters from those simply born somewhere other than Iraq, those really aligned with Al Qaeda as opposed to those anecdotally linked—and establishing the COIN [counterinsurgency] effort to disrupt recruiting/training inside the compounds. When Col. Callaghan and Maj. Gen. Stone arrived, a number of things had evolved, and they could afford to look at other facets of the program.

According to Lt. Gen. Gardner, the contract period for "reintegration programs" evolved over a period of months. They worked with finding individuals in the U.S. government who could assist in addressing extremists or reintegration, but had little luck. They also tried to contact Saudi Arabia with the same result. Lt. Gen. Gardner had several online sessions with Dr. Gunaratna and Ustaz Bin Ali in Singapore, but found that while some of the ideas could be applicable to the Iraq detention operations, many were not and "it took a while to sort the difference out."

CONCLUSION

Detainee operations were in a rough patch, but with the groundwork put in place by Lt. Gen. Gardner and inspired individuals like Gen. Petraeus now in command of Iraq, detainee operations were getting an overhaul. Changes were made and lessons were learned, but there was still much more to be done. Detainees were restless, and the strain and stress this put on the military guards responsible for keeping them calm continued to weigh heavy. TF-134 knew something had to change within the wire in order to placate the detainees and give them a sense of purpose and direction. They were acutely aware that previously moderate detainees were still getting radicalized, and that riots, escapes, and disturbances were bound to continue until something changed. Everyone knew *something* needed to be done, but what that something *was* remained elusive. Lt. Gen. Gardner was on the right track by being the first to acknowledge the precarious position by calling in the outside delegation to make an assessment. In essence, he set the groundwork for detainee rehabilitation, but as he tried to build and implement a plan, he received little to no support and basically ran into a brick wall. And without support from higher ups in its implementation, it was inevitable that detainee rehabilitation efforts would remain stagnant until *somebody* did *something* to make it all come together.

CHAPTER 4

In(To) the Fire

INTRODUCTION

Without reservation, the push for and actual implementation of detainee rehabilitation programs in Iraq were the result of primarily one determined man: Marine Corps Maj. Gen. Douglas Stone. In the face of adversity and resentment, Maj. Gen. Stone pushed an agenda that he knew was right, he knew would work, yet was virtually unsupported by anyone higher up in the chain of command. The result of his efforts not only outlasted him in Iraq, but with his continued influence and determination has since carried over to Afghanistan as well where they continue to improve the security of detention operations, and illustrate what a difference a fresh approach can do to overhauling stale detention operations. In essence, his controversial and innovative plan to incorporate rehabilitation programs into detention operations and, thus, irreversibly change detention operations as they were known, worked. But, it wasn't without difficulty.

MAJOR GENERAL DOUGLAS M. STONE

It all began to come together in April 2007 when Maj. Gen. Stone first visited Iraq for an initial 30-day appraisal at the request of General David Petraeus, who was then still only Multinational Force-Iraq (MNF-I) commander. What Maj. Gen. Stone found was a country in "such disarray" that he "decided against returning home and requested to be allowed to stay on." For 30 days, Maj. Gen. Stone traveled Iraq, talked with military personnel and detainees, and assessed the detainee population. As Maj. Gen. Stone became more knowledgeable about the detained Iraqi population, Lt. Gen. John D. Gardner (then TF-134 Commander) drew to a close his already extended tour. In May 2007, 30 days after his initial intake and a whole lot more enlightened about detention operations in Iraq, Maj. Gen. Stone became the new Detainee Operations TF-134 Commander reporting directly to Gen. Petraeus.

FIGURE 4.1   Detainees set their caravans on fire: Camp Bucca, Iraq, 2007. (Photo courtesy of U.S. Department of Defense.)

As Lt. Gen. Gardner had managed to successfully close both Fort Suse and Abu Ghraib prison during his tenure, when Maj. Gen. Stone took command, there were only two detention facilities left in Iraq to manage: Camp Cropper and Camp Bucca. However, the numbers of Iraqi detainees were at an all-time high as a result of the surge of American troops that peaked in the summer of 2007, just months after his arrival. By November 7, 2007, the detainee population was at 26,121, the highest number at any given point throughout the Iraq war. Maj. Gen. Stone knew something had to be done about the violence and overcrowding in addition to the lack of order and formalities (see Chapter 3). In the year 2007 alone, there were 25 severe mutilations (caused by detainee-on-detainee violence) and 6 detainee-on-detainee deaths. Detainees also started numerous fires in their housing quarters (Figure 4.1); created rogue weapons (Figure 4.2) that included darts, rocks, slingshots (Figure 4.3), and juice box grenades (Figure 4.4) for use against American soldiers; and made lists of requests that they demanded to be filled before they would cease the violence. Elaborate messaging between the compounds ignited anger and resentment and encouraged detainees across the camps to participate in the riots. "It made no sense to me that individuals were rioting at the level they were. So if they were rioting, there was no motivation to getting out. They obviously felt there was no rule of law, and no way to get out." Of course, "being incited and intimidated by a few hard-core extremists inside the compounds also did not help

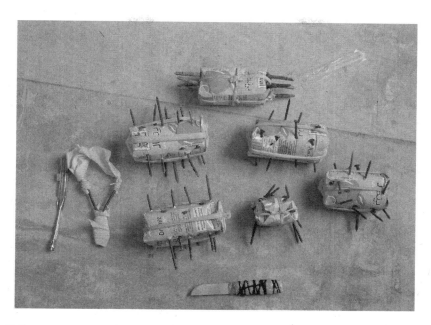

FIGURE 4.2   Handmade rogue weapons confiscated from detainee compounds: Camp Bucca, Iraq, 2007. (Photo courtesy of a U.S. soldier.*)

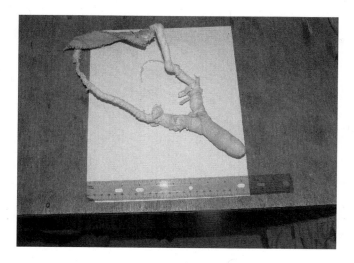

FIGURE 4.3   Handmade sling shot confiscated from detainee compound: Camp Bucca, Iraq, 2007. (Photo courtesy of a U.S. soldier.*)

FIGURE 4.4   Juice box grenades confiscated from compounds: Camp Bucca, Iraq, 2007. (Photo courtesy of a U.S. soldier.*)

the agenda. So I had to do something" (Maj. Gen. D. Stone, personal interview, October 25, 2009).

Among the first things he did was reform and ignite the idea of detainee rehabilitation programs, something Lt. Gen. Gardner had previously probed with little support and, consequently, little success. He called Dr. Gunaratna, in Singapore, to ask if he could come to Iraq; however, he was unable to make the trip at that point in time. So, Maj. Gen. Stone reviewed seven known programs and created his own effort from what others had learned through their efforts.

> The original program was a composite of all the successes, but it also had a huge part of Rule of Law because no detainee had ever seen or discussed his/her detention; it seemed to me, that while legal, it was not right. So, I created a process to better understand who was in detention, why they were there, and developed a process that would allow them to leave if we were certain that they would not return ... ergo, that some form of deradicalization had taken place.

And with that, Maj. Gen. Stone pushed rehabilitation programs' agenda to the forefront. He marketed his concept of rehabilitation programs being the next logical step in controlling and, subsequently, diminishing the violence that had taken over the theater internment facilities (TIFs). He briefed commanders that, as detainees felt there was no way out, no rule of law, they had no hope. He suggested that a total reform in detention operations would be key in reestablishing law and order

in the compounds, a necessary component of which must include rehabilitation programs and an improved method of structure. Detainees
needed something to look forward to; they needed to see that "there was
light at the end of the tunnel," according to Maj. Gen. Stone. "I started
pushing through when I got an idea. Everyone who didn't agree, I just
pushed them aside," Maj. Gen. Stone said. Unfortunately, this did not
come without cost. The response was immediate, and it was not positive. Most military personnel, including some of higher ranks, did not
agree with Maj. Gen. Stone and viewed his ideas as "too idealistic" with
"impossible implementation." Military police lodged complaints saying
that "detainees do not have a right to say their side of the capture,"
and "you cannot change detention … it's in the army manual!" The
result was no approved funding for the programs and a lot of heated
discussions between Iraq and even the White House. At one point, a
commanding four-star general met with Gen. Petraeus and demanded
Maj. Gen. Stone's relief as TF-134 commander, citing his approach to
detention operations as "eccentric" and "ridiculous." But this did not
sway Maj. Gen. Stone:

> My idea of change was based on principles that others did not share,
> or interpret as I did … that it would take my career to take on this
> establishment. I was certain that no one would support me, likely, but
> that if I did not do it … explaining all the way why I was doing it …
> I could not live with myself. After all, my hire, like the statement by
> John Stuart Mill, was a bit eccentric. But, [as Mill said] "eccentric-
> ity has always abounded when and where strength of character has
> abounded, and the amount of eccentricity in society has generally been
> proportional to the amount of genius, mental vigor, and moral courage
> which it contained." So, I have made it a badge of honor. The lesson:
> Stand for conscience before all else (Maj. Gen. D. Stone, presentation
> to the Naval Academy, 2009).

Fortunately, there was one man who did support him and it was
his direct superior. Gen. Petraeus, having worked with Maj. Gen. Stone
in the past and being able to witness on the ground the state of affairs
detention operations were in, felt as if he had nothing to lose by letting
Maj. Gen. Stone run his course. After all, he did hire him to fix the situation of detention operations in Iraq. He understood that if Maj. Gen.
Stone believed an idea would work, that invariably it did work. He kept
Maj. Gen. Stone aware of the lack of support from higher bodies so
that Maj. Gen. Stone could address concerns; meanwhile, Gen. Petraeus
made him aware of the support from himself, as MNF-I Commander.
While Gen. Petraeus did not get actively involved in the rehabilitation
plan of operations himself, he gave Maj. Gen. Stone the space and time
to work his ideas. "Gen. Petraeus never made any suggestions, per se,

but rather allowed my ideas to be put in place, and that is and was a big deal," said Maj. Gen. Stone.

According to Maj. Gen. Stone, he called up individuals who did not agree with his plans and he "invited them out to Iraq to see the TIFs and discuss in person." At one point the "entire funding for all the efforts were cut off by a single U.S. congressman." Gen. Petraeus made the first call. Then Maj. Gen. Stone called the congressman and invited him to Iraq. He had his constituents in the forces meet the congressman at the airport, and then Maj. Gen. Stone showed him around the facilities himself. After the visit, the congressman was so impressed with what Maj. Gen. Stone was trying to do that he turned the funds back on, according to Maj. Gen. Stone.

Maj. Gen. Stone conducted phone and video conferences, wrote countless e-mails, and put out reports on what he understood needed to happen in Iraq based on his interviews and observations for detention operations to move forward in a more productive manner. He explained that without rehabilitation programs, the United States is doing nothing to help the detainees, and that instead, once released, they will return to the very thing that got them detained in the first place. He discussed the frustration of detainees, and how they are causing problems because there is nothing to occupy their time. He talked about the low education of detainees: 60 percent of individuals in Iraq have less than a high school-level education; these individuals are more susceptible to indoctrination. Finally, he talked about how the United States is letting detainees with extremist ideology win the fight because of incorrect classification and compound placement, and how, eventually, if this situation is not corrected, more U.S. soldiers' lives will be lost because of it. With moral conviction, Maj. Gen. Stone passionately discussed with as many individuals as would listen his ideas and the way he felt the United States needed to move forward in detention operations if they want to leave something tangible for the new Government of Iraq to work with:

> By May [2007], I was making significant changes in how we were to engage with detainees. I was getting the verbal orders I issued upon taking command into writing, and the programs funded, the hiring started, and the changes being made. There was a tremendous amount of resistance to all of these programs, but we just kept going forward and I think it was all for the right. We influenced the population during the time of the surge in a manner that turned detention from a negative to a positive influencer not only in Iraq, but in papers across the Middle East. ... This change enabled the success of the surge because the worst offense was finally and respectively and effectively being addressed.

Origination of the TIFRIC Concept

When the rehabilitation programs were first conceptualized and implemented under Maj. Gen. Stone, they all fell under the term TIFRIC services, the shortened term for Theater Internment Facility Reintegration Center. However, later TIFRIC was sometimes referred to as Theater Internment Facility *Rehabilitation* Center (Stone, personal interview, 2010) before most recently being changed in 2009 to Theater Internment Facility Reconciliation Center (TIFRC) (Gen. D. Quantock, personal interview, January 26, 2010).

The origination and evolution of the term, however, is much more complex. Discussions concerning the name and intentions of the term took place over many meetings, which occurred both in the United States and in Iraq. According to Col. Michael Callaghan, who was in Iraq from March 2007 to March 2008, firstly as Deputy Commanding General (Effects) TF-134 (March 3–May 1, 2007), then as Commander of Task Force 300, TF-134 (May 1, 2007–March 3, 2008) under Maj. Gen. Stone, initial discussion of having rehabilitation programs occurred while in the United States.

> The initial concept for incorporating rehabilitation programs came in a discussion that I and Maj. Gen. Doug Stone had in January 2007 while still in the United States. We were discussing options on how to break the insurgency and what we might do to change the face of detention from just "warehousing" to something that allowed them to be turned into productive citizens. This was further refined during a meeting that involved Maj. Gen. Stone, Col. Anthony Lieto, myself with Capt. Dollard as the recorder within 48 hours of Maj. Gen. Stone's arrival into theater in April 2007 (Col. M. Callaghan, personal interview, June 11, 2010).

According to Col. Anthony Lieto,* who served as deputy commander of TF-134 under Maj. Gen. Stone during his second tour of Iraq from February 2007 to March 2008, the origination of the TIFRIC title took place while driving around a base in Iraq:

> Doug [Maj. Gen. Stone] came up with the idea for TIFRIC in the car on the way to Camp Cropper. The TIF part was already established as that was the name of the detention facilities at the theater level. The "RIC" came as we discussed reintegration, education, and the rehabilitation programs (Col. A. Lieto, personal interview, October 15, 2010).

---

* Colonel Anthony Lieto retired from the U.S. Army on July 1, 2008, after 31 years of service.

Likewise, according to Maj. Gen. Stone:

> Although I had initial brief discussions of possible ideas to curb the violence in Iraq—before I arrived in theater—the actual plan was solidified after I arrived, not before. When I got there [Iraq], I had no idea what programs or approach I would use, and had no idea how bad the situation was on the ground. The concept of TIFRIC, and the name, was developed in the back of a sedan, after reviewing the situation on the ground. Capt. Mike Dollard (my aide) and Col. Tony Lieto (my deputy commander) were there. Mike [Callaghan] was put in charge of finding the resources, and in helping to design how the intelligence flows might work.

Col. David L. Shakes,* who was in Iraq from February 2007 to January 2008, as the Rule of Law Advisor for TF134, confirmed:

> The idea of incorporating rehabilitation programs into detention centers started primarily when Maj. Gen. Stone assumed command in April/May 2007. Maj. Gen. Stone had the idea that we needed to prepare the detainees to be released under circumstances such that they would not return to the battlefield. He brought the perspective that sooner or later most of the detainees were going to be released and return to their communities. As such, we needed to ensure that they would not continue the fight against us. So job training and ideological training were important as both of these addressed the primary motivations of the insurgents. The paradigm shift that occurred with the arrival of Maj. Gen. Stone was that we went from a "hold them until the war is over" to a mindset of release under conditions that ensure they do not return to fight us. The paradigm shift was moving from traditional war fighting and detention thinking to counterinsurgency thinking and realizing that detention programs had a key role to play in counterinsurgency (Col. D. L. Shakes, personal interview, August 25, 2010).

Initial Challenges

Besides having command approval, there were a number of other challenges that went into trying to implement the rehabilitation programs. According to Col. Callaghan, one of the first challenges was socializing and gaining acceptance within TF-134 and the military police responsible for executing the detention mission. Another challenge was the socialization and acceptance of the MNF-I staff and Multinational Corps-Iraq (MNC-I), and then was finding the funding for the programs. While

---

* Colonel David L. Shakes retired from the U.S. Army Reserve in July 2008, after 33 years of service (5 active and 28 in the Army Reserve).

some initial money was provided to test the religious program and pro-cure textbooks for the Inside the Wire education program, true funding was not procured until late August 2007. Socialization of the concepts had to be conducted both internally and externally to the command. According to Col. Callaghan, development of the concept was a "contin-uous process through a series of discussions with the staff, MNF-I staff, [Department of] State actors, and others, while conducting day-to-day detainee operations." In addition, much of the effort was briefing the concept up to the Office of Secretary of Defense level to get the funding, working with contracting to put the contracts in place, all while work-ing with the antiquated processes and assessments that were being con-ducted by outside agencies. During the process, there were many hurdles to jump and rivers to cross. Col Callaghan said:

> We lost the opportunity to obtain money for the job training pro-grams initially when the State Department made an assessment report on the ability of the Iraqi government to take over programs. This assessment caused us to lose access to $150 million, money that could have been used to establish vocational training programs much earlier than we did.

Another challenge was convincing commanders outside of Iraq that reconciling detainees was a good thing in the middle of the surge. According to Col. David L. Shakes, there were several intensive chal-lenges that were constantly on the burner:

> Others can address the budget and funding issues. Let me address the issues that I dealt with directly. First, the Multinational Corps was a significant challenge. The Corps had the war fighters' perspective that the bad guys had to be held until the war was over. Any program that devoted resources to rehabilitating and releasing detainees was met with a great deal of resistance by the Corps commanders. From their perspective, the detainees represented threats to our soldiers and marines and should not be released under some "rehabilitation" program.

Meanwhile, however, the TF-134 perspective continued that they could not count on keeping huge numbers of detainees indefinitely, so a plan for rehabilitation and releases was necessary. According to Col. Shakes, the second major obstacle was resources. "There were not sig-nificant funds available for the programs Maj. Gen. Stone wanted to implement, so it seemed we were always begging, borrowing, and fight-ing for resources for these programs." The third challenge, according to Col. Shakes, was that the Iraqi government and officials were skeptical about rehabilitation:

For rehabilitation to work, we needed to ensure that the detainees who were released could find jobs instead of earning a living planting IEDs [improvised explosive devices]. It was a very tough sell to the Iraqis I dealt with (mostly judges and Ministry of Justice officials) to convince them that they should develop programs to employ former detainees when there were no jobs for the "good Iraqis" who had never been detained.

Closely related to the third issue was the fourth challenge, which was sectarian influences. It was no secret that the overwhelming majority of detainees were Sunni. Therefore, "the Shia leaders were not keen about working with TF-134 to develop programs that would be seen as helping former Sunni insurgents while not helping the 'good Iraqis'" (Col. D. L. Shakes, personal interview, August 25, 2010).

The fifth challenge was the Iraqi legal system. There is no concept of parole or probation in the Iraqi (or most Middle Eastern) legal systems. So, to make rehabilitation work, there needed to be a system of conditional release, like probation or parole, to monitor the conduct of the detainees after they were released back to their community. Col. Shakes worked directly with the chief justice of Iraq to develop a program of conditional release. He said:

> We used an existing provision of the Iraqi criminal procedure that allowed a defendant to be released pending charges on his promise to an Iraqi judge of his good behavior. This release on promise of good behavior became the core of our conditional release program.

As implemented, the detainees who were released made a pledge of good behavior before an Iraqi judge. If this promise was violated by the detainee, then he/she could be prosecuted in Iraqi court for the violation. Although the violation was a very low-level crime, it got the Iraqi courts involved, and the promise of good behavior in front of an Iraqi judge seemed to be taken very seriously by the detainees. "Our original plan was to have the conditional release supervised by a sponsor, i.e., a sheik that would take responsibility for the released detainee." However, the logistics in finding sponsors and concerns about possible corruption prevented TF-134 from implementing the idea. The conditional release was instead integrated into the MNFRC (as will be discussed below) according to Col. Shakes.

The sixth challenge was TF-134 proving that what they were trying to do was really possible. They were faced with U.S. and Iraqi officials who were very skeptical about the idea of rehabilitation in general and about TF-134's capability in particular. According to Col. Shakes, a particular aspect of this challenge was that:

> Maj. Gen. Stone was the creative genius behind the rehabilitation programs. However, some think he had a tendency to oversell our

rehabilitation programs. From my perspective at the embassy, I think over time people became skeptical [about] what we [TF-134] were trying to do as far as rehabilitation because of what might have been perceived as over-eager salesmanship by Maj. Gen. Stone.

Rehabilitation Pilot Program

Nevertheless, Maj. Gen. Stone succeeded in his conviction, and funding was approved for the rehabilitation programs to be tested on Iraq's detainee population. Fortunately, due to their initial (and continued) success, funding continued to be approved through the turnover of U.S. TIFs to the Government of Iraq in 2010. According to CSgt. Maj. Jeffrey Butler (personal interview, 2010):

> The money forward really came from Maj. Gen. Stone's time frame. He got the opportunity to talk to Gen. Petraeus. Gen. Petraeus was focused on counterinsurgency; and Maj. Gen. Stone showed him what counterinsurgency inside the detainee operations world means—that we need to give something tangible to the detainees that they can take away with them, so they won't attack us when they leave. And, he got funding for the programs. They were the ones to first hire the teachers, the Imams, the various vocational instructors—all the instructors we have now came from the funding he got when he was here (CSgt. Maj. J. Butler, personal interview, January 28, 2010).

Building on ideas garnered through the pilot programs in the summer of 2007, Maj. Gen. Stone evolved the rehabilitation programs to best meet the needs of the detained population as they went along. Most individuals familiar with the rehabilitation programs appreciate the very important role that Maj. Gen. played in the approval, funding, support, and implementation of them. Without doubt, the programs would never have been able to reach the capacity and strength they did by 2010 without his determination to make them happen in 2007. In fact, according to Maj. Gen. Quantock,

> The efforts to really look at detention efforts drastically changed when Gen. Petraeus took over MNF-I and Maj. Gen. Stone took over TF-134. His ability to resource the requirements and ideas of Military Police Brigades/Battalions at Camp Bucca and Camp Cropper turned the detainee operation around.

The evolution and implementation of the rehabilitation programs went through a lot of stresses through trial and error, and so, unsurprisingly, there are many individuals who feel encouraged and entitled to take credit for the detainee rehabilitation programs. But, when it boils down to it, those genuinely involved with the effort would invariably agree that it was the inclusion of dozens of small elements suggested by dozens of different people with dozens of different approaches that ultimately created and transformed the rehabilitation process throughout the 3 years it took place in Iraq. While there were many disagreements and challenges in the creation and implementation process, all agree that the programs were about the empowerment of the detainees while increasing security for the forces. The intent was that detainees, led by Iraqis, be empowered to want to transform themselves into being the persons they most want to be, and, consequently, not feel compelled to cloak themselves in extremism. And because of it, the world could be that much safer for the rest of us.

MNFRC Boards

Some say that the turning point in detention operations came with the establishment of the MNFRC. Before the MNFRC boards were created, a detainee never had the opportunity to plead his case. He never had the opportunity to stand in a court and defend himself/herself; some even claimed they had no knowledge of the charges against them. So, in essence, what the MNFRC boards did was to empower the detainee, give him/her a voice, and give him/her hope of release. Initiated a few months after Maj. Gen. Stone's arrival in Iraq as a way to curb the violence in the TIFs, the MNFRC boards were designed to be a process that gave every detainee an opportunity to stand in front of a three-member panel of military officers, at a minimum once every 3 months (for juveniles) or 6 months (for adults), and plead his/her case while hearing the charges against him/her (Figure 4.5). However, it did more than just that, as it allowed each detainee to participate in determining whether or not he/she posed a continued threat to U.S. forces or the Government of Iraq. It also gave the detainee an opportunity to have his/her day in court. When detainees found out that participation in the rehabilitation programs helped their chances for release at the MNFRC boards, their behavior improved; and they were more encouraged to pursue self-improvement. This spurred reconciliation among the different groups. It all tied together (D. Quantock, personal interview, November 4, 2009).

According to Maj. Gen. Stone, the MNFRC boards were developed because of the commitment of Col. Shakes and Capt. Bruce MacKenzie:

> The boards were developed with the idea to give the detainees a chance to personally appear before a board and explain their case, something that had never happened before. I believed that, culturally, it was

FIGURE 4.5   The MNFRC board in process: Camp Bucca, Iraq, 2008.
(Photo courtesy of U.S. Department of Defense.)

important for the Iraqi detainees to be able to face the board personally versus the paper reviews that had been done earlier. Additionally,
the idea was to have the boards manned by officers from the corps, so
they could see that the detainee had been rehabilitated or no longer
posed a risk upon release.

TF-134 was in charge of all detentions as well as releases; likewise,
it was in charge of the MNFRC process. Essentially, the MNFRC boards
allowed three things, according to Col. Lieto:

First, it allowed the detainee the opportunity to plead his case; second, it allowed for the detainee to understand the charges against him;
and third, the detainee received understanding of a way for him to get
released and back to his family, which was to do good, learn a skill,
and educate himself—all of which are supported by the Qur'an.

One of the biggest fears of detainees before the MNFRC board was
created was that they would be held indefinitely without due process.
Detainees wondered what was going to happen to them and if they
would ever see their families again. Detainees worryingly discussed how
under Saddam's regime anyone held in prison might never be seen by
his/her family again; they hypothesized if perhaps the same was true

when being detained by Americans. Dena Mansour (personal interview, 2009), a linguist who interacted daily with the detainee population at Camp Bucca, explained:

> Each of the detainees wanted to plead his/her case to whoever would listen to them in the American army, but they were not always allowed to by the detainees who were running the compound. The MNFRC boards and rehabilitation programs offered them that chance; it gave them something to look forward to.

After the establishment of the MNFRC boards, worries were laid to rest. As soon as detainees understood there was a process in place, one that they could actually influence, they became more cooperative and accommodating. MNFRC boards were always a big topic of conversation during the rehabilitation programs; they served as a meeting point between military and detainee on a higher level. Detainees who participated in any kind of programs would readily carry around participation certificates in their pockets, in the unlikely occasion that they unexpectedly get called to an MNFRC board. All detainees wanted to be prepared in the event that their file did not list the class completed; in which case, they could pull out their copy of proof. Talking about the MNFRC boards occupied many detainees' thoughts, as they devised ways of how to best illustrate to the board that they posed no security risk. Sgt. Matthew Sugars (personal interview, 2009), a military staff liaison of TF-134, recounted:

> The boards gave the detainees a hope they did not previously have. They were able to present their story of what happened and the evidence to prove if they were innocent or guilty. It gave them that "light at the end of the tunnel" feeling. I saw the impact in how many more programs started and grew from that point until we left. It was like an explosion of interest and desire of the detainees.

Under Maj. Gen. Stone, the MNFRC board consisted of three officers, ranked major or above. However, not everyone agreed that it should only be officers on the board: "Everyone tried to fight me on it because I said only officers on the boards. But, I thought experience was important" (D. Stone, personal interview, October 25, 2009). And yet, 6 months after the departure of Maj. Gen. Stone from theater, the composition of the board became a field grade officer, a senior noncommissioned officer (NCO) from the battle space (i.e., area where the detainee had been detained), and a junior officer, reported Maj. Gen. Quantock.

Camp Cropper, Camp Taji, and Camp Bucca had converted trailers where a makeshift courtroom was created for the MNFRC boards to be held in. The MNFRC board panels were rotated in and out usually weekly to ensure they were not overwhelmed or burned out from the continuously intense long days. MNFRC boards were held on every day of the week except Friday. Every evening, each panel trio would get a large box of documents pertaining to the detainees they would have in court the following day. They were responsible for familiarizing themselves with each detainee's case and preparing questions to ask the detainee in order to best assess if he/she was to remain in detention as a security threat. Few of the officers had a legal background. They learned as they went along, and, in some cases, they had to make judgment calls. On one occasion, an officer shared with me that after listening to a detainee justify his particular circumstances, he voted that the detainee should be released. However, the officer was later to learn that as soon as the detainee left the MNFRC board hearing, he was caught pocketing a sharp piece of metal he found on the ground. Discouraged, the officer had no choice but to change his recommendation for release to a recommendation of stay.

Others argued that the MNFRC boards were double-edged swords. While they provided a reason for detainees to do well (and the majority did), the board still caused problems. There appeared to be cases where even when a detainee had met the criteria, had recommendations from the intelligence agents, and participated in rehabilitation programs, he/she was still denied for his second, third, or fourth time based on information given by the capturing unit that was, in some cases, no longer even in the country and whose information could not be verified. This tended to cause some detainees to act out, sometimes mildly, and sometimes they joined extremists in the compounds (1Sgt. B. Emmert, personal interview, November 8, 2009). Fortunately, this was corrected as the process evolved. According to Maj. Gen. Quantock, individuals who worked on an MNFRC panel learned to appreciate the importance of proper documentation in a detainee's files; it encouraged them to better train their units to take pictures of the crime scenes and make sure all the required documentation was present. He recalls on one occasion at an MNFRC board, one of the officers opened up a detainee's file to find that the statement was written by Santa Claus. "Seriously! Santa Claus! The guy put that on the statement."

But, overall, the majority of detainees appeared at peace with the MNFRC board process. After the establishment of the rehabilitation programs and MNFRC process, it was determined that less than 1 percent of citizens released from a board had been recaptured due to criminal activity. Granted these numbers are hard to prove, as many individuals who were detained were apprehended on suspicion rather than proof. And, further, because the agreement between the United States and the Government of Iraq on January 1, 2009, meant that the United States no longer has anything to do with arrests or detentions, unless directly asked to be involved by the Government of Iraq. But, indisputably, it still illustrated some evidence of a process that worked for its particular circumstances. Prior to release, detainees were given a class that encourages harmony; then they took an oath before an Iraqi judge stating that they will not engage in terrorism or insurgency efforts (Sauret, 2008). A commanding officer also was present at release ceremonies to inform detainees that, if they are caught in criminal activity and returned to detention, leniency will be far less and that they will be housed in the least liberal (and most dreaded) of houses for a far longer period of time.

MAJOR GENERAL DAVID E. QUANTOCK

Maj. Gen. Quantock had the unusual experience of commanding a unit in Iraq during 2004 and 2005 while all the commotion was going on with Abu Ghraib, and then returning 3 years later in 2008. According to Gen. Quantock, the two different scenarios are worlds apart:

> When my unit arrived in January 2004, I commanded the 16th Military Police Brigade (Airborne) out of Fort Bragg, North Carolina. I was relieving two military police brigades: the 800th MP Brigade, commanded by Gen. Karpinski, and the 220th Military Police Brigade, commanded by Gen. Gahgan. Detainee operations were a complete disaster. On the 14th of January, I was first shown the pictures of the Abu Ghraib abuse right after the CID [criminal investigation division] team left Gen. Karpinski's office. From looking at those photos, I knew that it was going to be a very long year. Problems with detainee operations in early 2004 ... everything ... very little resources, minimal, if any, guard force training, approximately 8 medics and 8,000 detainees, the detention facilities were very temporary (detainees walked around in mud-caked fields), very little discipline in the units, very little leadership oversight in the detention facilities, everyone felt sorry for themselves, and very little force protection of the area because the facility lay on the fault line between two divisions. The focus was getting out of detainee operations ... [Coalition Task Force 7] CTF7's focus was stopping the insurgency ... little understanding or emphasis that detainee operations could be an enabler to stopping the insurgency ... not a byproduct of the system.

Nevertheless, according to Maj. Gen. Quantock, rehabilitation was an idea toyed with in 2004 to counter the Abu Ghraib abuse and attempt to give a better impression to the Iraqi population of what the Americans were about. However, nobody was interested. The issue was that nobody had an appetite for it because the insurgency was thought to be going away, and the plan was for the Americans to get out of detainee operations. In January 2004, there were well over 8,000 detainees in detention;

this number was raised to over 12,000 in the successive months before dropping to around 5,000 detainees on October 30, 2004, reported Maj. Gen. Quantock. According to the General, nobody looked at rehabilitation programs as an opportunity, but saw it rather as a by-product of the system. Abu Ghraib left many soldiers queasy to their stomach and everyone just focused on departing Iraq.

Obviously, a quick departure of troops from Iraq did not happen and, when Maj. Gen. Quantock was called back to Iraq in July 2008, he found a lot had changed:

> When I returned in July 2008, there were vast improvements in detainee operations. Vocational and educational programs were stood up [set up], the facilities were much better constructed, Camp Bucca had gone through a huge surge, and the modular detainee housing units were developed, unit training and leadership were much improved. Cropper and Bucca had full combat support hospitals. Visitation programs had grown exponentially, COIN [counterinsurgency] programs were in place added by Intel professionals versus what I had in 2004 [no Intel professionals looking inside the wire].

However, there were also some challenges, according to the general:

> The challenges we had were very little interface with the Minister of Justice and building capability and capacity of the Iraqi Corrections Service. As we approached the security agreement, we had many detainees that we had actionable intelligence on, but no actionable *evidence* to seek a conviction. So massive efforts were made to develop a close working relationship with the divisions to include the U.S. Embassy and the Ministry of Justice. After January 1, 2009 ..., we had to release all detainees in a "safe and orderly manner" while transferring the detainees with arrest warrants and detention orders over to the GoI [Government of Iraq]. We had about 15,000 cold cases that we had to try to figure out who were the worst detainees and develop as many cases as we could to keep as many as we could behind bars. It was a huge interagency effort to synchronize all the different agencies against the top tier detainees.

During his command in Iraq, Maj. Gen. Quantock left a deep impression on his troops. According to Command Sgt. Maj. Butler, Maj. Gen. Quantock is extremely approachable and that has worked greatly in his favor as he sought counsel with the GoI for devising the best way forward.

> His ability to work at that level with those key ministers and director generals, that's the real key to success of where we are now. And, he is just a real positive leader, doesn't get down, stays up, and everybody

knows he will work harder than everybody else. He will push himself harder than everybody else, and there's no doubt when he's leading you, you are comfortable in his decisions, you follow wherever he is going to take you.

Further, according to Sgt. Maj. Butler, "I think what Maj. Gen. Quantock brought was a military police background and different approach to things."

Maj. Gen. Stone understood that the services made a difference. But, I think Maj. Gen. Quantock kind of took those concepts and improved upon them; using the programs and also using our counterinsurgency inside the wire function to really stay ahead of any plans or violent acts inside the facility. I think the law enforcement background of Maj. Gen. Quantock in his approach to things was a big difference that really turned it to success.

Most probably, it was the military police background that had Maj. Gen. Quantock realize that there needed to be lawyers embedded with local division teams to ensure a certain amount of checks and balances when detaining individuals. In May 2009, the "blue cell" was created. Previously, there had been a lot of tension between those working in the detention sites and those actually out in the divisions around Iraq making the arrests. What happened is when detainees were released, many in the division who had made the initial arrest did not understand why. It created natural friction because here they had done the capturing, and yet it was TF-134 calling all the shots. It created "almost a hatred between the two divisions because we were the gatekeepers and we kept letting everyone go," Maj. Gen. Quantock said. The blue cell was initiated to bring harmony and credibility between capturing units and TF-134. It was two-fold: (1) It put lawyers into the division to help them work the cases and ensure all important documentation was handled correctly, and (2) Maj. Gen. Quantock personally went down and created relationships with division commanders, so that they knew directly with whom they were dealing. Maj. Gen. Quantock gave briefings to the divisions, "Don't complain about the fact that I have to release the detainees because you didn't do your piece in it upfront." Providing examples as evidence (Santa Claus!), he explained to them what was necessary in order to keep detainees locked up. Thereafter, fusion meetings were conducted weekly to address issues/questions. Eventually, what he found was that every case that arrived with a detainee was solid; the blue cell effectively did what it set out to do by creating harmony between the divisions and TF-134 and creating a more solidified course of documentation. All of the information on detainees was then put into a portal where lawyers could (re)examine it to make their case, the general reported.

Maj. Gen. Quantock was the longest serving detention operations commander in Iraq. He said that he enjoyed serving in Iraq because to him there "is nothing better than serving your country when it's at war." Further, he looked at it as a challenge. Having been in Iraq during 2004, he has seen it in some of its darkest days, and it was his passion to see his service end on a good note and see the operations come to an increasingly positive resolution. Maj. Gen. Quantock concluded:

> I believe that if you do it right, rehabilitation programs can be complementary to the war effort. This can be complementary in providing a valuable tool to stop the insurgency. But, is it everything? No. It has to work hand-in-hand with the battle space, with the people out there running around, knocking on doors, and working with the community to create jobs, political and economic. All that stuff is very important. The boats all gotta rise together. You can give these guys rehabilitation and vocational education, but if they've got nothing to go back to, other than vocational terrorism, that's what going to happen.

CONCLUSION

Changes had begun long before Maj. Gen. Stone arrived, prompted by the abuses at Abu Ghraib and by riots and disturbances at Camp Bucca and Camp Cropper. But, it was under Maj. Gen. Stone that positive changes received a boost in funding and support that allowed them to be carried forward. However, it also took individuals like Maj. Gen. Quantock who continued and evolved the rehabilitation programs during his time as detention operations commander to ensure the intent and purpose of the programs were not forgotten. But, the effort didn't stop there. The programs could have never happened without the dedication and determination of countless local Iraqi nationals who worked the programs, contractors who oversaw and evolved the programs, detainees who elected to participate in the programs, and the thousands of soldiers who maintained security for the programs to take place.

There are many other individuals who would like to take the credit for the rehabilitation programs and how successful they ended up being to the whole of Iraq. It did take a lot of people to make them happen, and even more to keep them going long after Maj. Gen. Stone returned home to his family. However, the indisputable fact is that the programs would not have received the support or gotten anywhere close to fruition if it were not for Maj. Gen. Stone's determination and his unwillingness to deviate from what he saw as an absolutely necessary overhaul of detention operations. His proven record and his position undoubtedly helped him to keep up the fight, but it wasn't without a great deal of moral courage in the face of grave opposition that kept him fighting. According to Maj. Gen. Stone, moral courage is putting ethics into action. "I argue that to stay loyal you must make moral judgments, that without it ... the democracy as we know it fails," he said. Most individuals understand very little about what it took for him to win the fight for funding and implementation of the rehabilitation programs. But, as hard as it is for some people to swallow, the facts are indisputable. Arguably, if the job demanded him to become an "over-eager salesman" in order to get the mission accomplished, he was prepared to give it his best shot.

Further, what is perhaps most remarkable—while greatly understated—about the introduction of the rehabilitation programs, besides what is mentioned previously, is what many have said since. That being, if the detention program had continued on the path set forth, prior to the introduction of the rehabilitation programs, that undoubtedly the entire detention process would have "blown up," according to Maj. Gen. Stone; which it most assuredly might have with all the numbers that the ground forces planned to detain. There was even suggestion that there might have been another incident that would rival Abu Ghraib, not necessarily by U.S. forces, but by those in detention. In fact, many officials have referred to those individuals involved in the rehabilitation programs as the unsung heroes of the surge, in that what Maj. Gen. Stone did, along with his support, was that they avoided this catastrophe, and in fact turned a situation from a net negative to a net positive. The ratings by the Islamic world in the papers and all over Iraq changed when they saw what was happening to their fellow citizens, and this changed the Iraqi public's attitude towards Americans and caused the other efforts being made seem like the Americans were being good and helpful. According to Maj. Gen. Stone:

> I think it changed the attitude of the [Iraqi] Government to favoring our actions and approach, and this is the greatest effect of all we did... not only did we make changes that caused de-radicalization...it massively effected the population of Iraq, and this was the unplanned, and wonderful outcome of making changes...Iraqi's finally felt there was a real rule of law, a sensitive U.S. Government, and that we were there to help, not just detain all their men.

It was all of this combined that really illustrated the kind of impact that the creation and implementation of the rehabilitation programs had, not only on the detained Iraqi population, but also on the Iraqi population at large. For the effort to be successful it was necessary for everyone to be engaged and on board in the rehabilitation process. For the most part, they were. Most individuals, once they were made to understand the importance and necessity of rehabilitation, were more than willing to be a part of it. However, it needs to be said that it was not always easy to conjoin military, civilians, and local Iraqi nationals together on a project; inevitably each brought their own chain of command, cultural differences, and ideas of what constitutes acceptable behavior and performance. And, in that, there was a whole other set of challenges and struggles with which to deal.

CHAPTER 5

Part of the Team

PROLOGUE

To fully understand the rehabilitation programs in Iraq, it is relevant and necessary to understand the circumstances of the individuals involved in the running and oversight of the programs. Their work environment, living environment, pleasures, and stresses that they may have experienced all contributed to whether the programs succeeded or not. The Operational Support and Services (OSS) contractors maintained uninterrupted direct oversight and supervision of the programs, and employed local Iraqi nationals who were responsible for the actual instruction of the rehabilitation programs to the detainees. The TF-134 military liasons—assigned to support OSS—provided valuable expertise and security to the operations. OSS and the TF-134 liasons were integral to the success of the rehabilitation programs. In Iraq, everyone endures his/her share of hardships. In the implementation of the rehabilitation programs, the OSS was no different. There were mountains to climb and challenges faced daily by everyone throughout the course of the programs.

OSS CONTRACTORS

Pilot Program

The first pilot religious rehabilitation program took place in June 2007 at Camp Bucca and ran for 6 weeks. Based on the outcome of the three sessions there, the programs were better adapted for the Iraqi population, but, it wasn't without controversy. There was a battle of wits that took place in closed rooms as individuals duked it out, each insisting that he or she knew the best way forward in detainee rehabilitation. According to Ken Reidy, an OSS contracted member of the first team to run the pilot program, "There were quite a few personality fights (between contractors, military, and employed local Iraqi nationals (LNs) and a constant learning curve in order to get the programs off the ground and running" (K. Reidy, personal interview, December 18, 2009). Likewise, according to Dr. Ann Speckhard, who after her previous involvement in 2006 with Lt. Gen. John Gardner and TF-134 was hired by OSS as head psychologist to lead training and counseling courses for the local Iraqi nationals, there were many problems from the outset:

> There was disorganization, poor leadership in the contractor side; colleagues in charge who didn't understand what such a program needs. … [There was a] lack of confidence on the military side with the contractor for these obvious reasons, which meant they dealt with me directly, which violated the contracting rules. Also the military had many conflicts among themselves and played many games with us and made it difficult to work (Dr. A. Speckhard, personal interview, July 26, 2010).

According to Dr. Speckhard, there were many things that happened in the shadows so as to try to make a good impression of everything running smoothly on the surface. Yet, views were varied. According to Col. Michael Callaghan (personal interview, 2010):

> Dr. Ann Speckhard believed that all the detainees were emotionally affected and that they need more psychological counseling than religious counseling. Her involvement in the program was during a very disruptive period, and her going in a different direction and leaving the program [was] good for everyone concerned.

Meanwhile, the local Iraqi nationals who worked for OSS in the rehabilitation programs appeared to have a different opinion. "I was lucky because when I was in Bucca, I met Dr. Ann [Speckhard], and she was a great woman. I was under her supervision for 2 months, learning from her about counseling, which I then used in the religious classes" (A. Sattar, personal interview, January 29, 2010). Due to conflicts of interest, Dr. Speckhard departed Iraq before the 6-week pilot program drew to a close, along with the top three clerics, who being disenchanted with OSS about the circumstances of her departure, decided to also depart.

Introduction

Linc Government Services, LLC (also known as REEP, Inc.), while doing business as OSS, was the winning bidder of the Theater Internment Facility Reconciliation Center (TIFRC) services contract on several occasions. In fact, due to productivity and success, OSS won and maintained TIFRC services contracts from the pilot programs in June 2007 through to the turnover of U.S. TIFs to the Government of Iraq in 2010. OSS mostly conducted the hiring for international staff from its offices in the United States. Consequently, all OSS-employed international (non-Iraqi) staff was hired with the status of independent contractor while in Iraq. While there were a select few who maintained longevity throughout the contracts, most did not.

From the start of the program in June 2007 to the closure of Camp Bucca in 2009, OSS had five different program managers come and go at just Camp Bucca; three in the first year alone. Because the first two were not performing up to par, according to the OSS Iraq headquarters office (located in Baghdad), they were each relocated under the guise that it was for each one's benefit. The next one got tired of what he felt was a "lot of crap" in OSS politics and work environment, and so resigned after 4 months of being program manager. All three of these individuals had military backgrounds, which fits the profile of OSS-favored hires. Some might say this preference for those with military backgrounds was to the detriment of operations. Some observers suggest this because those with military backgrounds and/or still in reserve duty were not as easily adaptable to the civilian lifestyle. They were more prone to fall into old habits of deciding who they had to listen to and to whom they didn't, based on their previous rank in the military. They also were more apt to be apprehensive about communicating directly with high-ranking individuals (i.e., generals) because their previous chain of command in the military did not permit it. On the flip side, civilians who were completely unfamiliar with military procedures did not easily adapt to (or understand) the military lifestyle, either. It was civilians who had been out of the military for extended periods of time and/or who were already familiar with the military environment that seemed to fare best. They appeared to more readily accept good ideas, regardless of the source. Likewise, they were more apt to diplomatically raise objections if something presented would complicate the mission and/or was inefficient, regardless of who suggested it.

Allegedly, there was what one senior management OSS contractor remarked on as "a lack of quality control" in OSS contractor hires. Although this was ironed out through the contracts as time went on, initial problems included inefficient skills for job performance. These problems often only came to light after arrival in the area of operation. One of the first reports was of a specialist, who was responsible for translating documents to/from English and Arabic, as well as providing verbal Arabic/English translations, and who was discovered to be incapable of reading/writing Arabic. This was only discovered after he arrived in theater and there was a document that needed translation. Another (married) OSS reports specialist was caught having sexual relations with an employed local Iraqi national whom she was supervising. Another OSS contractor arrived in Iraq impractically expecting to work

Monday through Friday from 9 a.m. to 5 p.m., and was surprised to hear that those specific work hours were unacceptable. And, yet, another OSS contractor (in a management position) lasted less than 6 months after it had been determined that crucial information about his recent past involving sexual relationships with patients while a practicing and married psychiatrist had been covered up. Other alleged problems with OSS contractors included poor job performance, public intoxication, laziness, and insubordination.

Another tension feature among OSS contractors was what was determined as a certain superiority emanating from those who had been born in the Middle East and emigrated to a westernized country over those who were still living in Iraq (most notably the employed OSS local Iraqi nationals). Not only did the individuals who had emigrated have a huge salary difference over those who did not, but it appeared as if those who were born in Iraq and moved abroad saw themselves to be of a different social level—rather superior—than the Iraqis who, for whatever reason, stuck with their government and remained put. Likewise, referring to someone as "Iraqi" who had been born in Iraq, but then emigrated and gained another citizenship could be a very sensitive subject. For instance, there were a few OSS contractors who, although Iraqi citizens at birth, claimed themselves to be of Syrian ancestry and were prone to get visibly and noticeably upset if anyone called them Iraqi rather than Syrian. Likewise, it was not uncommon to hear individuals who had been born in Iraq, emigrated and subsequently gained citizenship elsewhere, talking about other Iraqis with negative connotations: "All Iraqis are manipulative" and "Iraqis cannot be trusted" were two often-heard arguments. Yet at the same time, although some of these individuals might not have lived in Iraq for over a decade or two, they still referred to Iraq as it "used" to be, unwilling to acknowledge that Iraq could have changed during the 20 years they had been gone (as nations tend to do); instead preferring to project a situation and environment that was accurate over 20 years ago as accurate now. All of these contributed to what could conceivably be called a complex work environment.

On some Forward Operating Bases (FOB) in Iraq, contractors were referred to as "contractor scum" by military personnel and called other negative names. Usually, as a response to those contractors only in Iraq for the money (rather than for a patriotic duty or job interest), the "contractor scum" did the least amount possible to get by, were lazy, were always complaining. and acted irritated and/or rude when asked for, or directed to do, something that should have been done anyway. However, just like any profession, it all comes down to the individual and his/her personality. Contractors are acutely aware of which soldier(s) would be most helpful in accomplishing a project just as soldiers also are acutely aware of which contractor(s) can be counted on when time is of the essence.

OSS shared its own problems with implementation and undependable/ irresponsible hires, but they still got the job done, and the mission was still accomplished. Probably due in part to some key leaders, OSS is run by a mostly dedicated and determined team, which is why they continually won the TIFRC services contract. Most military officials familiar with OSS are bound to agree that there were both positives of having contractors engaged in the rehabilitation efforts as well as negatives. There is no doubt that contractors can provide a certain continuance that the military cannot. They essentially bridge the gap between incoming units and outgoing units, so as to not interrupt operational flow.

Sustenance

To put it simply, the food was much better than anyone who has not been to Iraq thinks it is. It also was much better than those who have been there think it isn't. Contractors ate at the exact same dining facility as the military; as such, they were bound to the same rules as well. Some rules included no sweaty gym clothes, no earphones on when entering, no bags, and a requirement to wear socks with shoes and wash hands before entering the facility. Interestingly, the military even provided a guard to ensure everyone remembered the hand-washing rule. The dining facility was open for four meals a day. There was breakfast, lunch, dinner, and midnight meal for those who worked the nightshift. Food was shipped in from the United States, and there was always an abundance of it. Sometimes, different convoys or shipments of food would get interrupted, so the dining facility might temporarily run out of certain items, but, a week or so later, the usual makings would be back. Each night there was a different special. For instance, on Thursdays it might be steak and lobster night and, on Mondays, it was cheeseburger night. Some larger dining facilities even had stir-fry, where you choose from a selection of meat and vegetables to be cooked in your made-to-order dish. Other dining facilities offered varieties of beef and chicken kebabs, sandwich buffet, and fruit buffet; all had a salad buffet. Most had made-to-order eggs available for breakfast.

On holidays like the Fourth of July, Thanksgiving, and Christmas, the dining facility was always decorated; Thanksgiving was especially impressive. Because of the special selection of foods available on these particular days, lines to the dining facility were always long. Sometimes, individuals would be in line for 45 minutes. During the holidays, different dining facilities would offer elaborate ice and frosting sculptures and extravagant cakes (Figure 5.1). Fresh turkey, roast beef, and ham carvings were often available along with all the hoped-for accompaniments like stuffing, deviled eggs, sweet potatoes, and pumpkin pie a la

FIGURE 5.1   An ice sculpture created and displayed during Thanksgiving in the dining facility in honor of fallen comrades: Camp Victory, Iraq, 2005. (Photo by David L. Butler, Jr.)

mode for dessert. Also standard during the holiday period was a small table set with a plate, silverware, and a glass just inside the entrance—a tribute to fallen comrades. During holiday meals, it was also customary for high-ranking officers to volunteer to dish up meals for the soldiers. In 2008, while in queue for the Thanksgiving meal, Dr. Angell noticed that Admiral Garland Wright was in front of her. After some brief chatting, he explained that although he volunteered to serve up meals inside, he didn't want to give the wrong impression by cutting in front of all the soldiers who had been queuing for such a lengthy period of time; instead, leading by example, he chose to wait with them.

Lodging

Lodging was disquietingly similar regardless of which FOB a contractor might be assigned. Usually, when a contractor first arrives on the FOB he/she will be assigned to a transition tent. The tents vary in size, but usually house between 20 to 40 individuals (Figure 5.2). Some house both military and civilian, but most house either military *or* civilian. Dr. Angell's first 4 months in Iraq were spent on a cot in a 20-women

FIGURE 5.2 Temporary housing for soldiers and contractors queuing for trailer assignments: Camp Victory, Iraq, 2007. (Photo by Jeffrey Folkertsma.)

tent (Figure 5.3). Toilets and showers were about 300 yards away. After being assigned a tent, a contractor's name is put into queue for two-person quarters (Figure 5.4). Usually referred to as a trailer or pod, it was the desire of every contractor to get out of the tent and into one as quickly as possible. Each quarters is assigned to two people of the same sex. Each person in the quarters receives a small twin bed, a nightstand, and a small closet for clothes. Depending on the layout, in many quarters, if one person lies on her bed and reaches out her arm, that person can almost touch the other person's bed on the other side. Some are strikingly similar to small single-wide trailers split into three separate living quarters, for a total of six people to live in, with three separate doors for entry. Others are almost like the sheds at a storage center. While "moving up" from a tent to a two-person quarters is the desire of most, unfortunately it does not necessitate that shower and bathroom facilities are any closer. Fortunately, for those late-night releases, when 300 yards in the dark and/or rain and/or mud is not so appealing, there were selections of porta potties located at strategic places throughout each FOB. Perhaps not so surprisingly, because most were sanitized and cleaned three to four times a day, they could actually be substantially cleaner than the flushing toilets.

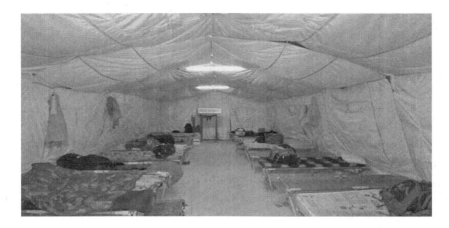

FIGURE 5.3   Inside temporary housing where soldiers and individuals might live for up to 6 months while in queue for a trailer opening. (Photo by Timothy Linza.)

FIGURE 5.4   One example of living quarters: Iraq, 2008. (Photo by Gerald House.)

Medical and Spiritual Services

The same multifaceted medical and psychological services available to the military also were available to contractors. Each FOB had a fully equipped general practice medical clinic, which included at a minimum a general practitioner, a dentist, and a psychologist. In the event of an emergency, all were available 24 hours a day. For nonemergency cases, the clinics posted their open hours for first in, first served. Complementary to the medical services available were also spiritual services. In the event a contractor requested spiritual guidance, there were representatives available from most major faiths. There was made available on every FOB a religious space where services for a variety of faiths were held weekly. The religious space also was made available for those who might practice a faith that did not have a regular scheduled service or for one who might just have wanted a place to meditate or reflect.

Extracurricular Activities

Without a doubt, there is plenty for contractors to get involved with outside of work hours (Figure 5.5). Every FOB has a well-stocked fitness center where it is not uncommon to find a variety of classes to participate in. During Dr. Angell's 44 months in Iraq, she was fortunate enough to have the opportunity to be in a marathon running club (Figure 5.6), play on league basketball teams (Figure 5.7), and be a Camp Victory member of Hash House Harriers (a different type of running club) (Figure 5.8). In addition, she participated regularly in boxing (there were spars every month or two in a ring flown in for that purpose),* Tai Kwon Do (with an official instructor who had been trained in Japan) (Figure 5.9), capoeira (an Afro–Brazilian dance), yoga, aerobics, and even fencing (Figure 5.10). Almost monthly, there was an organized race around the FOB, usually in partnership with a sister race in the United States, and almost unfailingly with the prize of a finisher's shirt for every participant (Figure 5.11). Some even gave away medals for the first three finishers. The Australians gave away stuffed Koala bears for the top finishers of their sponsored race. Fitness was an equal opportunity for everyone across the FOB. The military has a strong policy about fitness and thus went to great lengths to plan activities and adventures that were mutually inclusive of soldiers, contractors, and employed local nationals alike.

---

* It was up to the FOB commander whether or not to permit the boxing matches. On some bases, they were cancelled after participants got hurt.

FIGURE 5.5   U.S. contractors gather at "Baba's Place," an always fes-
tively-decorated group of trailers at Camp Victory, to celebrate Christmas
2005 with a BBQ and music. (Photo by James (Baha) Landi.)

For contractors not as inclined toward fitness-related activities,
there were other options. Certain nights of the week featured different music and dancing venues. Salsa and country line dancing were
two of the favorites. There also was open karaoke night, table hockey,
pool tables, and ping-pong available. Probably most impressive, however, was the large number of bands and performance artists that
came to Iraq pro bono to perform in honor of the troops. Toby Keith,
Rascal Flats, and Jerry Seinfeld were just a few that Dr. Angell managed to see in person. The World Wresting Federation (WWF) also
came out with all their fanfare, including a stage especially set up for
that purpose, to do some professional wrestling much to the enjoyment of the troops.

For those tired of the dining facility or wanting something different or just hungry outside of dining facility open hours of operation,
there was always Subway, Burger King, Pizza Hut (Figure 5.12), and
Green Bean Coffee. By 2010, these were almost standard on every larger
military base and offered the favored selections available at home. The
only difference was the location (Iraq) and the employees behind the

FIGURE 5.6   Paul A. Hunt, a U.S. contractor and member of the Camp
Victory marathon running club runs past Aw Faw Palace: Camp Victory,
Iraq, 2007. (Photo by Ami Angell.)

counter.* There was also a Post Exchange (PX) (also known as BX for
"base exchange") for housing/personal needs (Figure 5.13 and Figure
5.14). PXs had everything in them from books and magazines to shirts
and shorts to quality DVDs to knives to shampoo and conditioner; they
also had a whole assortment of food popular in the United States including items such as chips, candy bars, and protein bars. Unfortunately, all
the PXs located closest to the theater internment facilities (TIFs) were
quite small and were seldom well stocked. Therefore, most contractors working the rehabilitation programs either stocked up on desired
items when visiting a base with a bigger PX or ordered the desired items
online. Fortunately, the mail system to all the U.S. bases in Iraq was by
the U.S. Postal Service. Consequently, shipping to any of the bases was
charged at the same rate as shipping from one location in the United

---

* These places more often than not were run by other country nationals (mostly from
  developing countries) hired through contracting agencies in places like Kuwait. The
  majority of those hired were Filipinos. The Filipinos often lived in a confined area on
  base and were required to work a minimum of 6 days a week, 9 hours a day, in exchange
  for the monthly sum of 150 Kuwaiti dinar (approximately US $520) and a spending
  allowance of US $10 a week. They had a forced unpaid 4-week vacation once every 2
  years and often had their passports seized by their employers to ensure compliance and
  loyalty (Ditchon, personal interview, 2010).

FIGURE 5.7   "Team Mojo," a combined basketball team with both con-tractors and soldiers, part of a Camp Victory basketball league: Camp Victory, Iraq, 2005. (Photo courtesy of Ami Angell.)

States to another. Likewise, ordering online and shipping were charged at the U.S. rate of delivery. This made shipping and receiving quite inexpensive. So inexpensive, in fact, that Dr. Angell knows of one female who—being severely allergic to the soap used by the laundry facility on Camp Bucca—shipped all of her clothes home biweekly to be washed and returned.

For individuals desiring some local souvenirs made in Iraq, they didn't have to look far. For shopping therapy, most FOBs had a couple of shops referred to as "hajji shops." A hajji shop is essentially a makeshift store run by local Iraqi nationals who had passed security screening and were allowed to sell their goods on American bases. Some individuals tried to stop them from being called "hajji shops" on ethical grounds (*hajji* is also known to be used as a derogatory term), but it appeared that the workers themselves (local Iraqis) actually preferred the name and grew confused when people ceased its use. At least one of the shops, in every cluster, would be selling DVDs. In the DVD shop, copied DVDs and software disks would usually sell at US $2 to $5 each. There also were whole series of TV shows, such as *Heroes*, or *The Unit*, or *Sex and the City*, that would go for a flat rate of around US $25. Movies that had not yet made it out of theater were the favored among the troops who

FIGURE 5.8   Camp Victory Hash House Harriers ("a drinking club with a running problem") don red dresses for the annual "red dress charity run" in which they ran through base collecting donations for a sponsored charity: Camp Victory, Iraq, 2006. (Photo courtesy of Kristopher Malloy.)

FIGURE 5.9   Tae Kwon Do club: Camp Victory, Iraq, 2005. (Photo courtesy of Frank Jorge Ditchon.)

FIGURE 5.10   Fencing club: Camp Victory, Iraq, 2005. (Photo courtesy of Ami Angell.)

FIGURE 5.11   Soldiers and contractors conclude a half marathon with the reward of collecting goodies, which included socks, a water bottle, and a T-shirt: Camp Victory, Iraq, 2008. (Photo courtesy of Ami Angell.)

FIGURE 5.12   Two U.S. contractors, Paul A. Hunt and David L. Butler, Jr., wait for their Pizza Hut pizza: Camp Victory, Iraq, 2008. (Photo by Gene Williams.)

usually kept up to speed on the latest blockbusters. The copied DVDs did not always work and sometimes they were obviously videotaped in a dark movie theater by a shaky hand; however, the shopkeeper was always quick to exchange any problematic ones.

For the most part, all extracurricular activities available to the military were available to contractors. It was really just the punishment doled out for committing violations that varied between contractors and soldiers. For instance, the punishment for being caught drinking or having alcohol depended on your position. Obviously, when in a conflict zone, Americans are not permitted to drink alcohol or have any pornography for that matter. However, many individuals appeared to think of this rule as more of a guideline rather than an absolute. They would find creative ways to get around it. For many, it appeared to be the thrill of breaking the rules and not getting caught. Using the postal service to receive alcohol was the most popular method. However, as all packages still go through an x-ray machine, any package that looks as if it contains alcohol is opened and inspected, and, if any prohibited items are found, they are removed. This encouraged individuals to get creative in figuring out other ways to get alcohol on the bases. Creativity manifested itself in various ways: filling up a hydration bag's water bladder with vodka,

FIGURE 5.13   PX facility for shopping needs on Camp Victory, Iraq, 2008. (Photo by Jeffrey Folkertsma.)

pouring out a quarter of Gatorade and replacing the rest with alcohol before sealing it up again, or even just buying odd-shaped bottles or box cartons of wine. One contractor made his own wine in his trailer. That is, until the birds discovered his drip system, and started waking him up at all hours with their gleeful chirping as they drank. In some ways, Dr. Angell thinks the prohibition of alcohol in Iraq encouraged many to try getting it; the process became more thrilling than the actual pleasure of drinking it. The fact that the British were permitted alcohol-serving pubs on base as were the Italians permitted wine (a staple in their meal, ready-to-eat (MRE)), and the Russians allowed vodka (also a staple in their MRE), made the temptation even more irresistible for some people. However, this thrill came at a cost. Per military policy, U.S. contractors who were caught drinking or with alcohol had 24 hours to be removed from the FOB and were not allowed to return and work in Iraq for a period of at least 1 year.

Work Conditions

Work conditions for contractors varied widely. For the purpose of this book, Dr. Angell will only address the work conditions of OSS contractors

FIGURE 5.14 Entertainment square at Camp Bucca, Iraq. On the right is the PX, next to that is a jewelry shop, tailoring shop, and DVD store. Out of the picture on the left is a Pizza Hut, Green Bean Coffeehouse, and a hair salon: Camp Bucca, Iraq, 2008. (Photo by Sgt. Matthew Sugars.)

involved with the rehabilitation programs. For those, too, work hours and conditions varied widely. The only thing for certain was that nobody worked a standard 40-hours-a-week job. The hours of reporting to work varied depending on the program in session. However, on average, contractors in the rehabilitation program worked 6.5 days a week, from 12 to 16 hours a day. Half days on Fridays were sometimes suggested for relaxation, but were not always taken, as there was much that needed to be done in short periods of time. The first year when the rehabilitation programs were still in a trial phase proved most intense; often meals were eaten at the desk while working. Time would constantly come and go, leaving individuals no idea where it went. There was a saying in Iraq among contractors and military: "Every day is like 3 days back home." The only thing that regulated any semblance of days/hours was the opening hours of the dining facility, but even that was debatable.

Also impacting the work environment were military alarms and drills. Alarms would sound when the FOB was receiving incoming mortars or rockets. When an alarm would sound, all individuals regardless of where they were or what they were doing would grab their full battle protection gear (if immediately available) and run (sometimes crawl) to the nearest bomb shelter. There they would be required to stay until the "all clear" alarm would sound, after which they were free to carry on their previous undertaking. Other times, the military would run drills. Some of these drills included "lock down," which means that all contractors had to either stay in their office or remain in their assigned lodging until the drill was over. When the siren sounded, each individual basically had about 30 seconds to make the choice of which location he/she would prefer to be at for an unspecified amount of time. Drills are most common at FOBs with a detention center full of detainees. One common drill at Camp Bucca was nicknamed "code yellow," and was a mock escaped detainee drill. When the alarm would go off and the announcement would be "code yellow," then all military individuals, regardless of what they were previously engaged in, would be required to get in full battle gear and go to their units' prearranged location and report in. There they would be organized into search contingents. They would then set off to search for a dummy doll dressed in bright yellow (the color of the detainee uniform) hidden well somewhere on the FOB. Sometimes, the search would take 1 to 2 hours. More often, it might take 5 to 6 hours. However long it took, during this entire time contractors were required to stay in their office or trailer until the "all clear" signal was given. Soldiers go door-to-door to check inside buildings for the hidden dummy as well, so, if you choose not to be in your trailer, you risk potential disarray once you return to it. Of course, not all of them were drills, thus, they were all taken seriously.

When the pilot program began in June 2007 at Camp Bucca, OSS staff included a program manager (PM), program lead (PL), psychological subject matter expert (Psych SME), an Islam subject matter expert (Cleric SME), administrative assistant, and a radical ideology research specialist, in addition to a group of local Iraqi nationals. Other than the position of the "radical ideology research specialist," which eventually evolved into something else, all of these positions remained in some capacity throughout the life of the contracts. According to OSS's Ken Reidy, initially the program was off to a rough start:

> Everyone was going at a 100 miles an hour to get everything ready from the materials we would use, to finding LNs [OSS employed local Iraqi nationals] to run the programs to training the LNs to run the programs. We arrived to find that we had no office and nowhere to stay, so we were put up in transient tents, which were meant to be taken down. Indeed, they were always meant to be taken down! We were given an office a few days later, two computers, and access to a printer. There was a fair amount of misunderstanding by the

military with what we were supposed to be doing. Some had no idea, and others couldn't grasp the concept, which is understandable as it depended on how you wanted to conclude: Is it to get information? Is it to make them feel better? Is it to stop the riots? Is it to teach? Is it to listen?, etc. At the time, the specifics of the program were up in the air, and it has literally just been created. Some thought that it was merely a token effort, something they had to endure for a month before things would go back to normal—whatever that meant. For all the big talk in Baghdad, it seemed very little had trickled down to Bucca. Of course, other factors played into this. Namely, three of our clerical positions were filled by former detainees of Bucca or another TIF; can't remember. Having former detainees roam the FOB freely rightly got a few people worked up.

The chaos of getting lodging and adequate office space never quite went away. For the second pilot program, Dr. Angell with the OSS support staff arrived at Camp Bucca to discover that their assigned office space had been taken over by another military contingent. Fortunately, OSS military support liaison Chief Mark Crouch was able to work it out, and got OSS the office space returned within a week. In the meantime, OSS were forced to conduct operations from one tiny cubicle in the corner with one computer. They took advantage of the military health and morale center's computers to do online work, which helped progress. But, as OSS contractors were always on such a tight performance schedule, not having the space or capacity to run operations made this period very difficult. Fortunately, this too eventually got worked out as manpower grew and funding increased for the later rehabilitation contracts. In addition to the previous positions, OSS were fortunate to gain positions for Reports Specialists. These were basically glorified Arabic/English translators who were skilled at both written and verbal translations. They proved invaluable in the rehabilitation process for quality control as well as being dependable for other administrative and collective functions as needed.

Fortunately, for every OSS contractor who was sub par, there were two who were magnificent. These individuals generally went above and beyond while working the programs, simply because they believed in the mission, and what it was trying to accomplish. For these individuals, it didn't matter how many days or hours they had to work because they enjoyed the work and believed in the project and purpose. Unequivocally, they are the ones who drove the program to be a success. According to Maj. Gen. David Quantock (personal interview, 2010):

A lot of times, people have no appreciation for where you work— unless they've been there. I tell you, there's some dark phase in January and February [2009]. I thought, "Oh, my God, how are we ever gonna get out of this?" But we did. We've come an amazing way. Contractors like yourself who have come over and help us with this stuff. There's some real passion. Contractors who really believe in what they're doing.

EMPLOYED LOCAL IRAQI NATIONALS

Introduction

Instructors for all the rehabilitation courses were local Iraqi nationals (more commonly referred to as LNs). This is part of the effort to empower and promote from within Iraq. It also facilitates the comprehension of local Arabic slang and mannerisms unique to Iraq. Further, employing LNs to directly lead classes empowers the detainees who are able to see their fellow Iraqis in charge and instructing a course. Some have shared that it gives them hope and makes them determined to succeed, when they see that one of their "brothers" has. OSS was the contracting company responsible for employing local Iraqi nationals to fill the contractual positions of teachers, social workers, and clerics.

During the pilot program in June 2007, only eight LNs were employed, and all of them were acutely aware of the risk. Sheikh Abdul Sattar, a cleric who worked for OSS from the beginning of the rehabilitation programs on June 21, 2007, at Camp Bucca until the turnover of Camp Taji to Iraq control in March 2010, elaborated:

> The first time I was in Bucca, it was a difficult time. As you know in 2007, anyone who dared to work in a place with the Americans, he and his family will be killed by guns; it was a very big risk.

And yet, once hired, most LNs outlasted the contractors who worked for OSS.

However, hiring in a conflict zone always presents problems. One challenge was that LNs were worried about being targets in their communities if anyone found out they were working with U.S. forces on FOBs. This resulted in much tension and many of those called in for interviews ended up not showing up. Some interviewees would show up hours or days late, having been stopped on several occasions en route, but still determined to get to the interview. Other challenges OSS faced when hiring were faked documents. Some individuals starving for work were desperate enough to fake credentials, knowing that it was difficult for us to follow up to verify them. It was a chance they were willing to take for the possibility of a job to feed their family. This meant that OSS had to have a more in-depth hiring interview process. Once hired, individuals were required to go through another training process where it could be assessed that he/she had the right skills necessary for the position for which he/she was hired. Out of necessity, the hiring process evolved rapidly as we went along, and more positions were authorized for hire. It was a steep learning curve as Dr. Angell and OSS support staff learned to recognize and determine which individuals were most suitable to the stresses and culture shock of living and working on a U.S. military FOB; in addition to having individuals meet the qualifications to perform at the desired level.

However, even passing the U.S. military security at the checkpoint, passing the OSS interview, and proving oneself in the training did not always ensure an LN was a definite hire. Sometimes, employed LNs would show up on a security monitor as a "security threat" up to 3 weeks after the LN had already been on the FOB. During the more than a half dozen times this occurred while Dr. Angell was program lead, it usually fell on her shoulders to inform the LN of the upsetting news. Yet strangely, during her tenure as program lead, she never had an armed military escort while she did this. Usually, only a reports specialist (fluent in Iraqi dialect) accompanied her so that there could be no mistake over the information relayed to the LN. Of course, by this time, if the individual really was a security threat, he/she had the time to analyze the situation on the FOB and take whatever mental notes he/she wanted to pursue his/her aim. Yet, Dr. Angell never really had problems with any of the LNs when she told them the news. Their biggest worry appeared to be how they were going to now provide for their family and safety for traveling the roads back home. Safety was particularly relevant when she was required to inform the LN of his new status late in the evening. In those cases, she would try to gain commander permission for the LN to spend the night in a secure location (with guard oversight) until the morning hours when he could be escorted off the FOB in the daylight. On only one occasion did Dr. Angell ever feel any threat emanating from informing an LN that he had come up on security monitors as a security risk. He became intensely angry with her and then slowly let his eyes travel from her feet all the way until he met her eyes. His message was clear: He had implanted her into his memory and, given the opportunity, he wanted to cause her harm. In Iraq, sweeping someone with your eyes is a sign of grave disrespect.

Sustenance

LNs were permitted to eat at the same dining facilities as the military and contractors. As all the food was labeled, they could see what contained pork, what didn't, and make an informed choice. They appeared to greatly enjoy American cuisine and regularly tried to take loads of free Gatorade, boxes of juice, chips, and Otis Spunkmeyer muffins out the FOB gate when they went on leave. Initially, this was even overlooked. But, it was not long before certain military personnel realized what was happening and put a stop to it in November 2007.

Fruit appeared to be a particular favorite of the LNs. According to Salah Al-Hindawy (personal interview, 2010), an OSS BBA (bilingual bicultural advisor), the Saddam economy is likely the cause. "A banana would cost a dollar. In the time of Saddam, your paycheck could basically buy you three bananas. So, in fact, many Iraqis actually left Iraq having never tasted a banana in their life." This might explain why what fruits were available was always of interest to the LNs during each dining facility visit. Almost without exception, at the conclusion of each meal, they would enjoy an impressive amount of the available fruit to include grapes, bananas, oranges, and apples. Apparently, that was usually not enough because one out of two would also fill up a takeaway carton with additional fruit and nuts for later snacking.

However, having access to the same food and the same dining facility as the military and contractors should not imply that LNs were treated equally. LNs had to enter the dining facility through a separate entrance. One at a time, they would have to show their identification and then submit to a pat-down search. This would occur every time they wanted to eat at the dining facility. Those who ate in the dining facilities (which most did) three to four times a day found this a bit irritating. Fortunately, the irritation was not great enough to stop the frequent dining facility visits. In fact, the biggest LN complaint regarding the dining facility was that they were gaining too much weight from the American food.

Occasionally, when LNs would go on leave, they would return with a specially prepared local dish to share with the OSS contractors. Sometimes, this would be a whole fish filleted over rice. Other specialties included kebabs, falafel, soups, and sticky desserts. While some OSS contractors had certain reluctance about trying the food, a few of us always did and made sure that the LNs saw us doing so. It helped develop a stronger bond of trust, as they saw we appreciated their gift and culture, and that we trusted them. It also became a pleasure for us to experience native Iraqi food.

Lodging

All LNs working for OSS were required to live on the FOB. Both Sunni and Shiite were housed together. OSS maintained a zero tolerance for any kind of separation and segregation of those working the rehabilitation programs, and worked hard to that end. It was important that the detainees witness their instructors leading by example and getting along. The LNs lived in two extremely large tents. Each tent could technically house up to 80 LNs, but, fortunately, OSS never reached full capacity. Inside the tent, each LN had a bed and a closet. The beds were twin bunks. So, there was always some disagreement about who had to sleep on top. This was understandable as the beds were not the best of quality and sometimes shook when someone sat on them. Occasionally, they even broke apart. In 2008, there was an incident in which an LN taking a rest on his top bunk was rudely jolted awake as his bed collapsed on the one beneath it. While not visibly hurt, he was definitely shaken. Fortunately, his bunkmate had not been in bed when the incident happened.

Toilets and showers were about 100 yards away from the LN tents. Porta potties were put 30 feet outside the door for nighttime convenience. One of the challenges with the LNs as regards showers was to ensure they followed the military policy with wearing minimally a shirt and shorts when they were walking anywhere on the FOB, including the showers. We had a fair share of phone calls concerning LNs walking to/from the showers in only towels, and, a couple times, in just their underwear with their towel wrapped around their neck. But, overall, most LNs appeared to adapt fairly well to the living situation; they became creative in producing ways between the bunks to establish a certain amount of privacy and personal space. At one point, they lined all their closets to create a hallway down the center of the tent and produce zones of privacy. However, much to their dismay, their creativity was often limited, as the tent was still obligated to comply with the U.S. fire marshal guidelines.

LNs were never given (nor put on the waitlist for) trailers, and were required to live in the large tents a minimum of 5 nights a week. On Thursday after work, many of the LNs would leave through the FOB gate for their day off on Friday. Those who lived in the nearby town of Umm Qasr or knew a friend there would usually return to the FOB very early on Saturday morning before their work shift started. When Dr. Angell first started the rehabilitation programs, Sunnis were afraid to take their Fridays off by departing through the gate at Camp Bucca, preferring instead to just relax on the FOB. They considered Umm Qasr—being a Shiite village—too dangerous for them to be seen in. Yet, remarkably, by mid-2008, both Sunni and Shiite LNs were departing together out the gate. One quietly confessed to Dr. Angell, "Don't tell anyone, but we go and have beer!" One of them had found a bar and told the others about it. Excited, a couple more had gone along the following Friday. As it increasingly seemed safer, each week the group continued to grow.

Medical and Spiritual Services

It was a first for many of the LNs to have access to such quality medical care as provided on the FOB. Under Saddam's regime, medical care was extremely limited, and most could not afford any regular checkups, let alone the cost of a visit to the dentist. Many Iraqis have just grown used to the constant pain of a tooth needing to be pulled or the pain of a foot corn that makes walking difficult. Perhaps this is why, once they found out that pro bono medical care was available on the FOB, there was no holding back their curiosity and excitement. Stomach aches, headaches, earaches, and toothaches—the LNs competed with one another to find the most reasons for visiting the medical center. The dentist was the most popular; at least a few dozen teeth were pulled from OSS LNs by the dentist at Camp Bucca.

Abu Haji** gets tears in his eyes when he recalls the quality of care the military doctors provided him when he needed it most. Abu Haji was a social worker at Camp Bucca for the Islamic Discussion Program (IDP) and one of the most devoted and kindest-hearted persons one could hope to meet. An older gentleman, he had at one time even been a general in Saddam's army, but had eagerly decided to work the rehabilitation programs when he heard about them. Unfortunately, while instructing a class in May 2008, he started feeling pain in his gut and fainted. Another LN ran to get to Dr. Angell, and along with the military, she rushed him to the medical facility in the TIF. An examination showed that an allegedly botched operation years ago had resulted in his colostomy site getting badly infected. The medical staff determined that his situation warranted emergency surgery. As they did not have the proper equipment to perform the surgery at Camp Bucca, within an hour, they had airlifted him on a medical helicopter to a more equipped facility within Iraq. Although Dr. Angell followed his progress with limited phone communication, she lost contact with him when he went home for a couple months' recovery. It wasn't until January 2010 when she returned to Iraq that she had the unexpected pleasure of seeing him again. Working again for OSS at Camp Cropper, Abu Haji wept as he ran to her; calling Dr. Angell his daughter, he thanked her over and over for helping him and for the medical care that the military provided. Excitedly, using elaborate hand gestures, he related to Dr. Angell and the soldiers accompanying her about his experience during the Medivac and in the hospital where he had the corrective surgery. He told her, "I will never forget. You are good person. They are good people. They saved my life" (Abu Haji,* personal interview, January 26, 2010).

---

* An asterisk (*) is used throughout this book to protect the security and confidentiality of certain individuals whose lives might be threatened otherwise.

Extracurricular Activities

For the most part, extracurricular activities available to contractors and military were also available to LNs. But many LNs were quite apprehensive about getting involved. The favored physical activities outside of work, besides going on long walks aimlessly around the FOB, were playing pool and ping-pong in the moral and recreation center. One OSS LN even won the Camp Bucca pool tournament against contractors and military on two occasions. Another OSS LN won the Camp Bucca ping-pong tournament against contractors and military. While some LNs would regularly visit the fitness center, most did not. Probably because LNs were always searched when entering the gym, being searched at the dining facility as well as the fitness center undoubtedly did not encourage daily workouts.

Besides being searched for entry into the dining facility and gym, LNs had other concerns with living on the FOB. As many of them did not speak English, they often found it difficult to get around and fully participate in their environment. Soldiers and contractors would sometimes say something to them, and they were embarrassed that they did not understand. They missed their families and knowing they were so close, yet being unable to visit or call, was hard on them. This was made even more so by the fact that Iraq being at war was subject to constant random violence. Most had a fear that something would happen to their families and they would not be there to protect them. Others felt as if they were being treated unfairly or rudely by Americans. In some cases, Dr. Angell witnessed unbecoming behavior from Americans, some of whom looked at the LNs as potential security threats, not understanding (or wanting to) why they should be permitted on the FOB.

Throughout the rehabilitation programs, we had challenges concerning LNs and their use of Internet and mobile phones. For the first few months of the program, LNs were permitted to use the Internet in the military moral and recreation center. However, someone up the military chain became concerned that they could easily pass crucial FOB information through online communication, resulting in a breach of security. So, the permission for Internet use was suspended and never reinstated. The use of mobile phones to call home was another challenge. Every LN going to/from home would have a mobile phone. These mobile phones were required to be checked in at the base gate; no electronic items were permitted to be brought onto the FOB by an LN. The LN could then retrieve his mobile phone when he left the FOB again. However, with the constant violence, families were worried when they did not hear from their family member for a few days. This became problematic, particularly at Camp Bucca where phone signals were very difficult to get anywhere on the FOB due to the signal scrambles in the detention center. Fortunately this wasn't a problem at Camp Cropper and Camp Taji because each was located far enough from the TIF that individuals could still get phone reception; consequently, controlled phone calls home were permitted.

Much to their enjoyment, LNs also were encouraged to use the same laundry service as the rest of the contractors and military. They were very excited about this and as they had no Social Security number (the last four of which is normally labeled on every piece of laundry being dropped off), they would write all kinds of things on their clothing when dropping it off for washing. Usually, a bag of laundry dropped off has an inventory list attached. The person dropping it off fills out the list, has it verified by the laundry attendant, and then the washed, dried, and folded laundry can be retrieved in 3 days with proof of the inventory copy. The LNs were incredibly serious about keeping their individual laundry receipts in a safe place until pick-up day arrived.

As limited as they sometimes were, PXs offered LNs many items they could not purchase on the outside. While they were not permitted to purchase knives, military gym gear, or any other military-issued gear, they were permitted to purchase electronics if they had the FOB commander's permission. When an LN wished to make an electronic purchase from the PX, he/she would come to Dr. Angell (PL) and make the request. She would then write an official letter listing the LN's name and identification number and take it to the FOB commander. Once approved and signed by him, the LN could then take the letter to the PX and purchase the item stated on the letter. Per FOB policy, the item had to remain in an unopened box with the receipt and the approval letter taped to it until the LN was actually departing the gate on leave. In the meantime, the purchase would be kept in the OSS management office. Once the item departed the FOB, it could not be brought back on the base.

Work Conditions

Although OSS began its pilot program in 2007 with only eight LNs, by early 2008 at the height of the detainee population there were over 200 local Iraqi national civilians employed by OSS as social workers, teachers, and clerics. The LNs were hired to work 6 hours a day, 6 days a week. For most of them, this usually consisted of working a 3-hour period, followed with a 1 to 1.5-hour lunch/prayer break, and then another 3-hour period. Initially, when an LN was hired and brought onto the FOB, he/she would be given a temporary black-colored badge. Any LN with a black badge was not permitted to go anywhere without a U.S. contractor or military escort. Black badges would usually last from between 5 days and 3 weeks depending on how quickly the LN's particulars go through the security vetting system. Once approved to remain on the

FOB, the LN was given another colored badge, which permitted freedom of individual movement around the entire FOB. However, for the life of the contracts, LNs were never permitted to enter the actual TIF by themselves or even in a group of LNs. To enter the TIF, it was imperative that a U.S. contractor or military person accompany them. To that end, they were accompanied to the exact location where they would teach the class, and then were accompanied back out of the TIF to the FOB at the class conclusion. The only exception to this rule was a couple of special red badges that were permitted to key OSS LN leaders, which was based on additional English testing and proof that they were assigned a leadership position. Once approved, LNs with a red badge were permitted to go into the TIF without a military or contractor escort. They were not permitted to escort any LNs themselves, but they were permitted to walk freely around the TIF.

Undoubtedly, the LNs were very passionate about the work they did with the detainees. They would suggest needs to us and OSS would do its best to meet them. OSS encouraged and valued the information sharing; it was actually from the LN's request that it became standard for every class to be concluded with a graduation ceremony complete with snacks and certificates for the detainees. The rehabilitation programs grew so rapidly that OSS constantly ran out of supplies for the programs; either the military shipments would be delayed or we would have problems with the printer copying materials. On more than one occasion to address this inefficiency, some LNs went to the PX and purchased pencils and notebooks for the detainees in their class. Likewise, when we ran out of Qur'ans—usually presented as a gift to the caravan chief of each religious class—Sheik Sattar went around to the other clerics collecting Qur'ans that were not being used to offer in the interim.

An illustration of information flow from detainees to the LNs to OSS contractors to the military was during the October 30 to November 3, 2007, religious discussion class. The detainees requested, "When families come to visit, is there any chance the Americans can provide our children with slides and swings, so our children can play at the prison?" The result of this information sharing was an entire playground designed and built with the support and directive of the TIF commander at the time—Col. James Brown. Likewise at the request of LNs and detainees, and in line with respecting cultural norms, all Shiite and Sunni religious holidays were observed. During Ramadan, most classes were held in the evenings after the breaking of fast. During the summer months, when temperatures would sometimes reach 140 degrees and the air conditioning did not work well (if at all), to accommodate conducive learning and per detainee's request, classes were held during the evenings; and most classes were held from 7 p.m. to 2 a.m.

Because of the significant risk that each LN faced by being on the FOB and working for Americans, some requested that they be permitted to wear a mask covering their face while they worked. They saw that some of the translators were permitted to do this and felt that it would help ensure their safety. However, after much internal discussion, it was decided that wearing masks while working would not be permitted. Because of the nature of the programs, which was to help rehabilitate detainees, wearing a mask is viewed as counterproductive. An individual cannot effectively lead a discussion and establish trust and openness when he/she is hiding behind a mask. However, we offered them the choice to use alias names, which the majority decided to do. This is why an asterisk "*" has been used following several LN and detainee names throughout this book, in order to respect the security and confidentiality of the persons who worked the programs, most of whom still reside in Iraq.

Just like OSS contractors, some LNs truly worked hard, and some only worked hard enough to try to get others to do their tasking. Regardless, one thing could never be said against any of them: They put their life on the line just getting to the FOB to apply and be interviewed for the program, let alone work for OSS for an extended period of time. Every time an LN walked out the FOB gate, he increased his chances of something violent happening to him or his family. And yet, the majority stayed for a significant period of time. Fortunately and unquestionably, irrespective of any personal motive, their commitment to and passion for the mission evolved into a risk they willingly took for themselves, for their families, and for the good of Iraq. Without that risk, the programs would not have succeeded. According to Maj. Kevin Comfort (personal interview, 2010), who daily came in contact with the LNs:

> The Iraqis epitomize what true social investment in Iraq is. Their true investment of the heart is immeasurable. In my view, they represent some of the greatest people in the country. When many are self-absorbed or trying to exist day-to-day while overcome by the sheer magnitude of the trial of rebuilding Iraq, these small few easily seem to set all that aside. They have a true national spirit and see beyond the current situation. They set aside selfish advancement and strive to ensure that the meek and humble people in need are afforded a chance at a better life. Helping others help themselves whether it is intellectual, spiritual, or social investment is in my view the greatest thing one person can do for another. I hope that their example inspires more people to join them in the effort to see beyond self-fulfillment and join the cause of national advancement through investment in the people by giving them the life skills and personal tools they need to be successful

TASK FORCE 134 MILITARY STAFF LIAISONS

Fortunately, OSS was assigned military staff liaisons from TF-134 throughout the duration of the rehabilitation programs. For the first year of the rehabilitation program at Camp Bucca, Chief Mark Crouch and Sgt. Maj. José Morales provided enormous support for operations. A number of sergeants (including Sgt. Matthew Sugars, Sgt. Matthew Cantu, and Sgt. Kenneth Montage) were well liked (and respected) among the LNs and present throughout the first year of the programs. Other sergeants were rotated in and out in short durations, which proved beneficial as it always added a secure element and fresh insight. Chief Crouch and Sgt. Maj. Morales shared the same office with OSS at Camp Bucca. Having military support in the office proved helpful on several occasions. The TF-134 representatives acted as liaisons whenever the situation warranted. On several occasions when the programs first got up and running, there were conflicts between the LNs teaching courses and the guards in charge of maintaining security at the course site. Chief Crouch was able to alleviate the situation and get to the root of the cause. Likewise, when there were any misunderstandings or necessary clarifications between OSS management and FOB leadership, the military liaisons were able to use their position to ensure the information flow was uninterrupted and accurate. They were helpful as well in securing equipment for the office, such as desks, chairs, printers, and computers.

Transportation of the LNs was a huge challenge initially. For a couple of months in 2007, LNs were permitted on the military transport buses that travel around the FOB and to the TIF. However, for a never-clear reason, on a random day LNs were told that they were no longer permitted on the buses. Fortunately, through perseverance and determination, Chief Crouch and Sgt. Maj. Morales were able to secure two private buses for the transport of OSS LNs.

Meanwhile, the sergeants not only lived with the LNs in their tent, they were also responsible for escorting the LNs everywhere on base when they had a black badge; likewise, they took turns driving the LNs to/from their classes in the TIF in the two acquired buses. Sgt. Sugars, a military staff liaison at Camp Bucca from October 2007 to May 2008, noted in those early days, "Getting the program started was the biggest issue. Winning over those in the military command who had doubts was a real challenge" (Sgt. M. Sugars, personal interview, November 15, 2009).

We learned quickly that during drills, such as the escaped detainee drill, military units involved in the search would fly through camp upturning everything. Likewise, they tore through the LNs' tent, upturning mattresses and throwing what few possessions the LNs had into piles. This was upsetting to the LNs and, when the military liaisons understood this, they took over the situation. Thereafter, on every drill, a liaison would be posted on the outside of each of the LN tent's doors and informed the roving military units that the tents had been checked and were secure. This greatly aided the trust and appreciation of the LNs toward the military liaisons as well.

Initially, because of security concerns, LNs were not permitted to depart for, or return from, leave out of the Camp Bucca FOB gate. For most of the first year, the LNs would be scheduled on flights to Baghdad to go on leave. Unfortunately, flights were always problematic because the only way into Camp Bucca was by Blackhawk or Merlin (both helicopters). There were convoys, but they were not authorized for civilians or LNs to travel in them. So, LNs had to be scheduled for the helicopter flights to go on leave. But, as the LNs (being Iraqi citizens) were not authorized to travel through Kuwait, which is where the majority of the flights first stopped, they could only be manifested for the Merlin flights that go through Camp Basra to Baghdad. However, these flights were more seldom and were arranged by the British Armed Forces. Arranging the flights was surprisingly time-consuming, and could be incredibly frustrating as schedule changes happened frequently based on security and weather. Sfc. Dwayne Bowker, a TF-134 military liaison who usually spent his time based in Baghdad, did most of the flight scheduling. He also was stationed at Camp Bucca for a short while to better familiarize himself with the situation from the angle there. Both he and Sgt. Maj. Morales worked tirelessly to arrange and secure flights for the LNs, without which it would have been near impossible for the LNs to get anywhere.

The TF-134 military support liaisons for OSS deserve much more credit than the few examples highlighted here. Getting operations going without having the equipment, space, or manpower to be efficient was a challenge everyone faced, and fortunately one that the liaisons were prepared to handle. OSS contractors could have been nowhere as efficient and successful without the support and perseverance of the TF-134 liaisons attached. Dr. Angell refers mostly to the first year of operations at Camp Bucca, as that was the most trying one for everyone, after which most of the operations were that much smoother. Chief Crouch, Sgt. Maj. Morales, Sgt. Sugars, Sgt. Cantu, and Sgt. Montage all redeployed from Iraq by mid-2008. While she was introduced to, and met, many excellent liaisons to follow, there is something to be said for those who got the programs up and running when resistance was the greatest.

CONCLUSION

OSS contractors worked tirelessly in the continual oversight and management of running the rehabilitation programs in Iraq. According to Maj. Comfort:

> The contractors' relevance and involvement is impossible to describe as the army simply does not have the capability within its formation to provide the capability that the contractors provide to commanders. "Essential" doesn't even begin to describe their impact or capabilities. We could not have accomplished the mission without the very special skills set they contributed on a daily basis.

Undoubtedly the contractors, along with the TF-134 military liaisons and the LNs, contributed to the program's success. All the rehabilitation programs had value added to the detainee population. Notably, some of the most important moments occurred outside the classroom. Casual conversation, dining room chats, unexpected activities, informal gatherings, all of these interactions contributed to strengthening the bond between LN, contractor, detainee, and soldier. The monthly dinner party initiated by Col. Brown was one such example. It was first conceptualized to address misunderstandings between the LNs and the guards who kept watch over the rehabilitation programs. Most LNs could not speak English and most guards could not speak Arabic. Unfamiliar with each other's mannerisms, sometimes things could get tense when classes did not advance the way expected by either party. Col. Brown, then-commander of the Camp Bucca TIF, discussed with OSS how to alleviate the misunderstandings. Together, the idea was spawned to hold a dinner party with LNs, OSS contractors, and involved rehabilitation program soldiers invited (Figure 5.15). The first dinner party was held in October 2007 and was considered such a success, one that even had Col. Brown dancing along with the LNs to an Iraqi dance (Figure 5.16), that it was decided that the occasion should happen monthly. The party became a platform where the LNs sitting alongside the military could talk over dinner (Figure 5.17). The dinner offered was something other than the typical dining facility food, so it was seen as something special. In addition, having the TIF commander present and involved illustrated to the LNs how important their individual involvement in the programs was. Admiral Garland Wright also attended a couple of dinners, much to the pleasure of the LNs. At each table, there was a mix of both LNs and military. LNs who spoke English and translators were interspersed throughout the tables to encourage and facilitate dialogue. Guards who previously only saw "an LN" now knew that he was married with two boys and was from Sumaniya. Similarly, the LN who previously only

FIGURE 5.15 The monthly dinners and rehabilitation programs were due to the involvement and dedication of many soldiers, particularly including those above (from left to right) Cpt. James Elliot, Sgt. Maj. Larry Bull, Dr. Ami Angell, Sfc. Roy Walden, and CW3 Stan Kobj: Camp Bucca, Iraq, 2010. (Photo courtesy of Sgt. Walden.)

saw "a guard" now knew that the guard was taking classes for a degree in engineering and was single and lived in Texas. These dinners broke down the barriers that were preventing the programs from reaching full potential in the TIFs. Entertainment included music; initially, the LNs created a mix of Iraqi music on CDs and brought them to be played. Later on, they even sang and danced. Not to be outdone, the 130th Support Unit from Tennessee was encouraged to bring personal musical instruments to sing and play some country music to the enjoyment of the LNs. Some contractors even got creative and wrote their own songs to perform during the gatherings (Figure 5.18). Another time, the dinner party became somewhat of a talent fest with LNs reading poetry, reciting stories, and singing. Eventually, the LN population, the contractor population, and the military population looked forward to these dinners. Dr. Angell is convinced that having these dinners enabled OSS to retain far more LNs than they might have done otherwise. The dinners were enjoyable, but they also were so much more as they empowered the LNs into realizing that they are an important part of the process. They also helped to break down a lot of stereotypes and prejudices from all sides, as individuals who previously had never had the opportunity to talk engaged in frank dialogue (Figure 5.19).

FIGURE 5.16 During the first OSS/military dinner in October 2007, Col. Jim Brown dances along with some employed local Iraqi nationals to an Iraqi song. Camp Bucca, Iraq, 2007. (Photo by Maj. (Ret.) Guy L. Jester.)

FIGURE 5.17 Monthly dinner for OSS employed local Iraqi nationals and military: Camp Bucca, Iraq, 2008. (Photo by Sfc. Roy Walden.)

FIGURE 5.18   Contractors and military sing and play instruments for the OSS-employed local Iraqi nationals during a monthly dinner gathering: Camp Bucca, Iraq, 2007. (Photo by Maj. (Ret.) Guy L. Jester.)

FIGURE 5.19   Sheikh Abdul Sattar and Chief Mark Crouch at the monthly OSS/military dinner party: Camp Bucca, Iraq, 2008. (Photo by Ami Angell.)

Likewise, recognizing that empowering the LN population is an important part of the process, OSS management also put on a couple of events during the first year at Camp Bucca. One of the largest occurred in April 2010, when most of the OSS military liaisons, who had been present with us throughout the year, were getting redeployed stateside. Using it as an opportunity of appreciation for them in addition to recognizing outstanding LNs, Dr. Angell self-funded, organized, and designed a party of appreciation for the TF-134 liaisons departing and the OSS LN population. She ordered a sign of appreciation in addition to decorations and tokens of appreciation to be delivered to Camp Bucca. She also ordered bags with the OSS logo and personalized names for the LNs who had been with OSS for over 12 months. Certificates were created for those who had been with OSS for shorter periods of time. Chief Crouch and Sgt. Maj. Morales were able to secure special dining facility food and a large cake that was brought in for the occasion.

There were also a number of other individuals, although not assigned as OSS military liaisons, who had a significant impact on the rehabilitation programs. Maj. Guy Jester,* from the 181st Field Artillery battalion out of Tennessee, working 15-hour days, regularly found snacks, pencils, and gifts to use for the rehabilitation classes, often when OSS was in most desperate need. Maj. Ricky Shawyer, then-400th MP Battalion's executive officer, would also do his part in helping to find necessary items to enhance the rehabilitation process. He went out of his way to build an air-conditioned shelter for the LNs to wait and pray in, in between teaching classes. He also provided OSS regularly with candy and gifts to give the LNs, including a couple of large boxes of Frisbees and American flags for the July 4, 2008, American Independence Day. Lt. Col. Carol Haas also deserves mention as the only battalion commander at Camp Bucca at the time who was willing to give a released detainee a chance to lead a class of instruction; who was actually excited about the prospect, recognizing—as Dr. Angell already did—how much hope it would give to the other detainees to have a prior detainee instructing a class as a civilian. These are just a few, but there are so many others who helped make the rehabilitation programs a success, unfortunately, too many to have adequate space to mention. Once word got around that the programs were there to stay, people started stepping forward to do what they could to help. It became an enjoyable assignment for guards tasked with oversight of the rehabilitation programs, as they got a chance to talk and interact with detainees in a different type of environment. It would be a mistake to underestimate how important the relationship was between LN and OSS contractor, LN and soldier, and detainee and soldier. Because, long

---

* Maj. Guy Jester retired from the U.S. Army in November 2009 after 21½ years of service.

after they have finished their work with Americans, LNs and detainees will continue to play a significant role in daily Iraqi life based on those experiences. No longer was the detainee only a detainee or the LN only an LN. They became people with stories; it was about breaking down the barriers, one individual at a time; and, most importantly, empowering each to maximize his potential.

CHAPTER **6**

Detainee Care and Custody

INTRODUCTION

For detainees to open themselves up to participating in rehabilitation programs, they have to feel as if their needs and desires are being considered. Thus, the actual carrying out of the rehabilitation programs proved to be most effective when taking detainee needs, desires, and mindsets into consideration. Things that might seem relatively simple or even of little importance to someone not detained were sometimes the deciding factor of whether or not a detainee would participate in a course and/or be cooperative with soldiers. The care and custody of detainees, which involves correct classification, housing placement, medical care, motivation, extracurricular activities, and—above all—treating each with dignity and respect, all go into a detainee's choice on whether or not to cooperate with or inhibit detention operations. Every soldier and contractor who has dealt with a detained population understands that the way he/she treats the detainee inadvertently will affect how much information he/she is able to get from the detainee, as well as continued cooperation level.

BACKGROUND

"I think the rule of law in 2004 through 2006 was a pipe dream. Today, there's still a lot more to go, but we have come a long way. The mission has evolved," said Maj. Gen. David Quantock (personal interview, 2010). Some think detention operations are only a sideshow where detainees and guards interact in a postconflict space. This is a simplistic view that does not take into account the dynamic nature of the battle space. According to Maj. Gen. Quantock, care in custody is undoubtedly one of the most important aspects to consider when dealing with the detainee population.

Care in custody. This is underestimated, but to me, it's the most important. It's about treating detainees with dignity and respect. The key word is *respect*. I started this back in Abu Ghraib in 2004. I talked to every single one of my guard force. What people forget and what they lose sight of is that now many detainees, more than 90,000, have come through our facilities. If our long-term goal is a long-term strategic partnership with the Government of Iraq, then many of the future leaders of Iraq probably will have spent some time at our facilities. If we treated them with respect, they will have a positive opinion of America when they're released or gravitate to some leadership decision.

Soldiers were required to understand why it is important to treat detainees with dignity and respect. Commanders and generals regularly went around to their guard force to ask them why it is important. "And, if you ask a soldier, he'll say that we treat detainees with dignity and respect. Why? Because it saves soldiers' lives outside the wire in the battlefield," remarked Maj. Gen. Quantock. Akeel,* a former detainee who was then hired by OSS as a social worker, elaborated:

The military plays a big role in how detainees react to them, mostly because detainees perceive soldiers as those who came to kill and destroy. But over here, when they are treated with respect, which they have not experienced with Iraqi soldiers before and even now, that changes a lot of perspectives (Akeel,* personal interview, January 26, 2010).

The International Committee of the Red Cross (ICRC) has played a large role in advising the United States on the care and custody of the Iraqi-detained population. Since the war began, one of the functions of the ICRC was providing the military with working papers on issues of concern. Each quarter, ICRC representatives visited the theater internment facilities (TIFs) and talked with detainees; each visit generally lasted between 7 to 10 days. According to international law, during their visit they should be given full access to talk freely with any detainees they choose. At the conclusion of each visit, they wrote a working paper. That paper was passed up the military chain of command with their recommendations. Col. John "Mack" Huey (personal interview, 2010) commented:

Since the first time I was here, in 2003, as soon as the ICRC could get here, they were immediately in the facilities, making recommendations. You might think that these guys are a pain, but we opened the doors and openly listened for their comments. When you eat and

---

* An asterisk (*) is used throughout this book to protect the security and confidentiality of certain individuals whose lives might be threatened otherwise.

sleep here, sometimes the complacency factor sets in and you don't
see things clearly. For example, in Taji, ICRC was the one that recommended that there was not enough natural light for the detainees. And
$4 million later, we got it done. Now the detainees go, "Whoa, we've
got too much light, we can't sleep." So we've got to balance it out, too.

CLASSIFICATION CRITERIA

Proper classification of detainees is always a work in progress; it has
gone through many twists and turns throughout the Iraq war. But, one
of the first things Maj. Gen. Stone did after he arrived in 2007 was
to reevaluate and reclassify detainees in U.S. custody. Under Maj. Gen.
Stone's operational plan, when a detainee first arrived at a TIF, he/she
was assessed by a local Iraqi national three-person team consisting of
a cleric, social worker, and teacher for suitability for the rehabilitation
programs as well as compound placement based on his/her ideological
mindset. As a result of the assessment, the detainee was then placed in
a compound as a red (highest threat risk), amber (medium threat risk),
or green (lowest threat risk) detainee. This new detainee classification
assessment in combination with other important factors (introduction of
detainee rehabilitation programs and the MNFRC (Multinational Force
Review Committee) boards got the ball moving, and initially did very
well. Violence was greatly decreased, and extremists were for the most
part being separated from the rest of the moderate population. However,
by the end of 2008, the decreasing detainee population and longevity of
the Iraq war called for a more complex detainee classification system to
address those ideologically extreme detainees who were sliding between
the cracks unidentified.

According to Maj. Gen. Quantock, in 2004, when he was at Abu
Ghraib and then later when he was at Camp Bucca, detainees were classified by threat level alone. "The Military Intelligence community did
not have the assets to help us classify the detainees based on threat, so
we did the best we could... which was inexact at best," he said. At Camp
Bucca, after appearing in front of the MNFRC board, the detainee was
rated between 1 and 5 based on threat level, and then given a placement
based on his threat level number. However, then in October of 2008,
when the United States knew that a security agreement was being nego-
tiated, Maj. Gen. Quantock decided that a "more holistic evaluation of
determining threat level" was in order. Wishing he had done it 5 years
previously while at Abu Ghraib, Maj. Gen. Quantock supported Maj.
Gen. Mary Legere (Combined Joint Staff Branch for Intelligence "CJ2"
for MNFI-I at the time) who recruited a team of specialists from govern-

ment agencies, including the CIA and FBI, to do an intensive analysis of the Iraq-detained population. The general commented:

> In October of 2008, we brought in an extensive intelligence team with reach back capability to the United States. More than 100 intelligence specialists reviewed about 17,000 detainee files to give us an assessment score. We took their military intelligence assessment, which was Green, Amber, and Red; their MNFRC score; and their current location in their facility (Green, Amber, and Red). ... Then I had a mathematician on my staff normalize these three categories, and we developed the Threat-Based Detainee Review List (TDRL), which normalized every detainee from −1 to 1. So essentially, every detainee is given a score of .999 negative to .999 positive. We then rank-ordered all the 17,000 detainees to make correct compound placements. And, then in February 2009, we started releasing those detainees based on the least threat rating (Green Detainees) ... while we focused on developing cases against the highest threat detainees (about 2,000) for transfer over to the Government of Iraq.

The new way of assessing detainees created a more holistic model of determining detainee threat level. During the surge and the MNFRC, it had been how the detainee acted and sought self-improvement that determined his/her threat level. However, it was "discovered that the most dangerous detainees were often those who played the 'game' and let others act out for them. In fact, some of the most dangerous detainees did not have any negative reporting against them," Maj. Gen. Quantock confirmed. According to Maj. Gen. Quantock, it was not until the intelligence community became completely involved in the process that they were finally able to get a more "exacting determination" of threat. As far as the "modified detainee housing units" (MDHU), the least liberal of housing locations, detainees had to "earn" their way into an MDHU. Initially, a detainee earned his/her way into an MDHU by overt actions; however, later it evolved into a much more highly technical way of figuring out who were the real power brokers. It was these who were moved into the MDHUs. According to Maj. Gen. Quantock, very few detainees, who were in MDHUs, worked their way out of them, but they were still continually evaluated. In time, MDHUs were broken down into those who were violent, top leaders, and instigators and those who cooperated with the military. Most detainees appeared to prefer this method; it effectively gave them a "second chance" while at the same time empowering them to take charge of their actions during detention. Those who cooperated were given more privileges. He commented:

> I think our final system worked exceptionally well. The proof being the fact that violence did not escalate any worse than was already the

norm, and we were able to hand over the most dangerous detainees to the Government of Iraq with arrest warrants/detention orders/convictions ... nearly 8,000 in total.

HOUSING PLACEMENT

Detainees are not equal. Different threat levels of detainees required varying levels of secure housing. Depending on their TIF assigned, assessed threat level (TDRL), and continued behavior, detainees were housed in a caravan, a compound, a K-Span, an MDHU, a Specialized Housing Unit (SHU), or for the former Baath Party regime members—specialized studios. The only other factor impacting placement was that when it could be determined that detained family members were in the same TIF, but in different compounds, the military worked to ensure that family members who desired to be placed in the same compound were.

Caravan

A caravan (Figure 6.1) is similar to a large tent (like what is used in compounds), but usually air-conditioned and a hard structure with four walls and a roof. Porta potties and a wash area are located in close proximity. The caravans used at Camp Bucca for the rehabilitation courses had a fence that encompassed each caravan individually with a small courtyard for walking and/or playing soccer. Inside the caravan is a large empty space where up to 20 detainees can sleep on mats. Besides those used for the rehabilitation courses, some special compounds with extra privileges also had caravans, as did a couple of specialized populations, such as "third country nationals" (nonideologically extreme individuals with citizenship from countries other than Iraq), and "alternative lifestyle" (openly homosexual detainees).

Compound

Compounds were spectacular at Camp Bucca, which was responsible for separating and housing thousands of detainees (Figure 6.2). Some compounds were made up of several large caravans, but at Camp Bucca most compounds housed up to 1,000 detainees each; detainees were divided into groups and assigned to tents. Like Camp Bucca, Camp Cropper also had compounds. However, the compounds at Camp Cropper were smaller. Most had 13 tents, with each tent holding up to 25 detainees for

FIGURE 6.1   Inside a detainee caravan: Camp Bucca, Iraq, 2008. (Photo courtesy of U.S. Department of Defense.)

a maximum total of 325 detainees in the compound (Lt. Col. E. Mullai, personal interview, January 29, 2010). Some compounds were split into "quads"; four separately fenced areas that housed up to 50 detainees in each. Camp Cropper also had three large compounds that were broken up into four quads per compound; inside each quad was a type of open bay living accommodation, according to Maj. Gen. Quantock.

The advantage of a larger compound is more area for the detainees to move around. Many detainees had soccer matches (Figure 6.3). Other detainees would use the advantage of the large-sized compound to walk and/or run. It was also easier to get a "quiet" place away from the television in a larger compound in order to hold intracompound education classes. However, the disadvantage of a larger compound was that, with an increased population, the compound was more difficult for guards to maintain oversight and control. Detainees in larger compounds had greater numbers of violent incidents than did smaller groups of detainees. In addition, moderate detainees were much more susceptible to indoctrination and radicalization, as larger populations increased the odds of having the presence of ideologically extreme detainees.

FIGURE 6.2   Compounds separated by fences with catwalks (where soldiers can observe detainees) surrounding the top: Camp Cropper, Iraq, 2010. (Photo by Ami Angell.)

K-Span

The K-Span model (Figure 6.4) used to house detainees in Iraq originated in Afghanistan in 2001 and 2002, according to Col. Huey. However, in Iraq, K-Spans were only built and used at Camp Taji; each K-Span was two stories high. There were 20 cells per K-Span, 23 detainees per cell for a total of 460 detainees per K-Span (Figure 6.5). In the K-Span model, of the four walls of the cell, one is completely transparent (Figure 6.6). To the casual observer, it might almost suggest something similar to an animal viewing cage, but, in essence what this did was to permit the guard force greater oversight of the detainee population. Inside each cell were shower and toilet facilities; a curtain over the facilities provided for privacy. But, otherwise, all the detainees slept, watched television, and prayed in open observation by the guard force. They also each had their own area for daily recreation (Figure 6.7). The small size encouraged greater interaction (with the guard force) in addition to better protecting moderates from being attacked and/or indoctrinated by extremists. Maj. Gen. Quantock remarked:

FIGURE 6.3   Football, otherwise known as soccer in the United States, was a favored pastime of many detainees: Camp Bucca, Iraq, 2007. (Photo courtesy of U.S. Army.)

> I think one of the advantages of the layout of that facility is there's a lot more interaction between guards and detainees from many different aspects. You know, when you are in Cropper, for example, you're in these quads. So, you don't have the sensing. You have 250 detainees in there. A detainee can just stand there and not associate with anybody the entire time. But, when you go to Taji, the guards are a big part of your life because there are only 23 of them in a cell. So, there's a lot of interaction. There are good things and bad things in that. For example, if you look at our numbers, when I talk about incidents inside the facility—it's a 3 to 1 difference between what happens in Cropper and what happens in Taji because of the constant interaction.

Modular Detainee Housing Unit

The Modular Detainee Housing Unit (MDHU) (Figure 6.8) originated at Camp Bucca, Iraq, during late 2007 under Maj. Gen. Douglas Stone's command with the idea that for COIN (counterinsurgency) to be effective it was necessary to separate the real extremists from other detainees. Besides Camp Bucca, which had a number of them, the only other camp to get them was Camp Cropper in March 2010. It was the least liberal of housing options, usually reserved for the "worst of the worst" detainees;

FIGURE 6.4   K-Span: Camp Taji, Iraq, 2010. (Photo by Ami Angell.)

usually, those that are ideologically extreme and/or violent individuals. Basically, MDHUs were two 40-foot containers welded together (Figure 6.9). Each MDHU can house up to 10 detainees. Shower and toilet facilities were self-contained inside each one. MDHU detainees were only permitted outside (into a small open courtyard) for 2 to 3 hours per day, according to Lt. Col. Mullai.

Special Housing Unit

The Special Housing Unit (SHU) (Figure 6.10) was a building consisting of detainee isolation cells. Similar to what many might know as solitary confinement in the United States, detainees generally spent anywhere from 1 to 30 days there. SHUs were located at each camp: Camp Bucca, Camp

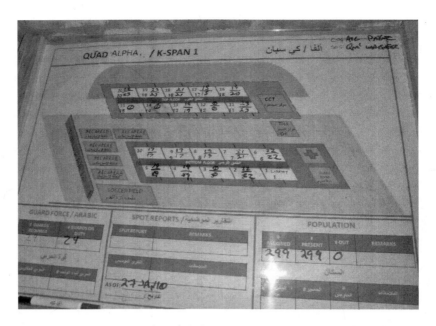

FIGURE 6.5   K-Span 1 layout: Camp Taji, Iraq, 2010. (Photo by Ami Angell.)

Taji, and Camp Cropper. Most had the capacity for at least 100 detainees. SHUs were utilized for detainees warranting disciplinary action, detainees who are medically ill and needing separation from the general population, and detainees on suicide watch.

Suicidal detainees, referred to more often as "self-harm detainees," are checked on every 5 minutes after being moved to the SHU. There were five self-harm cells at Camp Cropper made out of a special soft padded material, none of which had a window. Camp Taji and Camp Bucca meanwhile did not have any padded cells; self-harm individuals were put into the same cells as anyone else. Regardless of location, self-harm detainees were given a "self-harm smock" to wear, ensuring his inability to cause further harm to himself by ripping apart his clothing (Sgt. G. Hernandez, personal interview, January 28, 2010). Most SHUs had a sink, a bunk, and a toilet inside each individual cell (Figure 6.11). Individuals in the SHU for disciplinary purposes and on suicide watch were permitted 2 hours of recreation a day (similar to the MDHU). Detainees in the SHU for medical reasons were permitted 6 hours of recreation a day (Figure 6.12). Col. Huey remarked:

> We don't want to punish the people who are sick because it's not their fault that they are sick. We try to give them the same privileges that

FIGURE 6.6   Inside an empty K-Span. Note the transparent wall on the left side of the photo: Camp Taji, Iraq, 2010. (Photo by Ami Angell.)

they would get out there. They're just being isolated because of their sickness. We don't want an epidemic of TB [tuberculosis] or scabies. If we had an epidemic in the cell, then we would have 2,000 detainees with TB or scabies. That would not be a good thing.

Former Baath Party Regime Members Studios

The former Baath party regime members had different housing than the rest of the detainees. All the former regime members were kept at Camp Cropper in compound 5. According to Col. Huey:

There are less than 100 detainees in compound 5. What we have here are the former regime, former generals in the Iraqi army, former regime guys, politicians, minister of defense. Most of them have been here since 2003. We're holding them here now [in compound 5] at the request of the Government of Iraq, until they have the capacity and an appropriate facility to put them in.

According to Col. Huey, who oversaw Camp Cropper as Commander of Fort Hood's 89th Military Police Brigade and Task Force Griffin in 2009 and 2010, "This is a special population; given their background,

FIGURE 6.7   Recreation area for K-Span. Only one cell of detainees uti-
lizes it at a time. Every recreation area has a ping-pong table. Detainees
are also given a soccer ball if requested: Camp Taji, Iraq, 2010. (Photo
by Ami Angell.)

we give them a little more privileges than they get from the main TIF."
Each former regime member has his/her own little studio. Inside of the
studio, each has some personal items, a full-sized bed, television with
nine channels, and a radio. Outside of the studio is a small yard where
many of them have gardens and grow flowers, vegetables, herbs, and
spices (Figure 6.13). Unlike the housing for other detainees, in the former regime housing, there is no limitation on the recreation they get,
except during "lock down," which is about 8 hours a day. Each individual is locked in for breakfast, lunch, and dinner. Likewise, unlike the
other detainee housing units that serve meals in large coolers, former
regime members receive each meal on an individual tray.

Former regime members get more phone calls than the general TIF
population, and for visitation they can have as many family members as
they want visit them at one time. There is a specially built playground
for their visiting children and (in most cases) grandchildren and great-
grandchildren to play in while the adults can sit on a shaded picnic table
watching them and talking. Up to four former regime members might
have visitation at the same time, so 20 to 30 people could be in the courtyard, half of which are usually children. Family members are permitted

FIGURE 6.8   MDHUs (in the front) and K-Span buildings (the round shaped buildings in the back): Camp Taji, Iraq, 2010. (Photo by Ami Angell.)

FIGURE 6.9   Inside an empty MDHU: Camp Bucca, Iraq, 2008. (Photo courtesy of U.S. Department of Defense.)

FIGURE 6.10   The Special Housing Unit (SHU): Camp Taji, Iraq, 2010. (Photo by Ami Angell.)

to bring the detained individual (after a security screening) DVDs, clothing, and food when they visit. Said Col. Huey:

> These are the former Baath party members of Saddam Hussein. I think this is the least we could do. We're not here to punish, in that sense. We're here to hold out for the Government of Iraq until the Iraqi people are prepared to take control over their former government members. They're going to court right now to look at whatever crimes they committed while they were in power. We just hold them here.

According to Col. Huey, the former regime detainees are very cooperative and respectful; rarely is there ever a disciplinary report written about any of them. Many of the former regime detainees are older in

FIGURE 6.11   Inside a Special Housing Unit: Camp Cropper, Iraq, 2010.
(Photo by Ami Angell.)

age and have various medical issues, such as diabetes and high blood
pressure. There is also a blind man and a few who suffer from cancer;
"They're beyond capabilities at this point. It's terrible."

When a former regime member has to go to court for his trial, he
is put in a special holding cell for the working week; on the weekend
(Friday and Saturday), he is brought back to compound 5. Even after
all the TIFs in Iraq turned over to the Government of Iraq, a certain
contingency of former regime members are being kept under U.S. control in compound 5. This is to prevent, in the words of one commander,
a "very public and brutal mass execution." Instead, the United States
wants to ensure that democracy is followed, and each detainee, including the former Baath Party regime members, is afforded due process of
international law.

FIGURE 6.12   Recreation area for detainees in the SHU. Only one detainee at a time is permitted in each recreation yard: Camp Taji, Iraq, 2010. (Photo by Ami Angell.)

SUNNI AND SHIITE DIVISION

In Iraq, most compounds were first divided into either Sunni or Shi'a, then by extremism level into caravans, compounds, K-Spans, or MDHUs as available and as appropriate. Interestingly, according to Maj. Gen. David Quantock:

> The Shiites are causing us a lot more problems than the Sunni, even though the Shiites are only 20 percent of the population. If you look at the bigger disturbances, the Shiite has always been a greater challenge than the Sunni. Sunnis, when they take action, it's very calculated and probably a lot more destructive if they were allowed to do something. If they go after somebody, it's usually the guard force, to take him down. It's a little bit more of a warrior cult than I would say the Shiite stereotypes. I don't have any answer to why that is. ... But if you look at our disturbances, I would say 75 to 80 percent of the larger disturbances are Shiites.

Meanwhile, some compounds, notably compound 12 when Camp Bucca was open, housed both Shiite and Sunni together, and it worked. There was relatively little violence from compound 12; detainees there

FIGURE 6.13   Former Baath Party Regime members' specialized housing: Camp Cropper, Iraq, 2010. (Photo by Ami Angell.)

could be counted on to behave well when visitors would visit the TIF, causing it, in essence, to become the "model" compound. Besides a couple of other exceptions, the only other time this is replicated is at a compound called "Camp Liberty," also known as "Camp Tranquility," that was designed to encourage national unity for detainees who have been given their release paperwork (Figure 6.14). According to Lt. Col. Eric Mullai, commander of the 192nd MP BN at Camp Cropper:

> Camp Liberty was designed to let the detainees reintegrate—for national unity purposes—for 2 to 3 weeks before their actual release. What we do is we put them all together—Shi'a and Sunni—and we let them wear civilian clothes. They have a choice of traditional Iraqi or western clothing [jeans]. We also give them ping-pong tables, gazebo, open recreation, soccer field. ... Substantially more privileges than they had in their previous compound; we're trying to get them set to be released. We've been doing this for years.

Al-Hindawy, born in Iraq and now living in the United States, suggests a mixed population would have worked with more compounds, as both compound 12 and Camp Liberty illustrated.

FIGURE 6.14 Camp Liberty (on the left) and former Baath Party Regime housing (on the right): Camp Cropper, Iraq, 2010. (Photo by Ami Angell.)

> The right tool is by mixing detainees together. Have them see how it can work and remind them they are Iraqi first. Instead of treating them as a Sunni or Shi'a, we should be looking at them as an Iraqi, and they will look at themselves as an Iraqi (S. Al-Hindawy, personal interview, January 28, 2010).

MEDICAL ACCESS

According to Maj. Gen. Quantock, the first combat support hospital was put into Abu Ghraib in May 2004, right after TF-134 stood up. What it caused was an "enormous leap in capability," and "it eventually did more to quell the violence in the TIFs back in 2004" than anything else. "World class medical care really has a positive effect on the detainee population; many negative thoughts about coalition forces were forever altered because of our medical efforts" even though at that time there were only "about eight medics for 8,000 detainees."

According to Col. Judith Lee (personal interview, 2010), a medical/surgical nurse and then-commander of Task Force 14 in charge of detainee medical operations at Camp Cropper, Camp Taji, and Camp Bucca before they were turned over to the GoI., the detainees had access to doctors who were highly trained, including a "neurologist, cardiologist, internal medicine, family practice, orthopedic surgeon, general surgeon, psychiatrist, and even a nutritionist." Medics would go out to the compounds daily and check on the detainees while handing out prescribed medications. If there was something that requires more than what the medic could provide at the compound, then the detainee was given an appointment for the clinic to see one of the doctors, according to Col. Lee. Camp Bucca, Camp Cropper, and Camp Taji each had its own hospital, affording detainees the same access to medical care and expertise as U.S. soldiers received. There was an emergency room, internal medical clinic, optometry clinic, physical therapy unit, dental clinic, and more. On occasion when one location did not have the facilities necessary to best meet the needs of a detainee, he/she was flown to a better-equipped facility within Iraq.

According to the medical staff, the classification (or risk level) of the detainee, be it red, amber, or green, was not considered relevant when a detainee was brought in for treatment. At most camps, detainees shared the same pristine hospital as the U.S. soldiers, the only difference being that detainees were kept on a separate side of the ward. Detainees also were forbidden to speak to one another, and all were tethered to a bed.

Detainees received a variety of treatments at the medical facilities provided in the detention centers. At Camp Cropper, during the year 2010, the doctors had a population of around 200 detainees who had hypertension. The doctors also screened out about 25 insulin-dependent diabetics and approximately 80 noninsulin-dependent diabetics. According to Col. Lee, for these special populations, the medical unit provided specialized services and clinics; there was a hypertension clinic, diabetes clinic, and orthopedic clinic. Insulin-dependent diabetics had their blood checked in the morning and were given insulin every morning and evening.

Detainees also had hernias repaired, appendectomies, thyroidectomies, hemorrhoidectomies, and vein stripping. Medical staffs were on call at the TIFs 24 hours a day, 7 days a week. If something occurred that the medics could not handle, detainees were brought to the emergency room. There were trained emergency room physicians, and emergency room nurses and medics working in the emergency room. The detainees also had full access to dental care facilities, which were always particularly busy. The Camp Cropper dentist alone examined approximately 50 detainees a day. There were optometry services available as well; detainees had their eyes screened and were prescribed glasses.

There was both physical and occupational therapy at Camp Cropper. In 2010, there were about 10 detainees with prosthetic eyes and 12 detainees with prosthetic legs. According to Col. Lee, during a 6-month period, the medical unit was authorized a $50,000 budget to fit detainees with new prosthetics and/or adjust existing prosthetics; an Iraqi civilian came in and the limb was built to fit the detainee.

Initially, detainees prescribed medicine for medical ailments were left to their own devices in taking the prescribed pills. However, that proved ineffective. Military police doing sweeps found numerous bags of untaken pills; in many cases the pills were crushed into a paste. In other cases, it was discovered that chiefs were confiscating the pills. To counter this, in 2009, it was decided that all medicine given would require direct observation to ensure that the person the medicine was intended for was actually getting it. Enlisted licensed practical nurses would go out and give the medications directly to each detainee, who was then required to take the medicine while the medical team observed, according to Col Lee.

> I truly think that even as much as you can explain to them on how to take their medication, I'm not sure they understand. There is the language barrier, no. 1. They never had this kind of access to care. And I truly think that some of them just didn't take it because they didn't understand the difference it could make. So, the direct observation has done a lot of good out there. And, the MPs have really appreciated the fact that they are not finding hundreds of unused medications either.

It could be difficult for military interacting with detainees as well as the detainees in detention, which is why the psychiatrist team was important for both groups of people. At Camp Taji, there were five individuals who made up the mental health staff: a psychiatric nurse practitioner, a PhD social worker, a registered nurse (specialized in psychiatric nursing), and two psychiatric technicians. Together, the five individuals were responsible for taking care of the mental needs of between 3,500 to 4,000 detainees. According to Cpt. Sharon Lyles (personal interview, 2010), a nurse who was stationed at Camp Taji, there was a case load of approximately 200 detainees who suffered mental illness when the team arrived in July 2009. There were a number of detainees treated for being clinically depressed. Likewise, there was also a fair amount of detainees with psychosis (fortunately, controllable by medication). Among them included cases of detainees' head-banging, threatening suicide, cutting themselves, and swallowing foreign objects. Some of the foreign objects that detainees swallowed included pieces of wire and pieces of razor.

According to Col. Lee, the psychiatric staff does a great job of not only taking care of the detainees, but also taking care of the soldiers dealing with them on a daily basis. Something, she suggests, that has perhaps not been given enough attention. Particularly because of the situation, the medical professionals in Iraq are not allowed to practice necessarily in the same way they are allowed to when back in the United States.

> As a medical professional, at home you are taught about how compassion and touching [are] very important with patients. Getting to know somebody's family and their background and how that helps in their recovery. We don't do that here. There is no touching, no asking about family. The compassion part of you in a way, you have to turn off when you are dealing with them. So, how do you turn that back on when you go home? It is difficult; the guards get spit on a lot. The detainees who have been here a while are incredibly manipulative. Whenever you get a new—whether it's new medics or new guards—let the games begin. They will deliberately try to

drive wedges between us, and they are a very difficult population to deal with.

Likewise as an example, Col. Lee continued:

There was a young enlisted nurse; a licensed practitioner nurse. She took care of many maimed and burned Americans that took part in this war; and one day she saw this magazine and she saw one of the soldiers she had taken care of. And, he's got this melted face. She said to me, "I got so angry and then I had to take this detainee's vital signs." But, then she saw that he had a picture of his son. She said she realized then that he had a family, too. And, maybe his son is not so proud of him. And, it sort of brought her back to the reality of this place.

THE MOTIVATION FACTOR

At most intelligence gatherings, individuals can relate. If the motive of a detainee can be determined, it is much easier to decide on the most appropriate course of action to encourage cooperation and compliance. Sometime back in 2008, the idea was generated to provide the time, space, and environment to engage compound chiefs in discussion. As every group of detainees, regardless of their location, has an elected "chief" detainee, this became a central point of information gathering. At Camp Bucca, Camp Cropper, and Camp Taji, company commanders and the battalion commanders would arrange to meet with compound chiefs weekly in one large setting (Figure 6.15). Generally, what would happen is that all the military personnel and chiefs would sit in a large circle. Tea and snacks were served while issues were discussed. Chiefs were encouraged to bring up concerns from their compounds while the military was able to pass on crucial information. After the meeting, chiefs would return to their compounds and share the information garnered with the rest of their compound; likewise, the military would follow up on concerns. It became a very useful and effective mode of intelligence gathering and problem solving, while ensuring detainees were duly complying with compound rules, according to Lt. Col. Mullai.

The meeting of chiefs was about respect and empowerment, which is something important to detainees. Seemingly, something so easy can be very difficult when dealing with a highly secure environment. This was particularly true where one individual (the soldier) might have a very different idea of what qualifies as respect than the detainee. However, Sgt. Devin Daines (personal interview, 2010) realized its importance: "The detainees, they think very highly of respect; if you are respectful to them, they will be respectful to you in return." However, it was also

FIGURE 6.15   Council of Chiefs meeting, Compound 12: Camp Bucca, Iraq, 2008. (Photo courtesy of U.S. Department of the Army.)

about maintaining a leadership role while dealing with the detainees. Allegedly, detainees will experiment, particularly with new soldiers, to see how far they can bend the rules. According to Sgt. Daines:

> I haven't had much out of the ordinary happen. But, there are times when we tell them to go back into their zones and they'll say, "No, we want to stay outside for 5 more minutes." But, we respond, "No, you need to go in now." There'll be a small argument and all they are doing is wasting the 5 minutes they wanted to have anyway, and they go back inside their zones. They're fairly compliant, yet some are very manipulative. We always have to be on our toes.

Other than respect, many would agree that the ultimate motivation for detainees is the "Happy Bus." The Happy Bus is the bus that takes the detainee to the "Camp Liberty" (sometimes referred to as "Tranquility" or "Freedom") compound, after he has been given his release paperwork. Once a detainee is told to get on the Happy Bus, he knows that he is on his way to freedom and his family. So, naturally, this can be a very motivating factor for detainees. But, according to Ken Reidy, the answer might actually lie in something deeper than that:

Everyone's first answer is always the Happy Bus, but let us take a deeper look at it. It is, of course, that they hope to get their life back, see their family, etc. But, one must remember that many detainees do not know what happened to their families when they were detained. I have heard stories of detainees going home to find that someone else was living in their house and that their family was gone. Gone! Gone where? Were they detained? Were they killed? Did the area become hostile so they moved? Were they afraid of the area turning hostile so they moved? Ideally, detainees want to go home and start where they left off, but, I don't know how often this occurs.

Other detainee motivations can be a bit more simplistic and immediate. They often asked for longer recreation hours and the equipment for playing ping-pong. New soccer balls also are often requested, as those provided do not last long under the intense sun, sand, and frequent use. On one occasion when there were no soccer balls available, a soldier gave them an American football. "They looked at it and threw it right back over the fence at us. They had absolutely no clue about what to do with it," said Sgt. Daines. Ping-pong equipment, like soccer balls, was always in constant short supply due to frequent use. Ping-pong balls often get squished or misplaced.

Right now we have shortage of [ping-pong] balls. The detainees being what they are, they figured out that on their deodorant—which is roll-on deodorant—they can pop the balls out and use those as ping-pong balls even though they are not as nice and a little bit heavier. But, they work. Also, in between my two K-Spans, there is a common soccer field. Right now we are into the second rotation amongst my zone of having soccer tournaments—zone to zone. Another K-Span will do the same thing. We will take the winner of their K-Span and my K-Span and then have a soccer tournament, and the winner takes all, even though there's nothing to take, just the bragging rights. But everyone loves it (SSgt. S. Jarvis, personal interview, January 29, 2010).

Another strangely popular request is for chai tea. Although they get it at least three times a day with meals, many detainees always request more. Likewise, many detainees crave cigarettes. Just the act of being given a cigarette combined with the pleasure of inhaling/exhaling one is a stress reliever for some. Soldiers working in compounds are given a certain number of cigarettes to offer detainees at times throughout the day. During rehabilitation classes, detainees also are offered cigarettes during breaks. Yet, interestingly, only those who smoke got this extra privilege, since detainees are not permitted to hold onto cigarettes for later (to discourage the use of them for bartering). Those who do not smoke received nothing from guards during class breaks, which might lead one to assume that a number of detainees might have even taken up smoking while in detention in order to feel entitled to something. Military personnel that were asked about the logic of handing out cigarettes to detainees seemed unable to come up with a reasonable explanation; many just said they were following orders, and that cigarettes were the "one thing" they were permitted to give the detainees on a daily basis.*

When a detainee wanted to be heard, be it to participate in a rehabilitation or work program, visit with a medical person, or talk to an Intel guy, he would fill out a form called a 5-10. A 5-10 was filled out for any kind of minor or major problems/issues/concerns a detainee might have. Once filled out, this form was given to one of the soldiers working the compound, evaluated, and put into the system. After a risk assessment was conducted, a determination was made on whether to permit the detainee his request. Yet sometimes, understanding what the detainee was asking for could be quite challenging, particularly in light of the language difference. A lot of things can easily get lost in translation. Even a good linguist, if unfamiliar with the intricacies of Iraqi culture, can unintentionally mistranslate something. For instance, according to Lt. Col. Mullai:

> So, I got a complaint from a compound chief that the butter is bad. So, I'm thinking, maybe it's moldy or too soft or old, but the butter seemed fine when I examined it. Well, it turned out that they didn't like the butter because it was made in Denmark. And, they didn't like that because of the caricature of Mohammed. But, we had already purchased a bunch, so there wasn't much we could do. I told the Chief to just wait. But a couple months later, the Chief fills out a 5-10 to tell me that they were still getting Danish butter. Luckily for me, the other Chiefs were getting French butter by then. He was just the last person to get Danish butter.

Then, likewise:

> So, now it was the bread is bad. So I'm thinking, what's wrong with it? Well, because there was a fire in the normal bread-making machinery, we ended up buying the local bread, which they apparently loved. Eventually, we fixed the machines and we started producing bread again. But, the detainees preferred the previous local bread. They said this one is too thick and narrow. So, I asked my men about it and was told, "Sir, we're still adjusting the roller. We haven't gotten the right

---

* To encourage a healthier habit and reduce the chance of addiction, Dr. Angell wonders what might have been the response if rather than cigarettes something like an apple or pear (likewise, something they do not get as part of their regular meals) was offered in place of (or the choice of) a cigarette.

size yet." Eventually, we fixed that, too, but until then, the detainees were unhappy with us.

In detention, it is often the small things that make a big difference:

I keep reminding my soldiers: We're on this side of the fence and they're on the other side of the fence. If our roles were reversed, I don't know how we would behave. But, they're in there for 24 hours a day, 7 days a week. Some detainees have been in there for several years. We just provide basic services. So, if we could fix the bread, the butter, and that makes them happy, I'm happy.

Detainees are more cooperative, happier, and cause less trouble when there are incentives to look forward to. Besides the reward of participation in the rehabilitation programs, detainees also are occasionally given other incentives. Maj. Gen. Quantock initiated "Coke® Fridays" at Camp Cropper in 2009. "They love Coke, so we bring Coke on Friday, the religious day. Everybody gets Coke on Friday, we don't distinguish. They can choose whether to drink it or not, but they've got it." According to Maj. Gen. Quantock, he had relatively little disturbance in compounds after the initiation of Coke Friday. Detainees looked forward to it; yet, they also were informed that it was a privilege, not an entitlement. "When there was a disturbance in May in a Shiite compound, we took away their Coke Fridays for a month; it was surprising how well that worked, After that, we had fewer problems with them," remarked Maj. Gen. Quantock.

On other occasions, it appeared that just having active interaction with foreigners was enough to encourage cooperation. Most detainees had never encountered an American before they were detained, let alone carried on a conversation with one. So, to be recognized and listened to can be a big deal. On a few occasions, Dr. Angell was invited to eat with detainees in their caravan. They were taking part in the Islamic Discussion Program and asked a few of us involved to join them for a meal. The meal was the same one they ate most days. It consisted of bread, rice, meat stew, and oranges. There are different variations, but this was one of their staples. Sitting cross-legged and barefoot with them on the floor in a large circle, eating their meal with them in their caravan is not an experience Dr. Angell will soon forget. They were gracious hosts, insisting on serving us first before themselves, and ensuring that the best pieces of meat went to us, even the one of us who was a vegetarian. They were curious about our families and what the environment was like where we lived and the type of house we had. We broke down barriers as we found ways to relate— individuals who were being detained, soldiers who were doing the detaining, and contractors who were running the rehabilitation programs. There are many common elements between all three, but it appears most often that persons do not feel secure or comfortable enough to acknowledge them.

Another thing that encouraged cooperation from detainees was being allowed to listen to approved radio stations and watching prerecorded television for a few hours a day. Every compound also had a library available for detainees to check out books according to preference. At Camp Cropper, romantic novels were the second most popular (after the Qur'an) to be checked out by detainees. They also loved the The Da Vinci Code in Arabic; other favorites were books on the English language. Unfortunately, some of the libraries had their supplies diminished after a group of Takfiris (Muslims who accuse other Muslims of apostasy) feigning interest asked to check out a collection. Then after they received the books, they ripped them up.

Likewise, according to SSgt. Scott Jarvis, groups of detainees that have Takfiris among them will not watch television when it is their turn. Groups that did not watch television when it was on were usually monitored, as often it came down to just a couple of them being Takfiri. When the Takfiri were removed from the group, the rest would usually resume watching television. SSgt. Jarvis remarked:

> You can usually tell [that] the hardcore Takfiri will not watch TV or allow anybody in their zone to watch TV. We've had times when they go out to recreation, and a couple or three of the guys will stay behind and say, "Hey, chief, can you turn on the TV for me, chief?" So, it's like little lights start coming on that the TV has never played there for the last 3 weeks, and now this group of guys is out at the recreation yard, and these two or three are back there watching TV. We've sort of seen little signs like that.

In this particular case, there ended up being 13 Takfiris running that K-Span cell. While the group was on recreation, their area was searched. Within it was found a wielding rod, which was fashioned into a shank and a razorblade. All 13 were then sent to an MDHU, after being made to wait for transfer in the solitary confinements buildings next to the K-Span, according to SSgt. Jarvis (Figure 6.16). This illustrates only one example of the many challenges that guards dealt with on a daily basis:

> When we first took over, we were having a lot of hidden writing where they will put something on top of a picture and scribe on it so the picture is actually indented with names and phone numbers. We have to be keener and more aware on our searches and things that we do. When we get some unauthorized writing, we write the detainee a disciplinary report and send it to the battle desk here. Most of the time,

FIGURE 6.16 Solitary confinement buildings (also known as "time out") for detainees who need a few hours alone or who might be waiting for movement due to disciplinary action to the SHU. The K-Span that the buildings belong to is on the right in the photo: Camp Taji, Iraq, 2010. (Photo by Ami Angell.)

they end up 6 hours in the compound SHU; they get solitary for 6 hours if it is their first offense.

Detainees were incredibly creative with their messaging systems. Another type of messaging between detainees involved the use of "chai rocks." Although all messaging systems were prohibited (the result being the SHU if caught), detainees were fairly consistent in keeping it up. A "chai rock" is created by mixing the staple of Iraqi diet—chai tea—with the natural sand/dirt combination found outside of every caravan and compound. The combination together, once dried, creates a substance similar to a ball of cement. Detainees would then write messages on pieces of paper, crumble them around the chai rock, and then throw or sling-shot the messages between one compound and another by the weight of the chai rock. Some riots were organized via this communication method. Likewise, it was a method to incite and encourage indoctrination. When the detainees would riot, they would stock up on chai rocks and also use them as weapons to sling at soldiers.

CONCLUSION

Undeniably, the type of location a detainee must endure, as well as the food he eats, the way he is treated, and the activities he has the option to participate in, goes into how cooperative and engaged he is with his captors. Yet, all this must be taken in stride, as what one person does for a detainee can inadvertently affect his treatment of others. For instance, if a detainee is in a medical center, the medical staff is aware of how that person's actions might affect their comrades protecting the compounds. According to Lt. Col. Lee:

> If a detainee asks for a colder bottle of water, you have to ask the guards first because if I get a detainee a bottle of Gatorade or a bottle of cold water, these MPs may pay for it for months; it's that manipulation—The medics are nicer to me, and all that. That's why we all have to be on the same sheet of music. We cannot give them privileges that the MPs will not give them, and we shouldn't because somebody's going to end up paying for it. We take care of their medical concerns and treat them with dignity and respect. That's all we can do.

The care and custody of detainees, likewise empowering the detainee with choice, is key to having successful rehabilitation courses and, therefore, manageable detainees, which is why in every compound in every U.S.-run TIF in Iraq, the Geneva Convention is posted (Figure 6.17) and the sign, "Treat Detainees with Dignity and Respect," is very visible (Figure 6.18) because, in the end, happier detainees means less problems for everyone. Said Maj. Gen. Quantock:

> A lot of people don't understand what we do around here; they just think we warehouse detainees. We've done a lot of things to treat our detainees with dignity and respect. We talked about hearts and minds the other day, how we like to win hearts and minds. Because the bottom line is, it's about respect. This whole population and culture demand respect. The only thing that they have, in many cases of poorer individuals, is respect. If they respect us and we respect them, that drives a lot of things that's going through inside these facilities.

Understanding the Geneva Convention and Humane Treatment of Detainees

The Hague and Geneva Convention and the customary Law of War require that we, as American Soldiers and Iraqi Correctional Officers:

- Will treat prisoners of war, other captured and detained personnel, and civilians humanely.
- Will not obey an order whose execution is a crime in violation of the law of War.
- Are personally responsible for unlawful acts committed by ourselves.
- Are entitled to humane treatment if we are captured or detained by the enemy.

General Principle of Humane Treatment

- We can not harm or kill any one who, in the language of the Convention. Has "fallen into enemy hands".
- Murder or physical abuse never is, has been, or will be humane treatment.
- Once a person is under our control, we must treat him/her humanely.
- All captured persons are entitled to be treated as prisoners of war until their status is detained.
- The civilian population of the country in conflict is entitled to respect for their persons their honor, their families rights their religious convictions and practices, and their manners and costumes.
- They must be protected especially against all acts or threats of violence and against insults and public curiosity.
- Women should be especially protected against any attack on their honor. In particular against enforced prostitution, rape, or any other form of sexual assault.
- All persons are to be treated with consideration and with out any adverse distinction based on race, religion. Or political opinion.

معاهدة هيك و جنيف و قانون الحرب المتعارف عليه يطلب منا كجنود امريكان و كضباط الاصلاحين العراقيين:

- يجب معاملة سجناء الحرب و الاسرى و المعتقلين و المدنيين معاملة انسانية.
- يجب عدم اطاعة اي امر يعتبر تنفيذه جريمة و خرق لقانون الحرب.
- يجب تحمل مسؤولية اي فعل غير قانوني تم ارتكابه من قبلنا.
- يجب ان نتوقع معاملة انسانية اذا مانم اعتقالنا او اسرنا من قبل العدو.

المبادئ العامة للمعاملة الانسانية:

- ... اي شخص يعتبر تحت لغة ... (...)
- ... ليست ولم و لن تكون ...
- اذا كان ... تحت سيطرتنا فيجب معاملته معاملة انسانية.
- يجب معاملة كل الاشخاص المعتقلين كأسرى حرب حتى يتم ادانتهم.
- السكان المدنين للبلد الداخل في النزاع لهم الحق في احترامهم لاشخاصهم و شرفهم و حقوقهم العائلية و معتقداتهم و شعائرهم الدينية و عاداتهم و تقاليدهم.
- يجب حمايتهم بالاخص ضد اي تهديد او عنف و ضد اي اهانة و الفضول العام.
- يجب حماية النساء و بشكل خاص ضد اي انتهاك لشرفهم و بالاخص ضد اي عملية اجبار و اغتصاب او اي شكل اخر من الاعتداء الجنسي.
- يجب معاملة كل الاشخاص معاملة معتبرة و بدون اي تميز عنصري و طائفي و ديني وسياسي.

FIGURE 6.17 Understanding the Geneva Convention and Humane Treatment of Detainees is posted at every compound at Camp Cropper, Camp Taji, and Camp Bucca: Camp Taji, Iraq, 2010. (Photo by Ami Angell.)

FIGURE 6.18 These signs were posted at every compound at Camp Taji, Camp Cropper, and Camp Bucca: Camp Taji, Iraq, 2010. (Photo by Ami Angell.)

CHAPTER 7

A Method to the Madness

American efforts understandably have focused
almost exclusively on thwarting operations and
capturing terrorists—the visible tip of the iceberg.
We now have to expand the strategy to impede
recruiting and encourage rehabilitation.

Brian Michael Jenkins, Unconquerable Nation, 2006

INTRODUCTION

Brian Michael Jenkins has had over 40 years of experience researching terrorism—many of which involved working for the research organization RAND—and his conclusion is the same as it has been for many past years. Unless we address the root causes, terrorism will not go away. We have the capacity and knowledge to impede terrorist-related activity and, in this late hour, it is time to finally gather what we know and do something astounding with it. Understanding the purpose of rehabilitation, which directly complements counterinsurgency and information operations, and how the proper use of each method can ultimately transform individuals, as well as a society, should be the concern of every individual desiring an end to the countless number of violent activities and horrific deaths resulting from terrorist-related activity.

REHABILITATION UNMASKED

According to the *Oxford English Dictionary* (2002), rehabilitation is defined as: (1) restore (someone who has been ill or in prison) to normal life by training and therapy, and (2) restore the reputation of (someone previously out of favor [p. 703]). Derived from the Latin word *rehabilitare*, rehabilitation is "to make fit, after disablement, illness, or imprisonment for earning a living or playing a part in the world (*The Wordsworth*

Concise English Dictionary, 1993, p. 838). Consequently, criminal and terrorist rehabilitation is about reengaging, reediting, and reentry of those who have deviated from the mainstream back to society. Those exposed to, and convinced by, terrorist ideology do not lead normal lives. They adopt the writings and speeches of ideologues that espouse hatred and then transform themselves. Whether they are operational terrorists or extremist supporters, they believe that violence and other extreme measures are acceptable means to bring about political change. Terrorists and their supporters are not mainstream, but are extreme. To facilitate their return to the mainstream from the extreme, they must be rehabilitated. Unless an extremist is rehabilitated before his release from custody, he is likely to pose a security threat to the government and a societal threat to the community upon his return. Additionally, as his belief system did not undergo change, he is likely to contaminate others with his ideals and recruit them to advance his cause.

Unlike with purely economically motivated criminals, brief or prolonged incarceration is unlikely to change the belief system of ideologically driven terrorists. Terrorist and extremist rehabilitation is different from criminal rehabilitation. Those terrorists or supporters released from custody have repeatedly offended after their release. This includes those detained and released from the U.S. detention facility in Guantanamo Bay, Cuba. Interestingly, the Muslim world perceived Guantanamo Bay as revenge by the United States and not as justice by them. As such, many returnees received a hero's welcome in their own countries. Upon release, the extremists who were not transformed nor experienced deradicalization during detention, advocated, supported, or committed acts of violence. As those detained in Guantanamo Bay were not rehabilitated, they remained committed to the philosophy of Al Qaeda and its associated groups. One such example is 9/11 mastermind Khalid Sheikh Mohammed, who was quoted in a released transcript from a military hearing from Guantanamo Bay as saying, "I decapitated with my blessed right hand the head of the American Jew." And further, "For those who would like to confirm, there are pictures of me on the Internet holding his head" (Linzer & White, 2007).

There is no universally accepted definition of terrorist rehabilitation. Academics agree: "To date, there is no consensus on what constitutes success in reforming a terrorist, let alone what even constitutes reform in this context" (Horgan & Braddock, 2010). Criminal rehabilitation is defined as any "planned intervention that reduces an offender's criminal activity" (Walker, 2006). As there is no universally accepted definition of terrorist rehabilitation that exists in social science literature or within the security community, we seek to develop a working definition. While the goal of both criminal and terrorist rehabilitation is to reintegrate offenders back into society as law-abiding citizens, terrorist rehabilitation is designed to wean individuals from violence—terrorist or otherwise—and reeducate them about how political change can be achieved without resorting to violence, including terrorism (Prof. B. Hoffman, personal interview, April 5, 2010). Rehabilitation is a holistic process that addresses the drivers of conflict in an individual's life through education, vocational training, counselling, or therapy, and may include postcustody aftercare and community-connected services.

Rehabilitation is the answer to two grave challenges the world is faced with today. First, Al Qaeda and its family of groups specifically target the Muslim population. The contemporary wave of violence and counterviolence produces terrorist recruits and extremist supporters. Those exposed to the vicious ideology believe in the philosophy and methodology of Al Qaeda. They need to be ideologically and theologically rehabilitated. Second, contemporary detention and prison conditions contribute to radicalization. Unless detainees and inmates are kept in isolation, they become susceptible to indoctrination and training by fellow detainees and inmates. In most penitentiary and detention facilities, detainees and inmates are housed communally. In some facilities, both criminal inmates and security detainees are colocated, leading to an exchange of skills and will, as well as corecruitment and alliances that persist after release.

According to The Violent Radicalization and Homegrown Terrorism Prevention Act of 2007, which was passed by the U.S. House of Representatives in 2007 (H.R. 1955 [110th]), a working definition of radicalization is "the process of adopting or promoting an extremist belief system for the purpose of facilitating ideologically based violence to advance political, religious, or social change."[*] Based on a study of Islamist movements, Dr. Omar Ashour, an academic in the United Kingdom with extensive field experience in the Middle East, argues:

> Radicalization is a process of relative change in which a group undergoes ideological and/or behavioral transformations that lead to the rejection of democratic principles (including the peaceful alternation of power and the legitimacy of ideological and political pluralism) and possibly to the utilization of violence, or to an increase in the levels of violence, to achieve political goals (Ashour, 2010).

---

[*] The Violent Radicalization and Homegrown Terrorism Prevention Act of 2007 was a bill sponsored by Rep. Jane Harman (D-CA) in the 110th U.S. Congress. Its stated purpose is to deal with "homegrown terrorism and violent radicalization" by establishing a national commission, establishing a center for study, and cooperating with other nations. The bill was introduced to the House on April 19, 2007, and passed on October 23, 2007. It was introduced to the Senate on August 2, 2007 as S-1959. As of yet the bill has failed to win the approval of the Senate.

As ideological extremism is the precursor of operational terrorism, it is essential to counter radicalization, the "process whereby an individual or group adopts extremist beliefs and behaviors" (Homeland Security Institute, 2006, p.1). While most radicalized are vulnerable to supporting or advocating violence, categories of activity ignored and tolerated by many governments, only a tiny percentage actually engage in violence. Violent radicalization denotes a transition from radical thought to violent action (Center on Global Counterterrorism Cooperation, 2008, p.1). After radicalization occurs either or both in real and cyber space, recruitment into an organization mobilizes an extremist into committing terrorism or other violent acts (Borum, 2006, p. 7). The reverse of radicalization is rehabilitation, a nontraditional security tool that has wider applications.

One facet of rehabilitation is *deradicalization*, a term that academics are still in a stage of conceptualizing and defining. John Horgan and Kurt Braddock (2010) argue: "There is, in addition, confusion about whether any kind of rehabilitation is necessarily brought about by 'deradicalization' (itself a term that has not been adequately conceptualized, let alone defined) as opposed to other interventions for eliciting behavior change." In the context of governments engaging, including coopting Islamist movements, Dr. Ashour defines deradicalization as:

> a process of relative change within Islamist movements, one in which a radical group reverses its ideology and delegitimizes the use of violent methods to achieve political goals, while also moving toward an acceptance of gradual, social, political and economic changes within a pluralist context (Ashour, 2010).

Likewise, "extricating the negative ideology that had been imbibed into the mind of the beneficiary selected for rehabilitation, followed by negation of the misunderstood ideology, and subsequently replacing the negative ideology with positive ideology is deradicalization" (Horgan & Braddock, 2010, p. 268).

Deradicalization is a comprehensive process by which a terrorist's misunderstanding or extremist ideology is replaced with the principles of moderation, toleration, and coexistence. Only a small percentage of the population has extremist views that require deradicalization. Deradicalization involves religious engagements that seek to dissuade violence and extremism. Cognitive skills (sometimes called life skills) training is also employed. Such skills are used to inform terrorists that there are peaceful alternatives to violence. Changing the views and ideologies of terrorists and extremists is difficult, and may take more time than education and vocational training. The final stage of reeducation is to input the rightful understanding of theology or nationalism essential for moderation, toleration, and coexistence into the mind of the detainee. Upon completion of these stages, the detainee or inmate of rehabilitation would have undergone an ideological transformation that qualifies him or her to be reclassified as "no longer poses a security threat." A multifaceted process to meet a multidimensional threat, rehabilitation is much more than deradicalization. Although deradicalization is paramount to open the mind of the detainee or the inmate, successful terrorist rehabilitation can be achieved by improving the circumstance of the detainee, the immediate family, the extended family, and the wider community. By winning the hearts and minds in both through and after-care phases, one can enable an extremist of rehabilitation to transform. Yet, to abandon and reject violence and embrace and advocate peace, constant engagement is needed. For successful reentry, deradicalization should be continued after the custodial phase in the community phase by ideologically trained and intellectually competent clerics and community and other leaders.

In the counterterrorism toolkit, there are many pathways out of terrorism. In addition to deradicalization, there are other tools and techniques for ending violence. One of these includes disengagement, a behavioural change wherein the terrorist agrees to lay down his/her arms and stops fighting. While in custody, he or she must be persuaded to voluntarily disengage from the fight. Rehabilitation programs provide the skills and tools to voluntarily disengage. Terrorists in custody who are motivated by economic reasons or who are not totally committed to the fight are likely to shift from "compelled" to "voluntary disengagement" just by providing them education and vocational training. Those who are motivated by ideology will very likely require additional deradicalization efforts, such as religious engagement or cognitive skills training. Dr. Ashour (2010) argues that terrorists may suspend, abandon, or reject the use of violence, but may remain ideologically unchanged. John Horgan defines disengagement as:

> the process whereby an individual experiences a change in role or function that is usually associated with a reduction of violent participation. It may not necessarily involve leaving the movement, but is most frequently associated with significant temporary or permanent role change. Additionally, while disengagement may stem from role change, that role change may be influenced by psychological factors, such as disillusionment, burnout, or failure to reach the expectations that influenced initial involvement. This can lead to a member seeking out a different role within the movement (Horgan, 2009, p. 152).

As such, detainees disengaging or desisting "from terrorist activity are not necessarily deradicalized (as primarily conceived via a change in thinking or beliefs), and such deradicalization is not necessarily a prerequisite for ensuring low risk of recidivism" (Horgan & Braddock, 2010, p. 271.). Similarly, in return for cooperation with the state, an accepted government offer of incentives—such as early release— also should not be considered rehabilitation. Most academics agree that:

> Disengagement refers to a behavioral change, such as leaving a group or changing one's role within it. It does not necessitate a change in values or ideals, but requires relinquishing the objective of achieving change through violence. Deradicalization, however, implies a cognitive shift, i.e., a fundamental change in understanding (Fink & Hearne, 2008).

As such, to reduce the strategic long-term threat, whenever possible, it is important for governments to remain involved, deradicalizing individuals and groups who have disengaged from violence.

Terrorist rehabilitation is based on the theory that mere punishment through imprisonment is not enough to permanently reform and facilitate extremists' reintegration into society upon release. Particularly for the terror detainees, the ideological debate or religious counseling sessions are a very important component of the rehabilitation program. This is because their behavior and way of thinking are based on an incorrect understanding and/or misinterpretations of Islamic concepts. Hence, the counseling sessions serve to provide them with the correct understanding of Islam and its leading concepts. This correct understanding will not only forestall future criminal acts, but will also convince them that such behavior is inappropriate and misguided. This will bring about genuine feelings of remorse and repentance, hence permanently removing the source of motivation for their involvement in terrorist and extremist-related activities (M. Bin Ali, personal interview, November 16, 2009).

As different levels of extremism require different levels of response, there is the need to differentiate between terrorist leaders, members or operatives, and supporters and sympathizers. Just as there are circles of extremism, there are multiple target audiences; it is relevant to understand that not all detained are identical in their understanding of Islam. For instance, many foot soldiers of Islam do not know ideology. But, if told by a respected Imam, "To die as a *shaheed* [holy martyr] is the best thing," they will. To assess susceptibility to rehabilitation, detainees are classified into three distinct risk levels: high, medium, and low. However, this ideological risk level should not be confused with the U.S. detainee threat level classification, where detainees are classified as red, amber, or green based on a conglomeration of factors, only one of which is ideological standing.

Detainees classified as high risk are considered spiritual and operational leaders. They are usually those that form the core. They believe in their ideology and they are usually unwilling to move from it, despite many counseling sessions. Such people are very few. However, they generally have had contact with and received direct inspiration from a terrorist leadership. Even though Mullah Omar never completed his religious education and Osama bin Laden had no formal religious education, many extremists received instruction and guidance from them, and they believe that their beliefs are correct. To that end, they will do whatever they can to encourage others to think the same way they do, in addition to heavily encouraging violence against any Muslims who do not agree with their ideology, and non-Muslims. For the high risk detainees to open up their minds to counseling and religious dialogue, it is imperative to have prominent and respected clerics talk with them, otherwise, the clerics are unlikely to get anywhere. If granted release, these high-risk individuals are the most susceptible to returning to a violent lifestyle, particularly, if there is no after-release program.

Detainees classified as medium risk are operatives and the experts that form the bulk of the membership. They are ideologically and operationally active. They often experience intense hatred and are ready to commit violence. They generally look for justification and interpretation that suit their current mindset. They have usually served long in the organization, and not only are familiar with the ideology, but actively embrace it. Individuals from this group can usually be rehabilitated by a strong rehabilitation team.

Detainees classified as low risk are the active and passive supporters. They are mostly foot soldiers, inactive members, and those who are not involved in crimes. They do not know the ideology and are easy to mislead. Many joined thinking that their peers (relatives, colleagues, and friends) were fighting for Islam. However, through ignorance of Islam, they completely believe that whatever they do is justified by religion. Some only provide money without realizing that their contributions have been used for purchasing arms. For low-risk individuals, the minimum of counseling and rehabilitation is needed. However, that too needs to be given right away, lest the low risk become indoctrinated deeper by the medium- and high-risk individuals in the detention center.

IRAQ'S REHABILITATION PROGRAMS

As Maj. Gen. Douglas Stone's innovative idea of building and implementing rehabilitation programs for Iraq detainees evolved, so too did the rehabilitation programs. When the rehabilitation programs were first conceptualized and implemented under Maj. Gen. Stone, they all fell under the term "TIFRIC services," the short term for "theater internment facility reintegration center." However, later TIFRIC was sometimes referred to as "theater internment facility rehabilitation center" (Maj. Gen. Stone, personal interview, 2010) before most recently being changed in 2010 to "theater internment facility reconciliation center" (TIFRC) (Maj. Gen. D. Quantock, personal interview, January 26, 2010).*

The first TIFRC program was education. Education programs officially began in February 2007. The next program and the one that Maj. Gen. Stone fought the hardest for was the Islamic Discussion Program (IDP). It began in the summer of 2007. Following very shortly after this program were the vocational skills training programs in late 2007. In 2008, an official creative expressions program was introduced, followed shortly thereafter by the civics program. Officially, Tanweer combined all the TIFRC programs under one name (Tanweer) in May 2007. But it wasn't until late 2008 that the term *Tanweer* became often used. Under Tanweer, all programs fell under either Phase I (introductory), Phase II (maintenance), or Phase III (exit from detention). All the rehabilitation programs are discussed in depth in the successive chapters.

As TIRFC programs evolved, so too did the manuals for carrying them out. In 2006, ICPVTR (International Centre for Political Violence and Terrorism Research) worked with OSS (Operational Support and Services) in creating a religious manual for the IDP. Likewise, Dr. Ann Speckhard (personal interview, 2010) created a manual for the psychological counseling component of IDP:

> I orchestrated, created. and wrote the first version of the detainee rehabilitation program (the psychological side), and I organized for the Muslim scholars to write the Islamic challenge part of it. In its original form, I was listed as the author and I gave credit to everyone for the sections they wrote. The idea was to have half-day psychological group sessions and half-day Islamic challenge, and to work in tandem between these two so that the Imams and psychologists were working together and complementing each other.

However, after the pilot program of IDP ran during the summer of 2007, both manuals were set aside and new ones drafted to deal more specifically with the needs—both cultural and emotional—of Iraqi detainees. The new manuals took the lessons learned from Dr. Speckhard's input as well as ICPVTR's to create a program that, while using the valuable input of experts, was personalized by those on the ground more intimately aware of Iraqi customs and culture. Iraqi clerics and

---

* Under Maj. Gen. Quantock's command, rather than TIFRIC, it was spelled TIFRC, although the intent remained the same. To simplify, Dr. Angell will use TIFRC, being the most recently used.

social workers were questioned in-depth as the new manuals were created to ensure that the information and activities going into them would not cause conflict with cultural customs and norms. Nor would they offend anyone. The outcome of which were manuals widely accepted by the local Iraqi nationals who conducted the programs in addition to the Iraqi detainees who received the training. In addition to the manuals for IDP, as TIFRC services evolved, manuals were written for each individual vocational training program: the creative arts program, the civics program, and the education programs. All the programs that fell under TIFRC services had their own manual, written in both English and Arabic so that the military, civilian contractors, and Iraqi nationals could reference it as needed when carrying out the instruction. Anything questionable could be referenced back to the manual, hence, ensuring a certain amount of checks and balances.

THE PROGRAM

> If you know the enemy and know yourself, you need not fear the result of a hundred battles. If you know yourself but not the enemy, for every victory gained, you will also suffer a defeat. If you know neither the enemy nor yourself, you will succumb in every battle (Chinese author of *The Art of War*, Sun Tzu, c. 500 BCE).

The intent of introducing rehabilitation programs to Iraqi detainees has often been misunderstood by outsiders. According to Col. David Shakes (personal interview, 2010):

> This is a critical question and one that was much misunderstood. Unfortunately, too many military and Iraqi officials thought our rehabilitation programs were motivated out of some sort of desire to be social workers for the detainees. In fact, the real genius of doing rehabilitation programs with detainees was that is was a smarter way to wage a counterinsurgency. By rehabilitating the detainees, we could minimize the risk that they would return to the battlefield against us and increase the chances that they would spread the word that the United States was not the Great Satan that extremists were claiming. What was hoped for was that the detainees would be returned home in a condition that they would not rejoin the fight against us.

Thus, the first step toward understanding deradicalization, which is essential in order to most effectively introduce and implement rehabilitation programs, is to understand the motivations of those in detention. In Iraq, *the program* was looked at as a process. As such, the detainee is part of the program and the community (that which includes the detainee and his surroundings) is both part of the program and part of the process. A successful program must also deal with and address any underlying psychological needs of the detained population. It must address the needs of a population to continue educational fulfillment as well as address religious misinformation and misunderstanding. The Multinational Force–Iraq (MNF-I) plan to address these concerns was conceptualized in three phases:

- Phase I: Apply COIN (counterinsurgency) principles to TIF, separate extremists from population, and protect populations both inside and outside the TIF (theater internment facility).
- Phase II: Defeat the insurgency within the TIF, succeed in the battlefield of the mind, and identify ideas that are contagious.
- Phase III: Engaging populations of detainees, families, and releasees and establish a "social epidemic" that advances the objective of empowering the moderate Ummah to marginalize the violent extremists within Iraq.

The program tools utilized in carrying out the three phases involved varying amounts of:

- Mental assessments (education, religious knowledge, psychological, etc.)
- Observed behavior with others
- Counseling
- Basic, civic, and religious education
- Peers, family, tribe, community engagement and support group
- Material employment and job training and skills
- Role modeling
- Medical (physical and mental) treatment
- A "go-between" who can influence the "violent Islamist"
- Ideological tools (counterfatwas, dialogue with well-known Imams and Muftis)
- Repentant terrorists taking an active part
- Social measures (facilitating economic and social reintegration)
- Continued and subsequent monitoring to avoid recidivism

Finally, the overall objectives were determined as:

- Separate the violent Islamists from those nonviolent.
- Assess by degree of radicalization.
- Engage in a plan that "surrounded" the detainee with support options, while allowing for individual choice.

- Create an atmosphere of cultural understanding, clarity of mission, respect, and hope.

Essentially, the objective can be simply defined down to: "If a detainee returns to the fight, it is a failure in the process. If a detainee assists in reducing the fight, it is considered a success in the process," according to Maj. Gen. Stone.

Motivations are an important factor to consider when designing a rehabilitation course for a select detainee/inmate population. Of essence is determining the driving force behind participation and involvement in the activities that got the individual detained in the first place. Several motives were determined to have contributed to detainment including: sectarian animosity, economic motives, religious extremism, revenge as a motive, attitudes toward coalition, nationalism, male "youth needing to be a man," religious conviction/confusion, and personal/family honor (Maj. Gen. Stone, 2008). Among them, economic motives were among the most popular. Economic motives can be divided into two categories: (1) subsistence/survival (i.e., those who commit and/or support violent acts due to lack of viable alternative employment); and (2) opportunistic/greed (those who commit and/or support violent acts to supplement income that can provide a viable existence). The second category, namely that of opportunity and greed, is predominant. Many detainees are not completely unemployed, but rather they are *under*employed or employed sporadically (e.g., day laborers). Thereby, it is implicit that they may have ended up in detention by attempting to supplement their income by other means. The post-2003 environment has often been termed "the best of times, the worst of times," commented Maj. Gen. Stone.

Detainees interviewed during in-processing reported exponential increase in access to consumer goods; 82 percent reported an increase in income. Additionally, 92 percent had acquired a satellite dish, 56 percent a cell phone, and 43 percent one or more vehicles; other goods (post-2003) acquired included DVD players, refrigerators, computers, and air conditioners. From this, it might be determined that access to cell phones and vehicles may have enhanced their utility to insurgency. Similarly, DVDs (propaganda) may have attracted them to insurgency, although "absolute cause and effect were very hard to establish," said Maj. Gen. Stone. Meanwhile, the old patriarchal system of Saddam was gone, creating a chaotic environment. Hence, entrepreneurs willing to engage in criminal activity could prosper from activities ranging from oil smuggling to arms sales, thus, subsequently enjoy "the good life." All of this led to the very real danger that the insurgency was (is) becoming a vocation.

Revenge was another motivator for some detainees. Revenge seems to be a relatively rare, but at the same time, very possibly powerful motive. Questions probing "violence against friends/family" (from any source) had significant negative response from the detainee population. Meanwhile, forced relocation had relatively few responses. Some mid- to senior Al Qaeda leaders noted revenge-related themes (loss of business to JAM (Jaish Al Mahdi) or killing of a relative by the Coalition Forces) as their motivator to aid in violence.

Coercion was another motive provided by several detainees under questioning. In fact, within TIFs there was significant evidence suggesting it was a very powerful motive (e.g., forced adoption of or compliance with Takfiri views). Meanwhile, outside of TIFs, there was little evidence of coercion having as much power as it did from within the walls of detention. Unfortunately, like revenge, coercion was hard to estimate either way.

However, one thing is for certain. It was recognized that to develop successful rehabilitation programs, it is essential to understand the population that you are dealing with, "who" the enemy is, and how he/she got to be that way. In Iraq, some recognizable factors of indoctrination included the influence of:

- Political Islam (i.e., the legal interpretation of Sharia law, Islamic war-fighting historical lessons, and recent fatwas create an environment that both radicalizes violent Islamists and provides them support to continue their war-fighting approach).
- World Wide Web (i.e., the Internet has become the doctrinal source of self-radicalization).
- Detention (i.e., the failure of having or the misuse of a deradicalization process ensures further entrenchment to jihad. No detainee will stop fighting unless they believe the Ulema have so sanctioned it, or their own interpretation of the Qur'an and Hadith is wrong).

It is relevant to recognize that all detention facilities facilitate recruitment both inside and outside the wire. Therefore, Muslims living within, or confined within, the United States subsequently become targets for recruiting and radicalization. Likewise, transferring violent Islamist detainees into a U.S. system, or elsewhere, will provide an avenue for the radical movement to firmly establish and strengthen a presence within that new location. This is why it is increasingly relevant to be familiar with and understand the variables of countering violent Islamists in a detention and prison setting. According to the Iraq model presented by Maj. Gen. Stone in the summer of 2007, when considering the process of rehabilitation, it is necessary first to recognize the "basic principle," which suggests that only an empowered moderate Ummah can marginalize violent Islamists. The "war" is over when this condition is met; therefore, their involvement in any kind of rehabilitation process is critical. Otherwise, there are only two ways to change an extremist detainee's mindset: death or internment with a rehabilitation program. Maj. Gen. Stone preferred to go with the rehabilitation (to include a deradicalization component) programs. While briefing incoming commanders and officers at Camp Bucca in 2008, he identified seven steps in the rehabilitation process:

1. Assessment (motivation, commitment, ideological fervor)
2. Separation (moderate ideologies from those that are extreme)
3. Engagement (ongoing interviews, psychological counseling, voluntary religious discussions led by moderate Muslim clerics, physical activity)
4. Education (basic math/literacy, civics, art, vocational)
5. Reintegration (work with families/tribes to reestablish connections and incorporate families in the process)
6. Monitored release with economic incentives "for the families"
7. Follow-up and continued engagement (until approximately 50 years old) (Maj. Gen. D. Stone, Camp Bucca Briefing, 2008)

The optimal rehabilitation program would have all seven of these components. However, as it was recognized early on that the United States was intended to only remain in Iraq a short period of time, it became desirable to train and encourage the Government of Iraq to continue the rehabilitation effort. To that end, the Iraqi security forces were incorporated and utilized in training whenever possible throughout the implementation and running of the rehabilitation programs. It was in the hope that by the time they were handed control of all the TIFs, they had the know-how and desire to keep the rehabilitation programs in motion. That, however, remains to be seen.

COUNTERINSURGENCY OPERATIONS

Counterinsurgency operations, otherwise known as COIN, are the most important and effective way of protecting and motivating the detainee population. As a war-fighting concept, COIN is best utilized to obtain tacit and active support in putting down the insurgency whereby at the same time gaining the allegiance of detainees. Its importance to the process should not be underestimated. According to Maj. Gen. Quantock:

They [rehabilitation programs] were successful for moderate detainees for the most part, ... but I think the true impact of these programs, was that these programs facilitated the reconciliation efforts before the detainees were released. Many realized that Americans were treating them well and doing the best they could. I truly think what was just as important was our counterinsurgency inside the wire (COIN). Although I had suggested it in 2004, Abu Ghraib was still fresh in everyone's mind and no one wanted intelligence specialists inside the wire working with security forces. But, Lt. Gen. [John] Gardner (2006) and his team were able to assemble COIN teams that ran informants in the compounds to really sort out the population. Without the COIN teams figuring out the extremists from the moderates, none of the rehabilitation efforts would have worked. This has to be a phased approach. ... Rehabilitation is only one aspect of the entire detainee operation. I could go on for days about how COIN operations really made the difference then, and still makes a huge difference now. It is our only true offensive weapon in detainee operations.

The art of COIN is achieving synergy and balance among various simultaneous civilian and military efforts or lines of operation (Figure 7.1).

The intent behind COIN is the concept that counterinsurgency is all about separating those who are radical from influencing those who are malleable. Ultimately, you have your strong personalities and personalities that can be coerced one way or the other. According to the COIN team at Camp Taji on January 24, 2010:

Ideally, what we do here is identify those who are very extreme and those that have negative influences and keep them segregated from those that are possibly able to be rehabilitated. Through that concept, we hope and think we have positive results and reduce the amount of relapse.

In terms of actual application, the way the COIN team maintains operations is a combination of active involvement and observation by guard force.

Basically, our guard force is trained in what are indicators or warnings of possible extremist behavior, extremist recruiting, and just violence in general. When they see those indicators, they are obligated to inform the chain of command on what is happening so we can take appropriate measures to prevent those negative influences from infecting the rest of the population.

Further, the COIN team continued:

The other half is we want to allow our detainees a voice and the ability to say, "Hey, I don't fit in here. These guys are recruiting me. I don't feel comfortable with that. Please move me elsewhere." Those kinds of venues are what our actual agents and interviewers take into

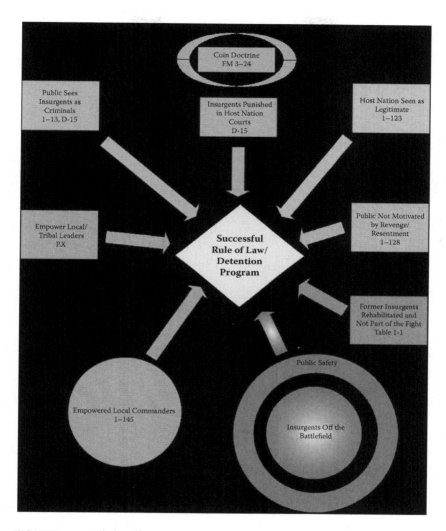

FIGURE 7.1 Slide illustrating the importance of detention policies in COIN. References are to the U.S. Army and U.S. Marine Corps *Counterinsurgency Field Manual*. (Slide courtesy of Col. (Ret.) David Shakes.)

account. What we do is offer basically the opportunity for any detainee to sit down with somebody, and that interviewer can ask questions like, "Is there anything you would like to talk about?" "Do you feel safe?" "Do you feel threatened?" These types of questions open a dialogue to enable the detainee to voice concerns or fears and, thus, say, "Hey, I don't really fit in here, please help me out." So, it is really the combination of the detainees' own voice combined with guard forces' observations that helps us formulate a clear picture of what would really facilitate the best stratification of the population to limit the amount of recruitment and negative influences on those who strive to be rehabilitated.

In order to effectively conduct COIN operations, it is useful to have a counterbalance of information operations and intelligence gathering. According to Maj. Gen. Quantock, "You are constantly studying your population to see if you have properly assessed the detainees and then try to influence positive behavior and create the hope of a better tomorrow, personally and societal." Through trial and error, studying what works and what does not, the U.S. military has made strides in its COIN and information operations. Previously, types of unsuccessful practices attempted included: "Overemphasize killing and capturing the enemy, rather than securing and engaging the populace; ignoring peacetime governmental processes, including legal procedures; and placing a low priority on assigning quality advisors to HN [Host Nation] forces," according to Maj. Gen. Stone. This old way of doing business is termed no longer as successful or desirable. In contrast, the new way of operating, with which there has been notable success, includes: emphasizing intelligence, isolating insurgents from the population, conducting information operations, providing amnesty and rehabilitation, having local police lead (backed up by U.S. military support), and expanding and diversifying the security forces. According to the U.S. Military Field Manual 3-24, "In COIN environments distinguishing an insurgent from a civilian is difficult and often impossible. Treating a civilian like an insurgent, however, is a sure recipe for failure."

INFORMATION OPERATIONS

"TIFRC services, to include work programs, vocational training programs, education, and religious discussion programs all are integral to the information operations fight" (Maj. Gen. D. Stone, Camp Bucca Briefing, 2008) and ultimately complement COIN doctrine. According to Maj. Gen. Stone's operations plan:*

We also can help turn or marginalize the Islamists by providing an alternative to the current system or the way of doing business. We must

---

* Every Task Force (TF) commander has an operations plan mandate that is written and provided to those under his command. Therefore, all military working in detention operations in Iraq during Maj. Gen. Stone's command were required to be familiarized with his operations plan (OPLAN).

never forget that this is an IO [information operations] fight, which we must conduct with a vengeance.

In Iraq, IO included the use of media, visitation, and TIFRC services (to include all the rehabilitation programs and the detainee work program) in order to encourage cooperation between the Americans and Iraqis as well as between Iraqis and Iraqis.

Effective counterinsurgency operations in any environment are all about collecting intelligence and influencing the perceptions of foreign, friendly, and neutral audiences. The doctrinal term for accomplishing these tasks is IO. IO in detainee operations must be tailored to reach objectives by shaping the knowledge and perception of the supporters, fence sitters, and threats. Hence, although IO is effectively its own discipline, it is considerably intertwined with COIN operations, aimed at influencing (or rather *informing*) the populace of available choices. IO has been an important part of military campaigns for decades. Doctors Ernest F. Bairdain and Edith M. Bairdain (1971) highlight the significance of one element of IO:

> Defection is most likely to occur as immediate response to PSYOP [psychological operation] messages when appeals are received in the context of some form of military pressure. Where timely persuasive messages are received, the opportunity exists, and defection is feasible to the situation. In the absence of exposure to immediate high external pressure, defection may occur because of the cumulative effects of a series of unrewarding, frustrating, difficult, and intermittently dangerous experiences, which greatly outweigh any positive features in the total situation.

The two major IO core capabilities necessary within detainee operations are psychological operations and operations security. In Vietnam, constant pressure utilizing IO was implemented. Psychological operations against Viet Cong or North Vietnamese soldiers were used through the Chieu Hoi "Open Arms" program, which had a significant impact on the enemy. More than 100,000 enemy soldiers defected to the South Vietnamese through offers of amnesty, job training, finance, and home assistance. Some reverted to the communist side, but overall the program was minimally dangerous and a more economical way of reducing a sizable number of enemy combatants. Although historically, it may sometimes be difficult to convert committed radical extremists, it is not impossible. There are many examples to support this. Take for instance the British, who in an effort to reduce the number of Irish Republic Army detainees, justified the release of individuals based on evidence that family and community ties could influence the detainee's move away from violence. This action created an effect that reduced both the population of detainees and the alienation in the communities from which they came. In many situations, the "repentant" provided crucial information and evidence that was vital in cracking the overall Irish Republican Army terrorists' campaign (Jenkins, 2006).

From the point of capture to the TIF, operations security (OPSEC) contributes to successful operations at every level. On the other hand, poor OPSEC may lead to missed opportunities to final defeat in turning a detainee in the U.S. favor. While most understand OPSEC as just keeping information from the enemy, it also includes countersurveillance. Security forces at every level must contribute to OPSEC. At the points of capture, the infantry soldier must practice good OPSEC by not providing information that could possibly be transferred to other detainees at other internment facilities. Additionally, the security force must practice countersurveillance of detainees by observing their actions, mannerisms, and other valuable information. This role of the security force must be passive, and information should be passed onto military intelligence analysts. The product of good OPSEC should satisfy the commander's critical information requirements, which leads to informed decision making. It was from this informed decision making that detainees were placed into the most appropriate rehabilitation courses in Iraq.

INTELLIGENCE GATHERING

Undeniably an excellent source of intelligence gathering has occurred during Iraq's rehabilitation programs. Away from their compounds, and involved in discussion where they are learning to differentiate between individuals who know what they are talking about (in terms of religious knowledge) and those who do not, detainees were often willing to speak against those causing problems in their compounds. In some sessions, detainees would hand the local civilian Iraqi nationals notes to pass on to the military. Other times when Dr. Angell was passing by a class in session, a detainee would come out and quietly request of her to speak to a security officer. And, sometimes, a bold detainee would even come right out and ask for a security officer to speak with directly. When the situation would warrant, the S2* would generally pull the detainee out of the caravan, take him to another secured location, listen to what he had to say, and then take the detainee back to where he had been retrieved. If done correctly, the other detainees

---

* An S2 is a manager in charge of gathering and disseminating information and issuing recommendations on how to best deal with the enemy's actions. The "2" stands for intelligence/security/information operations (1Sgt. B. Emmert, personal interview, November 8, 2009).

would never know why he had been pulled or, being that detainees were pulled frequently for varying reasons, neither would they usually care. In fact, according to Maj. Gen. Quantock:

> Sometimes detainees will complain of being sick to their stomach or something, then you will get them out to medical call and find out that they actually just needed a reason to get out of their compound … that they were tired of the extremists in it and were looking for another way out.

Notably, the function of intelligence in detainee operations is one of the most critical aspects that tie all other logical lines of operations together to reach the desired objective. As part of defeating an insurgency from within the wire, it is important to get into the threats decision-making cycle so that appropriate action can be taken. According to the Department of the Army and Marine Corps *Combat Development Command Field Manual* 3-24 (2006) and Marine Corps *War Fighting Publication* 3-33.5: "Intelligence and operations feed each other. Effective intelligence drives effective operations. Effective operations produce information, which generates more intelligence. Similarly, ineffective or inaccurate intelligence produces ineffective operations, which produces the opposite results."

Intelligence gathering is the method and the cornerstone of all efforts to curb, suppress, and prevent insurgent activities that are both criminal and disruptive to the safety and security of the outside society, the detainee population, and detention facility staff. There are primarily two types of intelligence applicable to the detention setting: tactical and strategic intelligence. Tactical intelligence is information that can be used to assist in the immediate or short-term investigation, operation, or problem. When there is a situation, tactical intelligence is gathered and action is taken. The action could be anything from apprehension of a wanted suspect, facility lock down, compound search, or transfer of detainees. Meanwhile, strategic intelligence can be used to support long-range planning, identification of developing problems, enemy combatants, radical leaders, trends, and patterns of detainee behavior. This information can be valuable to both the internment facility and the TIF commander. It can be useful to develop policy, allocate resources, and plan further contingency operations.

The intelligence cycle utilized by military and civilian law enforcement and corrections has variations in naming conventions, but come down to a four-step cycle. The intelligence cycle includes gathering and collecting, processing and organizing, evaluation and analysis, and dissemination. According to Maj. Gen. Quantock:

This is our offensive weapon. We deal with intelligence personnel on a monthly basis. They produce COIN collection reports. This has probably done more to separate extremists from moderates than anything else. And what helps us is these detainees talking to our Intel guys who are trying to figure who's pulling the strings inside each compound. This is a process that we work on every single day. There are 300 interviews, every 2 weeks; 300 here and 300 up in Taji; COIN guys talking to detainees is very powerful.

The first step is collecting or obtaining raw information. Collection methods include both passive and active collection. Guard personnel need to be passive collectors and submit as much information as possible about detainees on an observation report to the intelligence collectors. Serving as passive collectors reduces the risk of abuse. Yet, it is active collection that will generally result in the most significant and useful data. Active collection is conducted through "human intelligence." Human intelligence is collected through confidential informants, interrogations, and monitoring communication attempts with other detainees from other compounds, for example, passing of notes or monitoring mail and conversations that occur during visitation. Interrogations are considerably the most direct and intense of the active intelligence component. According to previous interrogator Matthew Alexander (2008), "Break is the jargon we use to signify getting a prisoner to open up a little—like cracking an egg." Critical to this step is to understand what is and is not important information; the objective is to create a series of collection networks that can serve as a vetting source for each other.

The second step involves organizing or processing the information, which includes putting it in a form that can be evaluated and analyzed by staff. This management of information may include entry into a database, such as a detainee management system and target packets. Target packets are hard copies of information collected about each detainee from his/her point of capture through his/her time in detention. It includes field notes from the unit that did the initial arrest to his/her actions and participation while in detention. Unfortunately, using hard copies of information too often resulted in misplacing of information from one detainee's file into another and/or permanent displacement, as occurred in Iraq during the early years of the war. To counter this, in July 2008 DIMS (Detainee Information Management System)—a more effective detainee tracking system—was designed and implemented under Maj. Gen. Quantock's command. All detainee conduct "operational and disciplinary; good and bad reports are all put up in DIMS. I don't care how small it is, like turning in contraband, because all of them impact in the decision of whether to release or not," said Maj. Gen. Quantock. DIMS connected all the TIFs in Iraq, which previously had been difficult to do as it relied instead on an archaic transport system of cartons of documents following detainee movement from one TIF to the next. The detainee information tracking system came a long way in Iraq from 2003 to 2010, but perhaps the model used in Afghanistan best illustrates the organization and processing of detainee information. Afghanistan probably has one of the most comprehensive and all-encompassing detainee management systems. When Dr. Angell and Dr. Gunaratna visited Camp Parwan (previously Bagram) in Afghanistan in April 2010, they were privy to viewing a complex and detailed global system that incorporates collected individual information for every detained individual (under U.S. custody) into a comprehensive global database. From his actual point of capture, to every letter he wrote and received while in detention (actual scans of the letters), to every report/observation about him to the result(s) of his interrogation(s) … every piece of information that had been collected on that specific detainee is entered into a database, accessibly by anyone with the appropriate clearance and qualification anywhere in the world. The detainee's entry also includes his eye scan, fingerprints, name, and all other identifying features (with photographs), such as tattoos and scars. This database cross-checks and ensures that all detained persons are indeed who they say they are, and permits someone with information about the same detainee elsewhere in the world to input the data that will automatically upload to the detainee's individual file for cross-evaluation and analysis.

In fact, evaluation and analysis are the third step in intelligence gathering. It requires the staff to determine the information's relevance, timeliness, reliability of the source, and validity. Information during this step is often incomplete, contradictory, or may not have a discernable meaning. This step may require some form of social network, pattern, or link diagram analysis to assist in identifying the information's usefulness. In 2005, at Camp Bucca, an informant provided information on a planned prison break. The significance of this information was that the detainees had been planning and digging a tunnel for more than a month. The intelligence pieces were there: Showers and portable latrines kept clogging, color schemes on the ground had changed, and guards even noticed rising of the ground. Yet, had the informant not provided the final piece of information, the detainees would have most likely escaped from within the compound before the military found the source of concerns.

Dissemination of the information is the last and perhaps the most important step in intelligence gathering. Information needs to be disseminated to those who need to know, especially the decision makers. The situation and value of intelligence may require verbal or written dissemination. It may produce orders to conduct a compound search or an increase in security, although, on the other hand, it may just be a verbal or written order at guard mount for guard personnel to be aware of a potential developing situation. The information also might feed the commander's critical information requirements, which may trigger decision points. An example of confirmed information might be that a detainee cleric is preaching and inciting malicious propaganda against the United States and its allies, which may trigger a decision point to relocate or isolate this detainee. It is a common practice to err on the side of caution when determining the value of gathered intelligence. In other words, it is better to be safe now than to be sorry later.

VISITATION

Detainee visitation, namely when family members come to the TIF to visit detained persons, encourages an optimal environment to engage in COIN and IO. Visitation began right after the creation of TF-134 in late 2004 and was such a success that it evolved and expanded as time went on. In Iraq, respecting cultural norms and customs was an important component of visitation and would often open the door to further engagement. For example, when visitors would initially arrive, women were searched by female soldiers in private areas, as were men searched by male soldiers in separate areas (Lt. Col. E. Mullai, personal interview, January 29, 2010) (Figure 7.2). There were also a number of rules governing visitation, including that all family members must have an appointment, without which they were asked to make one at present and then return another day for visitation.

The first thing to occur when family members would arrive is that they would interact with members of the U.S. guard force (Figure 7.3). They were asked if they had an appointment and the name of the detained person they were there to visit. The guards would then inform them of what was permissible and not permissible to have on their bodies and in their possession. Afterwards, they were required to have a body search. There was heavily mandated interpreter support so that there was little confusion throughout the process. Detainees were limited to six family members, and the military worked to ensure they were indeed family members, not friends. According to Lt. Col. Mullai, "We don't want strangers to come in here and influence our population to get into more trouble." At Camp Cropper, detainees were allowed a maximum of three adults out of the allowed six visitors. Meanwhile, at Camp Taji, Lt. Col. Richard Johnson (personal interview, 2010) said:

FIGURE 7.2 Individuals arriving to visit a detained family member come down this sidewalk past the initial and secondary security before being searched. The rooms on the right illustrate a couple of the search rooms: Camp Taji, Iraq, 2010. (Photo by Ami Angell.)

> They are allowed six visitors. No more than two children. Frankly, that is pretty much all they can handle. What we found out is that if there are more kids, it's very difficult for the detainee to have an adult discussion. So, it is actually more beneficial to the detainee this way.

Visitors were required to turn in mobile phones, cameras, videos, and all other electronic devices they had on them. A guard would take the prohibited items from the visitor, place them in a box, and give the corresponding box number to the visitor to keep on his/her person. At the end of the visitation, and before departure from the facility, the

FIGURE 7.3   The visitation process is posted clearly in both Arabic and English in all the visitation centers: Camp Taji, Iraq, 2010. (Photo by Ami Angell.)

visitor would exchange the number for the return of his/her prohibited items (Figure 7.4).

Next, visitors would go into in-processing. If it was their first visit and they had not yet gone through biometrics testing, they were required to have it done. They had to verbally state who they were, and then show documentation to prove it. Because there is no open visitation, it is then again confirmed that the actual visitors have an appointment for that particular day and time. If confirmed, the visitors go into a briefing room where they are informed of all the rules and regulations of visiting, the process, and the timing on when they will be brought to where. Approximately 30 minutes before their visitation, they would get on a bus and be taken to the reception area within walking distance of where they would have the official visit (Figure 7.5). There was always some sort of entertainment in the reception area, usually cartoons on television. The American cartoon *Tom and Jerry* was among the most favored to watch. In fact, it was one of the very few that never received complaints; some adults would even request that it be put on in place of others. Information operations campaigns, such as informational clips about upcoming elections, were also interdispersed with

FIGURE 7.4 The room where individuals (visiting detained family members) leave all prohibited items in exchange for a tag with their box number on it: Camp Taji, Iraq, 2010. (Photo by Ami Angell.)

the cartoons at the reception area. Children who wanted to color or draw while waiting were encouraged by American soldiers who were there for that purpose. Meanwhile detainees would also be waiting in a separate reception area for visitation to begin (Figure 7.6). Like their visitors, detainees were also held to following a certain number of rules, failure to do so would mean the visit either would not happen, or would end prematurely (Figure 7.7).

When the visitation hour arrived, family members were moved into a courtyard. There they were required to stand behind a thick (usually yellow or red) line painted across the ground. Fifteen feet directly in front of them, in a painted square, was the detained individual they came to visit (Figure 7.8). Families were required to stay behind their respective line—as was the detainee in his square—until the military gave the signal indicating that the 10 minutes of permitted physical contact had begun. At that time, family members could cross the line and approach their respective detainee (Figure 7.9). Children were permitted to approach and embrace the person they had come to see immediately upon recognition (Figure 7.10). Hugs, kisses, and touches were allowed during the 10 minutes, as long as the detainee did not move from his

FIGURE 7.5 Family members wait in the reception area of the visiting room for visitation to begin while the American cartoon *Tom and Jerry* plays on the television: Camp Cropper, Iraq, 2010. (Photo by Ami Angell.)

personal square painted on the ground. The square was about 2 feet by 2 feet, and the detainee was required to remain in it for the entire 10-minute duration. If he stepped over one of the lines, accidentally or not, one of the oversight guards (usually there was one directly behind each detainee) would tap him on the arm or shoulder so that the detainee could self-correct. Guards were instructed not to make a public display of corrective action, so as to limit insult and embarrassment to a detainee in front of his family. Only repeated abuse of privilege by the detainee would warrant a verbal response by a guard. But, as all the detainees were aware of the rules, as were family members, infractions were quite infrequent. For example, said Lt. Col. Johnson:

> Occasionally there are detainees who don't get along with mama. You think the detainees want to see their families; sometimes they don't. When you get there, there is a brawl, and you can tell by their language. Sometimes it happens within 2 minutes of seeing each other. And, they are on to each other, and the detainee might say, "Get me out of here, I want to be removed." We have more of those than we have disciplinary infractions. Husband and wife bickering. It's kind of funny and very human.

FIGURE 7.6   Detainees gather in a reception area watching soccer while waiting for family visitation to begin: Camp Taji, Iraq, 2010. (Photo by Ami Angell.)

During the 10 minutes allotted of physical contact, detainees and family members had the option of taking a photograph together, with or without an Iraqi flag as a background (Figure 7.11). If they chose to be photographed, a copy of the photo was provided to the family to accompany their departure from the facility; another copy was provided to the detainee for his/her return to his/her compound. However, some families did not wish to touch at all during the physical contact 10 minutes, or take a photograph together. Allegedly, one reason for not having a photograph taken was due to the embarrassment of being detained; other reasons included the fear that if the photo was found, it would illustrate that the family is without its main male protection and, consequently, subject to harassment or worse.

Also, during the 10 minutes allotted of physical contact, if a detainee had participated in a detainee work program and, thus, had earned money, he had the option of being paid up to the amount he had earned and giving it to his family. This is sometimes done to help with food costs and/or family transportation for visitation. Some detainees only withdrew part of what they had earned; some did not withdraw any. It was up to the detainee to decide what he would like to do or give to his family.

FIGURE 7.7   Detainee rules for visitation: Camp Taji, Iraq, 2010. (Photo by Ami Angell.)

After the 10 minutes of physical contact, the detainees were sent out one door and, on the opposite side, the family members were led out another. Both groups of people were then led into a special area where the detainees and family members were permitted to continue their visitation for another 60 minutes. No physical contact was allowed in this area, and detainees sat on one side of a wall while their family sat on another (Figure 7.12). Partitions between each detainee ensured that privacy was observed. Between each detainee and his family, there was a clear plastic partition with holes in it, which was used for ease of verbal communication. Some camps only had a metal screen, which made communication even easier. Only Camp Cropper visitation required telephones to communicate. Bolted down chairs ensured that proper distance was maintained and, thus, no violation of rules could occur between the detainee and his/her family. According to Lt. Col. Johnson, then commander of the 211th Military Police Battalion in 2009 and 2010, the military worked hard to ensure that the atmosphere was as enjoyable as possible under the circumstances. The facility was kept immaculate, the walls were painted regularly, and detainee-painted pictures were hung on the walls. "We will do anything to provide a comfortable atmosphere because it is the one time that the family gets to see the detainee and the detainee gets a release from it, if it's done right," he said.

FIGURE 7.8   Detainees impatiently wait in their respective painted red squares for their family members to be allowed in for the 10-minute con-act portion of visitation: Camp Taji, Iraq, 2010. (Photo by Ami Angell.)

It is usually during these 60 minutes that younger children grow restless and disinterested. To accommodate the situation, a playground facility was built in conjunction with each visitation center (Figure 7.13). A number of agreeable American soldiers (without their weapons) were assigned to interact and play with the Iraqi children. Most children knew very little English, and most guards knew very little Arabic; but there is definitely a universal symbol for "push me" on the swing and "play with me." This was a useful opportunity to engage in a simple information operations campaign, simply by playing with the children. It was incredible to witness the interaction and see how excited the children were to play with the American soldiers, who also were more than happy to escape mundane or more somber tasks through the contagious

FIGURE 7.9 Families interacting with detainees after being given the signal permitting them to cross their respective line and approach their detained family member for a 10-minute contact visitation; Camp Taji, Iraq, 2010. (Photo by Ami Angell.)

enthusiasm of the children. It also gave the adults (detainee and visiting family members) some "alone time" to discuss serious issues at home or just tell each other how important they are to one another, without their children being witness. At the conclusion of the 60-minute, no-contact part of visitation, every visiting child was offered something to take with him/her. There was always an abundant supply of stuffed animals in addition to clothing, school supplies, and toys from which to choose (Figure 7.14). Most of the items were provided by individuals and groups from the United States who, aware of the deprivation of many Iraqi children, would go on drives and solicitations to collect and buy the items for distribution. The individuals and groups would then ship them to units involved with direct interaction with Iraqi children. Most Iraqi families permitted their children to be given things by the Americans, but some families did not, usually to the obvious disappointment of their children. The families who refused gifts usually expressed that they wanted nothing from the people who were detaining their family member. These were usually the family members who also would not let their children play on the playground.

FIGURE 7.10   Children are permitted to greet detained family members immediately upon seeing them. Visiting adults must wait for the official signal that the 10-minute contact portion of visitation has begun: Camp Taji, Iraq, 2010. (Photo by Ami Angell.)

At the conclusion of the visitation, on the way out of the facility, family members were encouraged to schedule their next visitation appointment. For those who lived far distances, this was the best way to ensure that they did not show up without an appointment. Local visitors could usually visit detained family members about once every 7 days, while those who lived farther away would have an appointment around every 50 days. But, it fluctuated. According to Lt. Col. Mullai, sometimes if there was a cancellation or a rescheduling, then a family member might be able to get in after just a few days' request.

Visitation provided one of the best hands-on opportunities for U.S. military to interact with local Iraqi civilians. What happened during visitation was often communicated with villages when the families returned. Stuffed animals, school supplies, and anything given to the family by the Americans also indirectly impacted other family members who did not come, as well as neighbors and friends, who then had the opportunity to see and hear about the care the United States had taken with visitors.

FIGURE 7.11   During visitation, detainees and family members have the option of having a photograph taken with the Iraqi flag as a background. If they choose to do so, one copy goes to the detainee and the second copy is given to the family to take with them: Camp Taji, Iraq, 2010. (Photo by Ami Angell.)

CONCLUSION

The Global War on Terror is argued to be both a war of ideologies and a political war. Regardless, while there are many physical struggles, ideology and politics are tied by the one who dominates the information environment toward one view. The global U.S. detainee operations program must comprehend this fact and take proactive measures to influence the perceptions, decisions, and will of one's adversaries, specifically religious, political, and intellectual leaders.

Ideological and political warfare are an extension of armed conflict by other means. Likewise, it is a more humane approach, as physical violence is not a necessary component. Not only do they both focus exclusively on the U.S. enemies at large, but they also target those on their way into the enemy ranks, those who may be persuaded to resign, and those detained. Using resources within the wire, from talking with individuals detained to running rehabilitation classes and talking with visitors during visitation are all part of the ongoing battle to conquer religious extremism. Thus, every component is important to winning

FIGURE 7.12   Camp Cropper visitation booths for family members and detainees to use during the allowed 60 minutes of noncontact visitation: Camp Cropper, Iraq, 2010. (Photo by Ami Angell.) Camp Cropper, Iraq, 2010. (Photo by Ami Angell.)

the overall battle of hearts and minds while ensuring that no detainee is left behind. Ever more increasingly, emphasis is shifting toward understanding and dealing with the reasons that people become radicalized and resort to terrorism. This is the first step in combating it. In fact, even those in "detention of the mind" seek an alternative "narrative." For these detainees, embracing "radicalization" can be an expression of social need rather than purely the adoption of a political or religious agenda. Dealing with the motivator in radical extremism is essential, as is understanding the likeness and dissimilarities of cult and gang actions. To that end, counterinsurgency operations are a fundamental step in reducing extremism and violence within detention facilities. Winning the hearts and minds of the people, especially the children, may sound cliché, but it is believed by many to be an extremely valuable long-term strategy during a "Stability and Support Operation" plagued by an active insurgency. And, as Maj. Gen. Quantock was quick to point out: "If you don't keep them busy, they will keep you busy." Lt. Col. Johnson, who has experience within the U.S. prison system as well as detainee operations in Iraq, can relate to this:

FIGURE 7.13   U.S. soldiers interact with Iraqi children by giving them toys during visitation: Camp Victory, Iraq, 2007. (Photo by Maj. (Ret.) Guy L. Jester.)

I grew up in a city neighborhood. Half of my friends are convicts, and half of them are cops and firemen. I don't think any less of the bad guys because I understand what happens and how you can end up like that. Although there are people who are really bad people, and I do think less of them. But most of the time, there is some root cause of how you got where you got. If you don't help the person change somehow, that person is going to stay on that road, continue to menace the rest of us, and never recover from it. So, there is nothing positive that they could give back. It is our responsibility somehow to try and impact that. Not just for reparations, but for the rest of the Iraqis who need to live with that person, so that person can fit somehow. They are here in our custody and, so, if I can impact that, it is a positive effect, not just for me, but for Iraq

He continues:

I have friends and relatives that have gone through the prison system at home. They got nothing from their incarcerated time that helped them reintegrate. All they got from there was more time with the bad guys to network and do more bad things. But, then, it's different in a lot of ways because the anatomy of their incarcerations is a lot different than here because of the crime and politics and other stuff. But, the basic

FIGURE 7.14 Sgt. Taylor prepares stuffed animals to give out to children during visitation: Camp Taji, Iraq, 2010. (Photo by Ami Angell.)

concept is the same. You give a person a reason to seek reward and do better, and you open the means to do it. They will take it most of the time. But, for us military to be all of those things is frustrating. We want to be all these things. Yet, at the same time, we have to be always consciously vigilant. At the end of the day, you have to think about your family and get home. How far will you reach? That's a tough question for all of us.

It *is* a tough question. And it is these tough questions in this type of situation where you can really see how a person is made. A lot of men and women put their lives on the line to reach out and engage with detainees in Iraqi custody. Whether that was through interrogations, doing guard oversight, or direct interaction with visitors during visitation, each U.S. soldier and civilian played a part in causing that detainee to have a positive or negative experience while in detention. Based on what that result was, we have either helped create a more determined terrorist or we have helped to create a messenger of peace. So, yes, the challenges are strong, but the rewards can be even greater.

The global threat coming from violent extremist ideology requires captured terrorists to be rehabilitated before they are released. Unless they abandon the idea of violence before they are released, they will contaminate others with their ideas, support and commit acts of violence.

The disengagement strategy used should incorporate incentives, reeducation, and rehabilitation. As an essential element in the fight against extremism, detainee and inmate rehabilitation is the reverse of terrorist indoctrination. Rehabilitation is both detainee and inmate deradicalization and community engagement. Such rehabilitation initiatives can proactively and reactively counter the contemporary wave of extremism.

Through historical studies and contemporary trial and error, we now realize that rehabilitation should be made available in every facility housing terrorist detainees as well as those in danger of indoctrination. The mind is the most powerful weapon against their enemies and opponents. By unlocking the mind, an extremist can be made to reflect and reexamine his/her own ideas and thoughts. This is why terrorist rehabilitation is unique. Still in experimental phases around the world, terrorist rehabilitation requires visionary leadership, government–community partnership, and a well-resourced, specialist program of dedicated and trained staff. It was fortunate that Iraq met these requirements and was determined to carry them out. As Maj. Gen. Stone commented, "The bottom line was there was not going to be any change unless we did it. These types of programs never happen unless a leader takes chances. Who is going to reward someone for helping detainees? You know how it is. You have to take chances."

CHAPTER 8

The Secret Weapon

PROLOGUE

Hamid* first arrived at Camp Bucca at the end of August 2005. In his first week, he had a basic education evaluation where his literacy, language, and math skills were found to be at a primary school level. When the opportunity presented itself for him to participate in education classes, he readily volunteered. In 2007, he began attending a number of classes both at the intracompound schools and at formal schools. What he learned motivated him and, in 2008, he asked to be trained as a literacy and math tutor for his compound peers. He also started participating in other group activities provided by the military. As he strengthened his knowledge through the process of teaching his peers, he grew more confident in his ability to learn and grow intellectually. At his release, he asked to present the commander with his written story.

> When I was detained, I was totally illiterate. I had never been to school. I was like a blind man walking through life. I used to be embarrassed among my family and at work, and tried to cover up my illiteracy. But then, when I was detained, I was surprised to hear that there is a school where I can enroll myself. It was an honor to participate. It was run by the American army who supplied us with textbooks and stationery. I attended an 8-week course, where I learned reading and writing and Qur'an reading. I owe the American army to give me the chance to transit me from the dark corner to the light world. My thanks to the education program and my thanks to Allah. I was blind and now I can read and write. I wrote my first letter to my wife for the first time, by myself. I used to have other detainees write my letters to my family for me. But, now I write them. My wife is very happy. I am very happy (as translated from Arabic into English by N. Al-Jader, personal interview, March 20, 2010).

---

* An asterisk (*) is used throughout this book to protect the security and confidentiality of certain individuals whose lives might be threatened otherwise.

INTRODUCTION

A highly educated man, Maj. Gen. Douglas Stone (personal interview, 2010) was (and is) a key promoter in the right of education for detainees:

> For me, the key to understanding the Holy Qur'an is to comply with the first words of the Qur'an and to learn to read. Reading allows detainees to compare their own interpretation of God's word to that of other more radical detainee interpretations, and to reach the conclusion with guidance that violent Islamic behavior is not consistent with what the Qur'an teaches. Critical thought rests on the ability to reason, reason on learning, learning in part on reading and problem solving. Education is the foundation of the religious study and civics course; it powers critical thinking and challenges those detainees exposed to extremist dogma by allowing the detainees to think on their own.

Like Maj. Gen. Stone, Dr. Angell had the fortunate opportunity to witness many individuals in detention empowered and enlightened through the modus operandi of education. One such opportunity came in an unexpected fashion. In November 2007, Dr. Angell was asked by Lt. Col. Patrick Williams, then-battalion commander of the 705th brigade, to give a speech to a group of detainees graduating from primary education at one of the first formal school graduations at Camp Bucca. At the time, she wondered why he asked her, a civilian, to be the guest speaker. Especially as a well-respected commander and leader, he himself would be an excellent candidate. Besides, what could she possibly say to motivate these adult men, whose country was at war and who were detained? What could she, as an American and a female, offer them? The day didn't start off well. A trusted colleague had decided to oversleep with the keys to our Operational Support and Services (OSS) company vehicle in his pocket. Embarrassed, Dr. Angell walked in late to the ceremony, still unsure what to expect, and now ashamed of her late arrival. However, with the encouragement of hesitant smiles from the waiting graduates, she began to speak. She informed them that she knew the road ahead of them would not be easy, but that nothing worthwhile ever is. She told them about how she was the first person in her family to graduate from college and how some people told her that she would never make it. But, most of all, she told them to never let anyone tell them they are not good enough because they are all good enough. They have proved themselves by taking this first step and that, if they wanted it bad enough, it could be the first step of many more to follow. At the conclusion of the ceremony, several detainees walked up to thank Dr. Angell. One in particular told her:

I had no idea that Americans can also face some of the same troubles we do in Iraq. Now I know that we truly are all brothers and sisters. God willing, I am ready to continue my learning. And, perhaps one day I will be able to share with others what I have learnt here.

This simple dialogue, spoken from the heart of the new detainee graduate, illustrated what we knew all along: Education is a secret weapon. With it comes the power to reason, to question, to relate to and understand others, and, ultimately, to make informed life choices.

BACKGROUND

According to Maj. Gen. David Quantock (personal interview, 2010), the idea of providing education classes for the detainee population was quietly being discussed among the detention centers as early as 2005. However, it was not formally introduced and experimented with until the early months of 2007. With a new military command in Iraq and new funds allocated for the Iraqi detainee population, there was finally the operational space, capacity, and means to proceed. OSS, which had a long-running contract with the U.S. military by providing BBAs (bilingual bicultural advisors) across the Iraq theater, was consulted for starting an education module for the detainees. Encouraged, in March 2007, OSS hired an education subject matter expert (also often referred to as the teacher administrator)—Nadia Al-Jader—to develop, lead, and help instruct the education program. She was to become a valuable asset in developing a successful education module.

Without a building designated for holding formal schools, Al-Jader worked from an empty compound building. Rudimentary-style classes were held there while the military decided on a more permanent structure. Every day, all the supplies from detainees were put into black trunks and locked up to prevent displacement or removal. Because the buildings were used for other activities as well, it was necessary to transform the location before and after each education class. Finally, by mid-2007, a location had been selected and detainees in the carpentry detainee work program set to work building a facility that would eventually become the first designated formal school (Figure 8.1 and Figure 8.2). A groundbreaking ceremony occurred in September 2007, with detainees, soldiers, and civilians cheering as the ribbon was to be cut, symbolically opening the formal school to detainees. Curiously, nobody thought to bring a tool for the cutting of the ribbon. To compensate, a high-ranking officer brazenly pulled out a knife (knives are strictly not allowed in the TIF) and made the cut. While junior-grade soldiers gaped in surprise, detainees quietly stood nearby and watched in amusement.

FIGURE 8.1   The Bucca Freedom School being built by detainees in the carpentry work program: Camp Bucca, Iraq, 2007. (Photo courtesy of U.S. Department of Defense.)

The primary focus of the detainee education program was to address the fact that 60 percent of the detainee population lacked even a basic education. Understanding that detainees without a basic education are much more susceptible to indoctrination and recruitment to radical ideologies, education became a focus of the military. Accordingly, Maj. Gen. Stone made it a mission mandate to ensure that at a minimum, every detainee would have the opportunity to pursue basic education. There were two types of learning environments available: formal schools and intracompound schools. Formal schools took place in an actual classroom learning environment that detainees were transported to/from daily, while intracompound schools were makeshift classes that occurred inside compounds. Under Maj. Gen. Stone's command, the military on the ground made it a focus that every interested detainee would be offered education classes at least through to the fifth-grade level, and whenever resources permitted, beyond. Maj. Gen. Stone made sure to point out that education classes were available for all. While only those considered low-risk would be permitted to participate in the formal schools, everyone interested could participate in the intracompound schools.

After the groundbreaking, the classes being held in the temporary compound transferred to the new building, and classes in the

FIGURE 8.2 The Bucca Freedom School after being built, tiled, and painted by detainees as part of the carpentry detainee work program: Camp Bucca, Iraq, 2008. (Photo courtesy of U.S. Department of Defense.)

intracompound schools continued unaffected. However, there was noticeably a discontinuity in the education classes from the standards that the formal school had in place, from those that were in the intracompound schools. An even more marked contrast existed between the standards in place at Camp Bucca and those at Camp Cropper. The education program evolved and changed to meet the needs and demands of the detainees, yet they changed at differing paces, sometimes adding more chaos to the confusion. This discontinuity continued until early 2008, when the signing of the Memorandum of Understanding between the Iraq Ministry of Education and Task Force 134 would finally synchronize education standards within U.S.-run theater internment facilities (TIFs) across Iraq.

Iraqi Ministry of Education (MoE)

An official Memorandum of Understanding (MoU) between the Iraqi Ministry of Education (MoE) and TF-134 was entered into agreement on February 12, 2008. It detailed that the MoE would provide principals, teachers, syllabuses, and examinations in return for TF-134 ensuring that detainees would be provided the environment, encouragement, and supplies conducive to learning. According to the MoU:

Students will be eligible to complete each grade within a 4-month intensive study period per grade. Grades 1 and 2 will be combined for an 8-month period concluding with a Ministry of Education Assessment. Grades 3 and 4 also will be combined for another 8-month period of instruction with a second assessment conducted by the Ministry of Education. Each grade will constitute a 4-month period and final Ministry of Education Assessment.

It further stipulated that:

Upon completion of the TIFRC Services Program and release, those security detainees that successfully completed the program of instruction will be awarded a Certificate of Completion per grade by the MoE and may continue their education to higher accreditation levels by attending night classes offered by the MoE after release (Memorandum of Understanding between Iraqi MoE and TF-134, February 2008).

The memorandum declared that TF-134 would be responsible for building educational facilities (to include equipped classrooms) at all U.S. detention sites, be responsible for all movement of detainees to/from classes, pay for MoE-qualified instructors, and faithfully implement the MoE education curriculum as provided by the MoE. In return, the MoE would provide an Adult Literacy Program syllabus/Program of Instruction, Youth Program syllabus/Program of Instruction, refer MoE-certified Iraqi principals and teachers, provide and conduct the required examinations/assessments of each program of instruction, conduct regular visits to classrooms in order to ensure the program remains viable and retains its certification level, inform graduating detainees of their ability to continue their education upon release, and help with reintegration into communities. It further stated that the MoE would assume all financial responsibilities for the program upon transfer of detention operations to the government of Iraq, including, but limited to, payment of teachers' salaries, copyright expenses, and, of course, material expenses required for teaching. The MoU was officially signed on February 12, 2008, by Dr. Nihad Al Juburi, then-deputy minister of education in Iraq, and Maj. Gen. Douglas M. Stone, then-commander of detainee operations–Iraq.

Education Placement

Of all of our rehabilitation programs, the positions with those involved in education are the most diverse. There were seven positions authorized for the education component including the education supervisor, formal school civilian Iraqi principal, formal school civilian Iraqi teacher, intracompound civilian Iraqi teacher, intracompound detainee principal, intracompound detainee teacher, and detainee student.

Education Supervisor
In Iraq, the education supervisor was contracted by OSS. At any given time, there were between one and eight supervisors in the education program. These were civilian contractors, mostly Americans, who had a background in education. They were responsible for developing, enhancing, and the overall operation of running the education programs. They also were responsible for the direct oversight and supervision of the local Iraqi nationals who were employed into the education program. They were involved with hiring, report writing, giving presentations, evaluations, and other duties as needed by the local nationals (LNs), the military, and the OSS program lead and manager. Their immediate supervisor was the OSS program lead.

Formal School Civilian Iraqi Principal
There was one principal in every formal school. This was a locally hired Iraqi national who not only had a background in education and relevant experience, but also had supervisory experience in an extended capacity. In all of the TIFs in Iraq, the principals were male as the majority of the detained population was male. Each principal assigned teaching tasks to the teachers, prepared the schedule for the entire semester, helped conduct the trainings of the local civilian Iraqi teachers, and participated in teaching the formal school classes, among other tasks. The principal reported directly to the education supervisor and helped oversee the education programs running within his formal school.

Formal School Civilian Iraqi Teacher
The teachers in the formal schools were locally hired Iraqi civilians with an education degree and relevant experience. They went through intensive training programs at the detention facility prior to commencing work. Their immediate supervisor was the formal school civilian Iraqi principal.

Intracompound Civilian Iraqi Teacher
The intracompound civilian Iraqi teacher had the same stipulations on hire as did the formal school civilian Iraqi teachers. However, the duties varied. The intracompound teachers tasking, instead of teaching in a formal setting, involved supervising three to four intracompound detainee teachers as they taught subjects within their compounds. The intracompound civilian Iraqi teacher advised on curriculum, resolved any disputes, and served as the "go to" person for any needs the intracompound detainee

teacher might have had. In addition, the intracompound civilian Iraqi teacher was responsible for ensuring that the detainee school principal followed through on providing data, such as the list of all the internment serial numbers (ISNs) of detainees participating in each class, a list of detainee teachers teaching the class, and gathered reports of any problems/issues occurring during the class from the intracompound detainee principal.

Intracompound Detainee Principal

In large compounds, there might be three to four classes taking place. To alleviate problems and save time, the position of "intracompound detainee principal" was created. The principal was essentially responsible for consolidating all information within his/her compound. He/she was the single point of contact for the intracompound civilian Iraqi teacher. He/she was responsible for compound administration functions, and keeping the school running within that quad or compound. The principal was also in charge of recommending qualified intracompound detainee teachers to be trained and certified, responsible for opening classes at different levels of education, and assigning the detainee teacher with conducting the class according to the MoE- approved guidelines. In addition, he/she prepared a complete list of detainee teachers and detainee students who would be participating each term, reported to the local Iraqi civilian teacher all absences and/or releases with justification, and, lastly, helped with the final examinations at the end of each term.

Intracompound Detainee Teacher

Intracompound detainee teachers were detained Iraqis with a background and experience in education. They led classes inside of the compound next to the fence (i.e., in sight of the guard force and the civilian intracompound teacher). To be certified as an intracompound detainee teacher, a detainee had to pass a training and certification class given by the local civilian Iraqi teachers and OSS education supervisor. After passing, he/she was responsible for preparing a daily plan of instruction, following the MoE curriculum in teaching, creating lists of materials needed for teaching (textbooks, writing boards, markers, pencils, notebooks, etc.) for each semester, acknowledging advice from local civilian Iraqi teachers, conducting at least one quiz per week, and preparing the final examination with help from the local civilian Iraqi teacher and intracompound detainee principal.

Detainee Student

The detainee student was any qualified Iraqi detainee who voluntarily participated in any of the education programs, both in the formal schools and intracompound schools.

Training Program for Local Iraqi Civilian Teachers

The local Iraqi civilian teachers hired by OSS were noticeably apprehensive and anxious at first. Not knowing what to expect, many felt a certain measure of fear and trepidation about teaching those deemed a security threat by the United States. When Dr. Angell asked them if their family and friends knew they were working in a detention setting, they told me (in most cases) while their immediate family members were aware, they refrained from informing other relatives and neighbors for fear of reprisal. Amongst themselves, they shared stories of individuals, having been discovered working with U.S. forces, being targeted for violence and even death. Most came up with aliases for names in the hopes of helping to ensure their safety.

In an effort to alleviate fear and trepidation, the first intensive 2-day training program for new hires was introduced in April 2007. The program covered 10 general areas of influence: group teaching, multigrade teaching, effective methods of teaching, medium- to long-term planning, lesson planning, classroom management, monitoring students' work, time management, library organization, and, finally, doing assessments.

However, it was decided that while the 2-day intensive plan was useful, it did not meet all the desired objectives. It was too short to effectively prepare the new hires for teaching inside a detention environment, and it still did not address many of the underlying concerns of the local hires in dealing with the detainee population. In response, the training program was expanded from 2 days to 4 days, with a 2-week continued evaluation period at the conclusion of the training. The 4-day training covered what was previously in the 2-day training in addition to other TIF-specific subjects, such as: dos and don'ts inside the TIF, effective communication with commanders and guards, raising motivation, and dealing with difficult issues. During the training, there were many group exercises from which potential key leaders of the new hires could be identified and engaged to direct activities. In addition, the training was also utilized for new hires to practice detainee mock lessons while being evaluated by peers and supervisors.

Training Program for Detainee Teachers for Intracompound Teaching

While there were a large number of detainees who expressed interest in teaching within their compounds, we did not have methods in place to validate their skill or motivation. For quality control, we decided it was necessary to introduce an intensive detainee teaching curriculum before detainees would be permitted to teach subjects within their compound. This not only ensured that the detainee was qualified, but was also a way for the detainee teacher to earn recognition and be awarded a certificate of qualification after the training. Qualified detainees were very eager to be selected and participate, as not only did it break up the typical monotony of a day in detention, but leadership participation was also referenced during Multinational Force Review committee (MNFRC) hearings. The 1-day test and training included four main areas: effective teaching, assessment, lesson plans, and teaching methods. During the training, detainees were also briefed on who their representative would be, what they were permitted to request, where they were permitted to hold classes, and the procedures for requesting for, and then administrating, proficiency examinations for the detainee students in their class.

CURRICULUM

In accordance with the MoE standards, the curriculum for the first level of primary school included Arabic language for 10 hours a week, English language for 4 hours a week, and math for 4 hours a week. The teaching week was 6 weeks in length with 18 total hours of class per week. First grade, second grade, and third grade teaching also had 18 total hours of classes per week, but instruction lasted only 2 weeks and had a different breakdown of courses. These included 8 hours per week of Arabic language, 5 hours per week of English language, and 5 hours per week of math. By contrast, fourth grade was 3 weeks in duration and consisted of 6 hours of Arabic language, 4 hours of English language, 4 hours of math, 3 hours of science, and 1 hour of civics. Finally, the fifth grade curriculum—taught over 5 weeks—offered 5 hours of Arabic language, 4 hours of English language, 4 hours of math, 3 hours of geography, 1 hour of science, and 1 hour of civics per week.

Essentially, to make the process easier for detainee guards and the local Iraqi civilians teaching the courses, the grade levels (first through fifth) were broken down to two terms. One term was 8 weeks long. This was standardized for all the formal and intracompound schools. Most detainees entered the program with term 1, which covered first, second, and third grade. Term 2 covered fourth and fifth grade. It took a minimum of 8 weeks, including the review and final exams for a detainee to advance from one level to another. At times, there were opportunities for detainees to take part in grades 6 through 10, but because textbooks were more difficult to come by at the higher levels and because the majority of the population was illiterate, these classes were fewer and less in demand. If detainees passed the exam, then they were invited to the next level, which began around 2 weeks following completion of the previous term. With a successful pass on the examination, detainees were awarded an official MoE-approved graduation certificate stamped with an MoE seal of approval. The original was given to the detainee, while an official copy was put in the detainee's file. This helped prevent any mistakes if the data for the detainee's participation had been mistakenly left out of entry into the system. If a detainee did not pass the final examination, he had the option to retake the term.

Local Iraqi civilian teachers routinely worked 6-hour shifts, 6 days a week. This fluctuated depending on the season and holidays, but generally began with 8:30 to 11:30 in the morning. Then they would have an hour and a half to eat and pray before returning to work from 1 to 4 p.m. In a conscious attempt to involve detainees who already had basic education yet were eager to learn more, a series of 1-day classes and short-term classes were offered at various times, including but not limited to first aid, civics, and art.

INTRACOMPOUND SCHOOLS

During the surge of the detainee population in 2006, through to the middle of 2008, at any given time there were around 2,000 detainee students enrolled in intracompound education courses. By and large, intracompound education classes have had more detainees enrolled and graduated more detainees than any other rehabilitation program offered in Iraq. Providing education within the compound effectively reached out to the detainee population, who might not have otherwise had the opportunity to engage in such an exercise.

Intracompound schools had a detainee principal (sometimes, depending on the size of the compound), a detainee principal assistant (also sometimes, depending on the size of the compound), detainee teachers, and detainee students. Local Iraqi civilian teachers provided oversight and coordination while classes were in session. Classes were conducted in a corner of the compound, viewable by both the U.S. guard force and one local Iraqi civilian teacher who was not only there to address any needs the class might have, but also to serve as quality control oversight, i.e., to ensure that what was being taught was in accordance with class curriculum. Detainee students generally sat on mats on the ground while the intracompound detainee teacher stood at the front of the group over

FIGURE 8.3   Intracompound School class in session: Camp Bucca, Iraq, 2008. (Photo courtesy of U.S. Department of Defense.)

a propped-up white board to conduct the class (Figure 8.3). The guards and the local civilian Iraqi teacher were able to monitor the class in session safely through the fence.

Intracompound schools were tested at the same standard and with the same test as the formal schools. This ensured that no detainee was receiving any kind of favoritism and ensured equal opportunity for all detainees to progress. Except in exceptional circumstances, exams were organized and given during the same time frame for both the formal schools and the intracompound schools.

One compelling factor for taking part in intracompound schools rather than formal schools was that because there was no movement of detainees outside of their compound, there was no need to be individually searched. For many detainees, the process of lining up, being searched multiple times daily, and dealing with the time of transfer made attending classes exhausting and undesirable. This was particularly the case among the older population and/or those that had medical conditions. However, with the introduction of intracompound schools, curiosity and desire were satisfied with no compromise on comfort. In addition, intracompound schools provided the flexibility that formal schools could not afford. If there were not enough guards for detainee movement, sometimes detainees scheduled to attend formal schools would not get to participate. Intracompound detainee students never had this problem. Additionally, intracompound schools made it possible to involve the higher-risk detainee population, who otherwise were left out of many of the rehabilitation programs, as movement for them was necessarily much more tedious, thorough, and time-consuming as well as a higher security risk.

Effectively, by its very nature, intracompound education ensured that no detainee would be left behind. Some compounds had several hundred detainees. In these compounds, there might be several different classes taking place at the same time in different corners; this enabled the possibility of allowing different levels of learning to occur simultaneously. Security-wise, it also likens the fact that thousands of detainees could be kept busy at the same time, minimizing the chance of disruptive behavior, escapes, riots, or other security-concerned related activity.

FORMAL SCHOOLS

While intracompound schools provided education opportunity for the largest number of detainees, having the experience of attending and learning in a designated school building was still the favored amongst many detainees. For most, it was their first time inside a school, sitting at a desk, and writing on a chalkboard/whiteboard (Figure 8.4). For these detainees, it didn't matter how many searches they had to go through to get there because the end goal was worth it. As an added benefit of attending a designated formal school, the terms always concluded with a large official graduation (Figure 8.5). Officers, LN Teachers and others involved in education came to offer congratulatory handshakes to the new graduates (Figure 8.6). For most, it was the first time having their name called and being given a diploma. Because of this, graduations were sometimes very emotional. It was not uncommon to see tears of elation (Figure 8.7).

The fact that it was detainees who built the classrooms, painted the walls, tiled the floors, built desks, and created art work for the walls empowered the detainees learning within them. Detainees confided how it made the place feel more like "theirs," and that they felt proud to learn in a place that their "brothers" had built. Each formal classroom had 30 to 40 detainees per class, with meal times and breaks fitted into the curriculum.

FIGURE 8.4   Formal School class in session: Camp Cropper, Iraq, 2010. (Photo courtesy of U.S. Department of Defense.)

FIGURE 8.5   Detainees preparing to graduate at the Hasty School complex: Camp Bucca, Iraq, 2007. (Photo by Maj. (Ret.) Guy L. Jester.)

FIGURE 8.6 Detainees shake hands with military officers and local national teachers after being awarded graduation diplomas at the Hasty School complex: Camp Bucca, Iraq, 2007. (Photo by Maj. (Ret.) Guy L. Jester.)

FIGURE 8.7 A detainee is excited after being given his certification of graduating from fifth grade: Camp Cropper, Iraq. (Photo courtesy of U.S. Department of Defense.)

Curiously, during my tenure in Iraq, the formal schools at Camp Cropper and Camp Bucca underwent several name changes with new military units coming and going. However, one thing remained constant and that was the detainee's eagerness and willingness to participate. There were never enough schools to meet the detainee need and desire. The first school at Camp Bucca was called Bucca Freedom School, and that name, save for a few hiccups, stuck. In contrast, the other formal school at Camp Bucca was at one time referred to as the Hasty School owing to the fact that it was initially constructed using the military quick set-up construction called Hasties. After the arrival of a new military command unit, however, the name was changed to Bucca Enrichment School. Madrasat Dar Al Hikma (House of Wisdom) was another name that was often used to refer to all the education formal buildings across the TIFs, including the Bucca Enrichment School and the Bucca Freedom School.

The Bucca Freedom School was the first formal school at Camp Bucca and, as it evolved through moving to a new facility and under various military commands, it maintained its continuity with much of the same dedicated group of local Iraqi nationals who had been working there since the education programs started. From 2008 through to the closure of Camp Bucca in 2009, it had three classrooms equipped with air conditioning, desks, chalkboards, and storage cabinets for detainees' school supplies. It notably maintained a high standard of excellence throughout the years and, arguably, some of the best and most dedicated local civilian Iraqi teachers worked there.

The Bucca Enrichment School, also known as the Hasty School, began in two large military tents. Classes were held in the tents with detainee students sitting behind makeshift tables. The local national teachers had to shout to be heard through to the back of the tents. There were only two classes possible at a time, and no air conditioning. The side flaps of the tent could be put up to allow some circulation of air, but it still proved to be a sweltering hot environment during Iraq's summer months. Subsequently, fans were purchased in an effort to help the circulation, but they did little but stir up more dust and make it harder for the detainees to hear the instruction. The frequent sand and dust storms made having continuous classes nearly impossible. So, it was with great relief when the official Hasty School moved into a solid structure that had been quickly built by the military over a 2-month period. The two classes readily moved into the solid structure, wherein there was air conditioning and a respite from the dust and sand outside. Then, encouraged by enthusiasm of the detainee students, the military built two more classrooms in 2008. With four classrooms, the Hasty School became the largest formal school at Camp Bucca (Figure 8.8). The name officially changed to Bucca Enrichment School in mid-2008.

FIGURE 8.8 Inside a classroom In the Hasty School complex: Camp Bucca, Iraq, 2007. (Photo by Maj. (Ret.) Guy L. Jester.)

The tents previously used for the school evolved into the lunch and break area, and detainees lounged in them during their free periods in between classes as well as before and after school. A couple of ping-pong tables were put up inside to encourage detainees to release excess energy during breaks. In addition, the military, which has always encouraged exercise as a natural stress reliever, added the space and equipment for the detainees to have the option of playing soccer as well during breaks. Usually barefoot, soccer is so popular that sometimes it was quite difficult to get detainees back into classrooms when game challenges were particularly intense.

COMPUTER TRAINING

There was interest and discussion about starting computer training classes at Camp Bucca in early 2008, but, because of military concerns relating to security and information flow, the project was not approved. For most of 2008, employed civilian Iraqi nationals were not even allowed to use computers at the Morale, Welfare, and Recreation (MWR) facilities, nor were they allowed to bring or have anything electronic on base. Therefore, the idea of letting detainees participate in computer training was a stretch for many. However, all of that changed in 2009. Under the command of Maj. Gen. Quantock, computer classes began at both Camp Taji and Camp Cropper (Camp Bucca was closed by this date). Initially experimenting with just a few detainees, the class grew rapidly as word spread. Detainees were eager to learn to use the computer. Computers had been prohibited from use under Saddam Hussein's regime, but detainees realized the importance of knowing how to use one in the changing world. Hasanudin,* a detainee taking computer classes at Camp Cropper, elaborated (personal interview, 2010): "It is a highly developed world and the knowledge of computer is one of the most important tools in order to see it."

According to Maj. Gen. Quantock, computer training was introduced to complement detainees' pursuit in education. Detainees participated in formal instruction of Microsoft® Office® to include Word®, PowerPoint®, and Excel® (Figure 8.9). The training also covered other areas to include computer operations, safety precautions, maintenance techniques, basic project planning, and basic job skills. However, the class size was limited, as there needed to be one computer available for each detainee. As such, the wait list to participate was often long and classes struggled to meet the increasing desire of detainees to participate. As a component of the education curriculum, detainees had to be

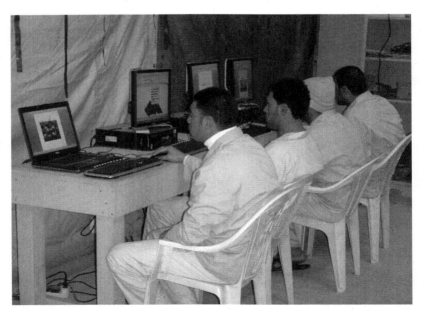

FIGURE 8.9 Computer class training: Camp Cropper, Iraq, 2010. (Photo by Ami Angell.)

literate in order to be selected for the computer training. Like the other programs, participation was voluntary and classes were taught by local civilian Iraqi nationals. The computer program was a 30-day course with instruction being 3 hours a day, 6 days a week. All hours spent in the class and during simulation exercises were recorded on a certificate that was presented to the detainee upon successful completion and passing of the cumulative examination.

When Dr. Angell spoke with detainees in January 2010, overwhelmingly, the computer class came out as one of the most favored. Mohammad,* who had been detained for a year and a half at Camp Bucca before being transferred to Camp Cropper, shared his thoughts about the computer program (personal interview, 2010):

> It's excellent. We benefit from this program. We can follow up with the progress happening around the world with computer. Saddam Hussein's regime left us very backwards. So, the computer class is a very good opportunity for us to gain knowledge about what is going on in the world.

Dr. Angell asked him what was so special about this particular class, and how he intends to apply the skills learnt at Camp Cropper after release.

> When we were young, we did not have this opportunity. The computer is like a window to the world. So, I want to experience seeing the whole world through this window. Computer now is similar to a glass of juice. You need it in your daily life. The same goes with English language. You need it and use it. English and computer complete each other.
>
> These programs help us develop ourselves and hopefully the knowledge will help us with our daily lives. This country needs this kind of educational programs for it to progress. And computer training is one way towards that. For example, perhaps when you have finished with your book, I can go to the computer and read it someday.

Maj. Gen. Quantock, who brought computer classes to the TIFs in Iraq, agrees about the class being important, but not only for all the obvious reasons.

> This is our most successful class. I just opened up our third computer tent, and you see some of the computer basics being taught like Microsoft. But it's more than just teaching computers. One instructor is a female. The first class was a Takfiri Sunni class. They walked in, and they saw a female instructor. They almost rebelled and walked out, but they sat down and tried it out. The first day there was no communication. They were just listening and going through the motions. The second day, they came back and gave her the greeting of the day. The

third day, the Iraqis cut their beard off to look good for the instructor. And, the fourth day, it was a wild class. So, you see it's also about breaking down barriers and breaking down stereotypes.

CHALLENGES

As with any program, running education programs in both formal school buildings and intracompounds within a detention center proved to be quite challenging at times. For instance, on one occasion in 2008, it was discovered that two of the local Iraqi civilian teachers responsible for oversight during an examination permitted cheating between detainees during a final examination. Because this situation had a credible witness (a linguist), action was immediately taken. Both detainees involved with cheating failed the examination, and both local Iraqi civilian teachers who had permitted the cheating were job-terminated. It was a no-win situation for all involved. But, it was necessary to preserve the integrity of the program and to prevent similar reoccurrences in the future.

Another challenge involved movement. Sometimes, classes would be moved. We would go to a particular compound expecting to find detainee students preparing for class and instead just find an empty compound. Dr. Angell can remember on a few occasions, detainees being split up and moved to other compounds in the middle of a school semester. While we attempted to locate each one again in order to continue the education they had been receiving, we often ran into problems. Sometimes, detainees were moved to a compound that was controlled by a few extremists on the inside who would not permit their detainees to take part in classes. Other times, the military seemed to be unsure of where the detainee had been moved and/or could not seem to access any records for the movement. Sometimes, it was just the location where they had been moved to that prevented continued participation in the education program.

Other seemingly smaller, but significant, factors also presented challenging situations at times. During certain months of the year, it would get quite hot outside. Yet, at other times of the year, it would be quite cold outside. It also rained quite often. For individuals taking intracompound classes, the weather could easily discourage detainee students from participating, especially if where the class was being held did not have a roof, as many did not. Also, the motivation factor was a constant concern; to keep detainee students motivated inside the compounds, while hundreds of other detainees are milling around, was not easy. It took increased innovation and motivation on the part of the detainee teachers and local Iraqi civilian teachers to come up with new ways of captivating interest and encouraging motivation and participation.

There were several ongoing areas of consideration and concern that also bear mentioning. Textbooks were always a great challenge. Getting the same textbooks for use in all the TIFs across Iraq proved problematic. There were never enough to go around, and often detainees had to share, and most were not permitted to keep textbooks in the compounds with them, let alone remove them from the formal school classrooms. This made memorizing and immersing oneself in learning even more of a challenge. Sharing did not help in such situations, when a detainee only had a limited amount of time to study the textbook and prepare for an examination. Detainees also talked about guards seizing their pencils and notebooks during searches, which, they complained, hampered their learning. Other detainees were upset about being searched so thoroughly on so many occasions as well as having to wait so long just to participate in class. They told us that these procedures were making them not want to bother with participating. On top of it all, there was also an extreme shortage of main school supplies that included writing boards, markers, notebooks, and pencils at any given time.

However, the searches and procedures were not without warrant. From another perspective, the military had to deal with constant acts of defiance from the detainee population while trying to maintain security in an environment that allowed education classes to succeed. Away from family and friends, the detainees often tested the soldiers ... amusing themselves by saying and doing things in an effort to elicit a response from the guards. One such notable act of defiance occurred in May 2008 when a small radical group of detainees decided to rebel against their compound guards, under claims of being disrespected. The detainees attacked the guards through the fence, spitting on them and throwing containers filled with human feces and urine at them. In this instance, the guards, being predictably very upset, made some regrettable decisions. Allegedly, with the approval of a commanding officer, they beat two of the detainees and sealed eight others in an MDHU cell filled with pepper spray overnight, with the cells ventilation ducts closed. As a result, a total of 13 Navy sailors* were initially accused in the abuse, including one officer whom the enlisted had accused of ordering the actions "to teach the detainees a lesson." Five of the sailors faced a court-martial for their actions. Four were found guilty of abuse and one was acquitted in March 2009. The point, however, is that this example illustrates how sometimes the action of a couple of detainees can have an immediate impact on the entire compound. There were education classes going on at the time when this incident occurred. In such acts, security measures

---

* Multi-National Forces Iraq included personnel from the U.S. Air Force, U.S. Army, U.S. Marines, and U.S. Navy all serving together. In the TIFS, certain compounds were often assigned to one contingent or another.

dictate the immediate cancellation of classes despite the desire of the detainees that were not involved to continue the classes. So, in the end, it was actually the detainees who were motivated and engaged in learning that suffered the most. If we want to take it even one step farther, in this particular incident, the extremists won. They are the only ones who got something they desired: the cessation of education classes for their fellow detained Iraqis and the criminal prosecution of U.S. Navy sailors.

CONCLUSION

According to Sgt. Matthew Sugars (personal interview, 2009), who as a TF-134 OSS military staff liaison helped oversee daily transportation of the local Iraqi civilian nationals to/from the TIF:

> I think all the programs stood out in one way or the other. But, if there was one that stood out the most, I would have to say the Bucca School (Dar al Hikma) was it. There were thousands of detainees going through the program covering a wide range of basic school topics. The feedback and the physical proof we saw from classrooms, students, teachers, and guards are hard to describe in one setting. These detainees went from being hard criminals and depressed nothings to someone with a future and the ability to use what they had learned to better their future and their families. It was something they had never seen, experienced, or even had a chance to partake in outside in their home towns.

Most individuals familiar with the education programs tend to agree with Sgt. Sugars. 1Sgt. Brian D. Emmert,* who was the Compound S2/COIN noncommissioned officer (NCO) from February 2008 to October 2008 at Camp Bucca, elaborates (personal interview, 2009):

> The education programs and the religious studies were by far the most beneficial programs to both the detainees and the coalition forces. Further, I see the future of detainee operations as having detainees long enough to give them a basic education so that they may determine for themselves their future and not rely on an *extremist's* interpretation.

One compound chief from Camp Bucca drove the point home: "Outside of here, I would not have been able to afford these books. Thank you for giving me the opportunity to learn." Accordingly, Col. Anthony Lieto, who on his second tour to Iraq was deputy commander

---

* 1Sgt. Brian D. Emmert retired from the Oklahoma Army National Guard in June 2009, after 22 years of service.

to Maj. Gen. Stone from February 2007 to March 2008, highlights education as one of the two most important rehabilitation programs (personal interview, 2009).

Throughout the TIF education programs in Iraq, many stories resonated of their success. One woman at visitation cried as her son told her about how he was learning to read and write and was learning carpentry. She begged the military to let him finish the program before releasing him, according to Maj. Gen. Quantock. Another detainee, who received his release paperwork 2 weeks before he was to take his final exam, begged to be allowed to stay so that he could graduate first and earn his diploma. He explained to us that he wouldn't have this opportunity outside detention and that he didn't have the money or means to make it happen, related Maj. Gen. Stone. Maj. Gen. Quantock elaborated:

> Of course, education is always the secret weapon. Literacy is critical in Iraq. We have less illiterate detainees now with this current population [2010] than we did before [2004]. When they graduate, they get a certificate from the Ministry of Education and they can actually use the diploma outside the wire. It's extremely beneficial when they can read. We knew this back in 2004 when we tried to start literacy class, that if they could read the Qur'an for themselves, they could interpret it more accurately. If individuals can talk about these things, they may be able to turn a different way.

The intent of any education program is to empower a person to change. With knowledge comes power and confidence, the freedom to pursue dreams, to make positive choices, and ultimately to transform oneself into the person one has dreamed to become. As such, arguably no successful rehabilitation program can exist without education as a necessary component.

CHAPTER 9

Religious Enlightenment

INTRODUCTION

A traditional Iraqi story goes something like this:

> A father intends to give his sons some important advice that will benefit them for the rest of their lives. The father gathers some small sticks and gives each son a stick. When each son has a stick, he tells them to break their stick. In turn, each son breaks their stick. Following this, the father gathers the same amount of sticks and binds them together with a piece of twine. He gave the bundle to his first son and asked him to break it. The first son was unable to and, so, it was passed to the second son until all the sons had an attempt at breaking the bundle. None of the sons was able to break the bundle. The father leaned forward and said, "When you are together nobody can break you, but, if any of you are alone, you can easily be broken."

Putting this into another context, Sheikh Mohammed Abdul Sattar (Sheikh Sattar), one of the top Operational Support and Services (OSS) local Iraqi civilian national clerics in Iraq, stated, "If the Shiites are alone and the Sunnis are alone, we can easily be broken. But, if we are together, then nobody [such as the militias] can break us" (Islamic Discussion Program (IDP), 2007, Nov. 10–13). Sheikh Sattar understood the nature of the Islamic program. Present from the first day of the program at Camp Bucca, all the way through to the closure of Camp Taji in 2010, he was a cleric whose natural insight, humility, and experience made him an invaluable asset. To those who knew him, it was no surprise that he became our top-trusted cleric at Camp Bucca in October 2007 before moving to Camp Taji (with the closure of Camp Bucca in September 2009) and becoming the top cleric there. A large part of the success of the religious program is owed in part to the very active role that Sheik Sattar, along with the other clerics, played. A man of much wisdom, his negative experience under Saddam's regime shaped him into a strong character with a heart full of compassion. It was often that his enlightened references and personal experiences encouraged detainees to open up to the religious education program.

Ideas of empowering religious Imams within U.S. detention centers across Iraq began as early as 2004. According to Maj. Gen. David Quantock, who was stationed at Abu Ghraib at the time, attempts were made to find the Imams inside the detainee population (personal interview, 2010). However, no structured plan was put into motion until mid-2007 with the arrival of Maj. Gen. Douglas Stone who spearheaded the effort. The religious education program began in August 2007 with the official name of Religious Enlightenment Program. The first pilot program consisted of two classes of 3 weeks in length and one class of 6 weeks in length. The 6-week class concluded just as Ramadan started, so the pilot program took a hiatus before reconstructing at Camp Bucca in time for the second pilot program to begin on October 16, 2007. During the break, the aim of the program reorganized to "reach and teach as many detainees as possible" before their release, related Maj. Gen. Stone (personal interview, 2010). This was when the short course, also known as the 4-day course, was designed and, subsequently, implemented. In December 2007, the title was changed to Islamic Enlightenment Program. In January 2008, the title was changed again to Islamic Discussion Program (IDP), and it is this title that remained through to the transfer of authority of all the theater internment facilities (TIFs) in Iraq to the Governmenet of Iraq's control. Undeniably, the IDP program was key to the winning of hearts and minds campaign. Without this program's success, the rest of the detainee rehabilitation effort would have been of little value.

BACKGROUND

The IDP consisted of three distinct programs of instruction. The "4-day IDP" was designed to provide a platform of discussion, with the overall aim of equipping detainees with the knowledge and ability to live life as proud and fruitful Iraqi citizens. The 4-day IDP was aimed at the moderate detainee population and, according to Maj. Gen. Stone, was an introduction to the basic tenets of Islam. As such, it was not considered a "legitimate deradicalization program" in its own right, but rather as a program to prepare detainees for after release. The "3-week IDP" had the same format, but was extended and aimed at those who had already been exposed to radical teachings and/or had already declared their alliance with extremist organizations. The third religious program was the "6-week IDP," which was aimed at the most extreme detainees—those who have been involved with and/or committed terrorist activities and were devoutly extreme in their ideology. The overall objectives of all three IDPs were to increase detainees' understanding of the Qur'an, provide a safe place for discussion and reflection, and, most importantly, prevent the [continued] allure of terrorist activities.

Each IDP program consisted of two components: the cleric component and the social worker component. Social workers also were referred to as counselors or psychologists, but in reality the local Iraqi nationals who worked these programs generally had little qualifications other than a Bachelor of Arts in a subject matter, such as counseling/psychology/sociology/liberal arts. To simplify matters, they will be referred to as *social workers* throughout this chapter.* The social worker component was designed to make the detainees reflect and discuss on topics important to them, to include detention, family, and life values. The other portion of each daily IDP session was the cleric component. The cleric component was designed to pick apart the Qur'an and challenge references that the detainees might have been instructed to follow and/or threaten to uphold, all while strengthening each detainee's understanding of the Qur'an and what it personifies. According to Ken Reidy (personal interview, 2009), as an OSS contracted radical ideology research specialist:†

> Were detainees enlightened to *other* means of interpreting the Qur'an? Almost certainly, but how much of this took place in the rehab programs? Hopefully, and this is how I would judge success, less and less, as more and more detainees moved through the programs and passed on their knowledge to others. Alternatively, many detainees may have had their first real Islamic encounter in the TIF, and it may have been an extremist one. So, in a short period of time, your average Iraqi will have been forced to obey extremist values, will also have had conversations with other Iraqis who will show him point-by-point why those views are wrong and how, if he wants to be a good Muslim, he should go about doing it. Then, as he goes about his daily life in the TIF, he will meet the seculars, the scholars, the homosexuals, the drug addicts, and the criminals, all of whom may be quite religious. Now that's got to be confusing. Hence, an important part of the IDP/RDP was the instilment of critical thinking, and we defined this quite simply: When in doubt, stop and verify. It could be opening up the Qur'an and finding the source of what someone told you; it could be looking back at

---

* In Iraq, it was incredibly difficult to find individuals certified in psychology or social work, as these types of programs were not offered under Saddam's regime. Iraqis would have had to attend school outside of Iraq to earn these degrees, and, unfortunately, most Iraqis who departed their country had no desire to return.

† Ken Reidy was contracted as a Radical Ideology Research Specialist only for about 4 months before the title was scrapped because most detainees were not too religiously informed. He was subsequently contracted as a "subject matter expert (SME) on psychology," although, according to Reidy, he mostly performed in the same capacity as previously.

what is right and what is wrong and choosing not to continue, etc. It also included the recognition that just because someone dressed in a certain way or spoke in a certain way, it doesn't mean that he is what he looks like; don't judge a book by its cover.

The social worker component went in tandem with the cleric component. All IDP programs had 6 hours of discussion a day, with Friday being the only exception. Days were broken down to 3 hours taught by a cleric and 3 hours taught by a social worker. Two 20-minute breaks and an hour for lunch and prayer were also factored in. All clerics and social workers went through intensive training prior to commencing any sessions with detainees. Those who had never worked on a military facility or with foreigners in general were unsure what to expect. Those types of issues were addressed in addition to detailed instruction about what to cover during the IDP sessions. Mock sessions were given to prepare clerics and social workers for classes. A guidebook also was prepared and given to all clerics and social workers to help with discussions, role playing, and activities. Before conducting their own classes, clerics and social workers would sit in active IDP classes as assistants, while a more experienced cleric/social worker would lead the class.

Clerics and social workers were responsible for writing a report about anything of interest that occurred during each IDP course. The report was summarily due at 10 p.m. the day after each 4-day course ended. Local Iraqi nationals were encouraged to recount interesting dialogues, concerns brought up by detainees, and/or any issues they might have had with conducting the class, and it is from these careful and colorful evaluations that the program would evolve to better meet the needs of the detainees.*

Each IDP session optimized the Socratic method: A form of inquiry and debate between individuals with opposing viewpoints based on the asking and answering of questions in order to stimulate critical thinking and illuminate differing ideas. The aim of the class was to make the detainees willing to think for themselves as well as give them the practice of trusting their own views. Besides the Qur'an, which was the principal book used in each class, the Taqrib was also used. The Taqrib was written by the jurist Abu Shuja Isfahani from the Shafti'i(te) School of Islamic Jurisprudence (d. 1197 C.E.). It is full of Qur'anic references, explanations, and clarifications (on *fiqh*, jurisprudence in Islam based on

---

* It is also from these evaluations that most of the personal experiences listed in this chapter were gathered. Detainee names have intentionally been left out for confidentiality and security reasons. Because of this, most references to detainees have simply been listed as "detainee" with the date of the IDP session from which the information was recorded.

the school of law founded on the opinion of the *faqih*,* Shafi'i. However, the Taqrib does not cover the Islamic creed (*aqida*) or ethics (*akhlaq*). It was most commonly known and referenced within the IDP as "Abu Shuja." It was chosen as a supplementary tool in the religious discussion classes because it was the recommended and favored book amongst the OSS-hired local Iraqi national clerics in teaching the Qur'an. In addition to the Abu Shuja, hadiths were regularly used in classes. Hadiths are narrations originating from the words and deeds of the Islamic prophet Muhammad, and are regarded by traditional schools of jurisprudence as important tools for understanding the Qur'an and in matters of jurisprudence for three reasons. Firstly, the hadith may consist of rules that merely confirm and reiterate the Qur'an, in which case, the rules concerned originate in the Qur'an and are merely corroborated by the hadith. Secondly, the hadith may consist of an explanation or clarification to the Qur'an; it may clarify the ambivalent (*mujmal*) of the Qur'an, qualify its absolute statements, or specify the general terms of the Qur'an. Thirdly, the Sunnah may consist of rulings on which the Qur'an is silent, in which case, the ruling in question originates in the Sunnah itself. Finally, other than these three collections (the Qur'an, the Abu Shuja, and the Hadiths), all of which were made available to detainees participating in the courses, Sheik Sattar would sometimes ask for copies to be made of other relevant articles, poetry, or verses for distribution in the program.

GROWING PAINS

The detainee rehabilitation pilot program for TF-134 took place in July 2007 at Camp Bucca. The intent of the program was to "develop the foundational framework of a detainee rehabilitation program, which will later be integrated into a wider theater information operations program." According to a TF-134 briefing, the desired effect of the programs on detainees was as follows:

> The treatment will deter the detainees from participating in or associating with those that are committed to violence, militant jihad, sectarianism, or other destructive behaviors. Facilitate the release and reintegration of militant, moderate, and juvenile detainees back into a still conflict-torn society. Detainees gain a sense of dignity, self-worth, a life purpose, and commitment to nonviolent tolerance (Maj. Gen D. Stone, personal communication, 2010).

---

* Faqih (plural fuqaha): legist [a specialist in law], jurisprudent, expert of fiqh or a person learned in the knowledge of fiqh who by virtue of his/her knowledge can give a legal judgment.

The pilot program included two 3-week programs and one 6-week program, aimed at the most ideologically extreme population. The first 3-week program began on July 15, 2007, while the 6-week program began on July 17, 2007. Each of the three classes had 10 detainees. Each of the 3-week classes ran simultaneously with the 6-week program window, one after another. All of them provided the resources and reasoning enough to challenge the most radical of extremists. The 6-week program was officially titled Militant Jihadi Redirect Program, and included exploring/debating topics such as: "political violence as a worthy and effective strategy," "exploring Qur'anic sources for and against militant jihad," and "the understanding of Daulah Islamiyah (Islamic State)." The 3-week program, officially entitled Psych-Lite by Dr. Ann Speckhard, was initially designed for detainees not related to the militant jihad and covered areas, such as: "humiliation, pride, and human dignity," "religion as a positive force for life direction," and "plan for the future—self, community, and country," in addition to many others. The optimistic end goals for both programs were that [detainees]

1. No longer believe that a militant jihad against coalition forces and the government of Iraq is sanctioned by Islam.
2. No longer believe in using Takfir as basis for legitimizing killing of fellow Muslims.
3. Has forsaken the militant jihadist ideology.
4. Has formed a clear articulation and commitment to a nonviolent form and expression of Islam.
5. Has taken significant steps to recognize and address the psychological vulnerabilities that led him/her to take on the militant jihadist ideology.
6. Has recognized and begun to work through the traumatic stress endured during arrest.
7. Among many others.

Yet, unfortunately, early on there were problems with the three central clerics hired to lead the clerical portion of IDP. They were a group referred to as the "Trio." and they were prior U.S. detainees who had been convinced into returning as civilian clerics for the program, once their paperwork was finalized for release. With promises of grandeur, the three were released, took a short break to visit their families, and then quickly returned to the TIF to work the IDP programs. However, the trio proved problematic to both OSS and the military. They refused to share what they were teaching in the classes and were upset that materials they wanted for instruction were not being provided fast enough. A couple other clinchers, including not being granted a longer vacation period and not being respected like they felt they should be, enhanced their frustration. Their favored psychologist, who was on staff with OSS at the time, was dismissed, and that was the "nail in the coffin for them," said Reidy (personal interview, 2010). They went on strike before the first pilot program was completed; bringing the programs to a halt as nobody was in a position to continue them. Fortunately, Sheik Sattar, who was also on staff during this trying phase, stepped up to the challenge and juggled the classes through to completion. However, as he was only one individual trying to conduct two classes, the classes had to be staggered, which proved challenging for the military who then also had to juggle meal times, movement times, etc. But in the end, it worked.

The 6-week pilot program concluded on August 24, 2007, and the second 3-week pilot program concluded on August 25, 2007. At that point, Ramadan was near, encouraging OSS management to give the employed local Iraqi nationals a 2-week paid vacation while the pilot programs were reevaluated and rewritten. The OSS management team returned to Camp Victory, and Reidy, with the munificent help of two Iraqi local national civilian clerics, went about writing the Islamic portion of the programs based on events that had been garnered from the pilot run at Camp Bucca. He related:

> Abdul Sattar and this other cleric [Sheikh Emad] hashed out the clerical side through my questions. I asked them specific questions; they answered, and we wrote the Islamic programs. I remember that pretty significant changes were made on the Islamic side. In fact, there were other Islamic programs we had that we didn't use. One had to be created specifically for the Iraqi population.

Reidy also spent a great amount of time working alongside Khapta,* another OSS employee who was dedicated to ensuring the social worker component of the programs was sound.

> So when we got back to Baghdad, Khapta* and I re-did some of the stuff to better reflect the reality on the ground. Compound 6 had become a little different than the rest, and word was spreading through the TIF. The detainees had found the experience engaging, fun, but also bizarre. We had to scrap a part of the program where Socials like Abu Haji* [an Iraqi civilian local national] would read a story, and the detainees were meant to close their eyes and imagine themselves at home or whatever. It just became a big laughing fest because Abu Haji* was so funny. Other socials were boring. Dr. Ali was great at it. But I can remember looking into one of the caravans and the detainees are hiding their faces so as not to look at Abu Haji*

---

* An asterisk (*) is used throughout this book to protect the security and confidentiality of certain individuals whose lives might be threatened otherwise.

prancing up and down the room pretending to be a "freedom bird."
Very funny.

"Freedom bird" was meant to be an exercise in meditation where
the detainees can, in their mind, go home and remember or even relive
being at home, noticing all the small details and generally get a feel
good sensation. However, not everyone is cut out to properly read the
script for the desired effect. Some local nationals (LNs) would read
it in a monotone and nonengaging fashion (copying the background
noise of the air conditioners), whereas others made it into a drama.
According to Reidy:

> Haji Abu Haji* would prance around the room with the vigor of a 6
> year old, arms flailing in an attempt at flight. He resembled what could
> only be described as a possessed octopus. Detainees would be on their
> sides laughing, trying in vain not to look at him and hide their faces
> so Haji wouldn't see them. This wasn't meditation, this was uninten-
> tional stand-up comedy. Sure, they loved it and they loved him, but it
> simply wasn't fulfilling what we needed.

Armed with new programs of instruction for both the clerical and
social worker components of the 3- and 6-week IDPs, a new OSS management staff, and more local nationals, we returned to Camp Bucca in
a motivated effort to implement the new curriculum changes. Yet, no
sooner had we arrived, than the IDP mission focus shifted. What was
realized was that while focus was being paid on rehabilitating the more
radical detainees, moderate detainees were being recruited into extremist networks while in detention. In addition, with the longer and more
concentrated classes (i.e., less detainees per class), there was little possibility that there would be time or resources enough to employ the many
clerics and social workers it would take to ensure the program would be
a success for the greater majority of detainees. For these reasons, as well
as others, Maj. Gen. Stone decided to strategically concentrate on implementing and excelling at a concentrated 4-day IDP program targeted at
the moderate detainee population.

Unfortunately, this transition was not easy for some. There was
a lot of confusion among guards, civilians, and detainees when the
religious programs began again. To counter the misinformation, two
one-page documents were created in October and November 2007.
One document, written in October, was for guards working with
the detainee population to address detainee questions about the program. At that time, we did not have Arabic printing capability in our
(new) office, so the rough translation into Arabic was handwritten by
Sheik Sattar (Figure 9.1). This document was followed by another in

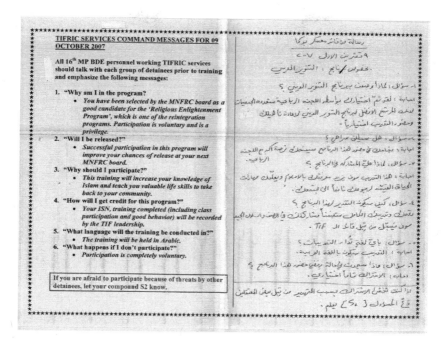

FIGURE 9.1   A one-page document, written for both guards and detainees, that addressed major questions on the purpose and scope of the TIFRC programs: Camp Bucca, 2007.

November 2007, as some guards maintaining oversight during the programs did not seem to understand the purpose of the programs nor the purpose of the locally hired Iraqi nationals coming in to conduct the programs (Figure 9.2).

Undeniably, these simple documents made a difference, as guards finally had something tangible that they could read about the programs, essentially countering misinformation and misunderstanding. But what really sealed the communication gap between the guard force and the intent of programs was when Col. James Brown, then-Camp Bucca commander, decided to hold a dinner to which individuals involved with the rehab programs—officers, guards, OSS management, and OSS local Iraqi nationals—were all invited. The dinner was such a hit that it became a monthly event, and grew to include dancing (Iraqi), music (Iraqi and even live music from a Tennessee unit), local Iraqi cuisine, and much chatting. Local Iraqi nationals would sit at tables mixed with the military, and through translators be encouraged to engage in conversation with each other. It was important, yet simple, moments like these

The Religious Enlightenment Program

The Theatre Internment Facility Re-Integration Center (TIFRIC) is part of an overall strategy by the U.S. government and Department of Defense to find a positive way to release back into society Iraqi security detainees currently being held in U.S. custody, in Iraq, with confidence that they will not become repeat offenders.

This commences in phase one with the **Religious Enlightenment Program (REP)**.

The detainee is then moved to phase two of TIFRIC–educating him to read and write in Arabic, and teaching him the basics of arithmetic and civics; onto phase three–a vocational education program imparting a skill that ensures the detainee is employable upon release; and finalizing with phase four–Possible release back into society.

- The REP will have vetted, moderate Imams and trained Behavioral Scientists work with small groups of detainees to engage them in religious discussions to enlighten them to a moderate interpretation of Islam as opposed to that of extremists

- As professionals, these Imams and Behavioral Scientists should be accorded every courtesy and respect that would be due clergymen and psychologists in Western culture... these gentlemen are our best weapon against the extremists, so treat them accordingly

- The program will commence with 4-day programs working with groups of moderate Sunnis and will sometimes conduct 6- and 3-week programs with other groups

FIGURE 9.2   A one-page document, written for guards, who are maintaining security during TIFRC programs, to understand the process that they are part of: Camp Bucca, 2007.

that finally broke down the barriers to trust and mutual respect between the employed local Iraqi nationals, civilians, and the U.S. military.*

FOUR-DAY PROGRAM

The "short program," also known as the "4-day program," was designed in an attempt to introduce the Qur'an to the widespread detainee population in a direct effort to address and reduce the probability of extremism while in confinement. To make the greatest impact on the greatest

---

* Unfortunately, these dinners at Camp Bucca ceased to take place after the arrival of new OSS leadership (for Camp Bucca) in August 2008, who never having been to one, did not deem them necessary, and, thus, felt no need to encourage new units to continue the tradition.

number, the program was designed to apply to the greater majority of those who were detained. Detainees selected for the 4-day program were already meant to practice a moderate version of Islam. Yet, this is not meant to imply that there is one clear-cut version of moderate Islam. Detainees often differed on their perception of moderate Islam through various means, which might include sect (Shi'a or Sunni), religious orientation (on a few, yet significant number of occasions, the 4-day program had detainees who are Kurdish; although Kurds are an indigenous ethnic minority, they endorse numerous belief systems, most of which do, however, overlap with Islamic principles), and place of origin (detainees from major cities tend to be more pious and educated in comparison to those from the countryside, who often are more tribal and less educated in nature). Hence, especially in the clerical part of the program, tailored approaches (teaching Islam on a strong religious line versus Islam as a cultural identity and peaceful means of living) had to be made depending on the sect, ethnicity, and origin of the detainees present in the session, according to Reidy. It was up to the cleric and social worker to find the right balance with which to engage and encourage the detainees.

Typically, 15 to 20 detainees were hand-selected (by the military) for the 4-day program per cleric–social worker team, with generally anywhere from 5 to 10 teams running simultaneously. The first day of the 4-day pilot program was October 16, 2007, and it was started with just three teams. However, by the summer of 2008, there were as many as 12 teams running simultaneously just at Camp Bucca. The program has been conducted in a variety of locations; but, by far, the best outcomes have been when the program took place in a secluded area. At Camp Bucca, this meant compound 6. Compound 6 had 14 caravans separated by fences. Detainees brought all personal effects, including their sleeping mats, sheets, and clothes when they were transferred from their compound to a caravan for IDP class (Figure 9.3).

Detainees who volunteered to participate in the 4-day program stayed in their newly assigned caravan during the entire course. Out of sight and hearing of detainees who might cause trouble for the participants, all were encouraged to participate fully. Each individual caravan of detainees, most of whom had not met previously, would attend class together, sleep together, pray together, and eat together. The local Iraqi civilian instructors would often join caravans for an evening visit and/or even meals. Some officers, such as Maj. Ricky Shawyer from Camp Bucca, while building rapport with the detainees participating in the IDP, provided snacks, soccer balls, or even newspapers/journals (*National Geographic* was their favorite) for them to read. Compound 6 also had a library; detainees were encouraged to check out and read books when so inclined. To make the caravans more attractive and

FIGURE 9.3   Islamic Discussion Program: Camp Bucca, Iraq, 2008. (Photo by Maj. (Ret.) Guy L. Jester.)

comfortable, paintings created by the detainee art program were hung up on the walls as decorations. To many, this was a little retreat—a home away from home—essentially an escape from the daily monotony of the average compound. That is what made it even more relevant that the detainees view participation as voluntary, rather than mandatory. It was a reward to be able to participate. In 2007 and 2008, with large numbers of detainees, the waiting list for participation was always high. Therefore, we could afford to maintain that standard. Obviously, as the detainee numbers started dwindling by late 2009 with the turnover of the TIF facilities to Iraqi control, so, too, started the dwindling of the waiting list.

Clerics in the 4-day program taught for 3 hours a day (Figure 9.4). Then a break was generally taken before the social worker would come in and teach for another 3 hours a day. Once a cleric and social worker were assigned to a particular group of detainees, they would stay with them throughout the duration of the 4-day program. While there was some amount of flexibility based on the group of detainee backgrounds and daily motivation, each day focused on a particular theme. At Camp Bucca alone, an average of 100 detainees participated in the 4-day IDP weekly. And, in fact, after some initial rough beginnings, most IDP classes began to combine both Shi'a and Sunni into each caravan. The

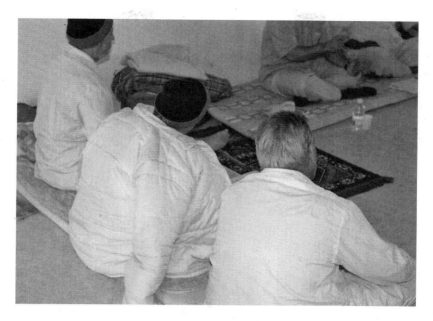

FIGURE 9.4 Detainees sit in a circle during the Islamic Discussion Program: Camp Bucca, Iraq, 2009. (Photo courtesy of U.S. Department of Defense.)

first combined Sunni/Shi'a class took place on November 4, 2007, amid much hesitation from the military. Many voiced disapproval, suggesting that the classes were going to end in violence. Interestingly, the greatest supporters of the combined classes were the detainees themselves and the local civilian Iraqi nationals who taught them. Fortunately, through the support of Col. Brown, a class was conducted successfully, and, thus far, not one act of violence has been documented as having occurred during an IDP combined sect class session. In fact, the initial combined classes worked so well that every attempt was made in following classes to do the same.

Day One

The first day of the 4-day program was probably the most important, as this was the day detainees would meet each other and meet the instructors. Movement of the detainees to their new compound occurred early on the first morning. Occasionally, movement issues caused delays on the first day. Likewise, misinformation could create issues on day 1, i.e., on a couple of occasions, we received detainees who were not told where they were being moved. Some groups were exuberantly happy when they found out they were being moved to participate in the program. However, we also had other groups who were bitter because they thought they were being moved for release.

Similar to most programs, the first thing to occur on day 1 was introductions between the instructors and detainees. Detainees were encouraged to say as little or as much as they preferred about themselves. Likewise, each cleric/social worker introduced himself and provided some background. After introductions, the signing of contracts would commence. The class contract at Camp Bucca included compound 6 rules in addition to the rules of participating in the IDP. The required physical signature of the detainee helped the detainee understand that each class was being taken seriously. Further, the contract detailed that the detainee was participating of his own free will and that nobody had coerced him into participating. It also highlighted that participation in the class would not guarantee release. All of these factors were important in gaining trust and maintaining transparency. Lastly, it outlined that at any point in time, if the detainee no longer wished to participate, he could request to return to his compound. Any detainee unwilling to sign the contract was automatically returned to his compound.

Cleric Component

The clerical portion of day 1 dealt with the topic of *prayer* or *salat*. Prescribed prayer is either obligatory (*wajib*) or supererogatory (*mandub*). The most important of prayers are the prescribed prayers performed five times daily. These prescribed prayers are among the "pillars" (*arkan*) of Islam. The goals desired were two-fold:

- Defining prayer and explaining the rules of prayer with a focus on the conditions of prayer being accepted by God.
  - Circumstances and events that lead to a prayer being rejected by God.
- Explaining the foundations of prayer in terms of the reasons behind praying. The session was presented as a means with which to understand prayer as something far more than merely a series of movements.
- Understanding the benefits of prayer in terms of the "bigger picture" within which it operates in one's life and how prayer can be used as a vehicle with which to show exact and good behavior as a lasting habit.

To this end, detainees were taught how to pray, and the topic of prayer was elaborated with discussion surrounding the shape of prayer. Extremists mainly pay attention only to the shape of prayer (where you should put your feet, how to hold your hands, etc.) rather than to all the integrals of prescribed prayer. Detainees were taught the preconditions for validly performing the prayer to include:

a. That one must not be in a state of minor or major ritual impurity.
b. That one removes all filth (*najasa*) from one's body, cloth, and place of prayer.
c. That one clothes one's nakedness (*aurat*).
d. That one knows or believes a prayer's time has come.
e. That one faces the direction of the Kaaba in Mecca.

According to Ustaz Mahfuh Bin Haji Halimi (personal interview, 2010), when performing the prescribed prayer, the "works of the heart" are the soul of the prayer, without which its outward form would be but empty words and motions. One's sole aim should be Allah Himself, offering the worship that is due to Him out of love and thanks. The prayer also should be performed with the humility and presence of mind befitting his relation to the nature of the Divine. When performing the prescribed prayer, the *arkanul salat* (the obligatory integrals of prayer that are the legally essential elements) must be fulfilled so as not to invalidate the prayer. The integrals of prayer include:

a. The intention
b. Standing
c. The opening *Allahu Akbar* (which must be pronounced, like all spoken integrals, correctly and without lengthy pause in between)
d. Reciting Al-Fatehah (the first chapter of the Qur'an)
e. Bowing (*rukuk*)
f. Straightening back up (*i'tidal*)
g. Prostrating twice (*sujud*) and sitting back between them
h. Reposing a moment in all physical postures of the prayer (*thuma'ninah*)
i. The final Testification of Faith (*tashahhud akhir*), sitting therein and saying the Blessings of the Prophet (*shalawat*) after it
j. The first of the two *Salams* that end the prayer
k. Observing the correct order of the above (M. B. H. Halimi, 2010).

Although they may appear to be the outer form, nevertheless, omitting them willfully will invalidate the prayer. These in *fiqh* are known as the *arkanul salat* (the obligatory integrals of prayer that are the legally essential elements), and must be observed together with the "*khusyu*."

Khusyu is feeling the presence of God (also means submissiveness, submission, humility).

Detainees are taught that fulfilling all the integrals of prescribed prayer in addition to observing *khusyu* is equally important when praying. While the extremist focus is on only one small aspect of prayer, that of the body, the moderate focus is on the personal and intimate connection between the prayer and God (LN cleric S. A. Sattar, personal communication, 2007). In a class from November 4 to 7, 2007, a detainee brought up a personal experience. "I was standing for prayer in Baghdad airport with other detainees. Someone said to me, 'Your clothes are so long, you must make them short.'"* Sheikh Sattar asked the detainee, "What does this mean to you?" He answered, "These extremists are only concerned with one's appearance and shape of prayer, but their hearts are empty." Later, on the same occasion, Sheikh Sattar told the detainees a story about a famous scholar. A person asked this famous scholar, "What should I wear when I pray?" He answered, "First wear your heart correctly, and then your body will follow."

According to Sheik Sattar, most detainees knew little about prayer beyond the basic movements. Also, most detainees prayed out of social habit. For example, some detainees said that their father would pray, and so they followed. Many learned how to pray in the TIFs from other detainees. Others confessed to not praying at all outside of the TIF. By watching the detainees pray, religiosity could sometimes be confirmed; in Iraq, extremists often hold their hands high toward their neck and angle their feet inward while praying. In addition to watching detainees pray, local Iraqi civilian clerics would also pay attention to a detainee's answers to particular questions. For example:

Iraqi civilian clerics: What do you think about the Shi'a?
Moderate answer: We are all Muslims with the same Qur'an and the same direction towards the Kabba.
Extremist answer: They are kafir (disbeliever).
Iraqi civilian clerics: What do you say about dealing with the Americans?
Moderate answer: It's up to you. It's a personal choice.
Extremist answer: Any dealings with the Americans make you kufr (rejection of truth).

Hopes of release and fearing for one's safety appeared to be the main motivation behind participating in group prayer inside the TIFs. Sheikh Sattar suggested that as soon as detainees are released, many

---

* Extremists usually demand that one's trousers are above the ankle; 3 inches below the knee is considered the premium length for extremists.

most likely will no longer pray; he emphasized this is quite normal in Iraqi jails/internment facilities.

Social Worker Component

Day 1 of the social worker portion is entitled Resilience to Religious-Based Extreme Ideology. The goal of this class is to distinguish religion from ideology through directed questions and answers. The social worker achieves this by having discussions on various topics, such as psychological contagion, the positive and negative points of group membership, group identity, the end goal of a religiously affiliated ideology compared with that of a pure religion, and the persuasion techniques that such groups employ in order to gain active members and supporters. The end objective of this session, and the 4-day program as a whole, is to instill critical thinking as the key to resilience so the detainees can (1) spread this knowledge and (2) protect themselves by being aware of the ideological groups' end objectives.

To this end, there are many question/answers posed in class, such as, "What is religion?" and "Why do ideological groups have so many followers?" and even "What techniques do ideological groups use to get followers?" By posing these questions and then encouraging the detainees to discuss possible reasons/scenarios, the topic could be explored in depth. Religion was discussed as following guidance, raising awareness, following religious teachings, obeying one's parents, understanding the constitution of Islam, being merciful with one another, calling for peace, and being forgiving. One detainee shared, "Religion can't be forced on somebody. I can't force you to pray or to fast; all I can do is advise you; the rest is up to you." Another detainee said, "I was unaware of a lot of things religious, but after entering here I began to believe in God. ... When I was outside, I was lost; I didn't know what to do. Now I know a lot and can choose the right path for my life" (IDP, 2008, March 9–12).

Ideologies were understood as entities that could tarnish religion. A detainee said, "There are some people who have a religious background and yet these [negative] ideologies enter through religious belief (a religious person using Islam as a vehicle to spread his own ideology)." Another detainee shared this:

> In 2005, Sunnis and Shiite would pray together. But, by the end of the year, Arabs from foreign countries began coming to the center of Iraq and they called for sectarianism; they demanded separation between Kurds, Muslims, and Christians. On the streets [of Iraq] they would cause problems between the Sunni and Shi'a and so they started killing each other (IDP, 2008).

Another detainee elaborated:

> They [extremists] made us hate religion and anything tied to it. They make us believe that whatever is forbidden is not forbidden anymore and vice versa. Truth is false and falsity is true; so, now we are confusing religious beliefs and teachings with facets that are not religious. We allowed these ideologies to seep through to our country through religion because we already had weak religious knowledge (IDP, 2008).

Social workers asked how these ideologies get transferred. Detainees said, "People adopt them because they are illiterate, poor, and lack religious knowledge. They may also need money, have weak spirits, and have weak personalities (hence, they are easy to control)." Social workers asked detainees what the characteristics are of people who transfer negative ideologies; some responses included:

> He will have lots of religious knowledge. He will also have a financer, a strong means of talking and a strong personality. He will be a powerful man and will always give reasons behind what he says [we must do X because of Y].

The social worker then asked what the goals of the extremist group are: "Their aim is to establish an Islamic country, kick the Americans out, spread the hate between people with the aim to make the social situation better" (IDP, 2008, April 6–11). Finally, social workers asked how these groups can be defeated. A detainee shared the following:

> People should be made aware of true religious meaning, and this education should be given to all people of the country. There is also a need to establish laws, which punish those who follow these ideologies as well as create jobs so people would have money and would not pursue illegal activities for financial gain (IDP, 2007, December 4–8).

During IDP class sessions, detainees were encouraged and often spoke openly about extremists:

- From the first day I entered Camp Bucca, the Americans put me in a Takfiri compound even though I'm Shi'a. They would call me *Kafir* and say that I don't believe in Islam and that my mother is a *zania* (adulteress/whore). They told me I had to ask for forgiveness and do the *shahada* again so I could enter Islam (IDP, 2007, December 12-16).
- "There's a Shi'a ideological ruling: If you kill ten Sunnis you enter heaven" (IDP, 2008, February 9–12).

- "The Takfiri's told me, 'If you were married during Saddam's regime, your marriage is illegal and your wife is *zania* as the government itself was illegal'" (IDP, 2008, February 9–12).
- "I remember an Imam in our mosque said to us during Jumaa (Friday prayer): 'Before you buy your TVs and other desires, you must buy a weapon so you can kill a Sunni. Do it before he kills you" (IDP, 2008, June 8–11).

Eliciting personal experiences is an important part of the social worker component of IDP, as it allows detainees to question what they have been told in addition to releasing suppressed emotions and/or anger. In a session on November 10 to 13, 2007, a detainee expressed anger and disappointment for the election 2 years previously. He explained what he understood as the first big victory for ideologies:

> Before the election, ideologies had already divided the Sunni, Shi'a, and the Kurds with the overall aim of dividing Iraq. But voting [the election] was the first step to officially dividing Iraq because on the voting billets the parties were divided by Sunni, Shi'a, and Kurdish, and people voted along these lines due to the ideological influence on society. This was the first flame for the war in Iraq. Why did they do this?

During the first day, social workers might also ask the detainees how ideological groups found resonance in Iraq. One detainee stated: "There are several ways: media, newspapers, religious figures, propaganda, by using the financial situation of individuals and threat." Another detainee said that the groups use teenagers because they still can't differentiate between right and wrong. He suggested they also choose boys who have certain issues with their families or who had been raised to be undisciplined. Or even that some of them were taught the wrong teachings of the Qur'an. One detainee gave a specific example of recruitment:

> A few of the Shi'a religious figures used "the mosque incident" [when Sunni extremists blew up Shi'a mosques] to blow up the Sunni mosques. These same figures also encouraged the Shi'a people to avenge for other instances as well. The people who follow them are those who have little or no religious education. They are illiterate and some are criminals (IDP, 2007, October 9–12).

A detainee added, "They [extremists] do this for personal goals. They try to gather the largest amount of people around the person who came up with that ideology, and then he makes them believe certain ideas." Another detainee agreed: "There are some religious figures who promised to fix social problems like water, power, but they lied to the people. They never fixed anything." A third detainee in the class added: "Most people are grateful to any person who attempts to solve their social problems like way of living, water, power, etc." He continued, "Like what the Americans did when they released some detainees, and the way they help them with medications and treatment." To nods of agreement from his classmates, another detainee summed up:

> Religion doesn't change the way people think, it just makes you closer to God. But [radical] ideologies permit people to kill or blow themselves up and also they make people believe that these suicide bombers will be awarded heaven. And that is just not true (IDP, 2007, October 20–23).

Day Two

Cleric Component

The clerical portion of day 2 dealt with the topic of *offenses*. This included informing the detainees what the Islamic position on killing is, regardless of one's intention. It also aimed to strengthen the detainee's mindset away from radical ideologies by teaching him to never follow those who use religion as a mask. The intended aims of day 2 included:

- Informing the detainees of the types of killing and their corresponding punishments
    - In this part of the session, killing will be highlighted as a dangerous endeavor not only for its punishment on Earth, but in the hereafter as well.
- Explaining the benefits of knowing what constitutes an offense and how it should be punished.
- Discussing the very topical issue, "Can a killer repent?"
- Informing the detainees that the human is a highly valued being as he is created by God's hands so nobody has the right to "destroy this building." [An Iraqi saying. Explanation: God, like a mason, created the human being so only he has the right to "destroy" his creation.]

In a class on October 21, 2007, detainees voiced the assumption that if anyone killed another by mistake, that God would forgive him. The detainees understood that if a person wanted to martyr himself/herself by performing a suicide attack, but killed 20 civilians in the process, that it would be understood as killing by mistake, and he/she would be forgiven. Unfortunately for those who believed this, the cleric had to point out that according to the Qur'an, there are big punishments in Islam for killing ... even by mistake. The detainees had gained their misunderstanding of this term, mostly through conversational means with other Iraqis. Hence, as often seemed to be the case in rural communities, it was street wisdom rather than a particular individual spreading faulty Islamic knowledge that contributed to this widely accepted misunderstanding. Fortunately, clerics were prepared to use Qur'anic reference and hadiths to illustrate that this was untrue, according to Sattar.

As on each day of the 4-day program, hadiths are utilized to emphasize points. On day 2, the hadith used was "God forgives everything to the martyr except the debt." Debt was explained in terms larger than financial. If a person kills innocent people while performing a suicide attack, then these people are the martyr's debt, and God will ask about these innocent deaths in the hereafter. This was backed up with another hadith, "In the hereafter, some people will come and they have a very big amount of merits, but their problem is that they killed or stole so God will take from his merits and give to those he wronged against." The prophet called these people "those with empty pockets," as in pockets without merits. Day 2 usually concluded with the following question: "Is there any connection between accidentally killing and being forgiven by God?" Detainees learn that undoubtedly, the greatest crime known to society is *qatl,* or the taking away of the life of another man. It is a crime denounced time and again by the Qur'an:

> And do not take any human being's life—[the life] which God has willed to be, sacred—otherwise than in [the pursuit of] justice. Hence, if anyone has been slain wrongfully, we have empowered the defender of his rights [to exact a just retribution]; but, even so, let him not exceed the bounds of equity in [retributive] killing. [And as for him who has been slain wrongfully], behold, he is indeed succored [by God] (Qur'an, 17:33).

Further:

> And who never invokes any [imaginary] deity side by side with God, and does not take any human being's life—[the life] which God has willed to be sacred—otherwise than in [the pursuit of] justice, and does not commit adultery. And [know that] he who commits aught thereof shall [not only] meet with a full requital Qur'an, [but] shall have his suffering doubled on Resurrection Day: For on that [Day] he shall abide in ignominy (Qur'an, 25: 68–69).

In addition, the punishment of murder as prescribed in the Qur'an is also addressed:

> O YOU who have attained to faith! Just retribution is ordained for you in cases of killing: the free for the free, and the slave for the slave, and the woman for the woman. And if something [of his guilt] is remitted to a guilty person by his brother, this [remission] shall be adhered to with fairness, and restitution to his fellow-man shall be made in a godly manner. This is an alleviation from your Sustainer, and an act of His grace. And for him who, none the less, willfully transgresses the bounds of what is right, there is grievous suffering in store: for, in [the law of] just retribution, O you, who are endowed with insight, there is life for you, so that you might remain conscious of God. (Qur'an, 2: 178–179).

By the end of day 2, detainees should clearly understand that killing never equates to forgiveness by God, related Sattar.

Social Worker Component

The topic of day 2 for the social worker portion is "self-sacrifice, martyrdom, and resilience against revenge." Detainees, by means of discourse through directed questions, learn to differentiate between martyrdom (sacrificing oneself *for a principle or a cause*) and self-sacrifice (sacrificing oneself or something of great personal value *for the good of others*). In Islam, these two principles are analogous as a person who dies through sacrifice or martyrdom may be distinguished as a martyr. However, they are separated here to identify good means of becoming a martyr, such as religion or family, from false means, such as a militant ideology. This session functions as a continuation of the previous session on ideology (as detainees are now able to distinguish between religion and ideology) where detainees learn to apply their knowledge and experience of ideology to the religious framing techniques of "martyrdom" as used by the extremists. The discussion is then taken to the cycle of violence created by sectarian-fueled (martyrdom) operations under the overarching theme of revenge and retribution as a means for achieving (a false state of) justice. Social workers facilitate the detainees to conclude that true justice is superior to being injurious or vengeful in nature, as it operates within a larger system that aims to be as reasonable and responsible as possible.

Throughout day 2, questions such as:

> "What does self-sacrifice mean to you and how would you define it?"

"What does martyrdom mean for you, and how would you define it?"
"Did you ever wish to sacrifice yourself?"
"What are the rules of revenge in your traditions?"

among others, are posed to the detainees. In most sessions, detainees were eager to brainstorm and share; the following were some varied responses shared on the subject of personal sacrifice:

"I was engaged to a girl, and I really wanted to marry her. However, there was a conflict between my tribe and hers, and so we called off the marriage. We sacrificed each other for our families and tribe."
"I am a farmer and I gave my neighbor, who's also a farmer, my water spraying machine as he couldn't afford one."
"I once found an injured person who had just been in a car crash. He needed medical attention, but we were in a rural area so I drove him to the hospital. He lost consciousness on the way there, but the doctors were able to save him. It cost me one million dinars."
"In 1975, I was a young student. My father became very ill and was unable to work anymore, so I quit university to earn money and help my family. I sacrificed myself for my family, so my younger brothers were able to go to university."
"My father died and my mother was very young. She put her whole life into us [her children] and refused to remarry. She worked day and night for us, and even to this day she still sacrifices herself for us."
"It was a very dangerous time during the Iraqi elections. Many people and groups had threatened everyone not to participate. Despite this, I went with my family to vote."
"I've donated blood numerous times" (IDP, 2007, November 14–18).

In this session, detainees concluded that should one sacrifice himself/herself for another person, he/she should not expect anything in return; and anyone who would not sacrifice money would never sacrifice his/her soul. They also concluded that sacrifice should be for a humane cause and done for God, country, family, and justice with the aim of living peacefully (IDP, 2007, November 14–18). During a February 2008 session, a detainee shared a heartfelt personal account of his experience with self-sacrifice:

Previously I was an officer in the old Iraqi army. I had a soldier who worked for me and he was my staff sergeant. One day I was shopping in *sinac* [a trading area in Baghdad] and the interior forces came and arrested many people without reasonable cause. I was one of these people. Those who arrested us took us to Sadr city, and inside there they separated us according to our sect. I was placed with the Sunnis; they knew my sect from my id. Next they took the Sunnis to the end of Sadr city [a place called *al sedeh*. This area is an open area, and it is used for killing people]. They hang a lot of people there. A man approached me as it was my turn to be hanged. He recognized me; it was my former staff sergeant. I couldn't believe it; he wore the rank of Colonel. He said, "Sir," like he used to say it to me, "just lie down and pretend you are dead." I did as he said and after all the killing, they all left. After that, I went back to my house very thankful.

After discussing sacrifice, detainees are then encouraged to brainstorm the difference between sacrifice and martyrdom. On the topic of martyrdom, many detainees had varying opinions. In a November 10–13, 2007, session, a detainee stated, "If anyone asks to God to be a martyr, then God will grant it to them. Even if that person is on his death bed, he is allowed to be a martyr." In other words, should anyone desire to be a martyr, then it is only for God to decide. Another detainee provided an interesting perspective to the question, "Would you want to be a martyr?"

> Before being detained, I would have said yes without a doubt. But being in Bucca has taught me a lot. I've learned lots about Islam in particular and understand that for a person to be a martyr, he has to follow certain steps. Thank God I was able to learn here. Coming to Bucca saved my life (IDP, 2007, November 10–13).

Other detainees stated they had never thought about becoming a martyr. One detainee speaking for a few others in a caravan said, "We never thought about being martyrs. We have goals and want to finish our education. My life is too valuable" (IDP, 2007. November 10–13).

After distinguishing martyrdom from sacrifice, day 2 discussions turned to the subject of revenge. Social workers would introduce the topic of revenge and ask detainees what they thought about it. Most detainees agreed that revenge in Iraq seemed to be mostly in the form of killing and torturing. In light of this reference, a detainee shared his story:

> I used to live in al-Zweiba [a Sunni district], which is close to al-Shalla [a Shiite district]. The Shi'as from al-Shalla used to kidnap Sunni children from al-Zweiba and kill them. They were paid $6,000 per body. Following this, the bodies were then hung from al-Maria Bridge, and anyone who attempted to cut the bodies down would be killed (IDP, 2008, March 4–8).

Another detainee contributed, "My cousin was married for 4 years, but was unable to have children with his wife, so he married another woman. His first wife asked her brothers to kill him because she wasn't happy. So, they killed him and his second wife" (IDP, 2008, March 4–8). Sometimes the conversation between the detainees would shift toward the "ridiculous" reasons for which people avenge. One detainee said, "I remember a fight between two tribes. Many people were killed, and the only reason was a marriage engagement." Another said, "I heard of a conflict between tribes where I live. It began over an egg and escalated to the point where seven people were killed." An elderly detainee got in the last word: "My neighbor used to fight with me all the time about our land. One day many years ago, I was sick and tired of it, so I hit him. When the war began, my neighbor wrote a report about me and that's why I'm here, paying for a mistake I did many years ago."

Day Three

Cleric Component

Day 3's discussion centered on judgment and testimonies. Through lecture and discussion, detainees were informed about the 15 preconditions in Islam required to be a judge. They learned that these conditions are very difficult to achieve and include vast quantities of knowledge, such as knowing the Qur'an with explanations, knowing all the hadiths and knowing the Arabic language, grammar, and syntax perfectly. The conclusion suggested that even the Imam of a mosque cannot be a judge due to the stringent conditions placed upon a judge. During day 3, detainees evaluated:

- What is a judge and what does being a judge constitute?
  - Who has the ability to be a judge?
- What are the characteristics of a judge and the 15 conditions one must fulfill in order to judge?
- What are the conditions that prevent a legitimate judge from passing verdict (such as being hungry, tired, etc.)?
- What is a witness and who can be a witness?
- What are the required conditions to being a viable witness?

Discussing judges, judgments, and courts is a popular topic among the detainee population, as most compounds have detainees who have declared themselves to be one or the other. Sometimes, these so-called judges have volunteered to attend the 4-day IDP class. On October 28, 2007, while leading the discussion, OSS local Iraqi national cleric Sheikh Hamid* made a comparison between the characteristics of real and fake judges. After doing so, he looked at the faces of the detainees and noticed that some detainees were looking at others with fear. Nobody dared to talk. Hence, Sheikh Hamid* repeated the lecture, but this time he posed questions at the end. "I saw some of the detainees look at the other detainees with a severe look in their eyes" [a warning to the other detainees not to say anything]. One of the detainees who was looking sternly at the others broke his pencil. From the above series of observations, Sheikh Hamid* could draw the conclusion that the detainee who broke his pencil was one of the fake judges in the TIF. A follow-up at the conclusion of the session indicated that Sheikh Hamid* was correct (IDP, 2007, October 25–29).

As Iraq has huge tribal influence, the influence of tribes in regard to judgments and the handing out of punishments also are discussed in day 3. In the greater part of Iraq, a meeting of tribes occurs whenever a serious incident takes place. A gathering of tribal sheikhs will occur in an agreed-upon location. (Tribal sheikhs are not to be confused with religious sheikhs. Tribal sheikhs are the bosses of the tribe, but do *not* necessarily have religious authority.) Usually, the aggressor sheikh will contact the victim sheikh and together decide where the meeting should take place. The meeting begins in a traditional manner. The aggressor sheikh comes to the victim sheikh's house and sits on the same mattress as him without talking (awaiting permission). Next, the victim sheikh allows the aggressor sheikh to speak. After listening to each other, the victim sheikh gives the aggressor sheikh the punishments, and they negotiate what punishment to give. It is always either money or women (marrying women from the aggressor's tribe to the victim's without dowry). Fortunately, the resulting punishment usually does not equate to loss of life as it has (local) political ramifications for the tribe. But, unfortunately, the lack of severity of punishment has led to increasing instances of intertribal killings, as some seek the punishment to fit the crime (IDP, 2008, October 30–November 3). It is this train of thought that many detainees have brought with them into detention, and which the clerics work to change. To do that, varying hadiths and Qur'anic references are used, among them: "He who kills anyone without the correct reason (a judge making a wrong judgment) is just the same as if he were to kill everyone on Earth. However, if you help somebody to live, then it is the same as if you saved the whole world" (The Holy Qur'an: Al-Ma'Idah; 5:32).

Detainees are taught the necessary conditions in order to set up and conduct a court, usually leading many to question "courts" and "judges" inside the compounds at Camp Bucca and Camp Cropper. One of the preconditions for being a judge is knowing how to read and write, which surprised several detainees. "We have a judge here in Bucca who can't even write his name," one detainee commented with a laugh (IDP, 2007, November 10–13). Another shared a recent event:

> An illegitimate court inside Bucca announced a verdict that some detainees had to be beaten. When the beaters [men who do the beating] came to give these detainees a beating, one of the detainees raised his Qur'an and said, "For the love of God, please don't beat me." The men kicked the Qur'an out of his hands and beat him severely. I attempted to stop the beating because the Takfeers kicked the Qur'an out of his hand. The Takfeers in turn wrote a false report to the Bucca management and told them that I was the Takfiri (IDP, 2007, November 4–7).

Another detainee said that in his compound, the judge said that all food from the Americans was *haram* (forbidden) to eat, and then he ordered them to all go on a strike.

> We obeyed him and did the strike. But, after the strike, the Americans punished us. And, then we found out that the judge and his Takfiri followers had a big amount of food, and so they could be without food for many days. In the end, I discovered that the American food was *halal* [lawful] for our judge and his followers, yet *haram* for us (IDP, 2007, December 26–30).

The detainees, after learning the Islamic references relating to judges, courts, and judgments, informed clerics about the many detainees they knew with big beards and clerical clothes who apparently knew nothing about Islam. With the subject of day 3, most detainee views of these men changed as they learned to compare [be critical] rather then merely accept knowledge. "Looking like the scholar of Iraq doesn't make you the scholar of Iraq," exclaimed a detainee (IDP, 2008, June 5–8). Another detainee told Sheikh Sattar about a man he knew with a beard down to his chest. Indeed, he looked very pious, and all the detainees respected him. When he would see Islamic scholars on television, he would call them *kafir* because he claimed they were ignorant. Yet, this detainee noticed this long-bearded man was taking a basic reading and writing class offered to detainees in the TIF. So, he has since come to realize the ignorance of this man despite his pious appearance (IDP, 2008, January 3–9).

Violence and intimidation are a very real part of many detainees' lives while in confinement. Although the U.S. military did what it could to eliminate the threat by moving problem detainees to more secure areas, there were still many who excelled at remaining below the radar. According to one detainee:

There was a detainee inside Bucca. Before being detained, he had a conflict with another man, and some time later, they ended up in the same compound. When this detainee entered Bucca, he recognized the other man. This other man set up an illegal court, and they sent two members of "the killers" to beat him to death (IDP, 2007, November 11–14).

Another detainee recalled an event:

Some days ago we were sleeping, and loud noises woke us up. There were detainees all around us and were preventing us from standing up. They were distributed throughout the room and were holding sharp objects. Within a minute or so, they were gone and had gouged out somebody's eyes (IDP, 2007, December 4–7).

Fortunately, the "courts" and "judges" did not always win. One detainee shared:

The extremists forced our camp to agree on a certain man being our Imam. When prayer began, this man began to read the Qur'an, but his reading was not good at all, so we refused him. However, the extremists insisted that we accept him. A battle took place between us and them, and lasted 2 days. Now we are in control of our compound (IDP, 2008, January 4–7).*

In a different session, a detainee shared the following:

When I was in Cropper, the extremists wanted to punish me with their so-called "legal punishment" as I wasn't praying. They demanded that I attend their court, but then at that very moment a U.S. guard came over and told me that I was going to Bucca. God saved me! You know, they have no mercy in their hearts and no brains in their heads (IDP, 2008, January 9–13).

Sheikh Sattar asked the detainees why they didn't tell the military what they had seen and experienced. They answered, "The Americans don't protect the detainees from the extremists. In fact, the Americans split up compounds and sent us randomly to other compounds. So, I

---

* According to the Hanafis, if equally qualified men gather for the prescribed prayer, the person most learned in its rules will be preferred for leading it, followed by one with the best recitation, then the most pious, then the one superior in character, then the most handsome, then the noblest in respect to lineage, and then the most cleanly dressed. If they are all equal with respect to these qualities, the selection will be by casting lots among them. Abu Hurairah reports that the Prophet said:
It is not allowed for a man who believes in Allah and the last day to be an imam for a people, except with their permission, nor may he specifically make supplications for himself without including them. If he does so, he is disloyal to them.
This is related by Abu Dawud (M. B. H. Halimi, personal interview, July 15, 2010).

keep my mouth shut in case I fall into extremist company." Another detainee answered, "I am not so afraid of the extremists in the compound. Rather, I fear that they would harm my family on the outside [by passing on information during their visitations]." Hussam Al-Khalidy, an OSS local Iraqi national social worker who worked in the education, civics, and IDP programs during 2008 and 2009, and who has had his own life threatened a few times from his work with the U.S. military, agrees. According to Al-Khalidy (personal interview, 2009), "Detainees are most afraid of their compounds and the extreme religious people who often control them. They also are afraid for their families from the militias. And rightfully so."

Many detainees blamed the violence and intimidation on militia members. Some suggested that the detainees who hold the illegal "court" and declare themselves "judges" are the same type of Iraqis that followed the orders of militia when they were free. Sheikh Sattar asked, "When were the militias first born, and how can we end their existence?" A detainee offered, "I remember watching television, and a militia leader was talking. He said he was going to make an army, and he would call it the Mahdi's army. To finish this militia, we must get rid of the head of the snake: Muqtada al-Sadr (IDP, 2008, January 14–17).

Another detainee added, "Nobody can do this except for the American military." Another detainee was not so sure about this and said, "After the fall of Saddam's regime, Iraq was so messy. Many gangs and militias entered Iraq from neighboring countries. I believe there is no way to finish them, as the politicians are only concerned with their parliamentary chairs, not with the Iraqi interests."

"Yes," said another detainee, "We must replace this government as their loyalties are with Iran, which relies on religious figures; and we want a secular government that can unite all Iraqis." Another detainee added, "We are unable to finish the militia, as our government protects the militia. Just look at each of our politicians, they have their own militia groups" (IDP, 2007, November 14–18). Similar sentiments were voiced time and again, particularly during sessions in 2007. In June 2008, the question was posed again, prompting a detainee caravan chief to respond:

> The militia is established by political parties because every party has his own militia. The solution is to get rid of these politicians from the government and to forbid the clerics to be in governmental positions because they destroy the country with their sectarian thoughts. The government needs to be replaced with secular politicians who have good credentials. The police and army forces need to be purified from the militia, which is funded by the Iranians with money and weapons. The most important point is to foster the unity, which is being established here in Bucca. This unity will end the militias (IDP, 2008, June 15–18).

Social Worker Component

The social worker topic for day 3 was "accepting difference through tolerance and the preservation of individual responsibility." This session encouraged the detainees to critically analyze concepts of difference. The "other" was elucidated as a positive addition to one's society by framing (social) progress as occurring through diversity in thinking and point of view. The session also considered tolerance as a means with which to live with social differences. This was reinforced by discussing how the extremists utilize perceptions of difference to achieve their organizational goals. En masse, people have a tendency to justify their actions by resting responsibility with the group. As a conclusion to this session, responsibility is constructed as something that rests with the individual.

Detainees enjoyed discussing difference through critical observation. One contributed, "Difference can be graceful, but it can also be awkward" (IDP, 2007, December 12–16). Social workers asked what Iraqis could do to make the most out of difference for the good of Iraq. Detainees responded that there are "thoughts that damage perceptions of religion and ruin people's lives. But there are also thoughts that enlighten people's minds." The conclusion was that if people are merciful toward each other, Iraq will prosper. Detainees explained that for Iraqi society to achieve this, merciful people should be put in power. A detainee said, "Through love, we will be able to put the benefits of the country above personal ones." Another said, "We must learn to accept each other. Acceptance begins inside a person, and from here it can spread to one's family, one's neighbors, and their relatives" (IDP, 2008, April 22–24). Social workers probed further and asked specifically *how* people can learn to accept each other. One detainee said, "Religion can teach us ... indeed, it can even order us to love each other." Concerning coexistence, a detainee mentioned an experience he had in Egypt:

> I met a British lady in Egypt [2005]. She asked me why Islam doesn't respect women. I told her that Islam has much respect for women, so much so that we consider our wives as diamonds. That's why men want to keep their women in the house, so nobody else can look at his diamond. I told her men work hard to keep their wife satisfied as she is a princess (IDP, 2008, January 24–17).

Another detainee added, "We should be smart and understand the implications of our actions before we take them. We should always ask ourselves if following a certain action is the right thing to do or will it harm people?" (IDP, 2008, March 4–8). Another detainee offered, "Look at us here; we are living in this caravan and the caravan next to us is Shi'a. We talk to them and listen to the news together—they have a radio. Last night when the rockets hit us, we hurried together and checked our neighbors to make sure everyone was safe (IDP, 2007, December 26–30).

The social worker asked what the reasons are for people not to accept each other. One detainee automatically responded, "Hate." This prompted an answer from another detainee: "Hate is the result of an action; it does not exist in isolation." Another detainee suggested, "Some people are just narrow minded and are not religious [so they have no moral guidance]." Detainees also mentioned money and faulty education (teaching Islam through the lens of the incumbent ideology). The social worker asked who should be the ones to pave the way for the new Iraq. A detainee said, "Somebody who has the ability to negotiate. Those people that are educators and have significant life experience; these are the people Iraq needs" (IDP, 2008, February 2–5). The discussion on leadership reminded a detainee of an experience he had:

> During Saddam's time, there were a lot of people who stole from the country's wealth. I found a man crying, and I asked him why he was weeping. He told me he was poor whilst many people obtain wealth by stealing it. "I need money," he said, "but I won't steal" (IDP, 2008, January 14–17).

From discussion and elaboration of the topic, the conclusion was reached that tolerating other people despite their differences will lead to an improvement in security as well as the economy. For example, a detainee who was a mechanic clearly understood the relationship between security and economy. If his city is safe, he can fix four cars; however, if his whole area is safe, people will travel to get their cars fixed and he can fix many cars. Another detainee was a shop owner who sold the same products as the other shop owners in his city. His customer base dwindled as people were unable or afraid to travel to his shop due to the violence and security situation. He received threats from another shop owner that he should close his store. He suspects that this shop owner reported him to the Americans as a terrorist in order to obtain more customers. Another detainee shared a similar story: "A man told the Americans that I was an insurgent. A while later when the security stabilized, he went to my family and with apologies told my family that he had mistakenly told the Americans that I was an insurgent. He said he was very sorry, and asked what he could do to reconcile the situation. My family said, 'It is up to God,' and they forgave him." The usual conclusion rested on tolerance as the result of peace and security (IDP, 2007, October 30–November 3).

Day Four

Cleric Component

Day 4 of the IDP was used for review. On this day, topics of all the other days could be elaborated on. In addition, the day was used to cover topics of interest in further depth while providing the space and time for detainees to bring up other subjects of interest or questions. The intended goals during this session were two-fold: (1) conduct an extended oral review that demanded elaborate answers to prescribed questions, and (2) open the floor up for whatever the detainees wanted to discuss. The review usually took place in the form of a round discussion, with opening remarks pertaining to how all the discussions over the past days pertain to Iraqi society. Through exploratory questions and answers, detainees were encouraged to think about what they wanted for their future, their families, and themselves.

Interestingly, the final class almost always brought about deep discussion and debate on the Takfiri population within the TIF. IDP became a safe place to discuss the influence of the Takfiri population, how to recognize them, what they do, and discuss/debate ideas on how best to counter their threat. In a class on November 10 to 13, 2007, a detainee stated, "The old Takfiris, we call them Wahhabiyya, are different from the new ones, who are Shi'a. I'm talking about the JAM [Jaish al-Mahdi]." A cleric asked another detainee specifically who the Takfiris are. He answered, "All the parties that call themselves Islamic parties, both Sunni and Shi'a are Takfiri." In another class, Shiite detainees stated that like the Sunnis have their Takfeers, so do the Shi'a; but some of the characteristics are different. According to the Shi'a detainees taking part in the class, characteristics of the Shi'a Takfeers include:

- They don't eat meat.
- Anyone who speaks with an American guard gets killed.
- If you don't pray to God during the night, you will be punished (especially after midnight, which is strange as there are no prayers after midnight. The final prayer is an hour and a half after sunset, with the following prayer an hour and a half before sunrise).
- They have their own courts in the camps.
- They consider the blood of the moderate Shi'a and the Sunnis as *Halal* (blood you can shed).
- They have secret sex with each other. It is acceptable to have this intercourse, but not to see it or talk about it. However, if a man comes into the compound and attempts to spread a moderate interpretation of Islam, the radical members of the JAM come together and coerce/convince a young man in the compound

(with feminine features) to make a speech in order to inform the other detainees that the man spreading moderate Islam had sex with him. In this way, the reputation of the moderate person is lowered, and nobody listens to him anymore.

- Another course of action involves a formal court in order to make him quiet. Possible results of the court include whipping by slippers, toilet prison (spending a specific amount of time in the porta-potty), or killing (IDP, 2007, October 25–29).

Sheikh Sattar asked, "So what's the job of the Takfeers [Sunni and Shi'a] inside the compound?" Detainees replied that is was "Killing, pulling out eyes, breaking legs, torture by slippers [as whips are not available], torturing in general, conducting "toilet prison" [house arrest inside the porta-potty,] and enforcing extremist rules, such as no smoking, no talking to the Americans. They also have a program inside the camp—a terrorist training class—where they teach detainees how to kill, how to kidnap, and other such things" (IDP, 2007, November 4–7).

Another detainee added: "The Takfiris have many punishments here. One of them is called '*Tizir*' [a form of punishment]. This is where a Takfiri will yell at somebody nonstop—the victim is not allowed to say anything back." Other detainees said that the Takfiris they have seen use many varying torture techniques, such as breaking hand and feet bones. Other tactics used inside the TIF include chopping off the tongue and the penis, and gouging out eyes (IDP, 2007–2008, December 31–January 3).

"They [the Takfiris] told us that it is forbidden to use ice as it wasn't available during the Prophet's life. They also told us that teachers should be treated like the police and lawyers: They should be killed" (IDP, 2007, December 8–11). From information passed during family visitations and through new detainees entering the TIF, detainees told the clerics that because of the Takfeers in Fallujah, women are forbidden to leave the house in the afternoon from noon to 8 p.m. They also are forbidden to sit in the passenger seat of a car and, when walking in the street, they are required to be at least one meter apart from their husband. Men are forbidden from wearing jeans, and nobody is allowed to have ice cream. This last rule intrigued the clerics, and they asked the detainees the reasoning behind this fatwa. The detainees said that according to the Takfiris, "Humans should eat food, not lick it" (IDP, 2007, November 10–13).

Sheikh Sattar asked, "Concerning the [U.S.] guards in Bucca, what do they do wrong?" The reply was:

Especially during the cold months (when there is fog or rain), the guards make the detainees stay outside for a long time in order to do a head count. The problem is that we have many elderly detainees who find this very tough. The result is that they get sick. The extremists use this sequence of events to inform the detainees that they are guarded by men without hearts and without mercy (IDP, 2007, November 4–7).

The detainees further detailed that while some camps are truly moderate, others are classed as moderate while an extremist presence still operates within them. In time, this extremist presence could once again seize the power in the camps. These extremists tell those who want to participate, or who have already participated in the IDP, that they are infidels. A detainee stressed that the extremists need to be separated from the moderates, as they are "the hurdles" preventing moderates from taking part in the IDP or other such programs. The detainee referred to an old Iraqi proverb: "If you have a sick animal, do not stick him with a healthy animal, as you will make the healthy animal sick." The detainees further elaborated that a good reason to separate moderates from extremists is that many detainees who come into the TIF are moderate; and when faced with a figure who seems scholarly, they will follow him without question (IDP, 2008, June 5–8).

Social Worker Component

The topic of the social worker portion of day 4 is "reintegration into society, educational and professional or job perspectives." Essentially, this subject involved citizenship responsibilities and roles one can fulfill in reconstructing Iraq. This session aimed to foster a sense of active citizenship within the detainees. Active citizenship is defined as working toward the betterment of one's community through economic participation, public service, volunteer work, and other such efforts to improve life for all citizens. The social worker aimed to empower the detainees to aid in the rebuilding of Iraq by furthering the discussion on responsibility (discussed during day 3) to social responsibility under the auspices of citizenship. He would then link this up with what the detainees could contribute to help their country, when/if they rejoin their fellow citizens, by focusing on their individual abilities (in education and profession/vocation).

However, first, this session began with a revision of the previous 3 days. Questions such as: "What does being a citizen mean to you?" and "How can you improve your educational level?" to "Do you have a profession? Do you like it?" are asked to provoke discussion and encourage critical thought. As an important component to day 4, social workers ask detainees to elaborate on what citizenship means to them and why each Iraqi needs to be a good citizen in order for Iraq to prosper. One detainee offered that each society is governed by laws like a honey comb. All the bees must work together, be organized, and function as one group to succeed (IDP, 2007, October 30–November 3). "A citizen is the person who defends his family, country, and flag. He is also responsible for every person in his country, whether they be Shi'a, Sunni, Kurds, or Turkmen," stated another detainee (IDP, 2007, November 10–13). And, yet another offered a more specific view of citizenship: "It is the person who protects his country from insurgents and helps rebuild his country" (IDP, 2007, November 10–13). A detainee said, "It is a love and belief in your country. It starts with the family." Other responses included, "Each citizen has rights and duties, and this defines their role in society. Some are farmers and others are soldiers, but they are all connected to their land; the more they give the land, the more the land gives them." Another replied,

> Just look here in Bucca, we have Muslims, Christians, and Sabeans.* We are all here in Iraq and we have the same language, history, and destiny. If we were hit by a bomb, you wouldn't be able to differentiate between us (IDP, 2008, March 4–8).

Others agreed, "I am a farmer and when I moved to a different country, I felt that the soil just wasn't as good as the one I was born and raised on." Another detainee described a country as the psychological environment for the citizen: "Even animals have a connection to the place they live." The social worker also encouraged conversation about citizenship responsibilities. One detainee said, "My duties as a good citizen are to protect my country from the extremists as they are destroying it." Another said that the key to rebuilding Iraq is through education. "Education is the key weapon against the ideologies. Through it, we can rebuild our country" (IDP, 2008, March 4–8).

With social workers' encouragement, detainees were usually eager to provide personal accounts of what they considered positive citizenship:

---

* With between 60,000 to 80,000 followers in Iraq alone, the Sabeans seem to have been a monotheistic religious group intermediate between Judaism and Christianity. Their name (probably derived from the Aramaic verb tsebha`, "he immersed himself [in water]") would indicate that they were followers of John the Baptist; in which case, they could be identified with the Mandaeans, a community that to this day is to be found in Iraq. They are not to be confused with the so-called "Sabeans of Harran," a gnostic sect that still existed in the early centuries of Islam, and which may have deliberately adopted the name of the true Sabeans in order to obtain the advantages accorded by the Muslims to the followers of every monotheistic faith. According to the Qur'an: "VERILY, those who have attained to faith [in this divine writ], as well as those who follow the Jewish faith, and the Christians, and the Sabeans—all who believe in God and the Last Day and do righteous deeds—shall have their reward with their Sustainer; and no fear need they have, and neither shall they grieve" (Qur'an, 2: 63).

My uncle is a mechanic in our local water plant in al-'Anbar. He loves his job and spends more time working there than at his home. Despite the fact that he does everything he can to ensure that his area is supplied with running water, his financial situation is very hard. Even under Saddam, his monthly salary did not exceed $3. We have offered him many other jobs that pay better, but he never accepted them as he cannot know for sure that whomever takes over his position in the water plant (if anyone takes it) will do the job to the best of his ability. He sacrifices easier and better-paid jobs for his fellow citizens (IDP, 2008, February 4–8).

Another detainee said, " I knew a man who had a government car. A Kurdish man approached him and wanted to buy the car. This man did not agree despite the fact that the Kurdish man offered a lot of money. He told the Kurd that he was waiting for a government to be established, so that he can give it back. As soon as the government was established, he returned the car. The government awarded this act with money" (IDP, 2008, March 8–12).

Replying to this, a detainee said, "The hard situation here brings the right ethics out of people, and they do help each other. We must foster this." Agreeing, a detainee added, "When we were children, my father always taught me to help others."

Detainees were also encouraged to discuss the more challenging aspects of the current situation. "One day I saw a man stealing batteries. His child was looking at him as he did it. I felt bad and said to my friend, 'This is not a good example for the child; his child will learn to do this.'" Another detainee concluded, "The presence of just one bad citizen can be a disaster for society." Another added, "And the instability of this country encourages people to move to another." Another said, "I have started to hate this country because of the lack of security and food" (IDP, 2007, December 14–18).

During the final part of class, detainees were encouraged to discuss what will happen, or how they will feel, when they are given their release paperwork. Responses included:

"I would feel like I'm leaving hell and going to heaven."
"My emotions and feelings cannot be explained."
"I will cry on my mother's lap."
"When I knock on the door, I can only imagine how my parents and family will embrace me."
"I have heard about the happy bus, and all I can think about is my family. When I imagine this, I always forget that I am detained" (IDP, 2007, November 10–13).

Some detainees who had already been through a previous detainment process shared their first release experience:

"When I was released the first time, I couldn't believe it; so when I went home, I was looking at the streets and the surroundings. It was like the first time I saw everything. I shook my whole family's hands many times. We made dinner and I just stared at everyone because I couldn't believe I was home. When I slept, I was scared to close my eyes as I didn't want to wake up in the detention centre" (IDP, 2008, February 4–8).

"I was also released before. When I went home I couldn't find anyone in my house. My neighbors told me that they were at the farm, and they gave me a ride there. My parents saw me approach the farm, and they were all waving. I felt like a bird in the sky when I was released" (IDP, 2007, October 22–26).

Unfortunately, not all first-release stories were positive:

"I was released after 14 months. When I returned, a neighbor saw me coming; and he told my family I was coming. My youngest child didn't recognize me and acted shy toward me. But, the rest of my children displayed a similar behavior; it was as if my kids were embarrassed at me—they didn't want people to know that I was their father" (IDP, 2007, October 16–19).

And some experienced mixed emotions:

"After I was released from *detention by Iraqis*, they only gave me underwear and took my clothes, my money, and my car. I had to walk home with nothing. I passed by the school where I used to be teacher; it was very embarrassing. Then I got home and saw my dad in the front yard. He hugged me and was crying. He thought I was dead; usually, if you're detained by the Iraqi police, your body is found in the trash" (IDP, 2007, October 16–19).

Four-Day Graduation

By far, one of the most exciting elements of day 4 is the formal graduation ceremony. Commanders, officers, and guards who have been a part of the process spread themselves between all the caravans, giving short speeches to congratulate the detainees on completing the course while encouraging the detainees to continue to learn and flourish. In

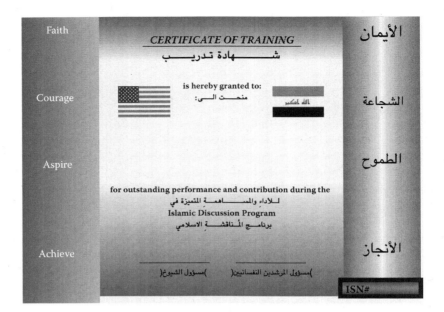

FIGURE 9.5 Islamic Discussion Program Certificate of Completion: Camp Bucca, Iraq, 2008.

2007 and 2008, from the suggestion of our local clerics, cookies and chai tea were consistently (and sometimes frantically) supplied by OSS leadership at Camp Bucca.* During the actual graduation, official certificates were handed out to the detainees (Figure 9.5). One by one, each detainee would go forward when his name was called and shaking the hand of the officer, he would collect his certificate. The cleric and social worker responsible for the caravan also were present to offer support and encouragement to the detainees. At the conclusion of the ceremony, the clerics at Camp Bucca would present the elected chief of the caravan with a Qur'an that he had personally inscribed.

That is what we most realized when conducting the IDP classes. It was the small things that proved to make the biggest difference in the IDP classes. When the first 4-day program concluded in October 2010, detainees were quick to give feedback when questioned. The top three remarks recorded by the clerics and social workers included:

---

* The cookies and tea were considered a "distraction" and were discontinued within two weeks of the arrival of new Camp Bucca OSS leadership at Camp Bucca in August 2008.

1. "The certificate for training surprised the detainees, as they realized that the class was serious, that we are concerned about the detainees, and that we were not merely passing the time."
2. "The giving of cookies was viewed as an 'act of generosity' and was greatly appreciated."
3. "What made the program look wholly legitimate ('top serious' in Arabic translation) was the coming of the Colonel and his fellow officers to share in the commemoration of the end of the program" (IDP evaluation, 2007, October 16–20).

And indeed, on weeks when the printer was not working and we couldn't get the certificates to the detainees, or the week in which a person responsible for creating the certificates hid them before she desisted work with OSS, and especially when we did not have the cookies and chai on hand to give the detainees … detainees let us know how they felt. With fallen looks and disappointment apparent on their faces, they would ask their clerics and social workers why they were being treated differently than previous classes. On these occasions, OSS would do its best to get together our deliverables, sometimes even showing up in the late evenings at compounds to personally present the detainee participant with what he was owed. Dr. Angell cannot recall ever visiting a compound where the detainee, even if asleep, was not excited to get up and get his deliverables. For some of them, it was the first paper symbolizing an earned accomplishment that they had ever received. To these detainees, it was quite exciting to have the attention of their entire compound, while being personally delivered it. All of them readily thanked us when we showed up as an OSS group to congratulate and deliver the certificate, and some even glowed with pride. On more than one occasion, from this simple act of keeping our word and delivering the earned certificate the same day we promised, other detainees were encouraged to ask about participating in the IDP. It was events like this that encouraged us to remember the small things. After all, if having that simple certificate boosts a detainee's self-esteem enough to rebuke the next extremist trying to convince him that his way is the right way, then in my mind it is worth all the extra effort to get it to him.

CONCLUSION

In mid-2009, the 4-day IDP program ceased to be voluntary. As the transition of U.S. authority to the GoI control started unfolding, detention populations were greatly reduced. With fewer than 9,000 detainees remaining under U.S. control in Iraq, Maj. Gen. Quantock decided that he wanted every detainee to take the 4-day IDP course. He remarked:

The Islamic discussion program is probably our most important program. We used to make it voluntary. But about a year ago, I made it mandatory. You will not get your happy bus papers unless you successfully pass the Islamic Discussion Program. This is like exorcism in some respect. Because extremists cannot survive 4 days of IDP, they'll do something dumb. Suddenly, we'll get a report stating some guys are refusing to go. If they refuse to go, they won't be going home. That's been pretty successful.

[Because]… Of all the programs that I thought could make the biggest impact, I thought Islamic Discussion Program to have the biggest impact. The other ones provide skills, but this one, if it's done right, it could change a person's entire perspective. Because many are under the impression that there is only one way, one understanding, when, in fact, there's multiple—there's other understandings of a particular sentence or phrase that they've been told, and looking from another perspective, it can mean something completely different, and that is tremendously powerful.

In addition to making the 4-day IDP mandatory for all detainees before release, under Maj. Gen. Quantock's command, the IDP was no longer conducted in an isolated location. Because of the lack of space in the smaller facilities, detainees were transported daily to/from their compound for class. Class sizes averaged 16 detainees with two clerics and two social workers per class, according to Maj. Gen. Quantock.

As in every innovative program, while there were many proven successes, there were also many challenges. Since the first class of IDP, we have been faced with many challenges in conducting the program, from relatively simple, but having a profound impact on lesson items, to class-halting larger issues. For example, one might consider the air conditioner breaking down in classes as seemingly minor. However, considering Iraq's climate, the air conditioning breaking down in caravans sometimes made the indoors temperature at +100° F. Conducting classes in such an environment was a near impossible task. Also, the movement of detainees to the caravans was always a challenge. Every time a detainee moves within a TIF, he must bring everything he owns with him. As they usually only have a few moments to gather their belongings after being informed they are going to be moved, often times toothbrushes or other necessities were left behind in the rush. Sometimes, there were not enough guards for the movements. Other times, it was the vehicles that were not in position, or a detainee might be in sick call or at visitation, and the group would be delayed while the military verified his location. All of these seemingly "simple" things from the outside are magnified when you are inside and have heightened emotions.

A larger challenge in the initial IDP programs was the use of Iraqi correctional officers (ICOs) as guards. While ICO guards had no noticeable impact when being utilized for education or any of the other rehabilitation classes, using them for the IDP classes proved quite problematic. It was acutely observable that when ICOs were present, detainees were less engaged and less willing to verbally participate in lessons. In addition, the amount of intelligence that we generated from the classes decreased substantially. Throughout the running of IDP courses, detainees vocalized their dismay and lack of comfort with ICOs present. While it was understood that the ICOs' presence was necessary in preparation for the eventual turnover of the facilities, it is arguable that their use as guards in the religious program was with too little preparation and, in 2008, much too soon.

Another challenge involved the education level of the participants. While it was desirable that all participants be able to read/write, in a country where 60 percent of the population cannot, it was necessary to amend the program to adapt for this population. Yet, as critical thinking was an important component of the IDP programs, classes would sometimes not receive the full impact of training, as they were unprepared to grasp the concepts. If they could not read or write, they could not follow along in the readings of the Qur'an, either. This directly relates to another concern regarding the shortness of the 4-day course. While essentially, it could be argued that with 4 days, the seeds could be planted for detainees to discover for themselves whether or not what they are being told is true, it was not effective for everyone, particularly those with either extremely low education levels or those with extremely high education levels. The former could just not grab the concepts quickly enough to meet a 4-day deadline, while those with higher education levels had too many questions to have them properly resolved over a 4-day program.

Finally, there was a neglected population of detainees that Dr. Angell thinks could have greatly benefited from personal interaction with our qualified clerics and social workers. When the focus of the IDP had shifted to concentrate on the majority of detainees, i.e., those with moderate ideologies, the extremist detainee population was left to their own devices. It might have been more strategically advantageous long term to invest a certain amount of time and energy in learning more about the extremist population, even if just in an attempt by interaction to create better arguments and discussions for dealing with the moderate population. In the words of Sun Tzu (c. 500 BCE) in his book *The Art of War*:

> If you know the enemy and you know yourself, you will not fear the result of a hundred battles. If you know yourself, but not the enemy, for every victory gained you will also suffer a defeat. If you know neither the enemy nor yourself, you will succumb in every battle.

According to Akeel* (personal interview, 2010), who spent 22 months as a detainee in Abu Ghraib before his release and subsequent hire by OSS as a social worker:

> Detainees are a lot better now. Before this, they used to be locked up, controlled by a few number of detainees, the extreme ones. You've been at Bucca, you know. They control everything that comes in, out. They couldn't even discuss anything without the approval of the extreme chiefs. This program actually opens some windows, as I told them. Some still believe that living outside is the same as inside here. But still, a lot of them have hope. Before, it was really hard. I remember when compound 8 in Bucca got hit by rockets. Other compounds thanked God because the infidel compound got hit because they are not extreme. So, you can see what kind of mentality they have. They believed compound 8 were not true Muslims, not true believers.
>
> [And yet] … The detainees now are a lot better than the ones in 2006, even 2007. You cannot compare them at all. And yes, I do believe that the programs play a role in this; even if it's small, it's enough. I believe if I can convince one from a hundred detainees to do the right thing, it's already a good achievement. Because just one guy can hurt a hundred.

Coming from an individual who was detained as a security threat, then turned his life around, and now is not only working side-by-side with the individuals who detained him, but also working directly with detainees who have threatened to kill him when they get out, that's pretty convincing. And yet, it also illustrates how important the Islamic Discussion Program has been to the whole of rehabilitation programs in Iraq. We have individuals who have been previously detained asking us if they can return as civilians to work this program. We have civilians and generals who wanted to stay longer to ensure the programs continued realization. You don't get this level of dedication and commitment in programs that don't work. IDP was essentially the core rehabilitation program in Iraq to winning the battle of hearts and minds, and giving anything less than everything we have got to its continuance and continual evolvement to best meet the needs of detained persons would undoubtedly be a grave failure on our part.

CHAPTER **10**

Teach a Person to Fish

INTRODUCTION

There is an old saying where Dr. Angell grew up: "Give a person a fish, and he eats for a day. But teach a person to fish and he will eat for a lifetime." The same holds true in teaching a marketable skill to a detainee. You can help a detainee change his religiosity to a moderate version of Islam. You can give him social and psychological counseling so that he is emotionally prepared and equipped to face life in the detention center as well as life outside of it. You can give him education classes to empower him, raise his self-esteem; essentially opening the door of personal and professional advancement more widely for him. However, unless a detainee has a marketable skill, once he walks out the gate, chances are high that in little time he will end up in the very situation that caused him to be detained in the first place. In cultures wrapped up tightly in ideals, such as respect, showing face, and providing for one's family, you will essentially set an individual up for failure if you do not equip him with marketable skills to succeed.

VOCATIONAL SKILL TRAINING

Among most soldiers and civilians in Iraq, the evidence is overwhelming. Keep a detainee mentally and physically busy, give him/her a sense of purpose and problems within a detention facility are bound to decrease dramatically.

> Education and vocational training for detainees is a topic upon which there is total consensus among Americans and Iraqis, regardless of religious affiliation, politics, or ideology. Providing detainees with improved literacy, job skills, and positive self-image prior to release will enhance their prospects to successfully reenter Iraqi society,

271

support their families, support the rule of law, and avoid a return to violence (Lt. Col. R. F. Johnson, personal interview, January 27, 2010).

Lt. Col. Richard Johnson, then-commander of the 211th Military Police Battalion, who directly oversaw the vocational and technical training provided to detainees at the Taji TIFRC (Theater Internment Facility Rehabilitation Center), has seen firsthand the difference in detainee behavior when they are actively involved in the programs offered on base. "There is no doubt that engaged detainees mean less trouble for my guard force," according to Lt. Col. Johnson.

"What we were essentially doing in 2008 was moving from an enemy prisoner of war [EPW] to a corrections model," suggested Maj. Corey Schultz, media and marketing officer at Army Reserve Communications, Office of the Chief, Army Reserve in Washington, D.C. "Trying to assess and prepare the detainees so that, upon release, they had some marketable skills and could support themselves that way, rather than being paid by insurgents to dig holes for IEDs [improvised explosive devices]" (Soza, 2010). Yet, according to Col. Michael Callahan (personal interview, 2010), getting vocational training approved for detainees was no easy feat:

> During September 2008, Task Force 300 developed, in conjunction with others within Task Force 134, a jobs training program [for detainees]. This program began at Camp Bucca. We eventually got a jobs program initiated at Camp Cropper, but this was much harder due to the 177th MP Brigade not supporting the programs that were developed, and they were very risk adverse.

Fortunately, persistence pays off and, by the time year 2010 rolled around, agriculture, masonry, sewing, carpentry, and heating, ventilation, and air conditioning (HVAC) were among the vocational skills training that detainees could elect to participate in. The training programs were voluntary, and the only requirement was that the detainees were on good behavior and willing to commit the time and energy to seeing the program through. The teachers of the programs, as with the other rehabilitation programs, were local nationals (LNs) trained and certified in the skill they were instructing. The LNs were responsible for carrying out the class curriculum in accordance with the respective Program of Instruction (POI). In addition, LNs were responsible for evaluating each detainee's performance and improvement throughout the course (Figure 10.1).

Similar to procedures for the other rehabilitation programs, detainees were selected to participate in the programs by filling out a 5-10 request form. They write their names and what their request is, and then

DETAINEE VOCATIONAL PROGRAM

Purpose

Task Force 134 is currently charged with the care and security of the Multinational Force–Iraq (MNF–I) detainee population in Iraq. The purpose of the Theatre Internment Force Reconciliation Center (TIFRC) Services Program is to provide an effective counseling and education program designed to reintegrate detainees back into Iraqi society, armed with the knowledge and life skills to make positive, productive, and peaceful members of society. This initiative supports Task Force 134's (TF134) overall counterinsurgency operations to increase safety and security of the detainees and soldiers serving in TF134.

TF134 Recognizes

- (a) That violent, radical Islamists exploit individuals.
- (b) Lack of education makes detainees vulnerable to extremist ideology.

THEATRE INTERNMENT FACILITY REHABILITATION CENTER (TIFRC)

TIFRC services help facilitate detainees in gaining the strength to develop into boundless individuals. Detainees are recognized as having physical, emotional, spiritual, vocational, and academic needs. Cognitive and practical lessons are combined to develop the individual strengths, potential, and uniqueness of each detainee.

Policies

To ensure a positive learning environment, detainees are expected to adhere to classroom policies and procedures. Prior to enrollment each

FIGURE 10.1 The standard first pages in a Program of Instruction (POI) for the Iraq TIFRC Detainee Vocational Programs. This is taken from the POI for the agriculture program. (Supplied by permission of Maj. Gen. Quantock.)   (continued)

detainee agrees to actively participate while in class, show respect for his/her fellow detainees, the instructors, and guard force. Detainees will be screened by S2 section prior to acceptance into program. Detainees are obligated to adhere to all rules and are subject to the disciplinary procedures outline within the REM II SOP. The primary objective is to create a positive learning environment that teaches detainees skill sets desired in the Iraqi labor market.

School rules are derived from the following principles:

- Respect for the guard force
- Respect for teachers
- Respect for school and property
- Respect for a positive and open learning environment

Teachers

Teachers will be qualified Iraqi local nationals, when available. Teachers are responsible for administering the agricultural curriculum in accordance with this program outline. Teachers also evaluate each detainee's progress throughout the course.

Goal

The goal of the TIFRC vocational programs are to offer detainees a skill that will help reintegrate them back into Iraqi society, help feed themselves and their families, and possibly obtain jobs.

FIGURE 10.1 (continued) The standard first pages in a Program of Instruction (POI) for the Iraq TIFRC Detainee Vocational Programs. This is taken from the POI for the agriculture program. (Supplied by permission of Maj. Gen. Quantock.)

submit the form to the officer-in-charge (OIC). The OIC then goes into the system and looks up the detainee's security risk. According to SSgt. Matthew Rogers (personal interview, 2010), an OIC at Camp Taji, "If they are low level, they get approved. If they are not a low-level security risk, they cannot participate."

Detainees do not get any special entitlements for participating in the classes other than being offered a cigarette during every break. Every break of the vocational programs is 10 minutes, and they have a break once an hour. During the break, detainees were offered one cigarette each by the guard force, which is authorized a supply on hand for this purpose. Sgt. Ryan Gaston was the squad leader of TIFRC services, and the non-commissioned officer (NCO) in charge of classrooms at Camp Taji from September 2009 to August 2010.

> As the squad leader, I have to make sure that they [detainees] follow the rules and make sure that everything is enforced to keep control of everybody's safety. We can't be giving more cigarettes to one detainee over another, as that may cause fights or make them think that we are into favoritism. Not being impartial will create a bad image of the U.S. guard force, and cause conflicts. We make sure one cigarette per detainee per break. Every break is 10 minutes. They get one 10-minute break per hour of teaching.
>
> Further, the incentive is the class itself. They come out from their K-span [living quarters]. They get to interact with each other here in class. They get to learn things they wouldn't be able to learn otherwise. They get a lot of privileges just being in the class itself, a lot of leeway and the fact that our supervision is very standoffish. I try to make it a point that there is no interaction between my soldiers and the detainees or as minimal as possible. We are not running the classes, the teachers are. We are just here as guard force and do our best to maintain the safety of the classroom (Sgt. R. Gaston, personal interview, January 28, 2010).

Detainees were held accountable for all tools used at the conclusion of each class. If a detainee is caught trying to leave with anything other than what he came with, no matter how minor, he may be removed permanently from the program. Officially, detainees in different work/vocational programs were not permitted to talk to one another, although inevitably it did happen.

There were relatively simple qualifying factors in order to be awarded a certificate of completion in any of the vocational programs. Firstly, detainees must have been involved in the program during the entire duration of the course (with the exception of scheduled appointments, such as a Multinational Force Review Committee (MNFRC) board hearing or visitation). If a student misses some classes (for a reason such as sickness), he will need to either start at the last level that was attained or be able to demonstrate his ability to be advanced to the next level/phase of training. Otherwise, if the detainee has not been present sufficiently to learn the skill as needed, he may request to retake the entire program or simply drop out.

AGRICULTURE

In July 2008, experiments with building an agriculture program began at Camp Bucca. From the beginning, there were problems. Experienced individuals were not the issue. The Army National Guard has an impressive amount of individuals skilled in a variety of disciplines happy to put those skills to use in Iraq. At Camp Bucca, two such individuals knowledgeable about agriculture developed a preliminary POI for starting a vocational training course. However, there were many problems in its implementation, including difficulty getting seeds, creating containers that would allow the seeds to take root, and conceptualizing a proper area, fertilizer/compost, and environment to ensure a detainee's security and participation. Nevertheless, the glitches were worked out at Camp Bucca in late 2008, and the agriculture program then expanded to both Camp Cropper and then Camp Taji in late 2009. National Reservists may have played a key role in helping that happen. "One of our lieutenants at Camp Cropper actually has a degree in agriculture; he has been an immense help in developing the program," said Maj. Gen. David Quantock (personal interview, 2010) during our [authors] visit to Iraq in January 2010.

According to the 2010 agriculture program POI, the 4-hour daily program was ongoing with a new group of detainees beginning every 3 weeks. Subjects were taught in a variety of mediums, depending on the class skill level and interest of the detainees and instructors. The intent being "to teach detainees skills necessary to assist in their reintegration into Iraqi society, provide nutritious additives to their diets and diets of their families, and possibly obtain a job in the agriculture field." As part of the program, detainees grew fruits and vegetables commonly grown in Iraq. Depending on the season, these could include potatoes, tomatoes, green peppers, eggplant, and even squash. According to Maj. Kevin Comfort, 89th MP BDE chief for the Long Range Plans & S-5/7/9/IO/HN LNO Fusion Cell at Camp Cropper, "pumpkins" were making a greatly anticipated appearance in April 2010 (personal interview, 2010). Radishes were also well-liked among the detainee agriculture students for their rapid growth and ability to persevere through a lot of stresses, including weather change and planter movement. Not being a part of the typical detainee meal, they were an appreciated luxury in the detention centers. "At Taji, they grew some radishes. They were pretty good size. So, once the guard force turned around, the detainees just started chomping on those radishes. They really, *really* liked them," according to Col. John Huey (personal interview, 2010). Although this was outside protocol and not necessarily approved (taking into consideration the possible risk of soil contamination, etc.), the guard force found it more amusing than anything else, and even Col. Huey, 89th Military Police Brigade Commander at Camp Cropper in 2010, grinned as he recounted the story.

The agriculture POI covers the core areas of horticulture. Through both classroom discussion and hands-on practicum, detainees learnt about such things as the temperature needed to optimize growth for the fruit/vegetable they were planting, the type of soil that is necessary to properly fertilize it, the proper way the fruit/vegetable should be planted in the ground (i.e., the depth and spacing), and how to properly harvest the fruit/vegetable once it was time to do so. They also learned about potential diseases and how the use of pesticide could affect the growth and/or production of the planted products.

Compost was also a very necessary component of running a successful agriculture program. For each class rotation, there was a lesson on how to build a compost pile, what common things to include in a compost pile, and the health benefits and environmental impact of having a compost pile. At Camp Cropper, detainees from the carpentry shop built a compost container, for which detainees participating in the agriculture program were able to create the necessary layers that a compost requires: two-thirds brown material (such as fall leaves, straw) to one-third nitrogen-rich green materials (such as vegetable peelings and fruit rinds, coffee grinds, etc.). Much of Camp Cropper's compost came from the detainee's dining facility, according to Col. Huey. Composts are required to be layered in a certain way, in addition to being mixed (turned) every couple of weeks, so perseverance, patience, and attention to detail are necessary. Unfortunately, although compost is ideal to fertilize a garden, it is not always feasible. For that reason, the detainee students also learned about fertilizer, how much to use, what kind was best for what they want to accomplish, and how to recognize the best macronutrients when purchasing fertilizer.

The outside portion of the agriculture class at Camp Cropper was next to the carpentry program. The detainee students used large wooden planters that the carpentry program students had (also) built, in which to plant their crops. These wooden planters have a mesh cover to protect the plants from bugs and sunlight. Some also had lattices for the plants to grow up and around as shown in Figure 10.2. At Camp Taji, the agriculture program experimented with both planting in the ground as well as using above-the-ground planters. A patch of soil that was agreeable for the agriculture students to use was specially prepared and properly fertilized to prepare for planting crops. Figure 10.3 highlights a small patch of land that was maximized for use between a classroom building used for learning and the sidewalk.

Detainees who were interested in continuing their education in agriculture were encouraged to repeat the class after the 3-week graduation. In fact, students who repeated were often utilized in assistant positions to help teach the new detainees joining the class. Progress in the class was continually monitored by not only the LNs teaching the class, but also by the soldiers doing the oversight through written records of individual development.

FIGURE 10.2   Transportable wooden planters used for crops in the agriculture vocational program. Camp Cropper, Iraq, 2010. (Photo by Ami Angell.)

BARBERSHOP

Detainees need and desire haircuts. It promotes self-esteem, good hygiene, and relieves visiting family members who are then able to see that their loved ones are being taken care of. It was from this concept that the barbershop vocational training program was conceptualized. According to the barbershop POI, detainees who take the course "will be familiarized with the tools, products, and techniques needed to open, run, and operate a barber shop." In addition, "The instructor teaches basic barbershop instructions, the practice of tool/equipment safety, overall safety techniques, how and why to use certain tools, and basic project planning."

The barbershop program was designed to be 30 working-days long, with 6 hours of intense training a day. Every day began and concluded with a safety review of proper equipment handling and ensuring the workspace was safe to work in. A wide array of subjects were discussed during trainings including "laws and rules," "salon sanitation management," "professional conduct," "occupational hazards and precautions," and "diseases and disease control." Once the safety and sanitation discussions were covered, detainee students then went on to

FIGURE 10.3 A small patch of land maximized for use in the agriculture vocational program. Camp Taji, Iraq, 2010. (Photo by Ami Angell.)

learn about "aspects of barbering (such as haircuts and shaves)," and "salon products (what is the best type to use for certain types of hair)," and even "hair arrangement" to include modern and popular styles, and short and long styles.

Conceptually, the most important component of the program was the hands-on daily practicum. After discussing hair arrangement techniques, detainees had the opportunity to test the styling techniques on each other and on wigs. Discussing and then experimenting in everything from dressing, styling, coloring (temporary and permanent) to bleaching, color mixing, and dimensional coloring, detainees got a relatively similar course to one outside a detention setting. They also got lessons in areas such as scalp and hair treatments and deep conditioning. Facial hair, to include beards, mustaches, sideburns, and the like, were discussed as well regarding various cutting techniques, after which detainees had the opportunity to test the styles on each other and other volunteer detainees. Learning the art of manicure and pedicure was also a component of the class. In the final class discussions, detainees were made aware of the necessity of accreditation and certification, the necessary tools to have in order to be in the business, and how to most effectively deal as management and with customers. There was a final review at the conclusion of the 30 days where detainee students were required to take and pass both a written and practical test in order to graduate. Provided they did well on both, they were awarded a graduation certificate that detailed total practicum hours at the official graduation on Day 31 of the program.

At the conclusion of the barbershop vocational program, detainees could request to be hired as barbers in the detainee work program. Depending on the size of the compound, each compound had a proportional number of paid barbers. As part of the detainee work program, barbers were paid $1 an hour to a maximum of $4 a day—money that they could choose to be paid out in one lump sum on their release, or give at any time to visiting family members.

While the intent was there, unfortunately the barbershop vocational program, as such, was short lived. Supplies and equipment were difficult to acquire, and support from the Department of Defense was allegedly low. Therefore, the barbershop program on Camp Bucca permanently ceased operations as detainees were transferred or released in 2008. It was never initiated at Camp Cropper or Camp Taji. According to Maj. Comfort (personal interview, 2010):

> It never took off at Taji or Cropper, in my view, because by then the detainee population had dwindled down to the more hardened security threat classification detainees. Instead, it shifted to a detainee work program position for only very select detainees.

CARPENTRY

The detainee carpentry program began in 2007 in both Camp Bucca and Camp Cropper. At Camp Taji, the program officially began in July 2009. The carpentry class was 16 weeks long with 4 hours of instruction per day. While both Camp Taji and Camp Cropper had a complete carpentry shop with many blades, saws, and tools (Figure 10.4), Camp Bucca was still in its infancy stage when it ceased operations with the closure of Camp Bucca in late 2009.

The first weeks of the program covered everything from safety of equipment to identifying tools, sharpening saws, and introduction of

FIGURE 10.4   Inside detainee carpentry shop tent: Camp Cropper, Iraq, 2010. (Photo by Ami Angell.)

pulling tools. As with the other vocational programs, safety was stressed. Detainees spent a significant amount of time learning about safety and safe practices before they were allotted the opportunity to actively engage in using the machines for precision and production. Detainees were introduced to drawing figures, using glue material, painting, and then to creation of simple objects, such as a first aid box and a ping-pong table. During the final week of the program, detainees were tested in all the areas they had learned during the previous 15 weeks and were allowed extra time to finish up individual projects.

At Camp Cropper, the carpentry program took place in four military-issue, general-purpose, medium-sized tents, the sides rolled up to allow circulation of air when it was hot outside (Figure 10.5). During the rainy season, the sides could be put down to keep the wood, projects, guards, and detainees dry. To ensure the safety and security of the area, there was one guard to every two detainees. There was also one guard armed with a shotgun (with rubber bullets) at the gate of the carpentry program, according to Col. Huey. At any given time, there might have been between 8 to 15 detainees working on projects. For example, "If it's a small project, like a ping-pong table, we might have 10 total detainees, but, we'll have two or three of them going at a time. Some guys cutting, some guys putting pieces together; they kind of rotate around"

FIGURE 10.5 Detainee carpentry shop tents: Camp Cropper, Iraq, 2010. (Photo by Ami Angell.)

(Lt. Col. E. Mullai, personal interview, January 29, 2010). After completion, projects were piled into a tent used as a store room until a request from a compound was put in for a replacement ping-pong table or picnic table (Figure 10.6).

When Dr. Angell visited the Camp Cropper and Camp Taji carpentry programs in January 2010, she was impressed with how complex and expansive the programs had grown since her departure in late 2008. Detainees were actively engaged in many innovative and increasingly complex projects, some detainees so inspired that class repeats were quite common. In January 2010, detainees Wasan* and Hamid* from Camp Taji both admitted that it was their second time participating in the carpentry vocational training program, albeit for different reasons. "I have been a carpenter for 18 years before I came here. I am skilled and comfortable here. What else do you expect me to do?" (Hamid,* personal interview, January 29, 2010). "I would like to take computers, but I also prefer to stick to carpentry till I go home so that I can get better and better, so that I get a job after. In sha Allah" (Wasan,* personal interview, January 29, 2010). Curious, Dr. Angell enquired of Hamid*

---

* An asterisk (*) is used throughout this book to protect the security and confidentiality of certain individuals whose lives might be threatened otherwise.

FIGURE 10.6   Detainee break area: Camp Cropper, Iraq, 2010. (Photo by Ami Angell.)

how this program could have been beneficial to someone already skilled in carpentry for over 18 years. He said:

> I am a construction carpenter. You know, build houses. But, of course, I learned something new here. I have learned to make some new designs. … The playground center, the cabinets, the [toy] boat [Figure 10.7]— all of these were not included in my job outside, but I learned to do them here. I have learnt new things. And I have new ideas. This was the first time I built a boat and if I make a new one, I'll do it better.

Many soldiers were actively engaged and invested in ensuring the program's success, in some cases going so far as to purchase additional ancillaries to enhance and enrich the program. According to Lt. Col. Mullai, "One of our soldiers bought a stenciling and woodburning kit. He purchased it out of his own pocket and then would make drawings on the project and then burn them into the wood. It really added a personal touch."

The Sunni Endowment for Iraq, an organization commited to funding Sunni mosques and discussing religious issues, was so impressed with the carpentry shop at Camp Taji that it donated tools to keep it running. "We donated tools as a gesture of peace, rebuilding, and

FIGURE 10.7   Hamid's boat: Camp Taji, Iraq, 2010. (Photo by Ami Angell.)

reintegrating the detainees into productive Iraq citizens," said Sheikh Mahmoud Ali Al-Falahi, president of the Sunni Endowment, at the press conference commemorating the donation of January 15, 2010. "The new tools will increase detainee interest and participation, as they will be more confident of our commitment to the program and feel better about the quality of their work," Lt. Col. Johnson confirmed at the press conference.

While the carpentry program was a vocational training program, designed for those with little to no carpentry experience, there were a certain number of detainees who, like Hamid,* come along with already advanced skills. When this happens, experienced detainees were drawn on in order that their skills and expertise be utilized in teaching the other detainees. In addition, detainees who were advanced in carpentry had the opportunity to engage in more difficult projects, such as making chairs, storehouses, and agriculture boxes. If detainees had the skills already and were not interested in advancing those skills or they could already complete all the advanced projects, they had the option of doing paid work in carpentry. Under the carpentry detainee work program, detainees could earn up to $4 a day creating projects for use in the detention center. The difference in earning money or not came from the decision of whether the detainee was doing was work or training. According to Maj. Comfort, "detainees are paid for work, but not for training." He elaborated, many detainees choose to enter the carpentry program initially to be trained and then, after their basic training was complete, decided to enter the carpentry work program to sharpen their skills, gain more experience, and earn money for their family.

When appropriate, the carpentry program has taken on special projects in support of renovation efforts. One such project at Camp Bucca involved the building of over 200 student desks for a nearby school in Um Qasr that had been destroyed during the fighting. Before the delivery of the desks in October 2008, students had been sitting on the floor and makeshift crates for their lessons (Sauret, 2008). To give some encouragement and show detainees in the carpentry program appreciation for the work they had been doing for others, the military command at Camp Cropper decided to do something a little different. Col Huey recounted:

> We put a project together for them. They come in, they do a lot of work to support the team. A lot of projects to help out everybody else. So, on this case, we give them a little bonus. They built something for themselves—they didn't even know that what they were building was for themselves. When they found out what they were really doing, they were really excited.

What the guard force had them do was build six elborate wooden lawn chairs, where a person can lay back and kick up his feet. Each group made one chair and got to pick out the design special to them. When all the chairs were complete, they were moved to an area at the end of the carpentry shop, thereafter termed the "break area," where during breaks detainees could sit in their crafted chairs, relax, and unwind (Figure 10.8).

Not being outdone, in December 2009, the detainees at Camp Cropper reciprocated their appreciation to the guard force by crafting a large wooden candle on top of one of the chairs and presenting it as a gift to the guard force. Predictably, as candles are more often than not associated with takfiri extremism in the TIF (theater internment facility), the soldiers were a bit taken aback with the elaborate candle and flame. "Candle, I said, what is this? And they said, "Well ... it's a Christmas candle specifically for the guard force. Thank you for treating us decent and kind." It was a surprise for us—for the Christmas season—and they did it to show that they respected us and our traditions," said Lt. Col. Mullai.

FIGURE 10.8   Detainee break area: Camp Cropper, Iraq, 2010. (Photo by Ami Angell.)

HEATING, VENTILATION, AND AIR CONDITIONING

HVAC is the abbreviation for heating, ventilating, and air conditioning (HVAC): the technology of indoor or automotive environmental comfort. The HVAC vocational program POI covers core subject areas as defined by the Ministry of Labor and Social Affairs (MoLSA) in Iraq. This particular in-depth training program involved 276 hours of training split over 51 lessons. The HVAC class started on July 10, 2009, at Camp Taji and allegedly continued through the turnover of Camp Taji from U.S. forces to the Government of Iraq (GoI) in March 2009. Unlike the other vocational programs, the HVAC class followed the school semester system. Each training program coincided with the weeks and hours of the school semester system, which was 4 hours a day for 3 months. This program was unique among the detention centers, as it has only been conducted at Camp Taji. At Camp Taji (Figure 10.9), it took place inside a solid metal structure that was cooled during the summer months and heated during the cooler months.

ACCA is the Air Conditioning Contractors of America and a professional organization/group of over 4,000 air conditioning contractors who work to improve the industry, promote good practice, and keep homes and buildings safe, clean, and comfortable. The ACCA offers

FIGURE 10.9   HVAC (heating, ventilation, air conditioning) vocational training class: Camp Taji, Iraq, 2010. (Photo by Ami Angell.)

online learning resources, and it was some of these materials that were used to instruct the detainees and evaluate their knowledge base to quantify and check on learning. The textbooks published by ACCA were used as teaching resources, and excerpts from the books were handed out to detainees to reinforce learning. Unfortunately, the budget did not allow purchasing of the textbooks for all of the students, according to Maj. Comfort.

The curriculum necessitated an unusually large number of various tools and equipment, to include a welding machine, grinder, wrenches (of various sizes), condensers (of various sizes and types), house refrigerator, capillary tubes (of different diameters), bi-flow valve, vaporizers (several types), pipe cutter, amphometer, filter dryer device, clamp meter device, thermostat, defroster, heater, deicer, capacitor, smoldering device, cooling fan, timer relay, iron saw, clamp, flare machine, tubing bender, copper pipe, welder kit, metal brush (to clean the inside and outside of a tube), pressure gauge, and electronic leakage detector, among numerous others. Many detainees had no idea what much of this was, let alone what it was used for, before taking the class. In lessons, such as "understanding heat transfer principles," "concepts of sheet metal skills and safety," and "fabrication with ACR tubing," detainees learned to not only recognize the tools, but when to use them, how to use them, and to what degree in order to complete the job.

The HVAC curriculum addressed the basics of electro-mechanic laws of refrigeration, including the study of thermodynamics and heat transfer. Detainees were also introduced to basic component identification and function. Through the curriculum, detainees developed a greater understanding of the proper use of hand and power tools in a work environment. Detainees also learned the basic refrigeration cycle and where to apply it to a live system. Basic electrical theory was introduced as well as recognizing and working in accordance to Ohm's law. Ohm's law defines the relationships between (P) power, (E) voltage, (I) current, and (R) resistance. Detainees were taught the principles of airflow and learned to work with sheet metal and ductwork. Refrigerants and refrigerant recovery were covered in-depth as well as retrofitting. Detainees also learned piping skills and system maintenance techniques.

The HVAC course was considered a basic program. Program theory was addressed in a classroom and then applied in a shop environment. Detainees were challenged to think through problems and develop a plan for repair work. Detainees were then called on to demonstrate their ability to work on fully functioning systems and to make alterations as needed. Class discussion and demonstrations were used to increase student comprehension of subject matter.

While Dr. Angell only had the opportunity to visit the class a couple of times in January 2010, the intensity and structure of the program appeared staggering. There were a surprisingly large number of equipment pieces available for the detainees to familiarize themselves with, and to utilize, for practical exercises. In addition, some complete refrigeration and air/heater/cooler units were available for use in examination and exercises.

The POI appeared to be mainly referenced from the 1999 book by Whitman, Johnson, and Tomczyk, entitled *Refrigeration and Air Conditioning Technology*, in addition to the *ACCA — Manual J — HVAC and Residential Load Calculation*, and *International Building Code Council Manual*. The program was noticeably more academically intense than the other vocational programs, and preparation of the detainee student's notebook/reference book was considered an important component of the class. At the conclusion of the course, detainees were presented with a graduation certificate and were given information on taking the ACCA exam, which was the first step in getting employed in the industry.

Unfortunately, the HVAC vocational program was instruction and training only, so as such, detainees were not given an opportunity to work as a part of a detainee work program after its completion. However, armed with their notebook, they were encouraged and supported to continue to familiarize themselves with different systems and keep up to date on the many varying components and procedures in preparation for the ACCA examination after release.

MASONRY

The masonry program was initially conceptualized with the ardent idea of a brick factory at Camp Bucca in 2007. After drawing up plans involving the spending of thousands of dollars in building a brick factory, ordering materials, and preparing for production, the program never had a fair chance. Tied up in legal affairs was a conglomeration of issues that included the necessity (or not) of paying detainees to be trained in masonry, hiring the appropriate personnel to oversee the training, and what to do with the bricks once they were created (i.e., storage, use in the facility, use outside the facility, destroy and recreate). According to Maj. Gen. Douglas Stone (personal interview, 2010):

> It was always an uphill battle to get the brick factory funded. I wanted it because they gave the detainees work, earnings, and money for their families. I also wanted the bricks to go out into the community as evidence that we wanted to rebuild Iraq. I am not sure whatever really held them up, only that of all the programs, this one moved the slowest. Nevertheless, it was the right idea, and I would do it again.

Allegedly, according to Maj. Gen. Stone, "The delay was due to the Department of Defense and Central Command's inability to find a category of funding that would allow for a work program to be funded in a U.S. detention center. Fortunately, with an untold amount of perseverance and determination, the brick factory, as a component of the detainee work program and not a vocational program, finally got approved and started operating at Camp Bucca in late 2007, early 2008."

However, it would not be until 2 years later that the masonry vocational program would officially launch at Camp Taji. It began in July 2009 and continued under U.S. direction through to the turnover of Camp Taji to the GoI in March 2010. According to Lt. Col. Johnson, when the masonry class first began, they actually had to borrow tools from the engineering unit as there was a delay in the arrival of masonry.

The masonry class included lessons, such as "building two perpendicular walls with half brick" and "building hollow poles" to "building arch structures." It taught both the English and German approaches to masonry in class and included films, discussion, practical exercises, and field trips to the brick factory. As a necessary component of the masonry class, detainees were required to learn about brick production, making bricks, the salt in the bricks, different types of bricks, and even the proper mixture and ideal seam to maximize capability. According to Maj. Comfort:

> The idea was to make bricks, and then teach detainees how to use the bricks to make things that benefit the facility or the community, i.e., sidewalks, patios, ornate walls and columns, archways, and so on. Kind of an idea that detainees could help rebuild Iraq one community at a time and also improve their facility and quality of life.

According to Lt. Col. Johnson, detainees built and took down several small structures when they were learning basics. Over a 2-month period, detainee students took part in 263 hours of specialized training. These hours of specialized training were split up to include 200 hours of practical work, 28 hours of technological learning, 7 hours of math, 21 hours of drawing, and 7 hours of humanities. The 2-month course concluded with a practical and theory examination lasting 17 hours.

As a necessary component of the masonry vocational training program, detainee students were required to spend a number of hours learning how to make bricks at the brick factory. The brick factory began operations on November 1, 2009. Those in the masonry vocational training program were able to view and ask questions about the construction of, and the process of, making bricks. There were a number of civilian contractors employed by Kufan Group (Iraqi engineering and construction company), who were contracted to work in the brick factory. They were responsible for operating the kilns and machinery, while the detainees in the work program moved and stacked bricks as necessary.

The detainees in the work program were paid for the strenuous work. Understandably, some detainees greatly enjoyed the work as it gave them exercise and got them out of the otherwise monotony of detention life, according to Maj. Gen. Quantock. The brick factory produced 35,000 to 50,000 "green bricks"* a day and had 50 detainees per shift working 4-hour shifts, said Maj. Comfort. But, the work was more difficult and demanding than the other detainee work programs. According to Lt. Col. Johnson:

> It was kind of hard for the guys who volunteered because they didn't know what to expect. So, when they found out how hard it was, they would quit. We were trying to gauge why we were losing detainees and could not keep a steady number. So, we talked to them. We found out that the guys who were hanging it out were the detainees who came from Bucca. They like the work. They knew what was expected. So,

---

* A green brick is a brick that has been formed, but has not yet been fired (hardened) in the kiln, so is unfit for use in construction.

they volunteered for what they knew would be exercise and decent pay. Pay is as much as the chief makes, and they only work for 3 hours. They suggested how to make it better. They said, "Can we get a snack? We come out to work for a couple of hours, and we are tired." A lot of guys didn't want to come back. So we got bread, cheese, and fruit. Next thing you know, we had five times the number of detainees over there.

Detainees had to choose what program they wanted to participate in, as they could only be enrolled in one or the other: the detainee work program or the detainee masonry vocational program. Said Maj. Comfort:

> The difference being was that in the brick program, they could make $1/hour for a total of $4/day, which they could give their family when they came to visit them. But, in the masonry program, they could learn the craft, therefore, getting that marketable skill for release.

At Camp Bucca, the work program was 4 hours long, while at Camp Taji the detainee work program was 3 hours long. Having the choice, many detainees elected to participate in the 2-month masonry program, after which they enrolled in the detainee work program. Thereby, they were able to earn money for their family, while still keeping their skills fresh and utilizing their new knowledge, albeit to a more limited degree. According to Maj. Comfort, "The bricks from the factory can be used for anything in the limits of your imagination, but they cannot be used to make money by the U.S. government, and they cannot be used for U.S. construction due to the material and U.S. construction standards, i.e., cinder block. However, they can be used on any type of civil improvement for the TIF or community as donated materials like septic and sewer cisterns, sidewalks, decorative columns, walls, patios, benches, façade, or siding. ... Again, whatever your imagination can think of."

Part of the problem seemed to be different approaches from varying commanders on what could be done with the bricks. One commander stated that the bricks could not be given away because they were created with U.S. funds. However, another commander suggested that they could be given away if they were used in the rebuilding effort. The only consensus appears to be that the bricks could not be sold, although even that was toyed with back in 2007 as an option to getting the brick factory going and then filtering the money back into the programs, thus helping Iraq rebuild itself. Another factor of consideration was that green bricks could not be formed and dried if the weather was too cool or too wet. So, based on the local climate, although the kiln may be fired year around, green bricks could only be formed between the months of April and October. According to Lt. Col. Johnson, in January 2010, Camp

FIGURE 10.10   A brick from the first batch of bricks produced at Camp Bucca, Iraq, 2007. (Photo courtesy of Maj. Gen. Douglas Stone.)

Taji had already baked 700,000 bricks. Yet, bad weather in November 2009 caused the loss of a bunch of unbaked bricks. Fortunately, "it's not really a big deal; you just put them back into the process," he said.

The first batch of bricks at both Camp Bucca and Camp Taji had a stamp on them. At Camp Bucca, it was an Arabic phrase meaning "brick-by-brick we build our nation," said Maj. Gen. Stone (Figure 10.10). And, at Camp Taji, it was stamped with "Kufan Group" and "Taji Brick Factory" in English. The initial concept for the stamp at Camp Bucca was so that if it were approved for an outside contractor to buy all the bricks at reduced prices, the bricks would go into buildings all over Iraq. Because the bricks would be marked with the Bucca symbol, they would be easily recognizable as something created at the detainee brick factory, and a way for detainees out on the street who had been a part of the process, to feel proud. It also would allow detainees to have a direct part in the rebuilding of Iraq effort. However, legalities kept the bricks from ever leaving the bases.

Because the turnover from U.S. forces to Iraq was foreshadowed, the United States began discussion with the Iraqi correctional system on how to proceed with the brick factory by late 2009.

> Right now we are using the brick factory for training only, but we have talked to the Iraqis. This is one of the areas where we've tried to encourage the Iraqis to be creative about a project. If they want to build a house with them, we will support it. We have moved 700,000 bricks, and we have put them in strategic locations around the TIF to

build footpaths and walkways. It's for them to use because we can't use them anywhere else, and they have to stay here. But, I don't know what their intentions are down the line (Lt. Col. R. F. Johnson, personal interview, January 27, 2010).

The bottom line is that the methods are in place for the vocational program to continue long after the U.S. withdrawal from Iraq. However, it is up to the GoI on how they best want to proceed. According to Lt. Col. Johnson:

What we are trying to do is leave in place something that will be of use to the Iraqis in running a vocational program. That is our goal. We are producing records so that we can account for the sale of bricks and the production of bricks. We are looking to leave in place an apparatus that would allow them to conduct vocational training and hopefully provide them a skill that they can use when they are released. We are working toward that direction. Right now, we are working with the contractor [Kufan Group] who helps us with the brick factory to leave in place the resources that will allow them [GoI] to continue operating this brick factory for at least 6 to 8 months. So, they will have enough raw materials for brick, and enough resources to fuel them until the end of August. Again, we have set the conditions for them to have the resources. They don't have to go around and look for project money. They just need to put some management in place, some ICO security in place, and then they will be successful running the masonry vocational program and brick factory.

The Taji brick factory, worth an estimated $5.2 million in 2010, was handed over to the Iraq Ministry of Justice with the transfer of authority on March 15, 2010.

SEWING

The detainee sewing vocational program unofficially began at Camp Bucca in 2007, with the introduction of two sewing machines by Col. James Brown, then-commander of Camp Bucca, to aid in the facilitation of the creation of the "Bucca Bears." As will be discussed in Chapter 11, Bucca Bears were a detainee initiative that involved sewing old detainee uniforms into bears to be presented to their children during visitation. However, the two sewing machines at Camp Bucca were often broken, leaving detainees frustrated and still sewing the bears by hand. By inquiry, we found many detainees were interested in sewing and tailoring; however, with the machines often broken and no instructor-approved funding for a sewing vocational

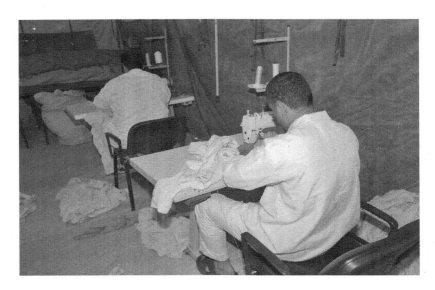

FIGURE 10.11   Detainees in the sewing vocational training program: Camp Cropper, Iraq, 2010. (Photo courtesy of the U.S. Department of Defense.)

teaching program, resources were not in place to satisfy the desire of the detainee population.

Fortunately, that all changed a year later, with the approved funding of an official sewing and tailor vocational program. The official program was never implemented at Camp Bucca, but rather was implemented at Camp Cropper in 2008. The program was 2 hours a day for 30 days. There were four students in each of the two classes each day, for a total of eight detainees who were permitted to participate in the monthly program. Occasionally, soldiers allowed detainees to attend the second session in the day, as necessary to complete a project on which the detainee might be working. However, as Figure 10.11 helps to illustrate, there were only four sewing machines; generally, each class timeframe was limited to four detainees. Others who were allowed outside their class time were permitted to only work on cutting patterns, practice hand-sewing, put stuffing in near-finished products, or similar tasks, in order that the machines be reserved for the detainees scheduled to use them.

Unlike the other vocational programs, this program was historically taught and led by U.S. soldiers, rather than by the LNs. Spc. Maria Wiggin, of the 536th Company at Camp Cropper, was given responsibility for maintaining and overseeing the detainee sewing program on December 26, 2009. When Dr. Angell personally interviewed her in January 2010, Spc. Wiggin divulged that sewing was a family tradition, and, thus, she greatly enjoyed teaching detainees a skill that she feels will always stay with them. "Everyone in my family knows how to sew. As long as people wear clothes, at some point, they will need to mend them. Sewing is useful and enjoyable." In most rehabilitation programs, the instructors are male in order to deal with the majority male-detained population, as well as to decrease the chance of sexist remarks and inappropriate behavior directed at female instructors by detained men who have been away from their wives for extended periods of time and might be frustrated sexually because of it. However, although she was female, the male detainees responded well to Spc. Wiggin. According to her, she never had any problems with any of them. She attributes this to her teaching style. "I just respect them and treat them how they want to be treated, and so they do the same for me," Spc. Wiggins said.

The only necessity to participate in the sewing vocational program was general sewing interest and ability, and the will to abide by the rules given. A detainee had to sign a waiver that he understood that the class was voluntary and that he was responsible for following the instructions of the instructors at all times. With his signature, the detainee also agreed to "waive any claims relating to an injury or damage that might occur during the training." According to the POI, the instructor taught basic sewing skills and explained the machine's component parts, to include needle clamp, bobbin winding, bobbin installation, thread routing, thread tension, along with adjustments, operational abilities, basic seams, advanced seams, patterns, fabric types, and before, during, and after maintenance of the sewing machine, among many others.

Like the other vocational training programs, the sewing program was subject to many basic rules. However, in addition to the usual basic rules (as listed in the introduction of this chapter), the POI for the sewing program also required additional vigilance regarding the needles used for the sewing machine. Only under direct supervision was a detainee allowed to operate a sewing machine and, according to the POI, "Only the instructors may replace broken machine needles," and even that "broken pieces must be itemized and accounted for" to ensure safety and security. This was made somewhat easier with the small number of machines and the one guard to every two detainees ratio. At Camp Cropper, the sewing program took place inside one small military-issue general tent. Inside the tent were a pile of detainee sleeping mats needing repair, bags of discarded and used clothing, bags of polyester stuffing, four sewing machines, and two large tables for cutting and arranging patterns. Detainees had plenty of space to move around, interact with each other, and participate in personalized training without interfering with one another.

The class was conducted with particular attention focused on using scrap material to learn new projects. According to Spc. Wiggin, detainees

FIGURE 10.12 Camel patterns and material: Camp Cropper, Iraq, 2010. (Photo by Ami Angell.)

"first start practicing how to start the machine, how to control the speed and move in straight lines. The first challenge they take is sewing a ping-pong net. Then they move on to mats. A little bit at a time." The making of the "Cropper Camels," essentially stuffed animals in the shape of a camel, came after the safety basics were mastered (Figure 10.12). Spc. Wiggin noted that the complexity of the seams in the camels helped detainees to practice seam accuracy while using a pattern. Seams are a mainstay to most sewing projects, and a must for a professional-looking project. Because of this, there was a disproportionately large emphasis on seams during the course. The camels helped detainees practice both straight and curved seams, in addition to giving practical experience in controlling the fabric and foot pedal speed. It also gave the detainee something tangible to hold and admire when completed, according to Spc. Wiggin.

At the conclusion of the program, the detainee student received a certificate of total hours of practical experience, in addition to having earned a sewing license for the class of machine that the detainee had been familiarizing with during the course of the class. Usually, each detainee was issued with a practical certificate of 72 hours, qualifying the detainee for an operator's license for the 301 class industrial sewing machine. The original was given to the detainee during the official graduation ceremony, and a copy made for inclusion in the detainee's file.

CONCLUSION

The detainee work programs, working in tandem with the vocational programs, were highly complementary. Being able to be paid for work that the detainees were just trained in was very satisfying and motivating to the detainee population. In addition, it keeps the skills fresh. With repetition, habits are formed and skills groomed. Ideally, detainee work programs should be offered to graduates of all the vocational programs in a visible effort to reinforce training and promote healthy competition and good solid skills. It also has undeniable mental health benefits. When a detainee has learned a new skill and then puts it to use, he feels happier, more empowered, and was far less likely to get into trouble. Being able to present one's family with money during visitation or having that nest egg when a detainee departs the facility, also helps with successful reintegration.

Many of the vocational training programs complement one another in their activities. For instance, while the carpentry class builds ping-pong tables, it was the sewing program that creates and repairs ping-pong nets. The carpentry class also has made it possible for the formal schools to operate, as it was responsible for building the formal schools from ground up. Together, the carpentry program and carpentry work program took care of everything in the formal schools, from tiling, painting, and structure to the student benches and tables that are used inside the building. The art program added murals and paintings to color the T-wall barriers surrounding the school as well as inside the classroom walls. Carpentry has complemented the barber shop programs as well by building barber chairs and boxes. The boxes helped to trap the hair and made cleaning up after haircuts and trims much easier (Figure 10.13).

However, not all government officials in Iraq understand what the detainee vocational programs in Iraq were meant to be about. In January 2010, Lt. Col. Johnson elaborated:

> In carpentry, to get a better product depends on the tools you use, and we recognized that. We now have a bunch of power tools donated by the Sunni endowment. The product improved immediately. It was

FIGURE 10.13 A chair and container made by the carpentry work detainees to assist detainee barbers. The detainee needing his hair cut sits on the chair and, as his hair is cut, it falls down into the catchall ensuring easy cleanup: Camp Cropper, Iraq, 2010. (Photo by Ami Angell.)

> more of an art program at first. That was one of those interesting gaps between their vision and ours. The director general of the ICS [Iraqi Criminal System] came and seemed disappointed with the product. He was thinking about the program they were running in some other place. He had a mindset about a prison industry program more than our mindset, which is vocational training. He was thinking we were finding these skilled carpenters to make beautiful things. That is not what the program is about for us. If you are already a skilled carpenter, we are not going to teach you. We are here to teach those that are not skilled. But, the ICS was not interested in seeing basic carpentry. Because of that, we had this separation until they understood why we are into this.

However, according to some soldiers, such as SSgt. Matthew Rogers, an OIC in 2009 and 2010 of the agriculture, masonry, and carpentry classes at Camp Taji, the vocational training was not useful. He notes many disruptive behaviors of the detainees during vocational training programs: "They try to sneak cigarettes. They try to keep as many as they can. It's all little things. They try to pass notes from different

K-spans." In addition, "A lot of time, there will only be two or three working; the rest of the time, they are talking to each other. It's the same ones doing all the work every day." So, when Dr. Angell asked him then what was beneficial about these classes for the detainees, he replied, "Socials. A lot of them in the carpentry classes were carpenters before they were here. They already know the skill." So, "overall, they're not useful. It's just a social, and they don't really get anything out of it."

Teaching detainees a marketable skill so that they can feel confident and empowered after release was important, but it was not the only thing. "We are hoping to give detainees a different perspective on Coalition forces," said SSgt. Steven Cotton, 66th Forward Support Company, who in 2008 oversaw the Bucca Enrichment School. "If out of 45 guys, one of them decides not to place an IED because they had a good experience here, then we did something right," Cotton declared (Bradford, 2009). According to Col. Huey, it is all part of the counterinsurgency effort. "We're trying to reach out and touch those who are willing, and educate them and teach them a vocational skill, so that when they're released, they can actually get a job and not be enticed back into the insurgency."

The original intent was that all vocational and educational training would be entered into a database called "Data Minor." Basically, Data Minor is a Microsoft® Access-based database that would contain all the information for education classes and vocational training that the detainee had participated in during detention. The data was then to be shared with the 24 MoLSA/USAID Vocational and Employment Centers throughout Iraq via the Multinational Divisions (MNDs). Overly simplified, there was to be a sort of Labor Guild in each division area or region that would provide training and résumés to potential employers with recommended employees. The detainees were supposed to be masked and treated like any other Labor Guild individual. This was also why the majority of POIs in the vocational programs were modeled after MoLSA standards. So, when a detainee was released and returned to his community, all of his education and training would be available for his community to assess his qualifications and skills, in order to recommend continued education and/or provide employment assistance. Yet, unfortunately, although the intent was good, it apparently never got on track with all the MNDs and started to "die on the vine" in October 2009. The program allegedly was abandoned, according to Maj. Comfort.

Fortunately, there was the possibility of other collaboration, support, and outreach within Iraq. With the help of a sycophant OSS BBA (Operational Support and Services bilingual bicultural advisor) at Camp Cropper, contact was made between U.S. forces and the Sunni Endowment for Iraq. Two of their main representatives—Sheik Ahmed Adbul Khafour al-Samara'e, head of the endowment, and Sheik Mahmoud Ali Ahmed al-Falahi, director of the endowment's human rights office—sat with Lt. Col. Johnson and discussed the needs of the detainee population and rehabilitation programs. According to Lt. Col. Johnson:

> The first visit was very modest. Sheikh Mahmoud came in a pick-up truck. We gave them access to the facility; we chatted for an hour and a half. He said, "You're here and you have to be here. I understand that, and I respect what you do, but, more importantly, I have people here, mostly Sunni, and I care about them." He understands that we treat them with dignity and respect, and knows that we run the prison good and orderly. He mentioned that he is concerned about the Iraqi transition. He wanted to impact how they would take this mission after us. His particular point of impact was vocational services and vocational education.

On January 15, 2010, the Sunni Endowment for Iraq donated a variety of useful tools to help ensure the maintenance of the vocational training programs. Saws, hammers, rakes, shovels, drills, levels, and screwdrivers were among the items presented as a gift to the U.S. armed forces for use in the agriculture, carpentry, and masonry vocational programs. At the press conference commemorating the donation, Sheik Ahmed explained that the first step toward rehabilitation for the detainees is to give them job skills that they can use upon their release. He also stated that he believes that recent violence has been carried out by some former detainees who did not have the opportunity to receive such training. Taji Warden Hassan Al-Mohammadawi of the Iraqi Corrections Service represented the Government of Iraq at the press conference commemorating the donation. At the conclusion of the conference, the Sunni Endowment expressed interest to Warden Hassan in continuing support in building the capability of future TIFRC services. A week later, the Sunni Endowment made another donation of 500 blankets for the detainees. According to Lt. Col. Johnson:

> [Sheikh Mahmoud] is a very strongly opinionated person about detainee rehabilitation. But, they are very interested about what we are doing here for vocational education and even more interested in how the Iraqis are going to take the handoff from us, because they really want to see them [detainees] succeed. They understand the tenets. The majority of the population here is Sunni. They understand that there is political value, too. It's not that they are totally altruistic. However, talking to both of them, they mean what they say. They are very focused on their message. Their message is that they believe strictly, no matter where you come from—Sunni or Shiite—that you should have access to vocational education. ... They believe that the bottom line is: Regardless of why you [detainees] are here, if we can provide you an option like a job skill, when you leave here, you will be less likely

go back to violence and more likely be able to feed your family and integrate back peacefully.

In January 2010, Dr. Angell asked a handful of Iraqis if there were other programs they think should be implemented or skills that they think should be taught. In a society that has a historical lack of encouragement for creative expression, the responses were predictable. Hamid,* a detainee working carpentry, responded, "There is agriculture, there is art. There is everything. I can think of nothing else." Trying to push for something that was not offered to gauge interest, Dr. Angell asked him about learning to cook. Shaking his head no, Hamid* responded, "I like ready-made food." When Dr. Angell asked Kawa,* an Iraqi LN who works as a social worker for OSS, what program was the most useful to have, he skirted the question. "It's all connected together. What they like, they can take. If somebody does not have a skill outside, he can take carpentry, or agriculture, or masonry. It depends on that person. What he would like to do" (Kawa,* personal interview, 2010). Meanwhile, Ziyad,* a two-star Iraqi general who had been working with the Americans for 4 years, had a more direct answer: "No. They should be happy" (Ziyad,* personal interview, January 26, 2010).

Fortunately for those unaccustomed to being creative, there are those of us who are. "There are many tools and many tool boxes. You can't just put all your tools in one box. Every day we figure out some other better way of doing something," said Maj. Gen. Quantock. According to Maj. Comfort, "OSS was very amenable and flexible in adding training to challenge those who had already attended and also to continue to offer positive outlets for the detainees to improve their life skills." Akeel,* a previous detainee who was released in 2007 and then hired back on as a social worker, had the (un)fortunate circumstance of seeing the situation from two very different angles: as a detainee and as a civilian. As such, Akeel* provided insightful advice:

> There used to be a barbershop in Bucca. They should have one here as well. I mention the barbershop because it was popular and simple. But, any program that will make them [detainees] think of something else, that will keep their mind busy, is a very good thing.

When Dr. Angell asked Wasam,* a carpentry detainee student, what he wanted to do when he gets out of detention, and how he was going to use his participation in these programs at home, he was quick to respond:

First thing I am going to do is start fixing things inside my house. Then after that, I am going to start working. I am professional now, so I know what to do. Because when I leave here [detention center], I am not coming back (Wasam,* personal interview, January 29, 2010).

And *that* is exactly what we are hoping.

CHAPTER 11

Art of War

INTRODUCTION

Ask any soldier or civilian who has worked with detainees in Iraq and he or she is certain to agree on at least one thing: Detainees are creative. Unfortunately, this knowledge initially came at a price. Knives, picks, chai rocks, tools to escape with—all of these have been created on numerous occasions by detainees applying their creativity to aid in violence against each other and soldiers and to pursue (or attempt to pursue) freedom through escape. The military has seized numerous instruments created for the express use of violence, passing information, or escape. So, there really was never a reason to doubt that detainees were naturally creative, but, rather, to understand what was going to be done with that creativity to harness it for something positive instead of the continued use of violence. It was from this mindset that the Creative Expressions Program (CEP) was initiated and subsequently created.

PROLOGUE

Before a structured art program was created, detainees were left to their own devices. At Camp Bucca, this meant that a small, special group of detainees, who were favored because of their consistent good behavior and cooperation, were allowed to have art supplies—given to them by the military—to create art at their leisure. As they embraced the challenge and obviously enjoyed being busy with projects, the military gradually gave them a space where a small number were allowed to visit on certain days and times to create their artwork. While there was no civilian or military leading the class, there was guard oversight, and the detainees were motivated enough to create a number of beautiful pictures, illustrating mostly unity between Iraq and the U.S. forces. It wasn't long before the art space became a favored stop among touring VIPs. Some visitors in 2007 were even permitted to depart with artwork created and given to them by the detainees. As the VIPs, military, and detainees increasingly appreciated the art house, it became apparent that we could do much more to involve a greater number of detainees.

However, it would not be until May 2008 that the first structured art program was written by Dr. Angell (author) in collaboration with Picasso•.* He is a character. As a detainee, he was well known among many high-ranking military officers, as well as visitors, some of whom visited expecting to meet him. Speaking fluent English (most of which he learned while being detained by Americans), with an engaging personality and usually wearing a baseball cap (the symbol of those involved in the arts in Iraq), he was a charismatic person to talk to. As a detainee, he was also one of Camp Bucca's best artists and a natural leader in the art space the military had created. Usually, once an Iraqi is released from detention, he/she is no longer allowed back on any U.S.-controlled base in Iraq to work as a civilian. However, as Picasso was such a unique case, he won the support of Maj. Gen. Douglas Stone who signed off on his return. "He was not an easy person to get approved, based on his past, but how could I not? Just look at his artwork! If that is not an example of a changed individual, I don't know what is," said Maj. Gen. Stone (personal interview, 2009). Dr. Angell could not agree more and also contributed with a letter of recommendation—based on his eager participation in the various rehabilitation programs offered, and her almost daily interactions with him—for him to take with him to his Multinational Force Review Committee (MNFRC) board. So as it happened, he was released and, a month later, he returned to Camp Bucca, but this time as a hired Operational Support and Services (OSS) local national (LN) art teacher. As Dr. Angell toured him around the facility, showing him the "other side" that he had not seen as a detainee, he laughed in amusement as he discovered paintings he had created over the years of his detention. They were showcased in many locations across the forward operation base (FOB) and theater internment facility (TIF), including the dining facility and conference rooms.

---

* Picasso is a nickname that was given to a detainee when he was transferred from Camp Cropper to Camp Bucca in 2006. Because of his interest and skill in art and because of the bright colors that he often chose to depict in his creative paintings, it only seemed appropriate that the name stuck even when he was released in 2008 and returned to work as a civilian art teacher. The asterisk denotes a fictitious name to protect the security and confidentiality of certain individuals whose lives might be threatened otherwise.

CREATIVE EXPRESSIONS PROGRAM (CEP)

The CEP was written in response to detainees' desire to have an outlet to express what they have gone through before detention as well as what they are currently experiencing while being held in an American/Iraqi detention facility. With this in mind, the program was designed to not only provide an environment where freedom of expression is encouraged through artistic means of creation, but also to be a forum of discussion on topics important to the Iraqi detainee population. The CEP was broken into two complementary components: the art program and the crafts program.

The art component's pilot program officially began on June 5, 2008, at the Dar Al Hikma (School of Enlightenment) compound located in the Camp Bucca TIF. It focused on the concept of detainees being able to create art as a means of everyday expression. Although necessarily evolving to effectively meet the needs of the detainee population and security concerns, the program was drafted to originally be 4 weeks in length with 18 hours of classes a week. The program theme (chosen by Picasso after discussion with detainees) was "Together WE Can Create Peace," and different variations of the same theme have persisted ever since. A unique component to meeting this objective was that there were an equal number of both Shi'a and Sunni voluntarily participating in the arts program at any given time. Half of the Shi'a detainees were skilled artists, as well as half of the Sunni detainees. Each class had a total of 20 detainees, 10 were Shi'a and 10 were Sunni.

Each week of the program presented a different theme with a different opportunity for encouraging the participants to creatively express oneself while in a safe environment. The premise was that the atmosphere would provide a forum for expression and discussion, which would help break down the barriers that were preventing the different sects from relating and understanding one another. Furthermore, the skilled artist participants were put in a position in which they could help those who were less skilled, and through doing so were able to further break down barriers by becoming a friend and mentor to a person whom they might not have ever talked to had it not been for the program.

The art program was designed to occur daily except for Fridays. Because of the number of detainees wishing to participate and because of the necessarily strict coordination and security considerations for movement of Iraqi detainees, they were broken down each session into two groups (Group A and Group B) with 20 detainees in each group. During the blazingly hot months, including Ramadan, most of the detainees slept during the day. In an effort to accommodate for this situation, initial Group A attended on Monday, Wednesday, and Saturday from

7 p.m. to 2 a.m., while initial Group B attended on Tuesday, Thursday, and Sunday from 7 p.m. to 2 a.m. Both groups had a 1-hour meal in between each 3-hour segment. In the middle of each 3-hour segment, each group received a 20-minute break.

The art program began (and remained throughout) hugely popular, so the selection criterion for participation in 2008 was a bit more difficult than that of the other programs. This situation appeared to cause an increase of desire and motivation from detainees, as the program at one point had the longest wait list of the many available options. To be selected for the art program, a detainee was required to submit a piece of artwork to his compound guard who then submitted it to his supervisor for consideration of selection. More often than not, as compound chiefs are the relative "authority" in their compounds, the interested detainee would first present his artwork to his compound chief, who then may or may not turn it over to the compound guard. Some compound chiefs did not allow individuals in their compounds to participate in certain programs, including the art program. This condition can stem from a few reasons, one being that the compound chief might think the program is a farce (i.e., maybe the detainee is actually not going to art class, but instead is giving compound secrets to the military). Another reason might be that the compound chief thinks the detainees might act out and cause trouble for his entire compound by their very participation. Or, it might be even as simple as the compound chief not liking the idea of any detainees in his compound being outside of his field of vision, thus, they then might be more easily persuaded and corrupted in the way of the "West," which to him is un-Islamic (i.e., the detainee might drink a Coke® or eat nonhalal food). However, in most cases, the majority of compound chiefs allowed their fellow detainees to participate, as it might give that compound extra incentives if many of its detainees were taking active roles in participating and cooperating with the military.

After a reasonable amount of artwork had been collected, the art pieces were then viewed and evaluated by U.S. military personnel, the art program instructor, and a cleric to determine compatibility with the art program and its then-current aim. The U.S. military personnel evaluated the pieces for particulars, such as extreme blood and violence, extremist-related propaganda, and anti-American hate, all of which would suggest instability in the detainee. The cleric evaluated the art piece for any traces of a radical ideology hidden within it. For instance, we had some pieces that featured individuals with missing or bloodied eyes. Taking the eyes out of those considered an infidel (Muslim or not) is a trait of the Takfiri detainees in custody; such pictures illustrate the individuals' extreme religiosity. Sometimes the pictures would not be so obvious; they might even have people in the background playing or eating with their family, with only shadowed eyes. To the untrained eye, it could look like an innocent picture of a family being together. However, a trained cleric can see that the eyes are shadowed because it is illustrating that the eyes are missing because the man in the picture did not follow Allah's laws and so had his eyes removed as punishment. The picture is now seemingly innocent with the man sitting with his family because he recognized the "errors" of his ways, according to Sheikh Sattar (personal interview, 2010). Finally, the art instructor would examine the piece for skill level and general creativity. Together the panel decided the suitability of the next class of detainees; factors of consideration being: the artwork, length of time the detainee has been in detention, and the behavior of the detainee. Sometimes it was necessary to have a further discussion with the detainee or compound guards before a decision of admission could be fairly determined.

In 2008, the equipment needs in order for the art program to run were quite straightforward. Foremost, the program needed a "safe" space where detainees could create and discuss without any interference from detainees who were not enrolled in the class. At Camp Bucca, this was a building beside the school house, quite removed from all the other detainees and very private. Yet, during meal times and breaks, it provided release and interaction with other detainees who were participating in education classes. There was a soccer [i.e., football] field outside the schoolhouse that many students utilized to stay active and release tension during breaks. Also, because it was a solid cement building, it provided a naturally cool environment, refreshing from the blazing summer heat. The first official art space for detainees is illustrated in Figure 11.1.

In terms of supplies, essentially what was necessary was an ample amount of workspace, paint, canvasses, charcoal pencils, colored pencils, and paintbrushes. Remarkably, when we began the first art therapy class, we had almost none of these. Yet, the detainees were so eager to engage that we all turned to each other to see what we could come up with. Soldiers and civilians stepped up, offering crayons, colored pencils, and markers from their care packages, and some even went out and purchased them from the PX on base. We called friends who were returning from leave or who were flying through Kuwait to buy watercolors and pastels from the stores. The turnout was remarkable. Everyone wanted to help the program to be a success. While we initially did not have any canvasses, we used old pine board pieces that had once been on the floor of detainee tents. It was only from the motivation and determination of the detainees themselves and the soldiers and the civilians who wanted them to succeed, that they did. Finally, about a month into the program, the supplies started arriving. Yet, it begs to be mentioned that while Dr. Angell was there, those products never seemed to arrive fast enough. There was a fire inside each detainee, a fire to create and express in a way

FIGURE 11.1   Picasso* stands in front of the first creative expressions art classroom for detainees: Camp Bucca, Iraq, 2008. (Photo by Ami Angell.)

that words cannot. As fast as we brought in products and supplies, the detainees would transform them into meaningful pieces of art.

Week One

The first week (18 hours) of the 4-week program was the most important. This was the week in which each detainee met the others participating in his class and, as happens, all were cognizant of the fact that the other participants were not only watching his skill level, but also were quite interested in what compound he was in, where he was from (i.e., what tribal clan he belonged to), and what he previously did for a living (i.e., his status in his community). In appreciation of curbing this curiosity, the first day included formal personal introductions of all the detainees in addition to an introduction from the art instructor and social worker to be present at all the classes. While lengthy introductions were given by the art instructor and social worker to put the new students at ease, when it came to each detainee's time for introduction, it was up to each to decide what he wanted to say and how much he wanted to share about himself.

The purpose and aims of the program (Together WE Can Create Peace) were elaborated on in detail during these sessions as well. The class was encouraged to discuss what the title implies to them and why they thought it was chosen as a theme for the class. The art instructor, after letting the class brainstorm for a while about the reason for the title of the class, would then proceed to elaborate on its significance in light of the aims and purpose of the program. He discussed how only by uniting as a whole can any of them ever hope to build a better Iraq. Further, how every single individual, regardless of background, religious preference, or even past activities, is a part of building a better and more peaceful Iraq, related Picasso (personal interview, 2008). Detainees were encouraged to interject with their thoughts and a free flow of dialogue was encouraged.

After an initial discussion of the purpose and aim of the art program, all detainees who were still interested in participating then agreed to a set of rules and guidelines that each would then sign, and which each would then be held accountable by one another for following. No two classes ever had the same full set of rules chosen. Often, the same rule would exist in each class's set of rules, such as "respect each other's artwork"; however, from that, the other rules might vary. Some classes would insist on rules, such as "never be late from break or meals," while other classes might have rules, such as "say at least one nice thing to every classmate once a week." The set of rules decided on and created by the 20 students highlighted the values of that particular group. What is most interesting about the set of rules is that once they were decided on and signed, they were generally taken quite seriously. Notably, detainees held each other accountable to the rules more often in the art program than in any other rehabilitation program we ran. The list of rules (with all the accompanying internment serial number (ISN) signatures) was posted by the door to remind detainees daily what they had agreed to.

The first week's actual art lesson consisted primarily of only colored pencils and paper. This helped to gauge the talent of those in the class and put everyone on a closer keel, as each was limited in his artistic creations. For their first piece, detainees drew whatever or whoever inspired them. Discussion would follow as the students finished their pieces or other detainees enquired about what others were drawing. During the last hour of week 1, all the detainees would form a circle and share what/who they drew and why they chose that subject. Interestingly, during this share period, we had everything from a detainee sharing that he drew his mother ("She fed and clothed me and my siblings and has the biggest heart of anyone I know") to another detainee who drew Gandhi ("He made a nation free using only nonviolence. What is not to admire when we are in captivity and every day it is a struggle not to violently resist!").

Week Two

By the second week of class, most detainee students were quite comfortable with each other. Without being prompted, they actively discussed their creations and engaged freely in dialogue and conversation. As it was both Shi'a and Sunni who were in the classes, a discussion about using art to bridge conflict was the topic in the beginning of week 2. During this week, detainees also were introduced to the idea of a class project.

The class project was a mural that every student would participate in creating and painting. Generally, the class mural would be completed on a T-wall barrier, which is one of the huge cement structures that generally protects and encloses within (and on the perimeter) all of the internment facilities. For this project, detainees were encouraged to draw and discuss their ideas of what message they would like to give by the creation of their mural. The mural had a theme, which everyone in the class would discuss and decide on as a group. The entire class would participate together in the painting of the mural. Thus, the beginning of the week would include a lot of sketches for ideas and, together, all the detainees determined what drawings best illustrated what they desired to say as a whole.

By the end of week 2, a mural sketch draft was decided on and plans for starting it during week 3 were determined. The mural sketch draft was vetted (checked by a cleric and U.S. military staff) before the work began. Besides the initial draft sketches for the mural, students also were encouraged to express themselves on the weekly theme: "How can we help stop sectarian violence?" They expressed themselves using colored pencils or paint of their choice.

Week Three

During the third week of the art program, work began on the class mural project. Having already decided what they wanted to create by the end of week 2, students split up the responsibilities and would begin creating their representative mural. During this week, detainees were asked to share their dreams about the future of Iraq: What do they want for their children? What do they want for their families, friends, and neighbors? In addition to working on the class mural, detainees were encouraged to work with pencils or paint to draw what they want the future of Iraq to look like.

Week Four

The last week of the art program was always an interesting week, as it culminated all the previous weeks' work with finishing touches to individual pieces as well as to the class mural piece. By week 4, detainee art students had a visible cohesive bond united by their sharing of emotions and artwork. At the last class, a "formal" graduation took place and certificates were given to all detainees who had actively participated in the art program. Involved military and civilians, in addition to other guests, were invited to the formal graduation. Copies of the certificates given to the detainees were submitted for inclusion in the detainee's official detention files. Graduations highlighted a detainee art gallery, showcasing individual pieces while reserving the top honor for unveiling the class mural piece. Once unveiled, an elected detainee would discuss the piece in detail: how/why it was selected and painted and what went into its creation. Afterward, guests and detainees would be invited to meander the gallery enjoying cookies and chai tea.

During the course of Camp Bucca's art program, there was an impressive array of murals chosen, as classes struggled with what they most wanted to articulate through paint. Sometimes they were as simple as highlighting "education is the key to empowerment." Other times the murals represented hope, or cooperation, as the key to a successful future. But, at the first art class graduation at Camp Bucca in July 2008, the detainees surprised us all with their design, as illustrated in Figure 11.2.

FIGURE 11.2 Picasso and Ami Angell in front of the first art class collaborative group mural: Camp Bucca, Iraq, 2008. (Photo courtesy of Ami Angell.)

What is considerably fascinating about this first mural is that it illustrates one of the few shining moments in Iraq since the war began. And, the fact that the class chose to illustrate this particular event to represent its hope and vision for the future, lauds the profound impact that the art program had on the detainees. The mural depicts an event that occurred on August 31, 2005. On that fateful day, a stampede occurred as Shiite pilgrims walked across a bridge over the Tigris River in Baghdad. The bridge connects a Shiite neighborhood (shown on the right in the mural) with a Sunni neighborhood (shown on the left in the mural). There is still some controversy over what started the stampede; yet what is not questioned is that the stampede led to hundreds jumping into the water in panic. Swiftly responding to the cries for help, several young men in Adhamiya, the Sunni neighborhood on the eastern bank, dived in to help. One of them, Othman Al-Obeidi, a 24-year-old Sunni, rescued six people before his limbs gave out from exhaustion, and he himself drowned. Nearly 1,000 pilgrims died that afternoon, but community leaders in the Shiite district of Khadamiya, on the western bank, lauded the "martyrdom" of the Sunni Al-Obeidi and the bravery of his friends. Adhamiya residents, for their part, held up Al-Obeidi's sacrifice as proof that Sunnis bore no ill will toward their Shiite neighbors across the river.

At graduation, a detainee spoke about why the class had decided to choose this story for the creation of their mural. "When we overcome our differences, we really see that we are all the same. ... Only by taking action together [Sunni and Shiite]—as we are all brothers—will we be a stronger, greater, and better nation," recalled Picasso* (personal interview, 2008).

Lt. Col. Kenneth King, while-commander of the 306th MP Brigade (and the final commander at Camp Bucca), said that art played an important role for the detainees at Camp Bucca. "It was one way to let them express themselves," he said, "It gave them something to help pass the time and the opportunity to have some degree of input regarding their environment." Lt. Col. King was preceded as TIF commander by Col. Rodney Faulk, who was at Bucca from 2007 to 2008. "The detainees always had a proclivity for art," said Col. Faulk, then-deputy commander of the 300th MP Brigade. Col. Faulk, in turn, inherited command from Col. James Brown, then-commander of the 18th MP Brigade, and said that it was during Col. Brown's time that the murals began to be painted. "He was working hard on giving the detainees alternatives to violence," Col. Faulk noted (Soza, 2010).

BUCCA BEARS AND CROPPER CAMELS

An interesting initiative that took place at Camp Bucca was initially conceived of because detainees wanted something tangible to present to their children when they would see them during visitation. Although the United States prides itself on having an ample supply of stuffed animals, crayons, coloring books, and the like to give Iraqi children as they come with their families to visit relatives in detention, detainees were still left feeling defeated, as they had nothing to present to their families themselves. While brainstorming one day, a few detainees in compound 10 at Camp Bucca came up with a creative solution. They called them "Bucca Bears," and they were created from pieces of detainee clothing that were too ragged or torn for detainees to wear anymore. Motivated by the purpose, detainees tore apart the old fluorescent yellow uniforms and sewed them together using an innovation of string from old prayer rugs and pieces of straw to create these rugged yellow bears. Soldiers donated buttons and, soon enough, the bears also had buttons for eyes. Col. Brown, appreciating the creativity of the detainees and the idea of empowerment behind it, supported the project and soon the detainees also had the space and materials to create as many as they could handle. The bears were nicknamed "Bucca Bears" and quickly became the desirable gift for detainees to present their visiting children (Figure 11.3). Some detainees would sew their children's names on the foreheads. Other detainees would do more decorative patterns on the bears. Still others, growing tired of only creating bears, started creating detainee uniform-yellow elephants, camels, snakes, and even rabbits for their children (Figure 11.4).

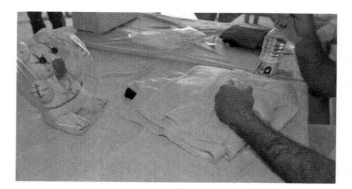

FIGURE 11.3 A detainee works on sewing a new "Bucca Bear" during class: Camp Bucca, Iraq, 2009. (Photo courtesy of U.S. Department of Defense.)

FIGURE 11.4   A detainee hand-sewn Bucca Bunny: Camp Bucca, Iraq, 2008. (Photo courtesy of U.S. Department of Defense.)

Meanwhile, motivated after a visit to Camp Bucca in May 2008, when soldiers from the 744th MP BN were able to see the "Bucca Bear" creation and distribution, ideas for a similar item at Camp Cropper started being tossed around. After much playful and heated discussion, the "Cropper Camel" was elected as the "logical" choice and work began to get the supplies and necessities for carrying it out. According to Gen. Robert Kenyon (then-commander of Camp Cropper detainee operations), the genesis of the Cropper Camel was with the 744 MP BN, then-commanded by Lt. Col. Enrique Guerra. According to Gen. Kenyon (personal communication, 2010):

It [Cropper Camel program] was the culmination of the sewing training effort since it required a more intricate pattern to be used by the detainee (work effort). It also enabled the detainee to develop a gift to be given to his children during his detention (outreach effort). It was also a response, in a competitive sense, to the "Bucca Bear" developed by the 42d MP, hence, our retort to it being a "far better product."

Rather than the harsh yellow material that might serve to remind released detainees of unpleasant memories of detention, the Cropper Camel is made of soft brown material, stuffed with genuine polyester

FIGURE 11.5 The original Camp Cropper Camels: Camp Cropper, Iraq, 2009. (Photo by Sfc. Rodney Brannon.)

stuffing and with buttons for eyes. Sewing machines, purchased to teach detainees seamstress classes and alterations, were utilized to ensure the camel would be able to stand up to the rigors of childhood. According to Lt. Col. Guerra (personal communication, 2010), "The camel flourished because there was a detainee that had owned his own tailoring shop. He spoke perfect English and was familiar with various types of commercial sewing equipment." Lt. Col. Guerra gives credit to Sfc. Brannon of the 220th MP CO (Colorado Army National Guard), who he claims was actually the "brains behind the camel." Just as the Bucca Bear, all Cropper Camels sewn by detainees were given to their families at visitation (Figure 11.5).

Meanwhile at Camp Taji, there was talk about having detainees make "Taji Tigers" for their visitors, but, according to Lt. Col. Daniel Deadrich (then-commander of the 705th MP BN at Camp Taji), there was not enough interest, and so the program "never materialized" (Lt. Col. D. Deadrich, personal interview, 2010).

ARTS AND CRAFTS

During the course of the various rehabilitation programs, many other creative initiatives also took place, as determined detainees found ways to constructively use their free time. Bracelets were one such use of free time. Detainees would take either prayer thread or ask soldiers for their combat boot shoelaces or other thick thread. This they would braid together to make bracelets for each other, soldiers, and visiting VIPs. Detainees also would use the thread/string to make hats, necklaces, or create scenes or names on their clothing. Although tampering with clothing is technically against U.S. detention policy, in some compounds of well-behaving moderates, the soldiers managed to overlook it as their relations with the detainees improved. According to one soldier who asked not to be named, it was all about "knowing when to pick your battle."

Other detainee initiatives included large-stitch cross-stitch, making bookmarks, building objects (such as a house) out of juice boxes, and even creating bags from juice boxes and/or meals-ready-to-eat (MRE) packs to take their personal items with them when released (Figure 11.6).

Col. Brown, two weeks before departing as commander of detainee operations at Camp Bucca, was surprised in 2007 with a 3 × 2-ft boat that a group of detainees had made for him. It was created from the juice boxes they received during meals. A bit of thread had been borrowed from guards to do some stitching on it, and straws added the finishing touch. It was a parting gift from a compound that looked favorably on him for his role as commander.

FIGURE 11.6 A detainee is released from U.S. detention carrying his belongings in a hand-sewn bag created from meals-ready-to-eat (MRE) packs. (Photo by Pfc. Springer, 16th MP Bde (Abn) PAO.)

LEAPING FORWARD

When Dr. Angell visited the CEP in Camp Cropper and Camp Taji during January 2010 [Camp Bucca was closed in 2009], much had changed. Foremost, most individuals had never heard of the CEP and instead referred to it singularly as the "art program." But impressively, it had a military-created and approved program of instruction (POI). With a POI, it had guaranteed funding and required evaluations, which keep the program running with little to no issues (Figure 11.7). The newly generated POI required that participants have completed the Tanweer component of the Islamic Discussion Program, in addition to at least having a basic education to participate. The newly structured art program was still voluntary, and interested detainees could still reapply for participation as often as they desired. The class also occurred in a more and larger formalized classroom complete with tables to work at, as seen in Figure 11.8.

According to the POI and what was observed during the January 2010 visit, the previously more complex (yet less structured) Camp Bucca CEP evolved into a more basic art course, designed mostly for detainees with little to no art background. However, allegedly, those with a solid foundation were warmly welcomed, albeit left to create pieces at their own leisure. Although it was still 30 days in length, it now had several components broken down into four skill groups. According to Teena,*

FIGURE 11.7   A detainee in art class: Camp Cropper, Iraq, 2010. (Photo courtesy of U.S. Department of Defense.)

FIGURE 11.8   Camp Taji art class for detainees: Camp Taji, Iraq, 2010. (Photo by Ami Angell.)

the 2010 art instructor at Camp Cropper, each student went to class for 2 hours a day for a total of 12 hours a week during the 4-week session. The average number of students was around 15, and there was one main teacher with two local Iraqi assistants, so it kept the ratio about five detainees to one instructor. During the course of the program, detainees were taught many basic techniques, such as using the line (straight and curved) to draw shapes and buildings, using shadow and light in relation to light sources and projections, experimenting with color combinations, painting buildings in relation to textures, still-life painting, floral painting, splatter painting, gadget painting. graded washes, and calligraphy painting, among many others. During the course, detainees were encouraged as well to experiment with various art tools available, including crayons, dyes, oil pastels, charcoal pencils, wood pencils, and markers among others. In the final class, a detainee had to demonstrate the skills acquired during the previous 4 weeks. This final exam determined what had been retained, whether the detainee had been present enough to get a certificate, and the amount of progress each detainee acquired over the course month.

According to Teena,* (personal interview, 2010) "The detainees leave with the basic skills of learning art. They can then apply that to all areas of their life. Many take it home to teach family members."

FIGURE 11.9   Calligraphy artwork: Camp Cropper, Iraq, 2010. (Photo by Ami Angell.)

Teena* also discussed what the detainees enjoy creating. "Other than art, we also create calligraphy; some are words of wisdom, some are phrases from the Qur'an"(Figure 11.9). Pointing at a few hand-painted portraits of U.S. President Barak Obama, she emphasized, "They also draw Obama pictures. They say they like him; he promises a lot." The art students at Camp Cropper also were sometimes allowed to give their pieces to their families during visitation. One detainee said that his wife had no idea he was taking the class. "So, when I gave her a picture I drew of her and the children, she could not believe it and shouted with happiness!" (Mohammed,* personal interview, 2010).

The art program at Camp Taji and Camp Cropper successfully included both adult and juvenile populations. During the 30-day art course, detainees were taught various other techniques including straw-blowing watercolor design, sponge painting, and ice painting, among many others. The July 22, 2009, graduating art class created a mural displaying the beauty of Iraq, as seen through the eyes of a citizen. Murals also continued to be created on T-Walls around the TIF (Figure 11.10). The mural was split into three parts: the Northern region, Baghdad, and the South. Each sector displayed three historical or geographical landmarks. One detainee who insisted on showing Dr. Angell the mural confessed that he had "no idea how to draw" before he took the art

FIGURE 11.10   Detainees create class murals on T-Wall barriers surrounding the TIF: Camp Taji, Iraq, 2010. (Photo by Ami Angell.)

class. Yet now "I [he] can draw with a flourish!" He elaborated how he enjoyed taking the art class so much the first time, "I had never taken art before," that he signed up for another 4-week class immediately afterward. He also adamantly requested that perhaps Dr. Angell could talk to the individuals who run the class to permit him to take it a third time, as he was concerned that they wouldn't let him take it again and, if so, then he "would go crazy with nothing to do" (Abdullah,* personal interview, January 26, 2010).

LESSONS LEARNED

Because of the nature of the art program and its location (i.e., in a detention facility), flexibility is key. Also key is that the detainee concludes the art program feeling more empowered to ask questions, make choices, give and receive input, and most importantly feels as if he has grown as a person. This is important on many fronts; security-wise it cannot get any more beneficial. It has been noted that if one allows detainees "space" to artistically express themselves in a safe environment, they feel happier, and thus more likely to comply with detention facility rules, in addition to being more likely to engage in constructive dialogue both in and out of class. Further, when they return to the compounds each day, their excitement about being in the art program is contagious and this enthusiasm spreads rapidly to other detainees. This, in turn, creates an increased detainee demand for the art program, which, in turn, causes more detainees to obey compound rules and be on good terms with compound guards in the hope that they will be considered for participation in future creative programs.

It is also about listening to what the detainees are saying, both verbally and nonverbally. Dr. Angell has found that soldiers and civilians, who opened themselves up to listening to detainees, often found that what the detainees were willing to divulge after that friendship is formed is priceless. Within the classroom, the bonding and closeness through the creation of art provides an invaluable setting for forming such friendships. For example, in July 2008, during the second week of the art course, Dr. Angell witnessed a remarkable display of kindred spirit, kindled by participation in the program. One of the 20 participants—a Shi'a—did something in his compound that caused the military to forbid his continued participation in the art course. When the other 19 students discovered that he would no longer be allowed to participate, they became upset. Acting together as a group, they decided that if the missing detainee could no longer be part of their class, then none of them would like to participate any longer either. They did not shout and they were not disruptive; they just quietly let the art teacher know that they had come to a conclusion that they did not want to continue without the missing detainee's participation. He had been responsible for a part of the mural and they did not feel that they could complete it without his involvement. In one way, this was exactly what the class was trying to encourage. It illustrated participation, cooperation, and trust between both the Shiite and Sunni elements. It also illustrated the impact that intimate sharing and discussion in a safe setting had on the detainee population. Dr. Angell personally felt the need to take this issue up to the commander level. Following much discussion, the detainee in question was allowed to rejoin the art program and classes continued as scheduled. Interestingly, this detainee, who inadvertently was given what could be conceived as a second chance by his fellow classmates and the military, at the conclusion of the art class asked a compound officer about the possibility of being moved to a new compound. He confided that his compound was being controlled by a few extremists, and that he didn't want to be pressured by them anymore.

THE WAY FORWARD

To date, the Iraqi art program has been considered successful with many hundreds of detainee graduates since its conception during the summer of 2008. However, much still needs to be done to shape and evolve the program to better meet the detainee's needs. There is no clear-cut or perfect way to run an art program. Each art program needs to be tailored to its participants. In 2008, it was concluded that it might be useful for a psychologist to be available during all class discussions. The psychologist would act in the assistant capacity to the art instructor; as a licensed practitioner, a psychologist would be invaluable in providing insight into each detainee's growth as he completes the full course. As an added benefit, the psychologist would be available to meet with the detainees one-on-one to discuss personal issues and/or complications that might (or are) impacting that particular detainee's progress. The evaluations and recommendations that the psychologist makes from his/her observations and dialogue with the detainee could potentially provide a helpful reference for military commanders who ultimately must decide whether the detainee remains a security threat or not.

However, after attending and presenting at the LaSalle College of the Arts (Singapore) inaugural conference on "The Internationalization of the Creative Arts in Therapy" in January 2010, Dr. Angell's initial conclusion of what would be most useful in conducting the art program courses for detainees shifted. Dr. Angell is now committed to believing that the ideal course of action would include combining the elements of the art instructor and the psychologist into one individual. Not only would this be more cost-effective and security conscious in the long term, a licensed and/or credentialed art therapist would effectively fill the void as educator, motivator, and therapist. According to the American Art Therapy Association (AATA):

> Art therapy is a mental health profession that uses the creative process of art making to improve and enhance the physical, mental and emotional well-being of individuals of all ages. It is based on the belief that the creative process involved in artistic self-expression helps people to resolve conflicts and problems, develop interpersonal skills, manage behavior, reduce stress, increase self-esteem and self-awareness, and achieve insight (http://www.arttherapy.org).

According to AATA, art therapy is based on knowledge of human development and psychological theories and is an efficient treatment for people with developmental, medical, educational, social, or psychological problems. Through the process of art creation, one can increase self-awareness; cope with symptoms, stress, and traumatic experiences; and enhance cognitive abilities. According to Elizabeth Coss, who is the program leader for the Masters of Art Therapy Program at LaSalle College of the Arts in Singapore, "An art therapist is more specifically trained to make verbal and nonverbal interventions during the art making as well as in the processing afterwards. They have a solid understanding of the art making process and the ability to process what is going on intrapsychically through images and metaphors" (E. Coss, personal interview, February 15, 2010).

An art therapist is trained in both art and in theory and principles related to psychology and psychotherapy. To be a licensed/credentialed art therapist, an individual must minimally hold a master's degree in addition to having had a clinical internship involving therapeutic art interventions. Further, a qualified art therapist brings his/her knowledge of art materials and art techniques to a therapy session and then skillfully tailors art activities and interventions that are therapeutic and goal-oriented. There are many ways this can be done, including using photographs to create collages, writing haikus to verbalize emotions, creating a sculpture out of clay, or even the more commonly known method of paint and brush. As a growing profession, art therapy is dedicated to improving the lives of others through active engagement in the creative process, which essentially could open a lot of doors in detainee rehabilitation. An art therapist, who is knowledgeable about art, can safely engage a detainee during a therapeutic process, and then articulate this back, when appropriate, to the military. Typically, an art therapy session involves both a verbal and nonverbal component, and an art therapist might use a variety of modems in order to get the best response. There is an emphasis on creating images as a vehicle of learning more about one's self through the discussion of one's symbols, metaphors, and personal experience.

In contrast, an art instructor may have a bachelor's degree with a solid understanding of art technique, but generally little-to-no art therapy understanding and experience. For instance, an art instructor tends to focus on the final art product, skill, and technique development; whereas an art therapist tends to focus on the process of engaging in the art making as well as the significance of developing the therapeutic relationship. Likewise, although a psychologist is trained to diagnose a mental state of mind, he/she may not be versed in the practical application of art or how engaging in art interventions can have therapeutic value. Honing in on all of these skills in one person will have lasting impact on the class structure and measures of effectiveness. According to Ronald Lay, who has been employed as an art rehabilitation therapist (ART) with the California Department of Mental Health at Napa State Hospital (one of five large forensic mental health facilities in California), since 1999 (personal interview, 2010):

> Art therapy has been successfully implemented in a variety of settings with a variety of populations with a variety of cognitive abilities. Developing trust is paramount in any therapeutic modality and must be

carefully considered and addressed by the therapist. Clinical supervision is an integral resource. They [detainees] are a very unique, different, and challenging population. In addition to the traditional therapy trust considerations, you also have to contend with historical, power, multicultural, and religious issues, to name a few. It can be expected that trust will take time. Consistency, predictable routine, and clearly defined expectations can assist in developing long-term trust. It is important that clients feel comfortable with this process, especially if engaging in art is a foreign concept or an activity that they haven't engaged in since childhood. If clients have effective verbal and communication skills, art therapy can be even more therapeutic and significant in that these can lead to increased insight, reflection, and change.

A limitation of having a licensed and/or credentialed art therapist may include the difficulty of finding one. Although art therapy is quickly growing as a field, its influence and particulars remain primarily within western countries. The notably few qualified individuals Dr. Angell has encountered in the Middle East received their training in the United States and England. While hiring outsiders to lead rehabilitation classes is tempting, it would be contrary to the intended purpose. The rehabilitation programs as run by local professionals are an essential and crucial component in the empowerment and growth of the detainee population. Detainees deserve to be motivated within their own community and have the role model on site to offer advice and guidance. Further, a locally hired individual is deeply rooted in the same traditions and culture as those with whom he/she is working. Finally, hiring locally reinforces the concept of giving back to the local economy and, by example, encourages the detainee participating to actualize his/her potential.

Across the board we have examples of detainees attesting to the fact that participating in an art program has improved their outlook on life and, in some cases, even made them realize the errors of their actions. However, our results are from detainees who have participated in the art program in conjunction with the other available programs, such as the Islamic Discussion Program. While it has been discussed on some levels, the feasibility of a stand-alone art therapy program to challenge radical mindsets is another matter. According to Lay, "It would be naïve and socially irresponsible to have art therapy as a stand-alone program in terrorist rehabilitation." If we have learned from the two individuals who went from Guantanamo to the Saudi Arabia art therapy rehab back to the forefront of the fight, it is that art therapy alone does not have (nor claim to have) all the answers. Instead, art therapy should be implemented as part of a comprehensive rehabilitation program and accessed as an adjunct to other therapeutic modalities. For those detainees who are at a very early stage of change, it may be appropriate to use art therapy to begin developing the therapeutic alliance, establish open lines of communication, and stimulate interest in actively and meaningfully participating in their overall rehabilitation, according to Lay.

However, could CEP be successful in enhancing the detainee rehabilitation process, and perhaps even help to achieve closure for some detainees who respond well to its methods? Most art therapists would agree that while there are always challenges, positive outcomes are possible in the detention setting. According to Lay:

> I've been employed full-time over the past 11 years providing individual and group art therapy services to those with ongoing relationships with the legal system. In my opinion, most curriculum-based therapy groups can be effectively aligned with art therapy interventions. An anger management through art therapy group quickly allows one to express anger and anger-related experiences in a safe and supportive setting, allows one to practice socially acceptable ways to express anger and frustration, and allows one the opportunity to explore alternative ways to express his/her anger in constructive versus destructive ways.

Class murals from graduating classes have been filled with warmth and personality, essentially illustrating unity, cooperation, and hope for Iraq's future. Detainees have attested to the impact that having an outlet to create has had on them. Abdullah,* a detainee at Camp Cropper, confided in Dr. Angell (personal interview, 2010), "When I am in art class, I don't feel like a detainee. I feel like I am at home. I wish for no sleep so I can be in the class." Other detainees have talked about how good it feels to "just leave the compound and create something," and "just be me." Art therapy, once considered a "softer" profession, is now aggressively spreading all over the world as countries are recognizing its significance, in particular, the well-being of individuals who have experienced some type of trauma, both physical and emotional.

Most probably the best example and most well-known art therapy program outside of Iraq is in Saudi Arabia. It began after the May 2003 series of Saudi citizen suicide bombings targeted at places where foreigners were known to live and work in Saudi Arabia. It was not long after this that the idea of art therapy and psychological counseling quietly began to be discussed within Saudi prisons. In 2007, the innovative art therapy approach targeted toward extremists began. Teaching in a former holiday resort outside Riyadh, the instructor—Dr. Awad Alyami— uses art therapy as part of a program to encourage ex-jihadists to express themselves on paper. Rather than using the word art, which in Arabic doesn't only mean painting or drawing, it also means dancing or singing (which is not accepted by most extremists at this time), Dr. Alyami refers to what they are doing as "taashkeely," which literally means "doing things with your hands" (Durham, 2008). Overwhelmingly, references to Saudi Arabia and the Qur'an abound in their work. At the end of what is usually a 2-month stay at the rehabilitation center, if the ex-jihadist has convinced the authorities that he sees the errors in his ways, the Saudi Arabian government eases the transition back into society by helping to pay for cars, apartments, and even brides and weddings ... "anything that might encourage the men to lead stable lives instead of turning back to violence" (CBC, 2008).

Other prison settings—even those without well-known (ex)jihadists—are also starting to embrace art therapy with its therapeutic benefits. The Art for All Foundation and Center in Thailand envisioned and created by Professor Channarong Pornrungroj, the head of Fine Arts at Chulalongkorn University, was originally started as an art program for disadvantaged and troubled children, but has since expanded to include art therapy for death row inmates. Prof. Channarong's initial concept involves putting a blind person, a deaf person, a mentally challenged person, a physically challenged person, and a volunteer into a group. Together these five individuals form one collective "genius" with each one compensating for what the others lack (Scrimshaw, 2010). Not long after, through the encouragement of Her Royal Highness, Princess Maha Chakri Sirindhorn, Prof. Pornrungroj extended his program to also include a special art program for prisoners on death row in Bangkok. According to Bang Kwang Prison Chief Chutinan Petcharoen, the art program is "most definitely a good thing. At Bang Kwang, all inmates are serving at least 30 years. They often end up brawling. Certainly those attending the art class have shown improved behavior" (Sa-ardsorn, 2008).

According to one inmate who was in jail for murder, "When I was sent to prison, I really lost hope and didn't want to do anything." He further explained:

> Because of a moment of passion I have to spend my whole life behind bars. Life is very much like a painting. When we are in a bad mood, just a single bad brushstroke by us can spoil the whole painting. Had I not killed anybody, I would have been able to enjoy a good life (Sa-ardsorn, 2008).

Thailand prison authorities have noted a significant reduction of violence from those participating in the art program. As an added encouragement to inmates, some of the inmates' paintings are sold to the public, after which the artist gets half the money from the sale.

On the other side of the fence, and potentially just as traumatic, art therapy has been utilized in treating Iraq war veterans with post-traumatic stress disorder (PTSD) as well as helping Iraqi children safely express their feelings surrounding the turmoil in their country. The Combat Paper project in the United States helps war veterans utilize art as a means to help "reconcile their personal experiences as well as broaden the traditional narrative surrounding service, honor and the military culture." According to the Web site (http://www.combatpaper. org), veterans cut up, beat, and transform their uniforms worn in war into sheets of paper. The transformative process of papermaking is used to reclaim their uniform as art and begin to embrace their experiences as a soldier in war.

Art therapy in the rehabilitation of extremists has grown substantially since the first time Saudi Arabia engaged in using it with the terrorist mindset in 2007, and Iraq embraced it in 2008. Yet, there is still much more to learn and much room for improvement. Although there is a great deal of anecdotal evidence about the power of art therapy, with very little scientifically supportable research on whether or not art therapy has a chance of working on the terrorist mind, there will always be critics. However, what we do know is that the ground gained from Saudi Arabia's and Iraq's experience of art therapy is not ground lost. We have individuals who have gone through the art therapy program in conjunction with other programs and have proved to be changed individuals. Many detainees chose to display their thoughts and emotions through creations of artwork, which they were then proud and excited to talk about afterwards (Figure 11.11 through Figure 11.14). This development

FIGURE 11.11 Artwork created by detainees: Camp Cropper, Iraq, 2010. (Photo by Ami Angell.)

FIGURE 11.12 Artwork created by a detainee. When asked about his inspiration for creating the painting, he replied: "All women are evil. If she loves, she kills. If she hates, she kills too. But I still love her.": Camp Cropper, Iraq, 2010. (Photo by Ami Angell.)

can happen from seemingly simple changes. "In the past, I didn't have any opportunity to learn art. But now I love it and will practice it. Also I will teach art to my kids when I'm released," said Abdullah.* To the more complex, "I was so angry before. I wanted to blame everyone for where I am today. Art has helped release the anger I have felt for so many years," remarked Mohammed.* But, perhaps most remarkably, the greater majority of individuals who have been through the programs have not returned to extremist activities. To those who have seen it in action, there is no doubt that with the right engagement from the right people, creative expression for rehabilitation of those in detention can become a powerful tool for change in the future.

FIGURE 11.13 Artwork created by a detainee that hangs in a battalion conference room: Camp Cropper, Iraq, 2010. (Photo by Ami Angell.)

FIGURE 11.14   The detainee who created this painting explained its significance as "… I created this painting that represents the Statue of Liberty as a gift for all believers and friends of freedom. This statue represents a woman wearing a crown with seven projections, which represents the seven seas. At her feet, there is a broken chain to symbolize the need to end inequality. The statue is 93 meters tall. The woman has been chosen because she represents the birth of humanity. As for the torch or flame, it represents that freedom is persistent and will always exist. The light can never be put out. And this is my hope for Iraq." (Photo by Ami Angell.)

CHAPTER 12

Widening the Scope

THE TANWEER CONCEPT

The appellation of Tanweer, *enlightenment* in Arabic, was toyed with for many months while the rehabilitation programs were running and transforming. Although introduced into the original fragmentary order (FRAGO) by Maj. Gen. Douglas Stone and TF-134 in May 2007, the different phases of Tanweer and the different elements involved were actually not formalized until May 2008; interestingly, only after all the other rehabilitation programs were individually in motion. With the encouragement that a busy detainee does not have time to get into trouble, the framework of Tanweer was designed to encourage and enable detainees to maintain a moderate way of thinking throughout detention by providing a range of activities from the time they arrive into detention to the time they are released. In addition, it was designed to simplify the rehabilitation process by integrating all the existing programs under one term, while at the same time leaving space for expanding the programs' options.

There were three original conceptualized phases of Tanweer. Phase I was Initial Tanweer, which intended to provide detainees with initial exposure to moderate messages prior to their placement in a compound. Phase II was Sustained Tanweer, which intended to provide detainees and families with long-term exposure to moderate messages during a detainee's internment. And, Phase III was Transition Tanweer, in which a detainee received formal instruction prior to release. Of the three phases, only Phase II was ever voluntary. Both Initial Tanweer and Transition Tanweer were nonoptional for detainees. Phase I occurred when a detainee first arrived at the detention site, after he/she had been in-processed, and was a total of 6 hours in duration. Phase II took place at any given time during a detainee's internment, and consisted of a variety of rehabilitation programs. Lastly, Phase III took place once a detainee was issued his release paperwork; it was 3 days in length with 6 hours of class per day.

Phase I: Initial Tanweer

The Phase I: Initial Tanweer program (more commonly known as "trans-in") officially began at Camp Bucca in June 2008 and consisted of 6 hours of a combined civics and life in detention lecture given to all new detainee arrivals. Active participation was voluntary, although listening to the instructors was not. It was created to inform new arrivals about detention policies, in addition to letting them know what to expect and what they could do to make their lives in detention easier. Opportunities of participation in the rehabilitation programs and daily procedures in detention were discussed in detail. The trans-in program was conducted in the same caravans as the Islamic Discussion Program (IDP). Usually, there were between 10 to 25 detainees per caravan. Operational Support and Services (OSS) civilian Iraqi nationals, to include one each of a cleric and social worker, would talk through the fence to engage in discussion with the detainees for a total of 6 hours (including two breaks of 30 minutes' duration). When they arrived to teach the lesson, all they would bring with them was two chairs, a whiteboard, and the instruction notes. On the other side of the metal fence, some detainees preferred to stand while listening, but most of them sat on the hard-packed dirt ground by the end of it. The topics included "Iraqi constitution," "rights and freedoms," "Iraqi government," "democracy," "Iraqi society structure," "adjustment inside detention," and, finally, "setting a path to success in detention."

During the 6-hour program, each detainee also had a brief one-on-one with the cleric and social worker leading the class. The one-on-one evaluation included being asked questions on such subjects as ethnicity, prior occupation, and literacy level. It also involved the cleric and social worker making observational notes based on each detainee's mental state, perceived religiosity, and interest in the class. At the conclusion of the class, copies of the detainee evaluations were given to the theater internment facility (TIF) commander as a factor of consideration for determination of suitable compound placement.

From Dr. Angell's observations, detainees seemed to enjoy the interaction with other local Iraqi civilians that Trans-In provided. Yet, this program only lasted a few months at Camp Bucca before space, timing, and manpower became issues in its continuance. In some cases, it was problematic because new arrivals to Camp Bucca would arrive late in the night (or early morning) and, as the local civilian Iraqi nationals could not be informed about the arrival time for security purposes, they would often be sleeping during the arrival. Being such, it became impractical and unfair to wake up the Iraqi civilian instructors to suddenly teach a class. At the same time, there was not enough TIF space to leave the new arrivals in the temporary compound until an appropriate time for instruction by the local Iraqi civilian instructors, as new arrivals were always incoming and the temporary compound barely provided space enough for each new group. The program was never instituted at Camp Cropper or Camp Taji, according to Col. Daniel Deadrich (personal interview, January 28, 2010).

All of this was unfortunate, as new detainees arriving onsite were in an ideal (vulnerable) position to be tested and asked any number of questions. Many were unsure of where they were or what was going to happen to them, and they were eager to be engaged. Because of this, it is highly recommended that in similar situations trans-in should occur, but rather in a modified form. A series of questions should be developed by a cleric, social worker, and teacher team in order to properly assess a compound placement and examine the new detainee's level of religiosity, so as to avoid misplacing him/her in an inadequate or life-threatening compound. As new arrivals are also in a unique position to be tested on their literacy level and interest in different theater internment facility rehabilitation center (TIFRC) programs, a set of tests to determine the educational level of the detainee, from basic level to college and beyond, should be written and given to the new detainee. At the same time, it might be advantageous to enquire of the detainee his/her experience and/or interest in particular vocational training programs. If he/she is experienced in a particular program, this could help identify a potential new leader. If he/she only has interest, but little to no experience, this could identify a potential new detainee student. Conceptually, all the data garnered from the trans-in could be entered into a spreadsheet to be given to the TIF commander to assist in compound placement. A permanent hard copy could be put into the detainee's file for comparison against data collected at other stages during the detainee's internment.

Undeniably, all interaction with a detainee during the first 24 hours of detainment has an impact and is crucial to a detainee's attitude during the entire time he/she will be detained. This is why it is considerably more important that during this period, information is gathered and put into a database for inclusion of future rehabilitation programs. As mentioned previously, it also will undoubtedly help aid correct compound placement (in hopes of reducing intercompound violence). Finally, a statistical summary of any changes a detainee undergoes while in detainment can be created on a chart after the detainee is asked similar questions every 6 months when going before the Multinational Force Review Committee (MNFRC) board. This information could then potentially give insight into issues in particular compounds (i.e., detainees becoming more radical in certain compounds or becoming more moderate in others) and provide clearer direction on the best way to introduce (or evolve) the rehabilitation programs.

Phase II: Sustained Tanweer

The Sustained Tanweer program was conceptualized to provide detainees and families with long-term exposure to moderate messages during a detainee's internment. Sustained Tanweer included formal instruction, detainee-led discussions, and family engagement. Formal instruction consisted of a variety of classes for detainees taught by clerics, social workers, and teachers. By 2010, all the rehabilitation programs, including creative expressions, vocational training, education, Islamic discussion program, and civics, fell under Phase II Sustained Tanweer. Detainee-led discussions were conceptualized to be an outcome of the "Train the Trainers" program, which was an attempt to empower detainees to lead other detainees. The final component of Phase II—family engagement—was targeted during detainee visitation through playing media and active interaction between U.S. military personnel and Iraqi nationals visiting detained family members.

10-Day Civics Course

Although changes in government and social status were (and still are) occurring daily across Iraq, many detainees remained ignorant of these changes when removed from their neighborhood and from selected media. Unaware, detainees often became disconcerted and confused, unsure of what to believe and whom to trust. Many were oblivious of the new Iraq constitution, and even the new Iraq flag, which no longer featured Saddam's handwriting across the front. Some detainees were unaware that Western-styled clothing was growing increasingly more acceptable as was women wearing jeans and holding positions of authority. To an individual who had been detained inside an internment facility while a country rapidly transformed with the ousting of an abusive government to the establishment of a new and more tolerant government, these were changes that could be quite intimidating to encounter. To address these concerns and others, it became apparent that there was significant need for a program that would better prepare a detainee for life after release by truthfully addressing the ongoing changes that were occurring across mainstream Iraq. This grew especially important as the TIFs transfer from United States to Iraq authority grew nearer.

As an increased number of Iraqi correctional officers (ICOs) started working at TIFs across Iraq, detainees became more and more accustomed to seeing them and being held accountable for following their orders. However, their hesitation and reluctance to trust the ICOs were evident. To address this and other factors, in the summer of 2008, particular special attention was paid to the initiation of a civics component in detainees' rehabilitation. It was developed as yet another alternative for detainees to involve themselves in learning about the changes taking place in the country of Iraq as well as more effectively keep them informed about changes in Iraqi government. The 10-day civics course began in May 2008 at Camp Bucca, and detainees were required to travel to/from it daily in order to participate. Participation was voluntary and, as with the education and other rehabilitation classes offered, anyone who did not wish to participate at any point in time could return to his compound without consequence.

The civics class curriculum included relevant explanations and examinations of the Qur'an and Abu Shuja; it started with discussing subjects such as patience, honesty, and truth. In addition, discussions on ancient and modern Iraqi history, the emergence of and continued existence of tribes in Iraq, and different religious beliefs found throughout Iraq were offered. Nationalism also was deliberated, with particular emphasis on the family and neighbors. The Iraq constitution, the Iraq national anthem, and the Iraq rule of law were discussed as well. Popular topics, such as women's rights, non-Muslims' rights, and human rights in Iraq, also were confabulated. Finally, the Iraqi government system was broken down into easy-to-understand language, and detainees were encouraged to ask questions.

During the course, detainees were given a copy of the Iraq national anthem, and time was given in class to practice learning the words. Detainees also were given a copy of the Iraq Constitution to keep. Daily quiz questions ensured that detainees were following the class and actively participating. Based on the detainees' answers, determination would be made by the cleric and social worker whether the detainee had satisfactorily passed the civics course or not. For those whose performance and/or attendance were not satisfactory, they would be invited to retake the course. Otherwise, for those who passed at the conclusion of the 10-day civics course, there was a formal graduation with chai tea, cookies, and graduation certificates distributed. Most classes also concluded with an inspirational Iraqi guest speaker. In the past, we had used both Iraqi and non-Iraqi as inspirational speakers. Our first inspirational speaker in June 2008 was born in Iraq, had emigrated to Canada, and then returned to work the OSS program as an education supervisor. He elaborated on his life choices that had got him where he was today, and encouraged all the graduating detainees to think before they act, and not to be afraid to follow their heart. It was a great speech and, from its success, encouraged us to attempt a speaker for each following civics class graduation. Although having a guest speaker for every graduation was not always feasible, we always had at least one officer present to end the ceremony with a celebratory and congratulatory speech.

Train the Trainer Tanweer

The Train the Trainer program was an inspiration of Maj. Gen. Stone, who had the idea that real change would come from within Iraq, so it was important to engage and empower natural detainee leaders to teach other detainees important topics. Essentially, the idea was to educate a group of detainees to become "peer Tanweer leaders," taking lessons learned in the Phase II, 10-day civics class back to their compounds in order to teach other detainees. In effect, by doing so, they allowed a larger population of detainees to benefit from the civics instruction.

The first class of Train the Trainer took place from June 10 to 28, 2008, at Camp Bucca. The class was 15 days in duration. Class hours were from 7 p.m. to 2 a.m. (due to the heat during the day making it unsuitable to hold classes), split up by two sessions: The first session was from 7 to 10 p.m., then an hour break, then the second session from 11 p.m. to 2 a.m. Each 3-hour session had a 30-minute break in the middle. Detainees were chosen to participate and be certified as peer trainers based on previously displayed leadership qualities while in detention. After the military identified and selected candidates, the detainees were then transferred to a caravan for the entire duration of the Train the Trainer course. The caravans chosen for the class were in the same compound—compound 6—at Camp Bucca as the IDP course. Throughout the 15-day duration of the program, ongoing evaluations and observations were conducted to ensure suitability and motivation level of each detainee participant.

The first half of the first day of the Train the Trainer course involved explaining the objectives of the course, detailing the participation rules, and signing individual detainee contracts. Afterwards, the class resumed with explanations on patience from the Qur'an and Abu Shuja. On day 2, the topics covered by the cleric were honesty, truth, and time, while the social worker discussed Iraqi history to include ancient Mesopotamia, Sumerians, and Great Babylon. The Islamic period, Iraqi monarchy, and Iraqi kings were also included in discussion. Day 3 began with a round-table on the multitribes, multinationalities, and multireligions that make up Iraq. Nationality as it relates to sectarianism also was discussed, as was traditional Iraqi customs. Thereafter, during the second half of day 3, the cleric covered women's rights in Islam. Day 4 began with the cleric leading a discussion on friendship and honoring one's parents, before the social worker deliberated on citizenship as a special status and as it applies to the rule of law. On day 5, the social worker began with a discussion about the Iraqi Constitution, encouraging each detainee to take a personal copy to familiarize himself/herself with it. The cleric followed with a discussion about neighbors' rights in Islam and peaceful heart against grudge and envy. Day 6 started with a deliberation on human rights and rights of non-Muslims in Islam. The social worker then took over with how the Iraq government now works and why the way it has evolved is important. Positions in government, such as what the prime minister is responsible for and the functions of the president, were also discussed. On day 7, the social worker led a discussion on democracy in Islam before encouraging the detainees to brainstorm on how to build a democratic Iraq that includes both social justice and economic development. The cleric followed by outlining giving and generosity in the Qur'an. Then from day 9 to day 12, the traditional 4-day IDP was taught, although more intensive, with extra time allotted for questions from the detainees. On day 13, the class worked on individual class outlines, breaking into small groups for discussion on which methods might be most practical for use in their future compound teaching. On days 14 and 15, there were individual practicals. Each detainee would lead a 30-minute discussion on a previously decided-upon topic. Together, the class of detainees would then help to evaluate the method used by the detainee "instructor" who had led the discussion. Each detainee instructor got his turn to lead and be evaluated by his peers. Finally, at the conclusion of day 15, there was a formal graduation with certificates presented to all the passing detainees. During this time, detainees also were given a handbook of notes and relevant clippings from the course content to use for teaching the 10-day civics course when they return to their respective compounds.

Provided they passed the course, detainees were then certified with the promise of returning to their compound and instructing others in what they had learned. Graduates were provided with the syllabus and course information, and required to follow the course content exactly the way they were taught it. As an added benefit and to encourage continued motivation and dedication to the program, according to the FRAGO, detainees who partook of the Train the Trainer course were given the opportunity to appear before the MNFRC board within 90 days of the course completion. This additional benefit was only explained to the detainees after they had been identified, selected, and moved to the caravan to wait for their class to commence.

Yet, unfortunately, while the concept was solid and looked good on paper, it didn't result in the desired effect. There was definite interest among detainees, particularly those who understood they could go before the MNFRC board in 90 days (as opposed to the typical 180 days) after participation. So, that was not the issue. Rather, it was determined that detainees in compounds had no interest in listening to, and engaging with, a program that was led by another detainee. They did not feel the program was legitimate without the presence of an OSS civilian. The same held true for the newly certified detainee instructors, who, once returned to their compounds, were met with disinterest by their fellow detainees. Both of these problems defeated the purpose, that of having detainee-led discussions. The final gripe was that there was no official graduation within the compounds after the courses ended. Allegedly, detainees were unwilling to listen and engage in a program that did not get recognition from the U.S. military, let alone did not offer a course completion certificate. And, unfortunately, without the checks and balances in place to verify which detainees had actually been active participants in the class, and whether or not the course material taught had been the full curriculum, conditions were not favorable to give them that. So, in the end, after just four Train the Trainers classes at Camp Bucca, the class ceased operations, and the focus returned instead to just ensuring that those who had the desire had the opportunity to participate in the many other rehabilitation programs available.

Phase III: Transition Tanweer

Phase III, Transition Tanweer (also known as "trans-out" Tanweer) provided the detainee with formal instruction and assessment during release. According to Lt. Col. Richard Johnson (personal interview, 2010):

> We found out that many of the detainees were getting ready to leave and were totally unprepared for the changes that occurred in Iraq since they left. That is essentially the objective of Tanweer [trans-out]. Tanweer is a civics class that discusses Iraqi politics, the changes in Iraq since the war, and it tends to prepare the detainee for what he will see when he leaves here. A lot of them have been here for a long time, and there have been a lot of changes in the outside world. Time stands still when you are doing time. Tanweer is one of those things that we like as a baseline class. We want every detainee to go to Tanweer because it gives them what we think is a decent basic level of what's going on politically in Iraq and since the war began, the security agreement, the U.S. presence, and what our intentions are. Those things are important to know. I think we need to provide as much information as possible, and Tanweer helps that to happen.

Clerics and social workers conducted this program to reinforce moderate messages prior to a detainee's release, the intention being to assist a smooth transition back to society. This class was mandatory for release; detainees who had been issued release paperwork had no choice whether or not to participate. The first class officially ran in April 2008 and was given only to individuals who had already been given release paperwork and were only waiting for transfer.* The 3-day long, 18-hour course was taught by a two-person team consisting of a cleric and social worker. It included discussion on human rights, women's rights, and non-Muslims' rights in Islam, post-Saddam Iraqi government structure, post-Saddam

---

* All detainees at Camp Bucca were out-processed through Camp Cropper. That is where they would receive any money due them from working during their detention, in addition to being returned all items seized when they had been initially detained.

Iraqi Constitution, and peaceful heart against grudge and envy. It concluded with both a cleric and social worker assessment in addition to a graduation ceremony. At the graduation ceremony, a high-ranking officer would give a sobering speech, congratulating the detainees about their release, but also reminding them that if they caused an infraction and were detained again, they would not be eligible to participate in the many extracurricular activities offered at the detention site. Instead, they would be housed in the highest security, modular detainee housing unit (MDHU), and limited to only 2 hours a day of recreational time outside. Photos of the MDHU and exercise courtyard highlighting the extreme conditions and limit of freedom were passed around to illustrate the point. According to commanders, they were instructed to make sure their speech was particularly somber, thereby eliminating any confusion on the detainees' part about what would be the outcome if they chose to engage in activities determined contrary to global security.

On some occasions, there was not enough time to give the whole 3-day program before a detainee would be released. So, for these occasions, a 3-hour civics course was developed. Usually directed as a last resort (as the intent was always that every detainee would have at least the 3-day course), the 3-hour course nevertheless gave the detainee a sampling of what to expect once released. After a basic introduction to changes that Iraq had undergone, it went through the topics of civics, religion, and Iraqi family in society. Detainees who got this brief course were also exposed to the Iraqi national anthem, had an opportunity to see the new Iraqi flag, and were given a copy of the Iraqi Constitution. Finally, they were also encouraged to ask any lingering questions they might have or bring up any areas of concern. At the conclusion of the 3-hour civics course, an officer with the rank of major or above would deliver the same sobering word-for-word speech as given at the conclusion of the 3-day course. The officer would remind each detainee to be vigilant and trustworthy once released, so that they were not involved in something that guarantees their return to detention.

TANWEER TRANSFORMED

Although Tanweer had been running under different names, and in different capacities, since Maj. Gen. Stone's arrival in 2007, it was with Maj. Gen. David Quantock's arrival in late summer 2008 that all the rehabilitation programs, including IDP, were pulled together to be referred to under one term—Tanweer. According to Maj. Gen. Quantock, in order to meet the changing needs of the detainee population, the 4-day IDP, which previously had been considered a completely separate program, was incorporated into a 12-day and 30-day class called "12-Day Tanweer" and "30-Day Tanweer," each falling under the Phase II: Sustained Tanweer intent. Both the 12-day and 30-day Tanweer combined the 4-day IDP with the possibility of a more intensive religious discussion component in addition to the 10-day civics course. Typically, the 12-day and 30-day Tanweer were aimed primarily at those set for release, so they dealt mostly with reintegration back into society. According to Maj. Kevin Comfort (personal interview, 2010):

> The contract with OSS required Tanweer as a Contract Line Item and the vendor and I as the COR [contracting officer representative] used the term Tanweer as it was IAW [in accordance with] the contract. However, I believe the term "Islamic Discussion Group" developed [continued] out of necessity to explain what Tanweer was/is by having a more understandable and self-explanatory name. The contracted hours for Tanweer were 12 days, but there were times and requirements for improvised and alternate educational opportunities for the detainees that altered the course, so there were incidents where the course was shortened locally at some facilities for small populations of detainees. This was usually done due to release date changes or to offer a population something they desired in an effort to again assist the more moderate detainees. Sometimes the 12 days could not be done. The 12 days were supposed to spread over the detention sort of an initial, interim, and just before release semester.

However, in reality, Camp Bucca, Camp Taji, and Camp Cropper all went about implementing the changes a little bit differently. Camp Bucca, which was the first site of the IDP, went about incorporating the Tanweer element by having two separate classes: the IDP and a 10-day civics class. According to Maj. Gen. Quantock (personal correspondence, 2010):

> The days when we were at Bucca (late 2008), I separated the two courses, so that all received the training, even those not being released; this helped us assess or identify the most radical of the detainees (some would never make it through the training without acting out). ... As releases slowed and changed into mostly transfers, we brought the program back together.

Meanwhile Camp Cropper had the 4-day IDP, 12-day Tanweer, and 30-day Tanweer. According to Lt. Col. Deadrich:

> The IDP was mandatory for detainees pending release. It not only discussed religious tolerance, but gave an overview of the Iraqi government structure (kind of like a civics class) to give them a better understanding of the changes in the government since their detention. It also talked a little about reintegration with family. The 12-day Tanweer was a mandatory class focusing on religious tolerance. The

30-day Tanweer was an optional class for those who wanted to get into more in-depth discussions about Islamic theory.

Detainees were assigned to one of the classes based on whether or not they had been approved for release. Detainees who were approved for release were required to attend the 12-day Tanweer before the official release ceremony. Detainees who were not approved for release were required to at least attend the 4-day IDP. It was somewhere during this time that the name of the Islamic Discussion Program became synonymous with 4-Day Tanweer. As there were many extra safety cautions for movement of those designated as extreme, the 4-day Tanweer program was brought to the detainees at the MDHU. "Our Imams would go to them [the extremists] and sit in the recreation yard on the other side of the wire and teach them about the Qur'an," commented Lt. Col. Johnson.

Finally, Camp Taji, which did not open until late summer 2009, only had the 12-day Tanweer and the 30-day Tanweer. According to Maj. Gen. Quantock:

> Yes, to be clear, the 4-day IDP was in the 12-day Tanweer when you were at Taji. Everyone had to participate in the IDP portion. ... The rest was mostly provided for those being released or programmed for release (sometimes the truth changed, we got a late arrest warrant/detention order).

12-Day Tanweer

Although there was no difference from the subject matter taught during the initial 4-day IDP discussed in Chapter 9 and the 4-day Tanweer program, the 12-day Tanweer offered the time and space to expand on topics. The 12-day Tanweer was set up similar to the 4-day IDP, with most days including 3 hours of classes being taught by a cleric, a break, then another 3 hours being taught by the social worker. According to the 12-day Tanweer program of instruction (POI), on days 1 to 6, clerics taught the morning classes while the social workers taught the afternoon classes. On days 7 to 8, it was a clerical immersion, and on days 9–10, it was a social worker immersion. On day 11, the clerics taught morning classes and the social workers taught the afternoon classes, while on day 12, the clerics conducted the morning assessment before the social workers wrapped up the afternoon assessment. Lt. Col. Johnson described the 12-day Tanweer as:

> It's a religious discussion and it is also a civics discussion. It is limited by that definition, but the civics piece of it talks about the changes in Iraq now, the politics of Iraq, and the new government. Lately, we are

talking about the election coming up. We were just polling our detainees: Who wants to vote? Who is registered to vote? It grows to be a
larger discussion, but there is a religious discussion as well.

Clerical topics in the 12-day Tanweer built on the 4-day IDP topics
to include such topics as "non-Muslim rights in Islam and Friendship,"
"human rights and Islam/women's rights," and "honor thy parents/
neighbors' rights in Islam." Similarly, social worker topics built on the
4-day IDP to include "Iraq government structure," "reintegration into
society," and "tolerance and humaneness," according to Maj. Comfort.
From retention, Sheik Adbul Sattar (personal interview, 2010) outlined
the clerical elements of the 12-day Tanweer program to include:

> Day 1: For introductions. Introducing yourself to everyone. Day 2: We
> start the POI with the topics of Purification and Prayer. Day 3: Honesty.
> Day 4: Repentance. Day 5 and 6: Offenses (two days because this is
> a very important subject). Day 7: human rights including Muslim,
> non-Muslim, and Women Rights. Day 8: The good heart against envy
> and hatred. Day 9: Respect the parents. Day 10: Neighbor's rights.
> Day 11: Power of tongue. Between 2 hours: lies and slander. Day 12:
> Assessment and graduation.

In addition to in-depth discussion, the 12-day Tanweer also included
role playing and homework that detainees were encouraged to complete.
These included activities such as "judge yourself and clear your heart
before you sleep" and "list two hadith verses related to a peaceful heart,"
after the conclusion of the day dealing with peaceful heart against grudge
and envy. Other activities included discussing "what would you do if
your parents ordered you to do something sinful," to complement the
day's lesson honoring one's parents' and neighbors' rights in Islam, and
"recall three verses that reference patience," to complement the day on
patience and time. Each day detainees would conclude the lessons with
a homework assignment, usually involving something to think about or
research in the Qur'an and/or hadiths.

30-Day Tanweer

The Tanweer 30-day was an extension of the Tanweer 12-day, but with
the added intent of exploring topics even further in-depth. According
to Sheikh Sattar, the Tanweer 30-day was designed for those with less
religious knowledge or for those who would benefit from having a longer class length. Often, the 30-day Tanweer would have three clerics and two social workers per class. The books used were those in
the 4-day IDP to include the Qur'an, hadiths, Abu Shuja, and Islamic

history. The Islamic history component did not come from a specific book, but rather from the cleric's knowledge "built through a lifetime of studying the Qur'an." Sheik Sattar outlined the clerical topics of 30-day Tanweer to build on the topics of the 12-day Tanweer by discussing. He said:

> Punishment in Islam is very important and takes sometimes a few days to cover. Also ... inheritance according to Islamic law. On the topic of jihad, we explain to them how to distinguish between martyrdom and suicide. This is very important to let them know what the punishment in Islam is when a human kills himself. It happens in Iraqi streets a lot, so it is very important and relevant to discuss in-depth.

The cleric portion of the 30-day Tanweer was an intense examination of the Abu Shuja text. Pairing it alongside the Qur'an, detainees were encouraged to read and discuss topics such as "the benefits of testifying," "truthfulness," and "nationalism in Islam," while exploring the Abu Shuja justification of the topics. The social worker portion of the 30-day Tanweer elaborated on topics such as "patriotism," "Iraqi Constitution," and "life values and life goals" in addition to the topics covered during the 4- and 12-day Tanweer. The social worker content during the 30 days also included many role-playing activities. One such role-playing activity is where the instructor divides group members into pairs where one person in each pair pretends to be an extremist leader intent on trying to convince the other person of the validity of his views while that person resists." After, group members change their roles and repeat. This particular role play complemented the lesson on "leadership and dependence from leaders in extremist groups." Another role play involved splitting the detainees into pairs where each pair has both a grandfather and a grandchild. The grandfather was instructed to tell his grandchild the story of his life, the good things he did in his life for himself, for his children, for his grandchildren, and for his country. He was then encouraged to give his grandchild advice. Again the roles were flipped and repeated.

During both the clerical and social worker portions of the 30-day Tanweer, detainees were encouraged to question anything they were being told or have been told in the past. They also were encouraged to go outside the topics presented in class to research particular areas that most interest them. Class was presented as a time not only for discussion and debate, but also as a time to reflect and absorb the information that was being offered.

CONCLUSION

Most soldiers, detainees, and Iraqi civilians who have worked the Tanweer program agree on its usefulness. According to Lt. Col. Deadrich, the way Tanweer is structured is both necessary and productive in managing and preparing the detainee population for release or transfer to Iraqi control. He said:

> I think these programs are useful, after being in this environment. You have to keep them busy. You have to keep them thinking about something, or they will think about ways to hurt you. I'd rather them think of ways of what they want to paint or build than think of ways that they would want to escape or hurt my guard force. You have to keep them mentally challenged, keep them physically challenged, and keep them occupied with things to do rather than let them think of bad things to do. The program provides a very good thing in reducing the level of anxiety of this population as it gives them things to do. It gives them something to look forward to and they enjoy it. It also provides a basis of opportunities that they didn't have and maybe would never have had. To get a chance to get a class to learn more about the Qur'an and the different meanings of the same verse or even a chance to learn how to read and write … that's definitely something useful.

In addition to making the 4-day IDP mandatory (by its inclusion into the 12-day Tanweer) for all detainees before release, under Maj. Gen. Quantock's command the IDP was no longer conducted in caravans for the course duration. Instead, detainees were transported daily to/from their compound for class, according to the general. The only exception were those who were most extreme, who were taught in their compound through the fence. For those who were transferred daily to/from class, class sizes averaged around 16 detainees for both the 12-day Tanweer and 30-day Tanweer.

Otherwise, another noticeable difference between the 4-day IDP and the Tanweer classes was that detainees were unfortunately not given copies of the Abu Shuja or any other documents for personal use. When Dr. Angell returned to visit Iraq in January 2010, it was not clear if this was because of a security concern, lack of supplies, or just lack of knowledge about their importance. But, according to Sheik Sattar:

> Is it good to give the detainees a copy of the Abu Shuja to read? I can only answer you based on my experience in Bucca. But, I think it's good to keep the detainees busy reading. Otherwise, maybe they will listen to others talking about religion. Maybe they will get the wrong answer. Maybe if they had important books to reference, that wouldn't happen.
>
> Nevertheless, we have many great programs. It's like a string of beads, something to complete the other. For example, we need

education for those who cannot read and write. When they finish this program, they come to us so it's easy for us to teach them the Qur'an or the prophetic sayings so they can understand what we say. Otherwise, without the ability to read and write, anyone can deceive them by saying, "God said this in the Qur'an," and they can't say yes or no. For example, what happened in Bucca, and Dr. Ami knows that well because she was my mentor there, in one of my classes I met a detainee. I said to him, "I know Bucca is a place where you are so far away from your family, but, in spite of that, how do you find Bucca?" He said, "In the 30 years of my life, I didn't touch a pencil, but now after I finished the education program in Bucca, I can read and write." To prove that to me, inside the class, he quoted from the Qur'an and started to read, and he was very happy.

According to Maj. Gen. Quantock, "Tanweer was tailored and changed as our mission evolved." Lt. Col. Johnson supports Maj. Gen. Quantock's interpretation and transformation of Tanweer. According to him:

> We start with General Quantock. He drives everything here. Because his mission is unique, General Quantock is unique. For a general officer, very rarely will you see a guy who knows his mission so well. General Quantock knows right down to which detainee is to which zone. He knows the details better than anybody in this mission. That is why he is seeing through the mission before he leaves. He drove this from the top.

Maj. Gen. Quantock redeployed in March 2010, after almost 2 years in Iraq as detainee operations commander. During his time as commander in Iraq, he became well known among the troops as he actively engaged in an attempt to learn as much as possible about how to complete the mission to the best of his ability. Many have questioned his concept of combining IDP with civics to form the 12-day and 30-day Tanweer (Figure 12.1), in addition to making IDP participation no longer voluntary. But, his seemingly simple logic has an unusual complexity to it, one that he will voluntarily elaborate on when questioned. Does it make sense to group the IDP and the civics under one program? Does it make sense to make the programs no longer voluntary? According to him, "absolutely." And as Dr. Angell didn't hear any disagreement while interviewing soldiers, civilians, and most importantly detainees, she is bound to venture that he just might be correct. Apparently, time, place, and circumstances sometimes call for extraordinary, if unusual, measures.

FIGURE 12.1   Civics class in session: Camp Cropper, Iraq, 2010. (Photo courtesy of U.S. Department of Defense.)

CHAPTER 13

The Future of Extremist Rehabilitation Programs

THE CONTEXT

The global campaign against terrorism has been dominated by an overwhelming kinetic response. The lethal operations have temporarily disrupted terrorist operational infrastructures, but have not disrupted the conceptual infrastructures driving extremism and terrorism. The modus operandi to catch, kill, and disrupt terrorist organizations is having a boomerang effect. Although the operational capabilities of terrorist groups have been reduced in some theaters, the motives and intentions of the terrorists to fight back have grown, protracting the fight.

In some countries, soft power has been cast aside as hard powers are wielded. The combination—smart power—is used only by very few nations. While the use of operational measures should not be disregarded, an equal amount of attention has not been given to the strategic fight—the battle of ideas. The ideological and intellectual infrastructures form the foundations of the terrorist movement. As the environment remains permissive, ideology remains the lifeblood of contemporary terrorist groups and movements. Terrorist ideologies can only be delegitimized by ideological and theological refutation. To safeguard the next generation of youth from the lure of fighting and the appeal of extremist ideology, counterideology must be incorporated into the counterterrorism toolbox. Ideally, the two counterideology prongs of community engagement and terrorist rehabilitation should be used in parallel.

By building community-based programs that aim to engage indoctrinated extremists and rehabilitate operational terrorists, regeneration of violence can be prevented. These programs should be built in partnership with the government. Terrorist rehabilitation is a vital tool in the fight where incarcerated terrorists are actively engaged to recant, repent, and express remorse for their thoughts and acts of violence.

THE BACKGROUND

According to the International Committee of the Red Cross (ICRC), there are over 100,000 convicted and suspected terrorists languishing in penitentiary and detention centers from Europe to the Middle East and Asia. Although there are vocational and educational programs to rehabilitate criminals, there are very few initiatives to rehabilitate terrorists. Though terrorist rehabilitation has been the topic of significant interest and debate from academic circles in the United States to the officials in Europe, there has been very little effort to examine the concepts, processes, and outcomes of terrorist rehabilitation. Despite significant study into terrorist mindsets and the ideologies driving them, terrorist rehabilitation remains the exception worldwide. Terrorist rehabilitation is not the norm.

During the George W. Bush presidency, the United States had a golden opportunity to start a rehabilitation program in Guantanamo Bay (Gitmo) in Cuba. Instead, the United States earned the anger of the Muslim world by portraying images of muffled and chained men wearing orange jumpsuits. Arguably, Gitmo should have been divided into two sections: (1) a privilege section where detainees, who cooperated, received counseling, learnt livelihood skills, played with their children, and met with their families; and (2) the other section perhaps being for those who did not want to cooperate nor participate in any activities. But, unfortunately, there was no difference in sections; instead, all detainees were grouped together and did not have any access to counseling or any other privileges. The outcome of the U.S. choice of inaction was that the Gitmo detainees departed Guantanamo Bay even more radicalized than when they were brought in. Instead of giving up the habits that had put them there in the first place, they built on and solidified their impaired ideologies by their very isolation. As such, it should have been no surprise that after their release, nearly 100 former detainees returned to the fight (Morgan, 2009). U.S. President Obama signed a decree on January 22, 2009, commanding the closure of the Guantanamo Bay detention centre (Priest, 2009, p. A1). While this was an unavoidable promise that likely helped him win office, the fact that most countries receiving Gitmo detainees didn't have rehabilitation programs perhaps should have been taken under consideration.

Egypt pioneered the idea of contemporary religious rehabilitation as early as the 1990s. Al Azhar scholars and counselors working under the historical leadership of Al Gama Al Islamiyah Al Masri (Islamic Group of Egypt) began to influence detainees and inmates to abandon violence and build peace (Blaydes & Rubin, 2008, pp. 461–479). There were efforts in rehabilitation earlier, in the 1960s and 1970s, when Malaysia and Singapore developed programs for rehabilitating the communist terrorists in Malaysia; however, these were not elaborate. Communism in Asia was not yet a global threat and religion was not the basis for the ideological mindset in that era. Resolution of the problem at the time was contextual. In fact, it wasn't until after realizing the scale of the threat following the Al Qaeda attacks against the United States on September 11, 2001, in combination with uncovering threats/arrests in their own countries, that Singapore, Saudi Arabia, Iraq, Uzbekistan, Indonesia, and Malaysia developed national rehabilitation programs. Since then, the process of detainee and inmate rehabilitation has been gaining momentum worldwide. As a new frontier in counterterrorism practice, rehabilitation programs have provided varying degrees of success in the countries that have adopted them. Some countries, such as Singapore, have leveraged community involvement to strengthen intercommunal bonds. In times of crisis, the focus is on preserving harmony and trust in society. Clerics and scholars have volunteered to counsel detainees, their families, well-meaning individuals, and even institutions in their effort to promote and encourage extremist rehabilitation. Although requiring a much-higher commitment level, the participation and ownership by the community is an important fundamental step in the right direction.

HUMAN TERRAIN IS KEY

The contemporary wave of ideologically driven violence presents a series of new challenges. Most countries have built the skill and will to fight using security and intelligence services, militaries, and enforcement authorities. But, unfortunately, most countries have not yet adequately developed the ideological and intellectual understanding, knowledge, and structures to counter the conceptual terrorist infrastructures. To reduce the immediate threat, operational terrorists should be sought. However, for strategic peace, the reality of the global viewpoint needs to be corrected. For long-term success, the government needs to understand that human terrain is the key.

Unlike the previous generation of threat groups, Al Qaeda understood the importance of the human terrain and placed a premium on using New Media and technology to spread its message. Many years have passed since Al Qaeda attacked America's most iconic landmarks on September 11, 2001, but governments are still only best at using lethal, kinetic, and hard power. And, regrettably, in this operational counterterrorism method—catch, kill, and disrupt—we cannot win the fight in totality. To reverse the current global trend, greater strategic capabilities (to win hearts and minds) and platforms for engagement should be built. The future is about grass roots initiatives; it is about preventing the making of extremists and terrorists through active community engagement, and offender reintegration into the community through rehabilitation.

Terrorism represents the tier-one national security threat to most countries. No country is immune from the threat of extremism or its vicious by-product: terrorism. Even if governments built the most capable military, law enforcement, and national security agencies, no government can guarantee its citizens total security from terrorism. The threat is diverse, complex, and global. Truly transnational threats, terrorism, and extremism permeate territorial borders and communities. If any single country or region is producing terrorists and extremists, other countries and regions will remain at risk. There should be recognition that no country is great enough to secure itself without the cooperation and expertise of others. Similarly, no country is too small when it comes to contributing to global security.

Currently, cooperation and collaboration are largely on the operational arena and not yet at the ideological frontier. To make rehabilitation a part of the solution at a global level, a more concerted effort is needed. Leaders and visionaries need to fully engage themselves; their expertise and dedication are greatly desired to make the ideological transition from local to regional, and national to international.

THE NEGLECTED BATTLEFIELD

Today, the most significant terrorist threat emanates from a global movement, underpinned by a violent politico-religious ideology. Political incompetence drives it and religious misinterpretation legitimizes it. Members of this movement seek to overturn regimes they consider to be apostate through violent and undemocratic means. The local and international grievances of the Muslim masses are exploited to help construct a picture of a modern world hostile toward Islam and Muslims. This threat driven by a volatile ideology can never be adequately addressed by military and law enforcement actions. A paradigm shift must occur.

A terrorist suffers from exposure to extremist propaganda and indoctrination. A vicious by-product of society, perhaps he/she was more susceptible and vulnerable to the extremist message than other members of society. By skillful approaches and interviews, it is possible to map the person's ideological, theological, and intellectual makeup as well as his/her orientations and inclinations. After discerning the terrorist narrative that affected him/her to cross the line, the factors that radicalized him/her to hate, conceive, plan, prepare, and attack can be identified. The understanding and knowledge to strategically fight the contemporary wave of radicalization and violence rests within that extremist.

Rehabilitation allows communication with the captured extremist, challenging his/her thoughts and ideas as well as allaying any misgivings he/she might harbor. Such a careful and involved approach will eventually defeat terrorism by decreasing the need for militaristic means.

The battlefield of the mind is a neglected battlefield. A strategic investment, fighting the battlefield of the mind is less costly, albeit a larger commitment. Extricating the negative thoughts and replacing them with realistic thoughts are also a more humanitarian approach. Making terrorist and extremist rehabilitation mandated by law also will have other benefits; it will reduce humiliation, abuse, and torture, and, in the process, remove another justification from extremist indoctrination about how the West tortures Muslims in detention.

MODES OF REHABILITATION

Rehabilitation requires engaging the extremist on all his/her facets. A successful program that can withhold long-term must recognize and incorporate all modes of rehabilitation. It also must be flexible enough to evolve based on the country and persons for which it is intended. Within each mode of rehabilitation there are various styles, which also might need to evolve depending on the ideology of the particular extremist. But, in general, the seven ideal principal modes of rehabilitation are religious, psychological, family and social, vocational, educational, creative arts, and recreational. Many of these might overlap with each other, which is beneficial to the extremist. In fact the more involvement an extremist has in all aspects of the various modes, the more potential there will be for him to destroy his destructive ideology at an accelerated pace. Often, different modes, such as "religious rehabilitation" and "psychological rehabilitation," might coexist at the same time in the same program. The important thing to remember is that a successful program is constantly evolving, and as such there are no absolutes about the way each part of it should happen; rather, just general rules and guidelines. The modes of rehabilitation are discussed below.

Religious Rehabilitation

Every religion promotes peace and harmony, and values tolerance and moderation. Nevertheless, the ideas of religion (i.e., religious ideology) have frequently been used to provide legitimacy in the justification for violence. As such, religion is often misused as a means to influence and convince persons to believe and act in a certain way. In the past two decades, we have witnessed terrorism stemming from the propagation of deviant versions of Hinduism, Judaism, Christianity, Buddhism, Sikhism, and others. Only religious teachers and scholars can correct this by addressing the incorrect interpretation and incorrect teachings. Many terrorists believe that the United States, its allies, and its friends are deliberately attacking Islam and killing Muslims. They are made to believe that the West is "Satan," and a religious obligation binds them to attack the United States and its allies. Through the imposition of an extremist and militant interpretation of Islam, the terrorists are committed to reestablishing the caliphate. The term *caliphate* refers to the first form of government inspired by Islam. It was initially led by Mohammed's disciples as a continuation of the political authority the prophet established. To extremists, this is the ultimate aim—to have a global caliphate—and, to that end, they justify any amount of violence.

To derive legitimacy for their struggle, Muslim extremists interpret the Qur'an and other religious scriptures in a manner that portrays them as the true guardians of Islam. Learned Islamic scholars and clerics have the understanding, knowledge, and authority to correct the Islamic misconceptions a terrorist holds and believes in. Unfortunately, among religious communities, the realization of the dangers of extremist ideas has not been significantly and adequately addressed; and many do not understand the necessary sensitivity that is required when working with dangerous ideologies. A systematic and compassionate methodology is needed to bring the misguided back to the intended path. Singapore originally took the initiative in 2003 in guiding religious counseling by producing a manual to assist the religious counseling of individuals who were found to have subscribed to terrorist ideology.* (Bin Ali, personal interview, November 16, 2009). In addition to being offered structured counseling sessions conducted by clerics and psychologists, the detainees are provided with and coached in complementary religious texts, including the Qur'an, books on *Tafsir* (exegesis of Qur'an), *hadith* (sayings and deeds of Prophet), *Fiqh* (Islamic Jurisprudence), and *Sirah* (Prophet's history), all of which were to some degree also utilized during Islamic Discussion Program (IDP) courses in Iraq.

In the process of religious rehabilitation, the extremists' errors in thinking about the world need to evolve. For example, their tendency to think in a binary mode (*I am good, everyone else is evil*) as well as their

---

* Ustaz Haji Ali Haji Mohamed and Ustaz Hj Md Hasbi Hassan were approached by the Ministry of Home Affairs (MHA) to assess the JI detainees, early in 2002. Ustaz Ali and Ustaz Hasbi came forward and led a small group of Islamic teachers and scholars to study the JI ideology. After several interviews with the detainees, both Ustazs concluded that the JI had misunderstood different Islamic concepts. They decided to volunteer themselves to form the Religious Rehabilitation Group (RRG), primarily with the objective of counseling the JI detainees. The RRG Secretariat then embarked on research for the production of an RRG Manual in May 2003. In 2009, the RRG produced a second manual.

sense of exclusivity (*us* versus *them* mentality) should be challenged. There is also the need to shatter the myths surrounding commonly misunderstood Islamic concepts, e.g., being a suicide bomber guarantees a person (and his/her family) entry to the "eternal afterlife." Other myths, including the concept of allegiance versus nonallegiance and the belief that it is a "devout" Muslim's duty to pay respect only to Allah and, therefore, shun and abhor all other Muslims and non-Muslims alike, are also hazardous ways of thinking that need to be challenged.

After extricating the negative ideology and concepts, there is a need to replace them with accurate mainstream religious concepts, e.g., the true meaning of *jihad* in Islam and the correct way to treat non-Muslims. Finally, extremists and those in danger of becoming such are to be immunized against future challenges by providing them a wholesome and thorough understanding of the many facets of Islam.

As wives are usually close to their husbands, the services of *Ustazahs* (female clerics) also should be made available to counsel wives, when available. In most cases, extremist-minded husbands will have indoctrinated their wives and children with their same beliefs and thoughts. Attending a service from an Ustazah will help to lend support to the confused wife, while her husband is going through counseling and education on the correct and intended interpretation of Islam. Counseling extended to the wife must challenge any extremist thoughts and beliefs within the family as well. This will help when the detainee is released because the wife also must take an active role in encouraging the true study and practice of Islam in their home. Some wives, especially those who might have attended extremist classes alongside their husbands, might have been exposed to a significant amount of radical ideology. It is even more important to address these wives' concerns and needs, so that when the husband returns to his family, everyone agrees and is committed to practicing the correct interpretation and values of Islam. Children of the detained extremists also might be advocates of, or at least exposed to, the extremist ideology that landed their fathers in detention to begin with. When this is the case, it is not only the wife who needs to be counseled, but it is also important not to neglect the children, as they are most at risk of becoming part of the new generation of extremists.

Through the right combination of tools, a terrorist who needs help can be reformed. While psychological, vocational, education, social and family, creative arts, and recreation rehabilitation can change one's heart and mind, the most powerful component is religious rehabilitation. Religious rehabilitation has the power to unlock the mind of a detainee or an inmate. It has the power to make a detainee of rehabilitation repent, become remorseful, and successfully reenter the mainstream.

Psychological Rehabilitation

The psychologist adds an important dimension to the rehabilitation process. Psychology enables us to understand why extremists cross the line and kill (or support those who do). The methodology involves psychological profiling, assessment, and solution. From a psychological perspective, it is much easier to change behavior with rewards than with punishment. The fact is that long-term reformation of terrorists may be much less costly than to just ignore them. By showing the extremists that they can benefit from both denouncing a violent ideology *and* from adopting prosocial behavior/ideology, they hopefully will be empowered enough to come to believe their reasons to fight are nullified.

This leaves counselors with an imperative commitment. The captured terrorists must be convinced that their imprisonment or detention is to allow them to participate in a rehabilitation program. They must be assured of getting all the help they need to understand their current situation in addition to knowing that after release, they will have the support they need to avoid falling back into old behaviors. For this, they must be given access to enter into dialogue with qualified clerics and scholars of Islam. Opinions, such as an extremist's genuine concern for the suffering of Muslims in places such as Gaza and the West Bank, Iraq, and Afghanistan, must not be merely dismissed as extremism. On the contrary, these opinions should be used as a window of opportunity to gain greater understanding on how his/her mind works. This might also present counselors with an opportunity to strengthen any poor reasoning capacity and/or poor communication skills that the detainee might have. Whenever an extremist manifests emotional attachment to a certain issue, counselors must help them develop a realistic attitude to dealing with the issue, while also capitalizing on any opportunity to diminish extremist thoughts, beliefs, and behaviorisms.

Social and Family Rehabilitation

When the head of a family is detained, he ceases to be the breadwinner of the family. This can present quite a problem because then the family will suffer, not only emotionally from his absence, but also financially. As the family starts to suffer, both the wife and the children often need assistance to survive. Social rehabilitation becomes essential because the family is traumatized by the detention and, as such, might be prone to the same activities that landed the extremist in detention to begin with. The means of livelihood for the family, the need for school for the children, and making sure the wife and children have a roof over their heads are all aspects of social rehabilitation.

As a part of the community aftercare initiative, ideally the wife of an extremist should be visited by community and social workers. Children need not be socially isolated or treated as if everyone in the family is an extremist or in legal trouble. In order to prevent this, the social workers must be very inclusive of all the family members. Naturally, by being inclusive while preventing isolation and trauma, the family's reassimilation back into mainstream society is facilitated and made easier.

As a part of social rehabilitation, social workers assigned to the program might provide the extremists' children with required play items and tutor them with schoolwork. To give them strength to excel, the community and social workers regularly visit and encourage them. It is important to engage the entire family, mentally and socially, to prevent the buildup of anger and resentment. If not, it would create the opportunity for extremists and extremist groups to reach out to them. To discourage resentment and counter extremism, community and social workers provide aftercare in a variety of ways to include jobs, monetary assistance, and, most importantly, *a fresh outlook*. This way, by the time an extremist detainee has been transformed and released, his/her family is also transformed and ready for his/her return. In some cases, community workers and social workers might continue to work with the family even after the detainee has returned home, when asked for and/or needed.

While this was not necessarily possible because of the unique circumstances of the detainee rehabilitation programs in Iraq, Singapore is an excellent example of a workable social rehabilitation network. Its Interagency Aftercare Group is a voluntary community effort between different Malay/Muslim agencies and organizations that provide assistance to the families of the detainees, including their wives and children. Within the aftercare framework, the unique approach by these agencies and organizations is aimed at supporting the families of detainees during the transition period. Yayasan Mendaki (YM), Association of Muslim Professionals (AMP), and Taman Bacaan focus on their specialized expertise, consolidate expert areas, and coordinate efforts between different agencies for the benefit of each client. YM covers the educational program and assistance in the form of tuition fee subsidy or program fee waiver that it provides to the families. In addition to coordinating with Taman Bacaan and AMP to help the families, YM also refers such families to relevant agencies and organizations that also might help with financial assistance.

Education Rehabilitation

If an extremist is not intellectually prepared to recognize faulty ideology, he/she is more prone to be misguided or even wholeheartedly embrace it. Education is an important component of rehabilitation, particularly for those individuals who have not had many academic opportunities. Education is important from the very basic level; an individual cannot be effectively rehabilitated if he/she cannot read or write, up to the university level. An individual cannot effectively be a champion of peace if he/she cannot fully comprehend or refute faulty teachings. Until he/she learns to do so, he/she can easily be indoctrinated by other individuals who can readily reference the Qur'an, or even make up references, knowing that the individual in question is in no position to challenge them. The intent of any education program is to empower a person to change. Being such, arguably no successful rehabilitation program can exist without education as a necessary component.

Vocational Rehabilitation

To successfully reintegrate the detainees and inmates back into society, they need to be guided and empowered through development of skills and advanced education. Designed to provide necessary skills for a job, vocational rehabilitation imparts useful skills to detainees and inmates before release. This may include relevant vocational training, such as metal and woodwork, carpentry and masonry, dairy farming and agriculture, computer and language skills, and art and sewing. Unlike the other modes of rehabilitation, vocational rehabilitation runs a higher security risk. To minimize the risk, detainees and inmates generally should not be taught certain skills that can be counterproductive, such as electronics—a capability that could be used to build circuitry for bombs. More than perhaps any other country, Iraq has proven success with vocational training of detainees, as highlighted in Chapter 10. Likewise, the Kingdom of Saudi Arabia has been significant as well in its establishment of a care center outside of Riyadh complete with games, cooking, and the study of arts. A beneficiary of the center, Mohammed Dousery, a Guantanamo detainee for 6 years, said:

> The centre prepared me to engage gradually with the rest of society. You can't go directly from Guantanamo Bay to normal life. This is an extremely difficult thing, and everything changes. Saudi changes and so does the rest of the world. I have a great wife, and she is encouraging me to try and forget Guantanamo, and she says to me, "Forget that prison, you are a new man and you have a new life in front of you and you have your family. Focus your concerns on this. This makes me feel much better" (Gunaratna, 2009).

The five compounds, each with a capacity for 1,200 people, support reintegration back to Saudi society. The beneficiaries, as they are called, are able to swim, and play football, table tennis, and TV games. In an air-conditioned tent converted into a dining hall that serves traditional food, they also engage in dialogue and religious discussion. After vocational training, most detainees are equipped with new skills to ensure their survival and happiness when returning to mainstream society. However, what must not be neglected is that the government and community need to take an active role in encouraging and helping released detainees find meaningful employment in their new skill set. Government's involvement might even include encouraging local businesses to hire newly released detainees, either for tax breaks or some kind of subsidization. In vocational rehabilitation, as in other modes, the range of activities is only limited by human imagination; the vocational training opportunities should fit the community to which the detainees are returning. So, whatever services and needs the community most needs—be it painters or woodworkers—the internment facility should mirror that.

Creative Arts Rehabilitation

Not everyone finds a classroom setting comfortable or useful. For some individuals, it is much more valuable and motivating to use creativity, as an outlet of expression. The Creative Arts Rehabilitation mode recognizes this and encourages the expression of emotion through the creation of something as a useful and necessary component in the rehabilitation model.

Most probably the best example and most well-known art therapy program outside of Iraq, like the vocational training program, is in Saudi Arabia. In 2007, an innovative art therapy approach targeted toward extremists began to counter the rising extremism. Overwhelmingly, references to Saudi Arabia and the Qur'an abound in their work; detainees are encouraged to create/draw/paint/write as an elongated expression of what they would like to say. Overwhelmingly, the classes have been deemed a success, and the director (Dr. Awad Alyami) has talked extensively about arts usefulness when combined with religious education for mainstreaming extremists. Notably, while the creative arts component might be useful on its own when dealing with criminals or other non-ideological extreme individuals, it has proved to be ineffective when countering any kind of radical thought. In those instances, it is essential that a religious element is introduced and combined for optimal detainee and extremist rehabilitation.

Recreation Rehabilitation

The newest additional mode to detainee and extremist rehabilitation is the recreation element. Studies have long shown that individuals who get daily physical activity have sharper minds and are less prone to suffer from stress, depression, and poor health. Invariably, adding a release element to the rehabilitation mode will help get out excess energy while mentally focusing the detainee for religious deradicalization.

However, as the newest component, recreation rehabilitation has yet to be formally tested in an extremist or terrorist setting. Yet, there are good indicators of its usefulness in prisons and detention centers. Perhaps one of the best examples is that at the Cebu Provincial Detention and Rehabilitation Center (CPDRC) in Cebu Province, Philippines. The prison is maximum security with about 1,400 inmates; 70 percent of the individuals there have been convicted of serious crimes, such as narcotics trafficking, murder, and rape. In 2007, two prison gangs were gearing up for a confrontation within the prison walls. Guards noticing the impending confrontation fired warning shots into the air, but, the prisoners took no notice. A confrontation seemed inevitable when in a last-ditch effort, one of the guards (Byron Garcia) turned on the prison speaker system and started playing the Queens song *Another One Bites the Dust*. As the music blared throughout the prison, the gang members grew distracted, and, beguiled, they joined in with the other inmates who were singing and dancing to the music. It was from this incident that the idea was conceptualized to combine music with a fitness regime as a redirect from innerprison violence. Because the inmates enjoyed music and dancing, Garcia decided to use this approach to bring in qualified dance instructors and teach the inmates professional dance moves. Every day for 30 minutes, popular music plays as inmates learn new dance steps; Michael Jackson's music is particularly popular. But, perhaps most impressive is that since the introduction of the dance regime, as of 2011, there have been no serious violent incidents within the prison. Further, the guards have noted better inmate health, improved attitudes of inmates, less violence overall, and reduced recidivism.*

WORKING MODEL

There are obviously practical difficulties in developing a universal model to rehabilitate terrorists seeking to justify their actions through Islam.

---

* YouTube clips at http://www.youtube.com/user/byronfgarcia highlight the story of Byron Garcia and display dance moves performed by the Filipino inmates. (Still accessible on March 20, 2011.)

To start with, Islam comes to every country in different ways. As such, there is a need to understand diverse values and traditions of the Muslim community: how they practice Islam, how they relate to each other, and how they see the world. The economic context, political environment, and unique language and culture make standardization a challenge. As the security landscape in every country is different, the terrorists are also different. As the conditions of capture, treatment during incarceration, as well as release, differ, there cannot be one standard rehabilitation program. A government can develop a standard model, but it will only be applicable to a specific threat group at a specific place and time. Every rehabilitation program operates in the context of a community. Although criminal justice and prison systems are unique to different countries, an approach to rehabilitation can exist. Instead of a standard universal model that applies to all situations across the globe, it is perhaps more practical that a working model on rehabilitation be taken into consideration.

The working model on rehabilitation includes the following nine fundamental aspects.

First Fundamental Aspect

Those selected or volunteering to undergo rehabilitation should be viewed as beneficiaries and no longer as inmates or detainees. Many security prisoners and detainees are treated poorly, at times harassed, and sometimes even tortured. Most guards have preconceived notions of how to "educate" detainees and inmates which lead them to behave aggressively toward the detainees. By referring to detainees as beneficiaries, it changes the mindsets of the guard staff, the government, the community, the rehabilitation team, and the detainee himself.

Second Fundamental Aspect

Rehabilitation efforts should begin on day 1 of detainment. If the captured terrorist is beaten and treated unkindly, he/she is likely to harbor a grudge and will be much more difficult to work with. The best form of interview with a detainee is rapport-based. As highlighted in Chapters 2 and 3, threats and torture are unlikely to yield truthful information (M. Alexander, personal interview, November 14, 2009). To facilitate this, as Iraq's rehabilitation program highlighted, day 1 of the detainee's internment should include a sit-down with a psychologist, cleric, and teacher. In tandem, the three assess the new arrival. They assess his/her openness to discuss religion, his/her education level, and his desires/aims for the future. The cleric can help determine, based on the detainee's religious ideology, if he is of low, medium, or high risk. The teacher will profile his education and vocational skills (Does he have the knowledge and means to gain meaningful employment if he was to be released in 6 months?). The psychologist will analyze his thinking, his reasoning of logic, and consider if the detainee suffers from any mental illnesses. From these initial assessments, the correct type and amount of customized rehabilitation can be determined.

Third Fundamental Aspect

A government must decide whether or not it wants one-on-one sessions or group sessions, or maybe even a combination of both. For instance, in Malaysia, detainees stay in a dormitory. They live together and receive both group as well as one-on-one counseling. One-on-one counseling is generally ideal, if a country's government and resources can support it. However, countries with thousands of detainees may find they do not have the resources or manpower to conduct such intensive and time-consuming sessions. In this case, they may want to opt for group sessions. The time factor also should be considered. In a country where time might not be an issue (i.e., perhaps a detainee has a "life sentence" or other similar long length of prison commitment), it might not be seen as crucial. However, in a place like Iraq or Afghanistan, where the U.S. government is on foreign soil and only has a limited amount of time to run programs before turning the country back over to the local government, time is a much more decisive factor. Conversely, a place like Singapore, which has an extended amount of time to work with detainees, is able to conduct intensive one-on-one sessions for many years as well as greatly involving the community. What we know from these different approaches is that they all work on some level, ... but, as a general rule of thumb (and as Singapore has proved), the more resources and time a government has to run a program, the more likely the results will be as they hoped.

Fourth Fundamental Aspect

Resources are needed to create an environment conducive to rehabilitation. As most detention and penitentiary facilities are overcrowded with many detainees per compound or cell, the environment is generally not conducive for rehabilitation. In such a situation as that, stipulations need to be produced for successful rehabilitation to occur. A "safe" place far from the eyes and ears of other detainees needs to be created for the counseling sessions to take place. If it is one-on-one sessions (i.e., just the cleric or psychologist and the detainee), then the room should be small, inviting, and comfortable. If it is a larger group discussion, then the room size and comfort needs to also fit proportionally. If the government has the means, a new and remote facility, such as the one built in Saudi Arabia, would be ideal. However, if the government is limited on funds, then creating a place removed from the other detainees is a basic requirement. This could even take place as part of a vocational training rehabilitation component. In Iraq, because there was no space for sessions, formal schools were designed and built by detainees so that education classes could take place. Similarly, Iraqi detainees also built and designed the Art School and a woodcrafting workshop, so that they could take lessons. From the initial assessments of individuals, detainees who are gifted with construction and architect skills could be paired with detainees needing/desiring such skills, thus creating a volunteer team for carrying out the building projects for the good of the center, while still imparting useful skills for the good of the detainees.

Fifth Fundamental Aspect

As it was religious justification that was used to bring about the concept of hate and violence, counseling by clergy must be an essential part of any rehabilitation program. In countries where church and state are separate, there might be more of a reluctance to use religious counselors; however, by neglecting this area, other modes of rehabilitation will be unbalanced and are unlikely to work. Naturally, the clergy must be trained in dealing with extremists and have the mannerisms to suit. It is plausible that many clergy will come forward to offer their services in order to protect the sacred values of Islam through rehabilitation of extremists, if given the opportunity. Once committed to working with extremists, the clergy also must still be monitored in order to ensure the target object—turning an extreme viewpoint of Islam into a moderate one—is achieved. It is imperative that no cleric projects his/her own school or orientation as the right (only) interpretation of Islam, otherwise, that may lead to discord between the clergy and be counterproductive to the detainee. It is ideal for clerics from diverse schools and orientations to work together, thereby ensuring a balance of religious logic and reason to the maximum benefit of the detainee.

Sixth Fundamental Aspect

Continual training and education of the professional and support staff at a rehabilitation center is essential. It should be a collective effort, not only by investigative officers and operations officers, but also by the clergy, psychologists, and academia. Whether it is a guard, psychologist, or sports instructor, no one should be assigned to a rehabilitation center without undergoing an orientation course outlining the intent, purpose, and modes of rehabilitation. Otherwise, if even fleetingly, an uninformed guard on duty disrespects a detainee, the goodwill built by others will be damaged.* In Iraq, it was only a one-page handout and 5-minute introduction that were given to guards securing centers where rehabilitation programs were taking place. For that purpose, it was enough to make a difference to many who didn't understand what was taking place. Obviously, for individuals more involved, it will be necessary to create a more complex program of instruction, guidelines, and modules to follow. Training and education, to include a manual for reference, should be customized to reflect the duty of the persons they are intended for; this saves on time and prevents misinformation. Additionally, it also is necessary to create, implement, and manage a comprehensive security framework when rehabilitating detainees and inmates. The framework should involve both security and religious screening of staff. Depending on the environment, it is necessary for professional and support staff to be screened routinely and maybe even continuously. The detainee should be closely monitored as well during counseling sessions and when he/she interacts with his/her family, visitors, and other detainees.

Seventh Fundamental Aspect

No one can guarantee that a person's mindset will be changed through rehabilitation, no matter how good the cleric is or how engaged the government might be in supporting it. To ensure he/she will not become a contaminant upon release, it is desirable to support a detainee's gradual reintegration into society. Ideally, prior to full release, the detainee should be placed in a halfway house where he/she can spend time with his/her family and friends while remaining committed to understanding the intended aim of Islam. While there, the counselors who helped him/her through detention will remain in contact with him/her and be ready

---

* The Governor of Helmand Province in Afghanistan, Mullah Abdul Salam Zaeef, the former Taliban ambassador to Pakistan, spent 3 years at Guantanamo Bay. In his book titled Da Guantanamo Anzoor, Zaeef "admires a few Americans who were nice to him, did not 'torture or beat' him and spoke to him kindly."

to help out in any way should the need arise. This is important because, if an environment is hostile, the revival of earlier beliefs may lead a released detainee to violence again. A classic example is Said Ali al-Shihri (alias Abu Sayyaf), a detainee released from Guantanamo in November 2007, who had gone through the Saudi rehabilitation program (Worth, 2009). After he was released, he was approached and successfully recruited by the Yemeni branch of Al Qaeda. Soon after, he traveled to Yemen with them, and was appointed deputy leader of Al Qaeda in that country. He then participated in the bombing of the U.S. Embassy in Sana during September 2008 that killed 16 people. On the contrary, Abu al-Hareth Muhammad al-Awfi (alias Muhammad Attik al-Harbi) was another Saudi beneficiary who was approached by Al Qaeda in Yemen after he was released. Although he initially joined Al Qaeda in Yemen, he didn't stay for long and instead opted to return home after his clergy and his family spoke with him (The Associated Press, 2009). When dealing with hearts and minds, there are no absolutes, but. we *can* stack the cards in our favor if we are smart about it.

Eighth Fundamental Aspect

Governments should work to involve their communities. By engaging a community, the community is empowered to become more aware of suspicious persons and/or situations. Communities also are aware of what to do if they encounter and feel threatened in a situation. Governments encouraging mosques and interfaith community centers to take active roles in community development also help to facilitate cross-religious understanding. Having community gatherings and events where persons from many faiths participate helps to prevent misinformation and prejudice from festering. Singapore takes an active stance in community engagement by posting signs in the transportation systems, education facilities, and elsewhere around the country, informing persons what to do if they see any suspicious activities.

In addition, calling on nongovernment organizations and other charitable organizations to rally to the call for terrorist and detainee rehabilitation can be effective. There are a number of organizations that, if given the chance, would be pleased to help in a detention situation. Some might even be in positions to grant jobs to detainees after release. The Sunni Endowment of Iraq is one example of a group that stepped forward to donate tools and blankets to detainees participating in vocational programs in Iraq. And, to that end, they were willing to create a partnership to foster understanding. According to Sheikh Mahmoud, the representative from the Sunni Endowment, "No matter where you come from, Sunni and Shiites, it doesn't matter; if you are here, we need to provide you with help so that you can better reintegrate with all of us for a peaceful Iraq" (Lt. Col. Richard Johnson, personal interview, January 27, 2010).

Ninth Fundamental Aspect

Successful rehabilitation requires the continuous study of the evolving narrative and ideology of terrorists as well as their perceived and real grievances and aspirations. It requires access and comparison to studies by scholars and writers and by other programs and institutions. Many terrorists and their supporters believe they can help Muslim brothers by doing *jihad* in places like Somalia, Iraq, Afghanistan, Pakistan, Israel, Chechnya, Thailand, Indonesia, and the Philippines. Clerics and scholars need to be aware of this, so that they can develop an intellectual mindset to refute the ideology and deliver an Islamic alternative to traveling and fighting in conflict zones. When this is brought up in counseling sessions, it is essential that a cleric be prepared with the correct rebuttal to the extremist deviation that permits Muslims to carry out jihad for the killing of non-Muslims. To this end, it would be helpful for the rehabilitation team and the government to have a strong relationship in working together for a successful rehabilitation program. As such, it is relevant to relate the importance of establishing and maintaining specialized centers of academic research in political violence and terrorism research. In order to understand and counteract violent ideology, a localized principal research center cannot be understated. As ideology is evolutionary, constant research and analysis are needed to both produce and update rehabilitation manuals. A specialized academic community generates new ideas, looks at the antecedents, observes success and failure, scans, analyses, and fills potential gaps. The academics look beyond the immediate and the urgent, and provide strategic direction. Research centers also will provide an avenue that focuses on problems of understanding global terrorism and its occurrences, while at the same time providing databases and resources that both the government and the rehabilitation team can gain and benefit from. It can provide the necessary orientation and trainings as well, as new clergy, psychologists, teachers, and guards join the rehabilitation programs in internment facilities.

GUIDING PRINCIPLES

Detainee and extremist rehabilitation specifically deals with incarcerated extremists who either have, or are risk of becoming, engaged in violence. While it is arguable that not all security detainees and inmates can be rehabilitated, nevertheless, it is the moral responsibility of every government and well-meaning citizen to advocate the establishment of rehabilitation programs in every penitentiary and detention center worldwide. No one is born an extremist or terrorist and, if we can establish programs at the grassroots, perhaps we can decrease the numbers of those drawn to that lifestyle. However, for those who are already in it, rehabilitation is the only intelligent proactive means to impede the spread of terrorism. Although the transformation of a terrorist into a person who is actively compassionate takes time, rehabilitation has the potential to influence our threat landscape greatly. But, in order to do this, there are a few guiding principles worth mentioning. First, there must be a zero tolerance policy at the state level toward any promotion of hate and violence that uses religion as justification. We have witnessed the ramifications of allowing hate to fester in places all over the world. We cannot afford to keep tolerating hatred using religion as justification.

Secondly, terrorist rehabilitation should not be symptomatic or reactive, but a proactive intervention. It should address those who are radicalized as well as those who are in danger of being exposed (or already have been) to extremist ideology. Some individuals are more prone to radical ideologies. These individuals are more likely to collapse into it when confronted. Being regularly bombarded with propaganda while searching for meaning can cause many to fall. To prevent this, detainee rehabilitation programs should be complemented with public education and awareness. If we can get to individuals in danger before the extremists do, then we have already won them to our side. If we do not attempt to do so, then chances are great that we will be spending government money instead on their incarceration and intensive rehabilitation.

Third, as mentioned above, a successful rehabilitation program requires the support of a range of actors: endorsement at the highest level of government, community participation, and a good press. Media can shape public opinion and build support across the spectrum. In many Muslim countries, the media promoted and projected Osama bin Laden, but, media did not give space to Muhammad Sayyid Tantawi, a mainstream Islamic leader. Many Muslims did not realize that Sheikh Tantawi was the Grand Imam of Al-Azhar Mosque and Grand Sheikh of Al-Azhar University, the highest seat of learning in Sunni Islam because he did not get much press.

THE FUTURE

After 9/11, the Western-led kinetic, lethal, and punitive approaches have emerged as the dominant strategies to fight terrorism. These tactical and operational responses have produced mixed results. Although several important terrorists have been killed or captured, the strategic threat has not diminished. Unless governments share and adopt nonkinetic, nonlethal measures to fight terrorism and extremism, the threat will persist in the foreseeable future. The radical Islamic ideology driving violence is growing. Extremist rehabilitation is a classic example of using smart power. It is neither soft nor hard power. It is a combination of not only integrating our laws to detain and hold, but also using our goodwill and judgment to correct the misled and the misguided. As no one is born an extremist or a terrorist, it is necessary to reverse the global trend of radicalization before more lives are lost to senseless violence.

The science and the art of terrorist rehabilitation rest within the rubric of counterideology. Ideological and intellectual response presents a positive and plausible avenue to create an environment that is hostile to terrorists and unfriendly to extremists. For this to be effective, it must come from the Muslim community. However, unless the Muslim majority and minority governments and all other communities work with and support the Muslim leaders, it is unlikely to happen. As the urgent and the immediate take priority over the important and strategic, terrorism will remain the tier-one national security threat to most countries. If not stopped, Al Qaeda and its associated groups will continue to inculcate the Muslim world with their vicious ideology, producing the next generation of terrorists.

The world is at an early stage of understanding both extremism and terrorism. An evil political ideology espoused by a violent group masquerading as religious men has driven youth from around the world to fight thousands of miles from their home. For three decades, many participated in all facets of the global terrorist network's support activities and operations. For every active terrorist, there are thousands of active supporters and tens of thousands of passive sympathizers. As every supporter is a potential terrorist, early ideological intervention is an absolute necessity. As heightening of extremism is prone to violence, approaches of engagement and legislation should be applied to prevent, punish, deter, and cure.

TOWARD A GLOBAL REGIME

The United States of America was comparatively late in buying into the idea of detainee and extremist rehabilitation. After 9/11, the U.S. leadership did not see rehabilitation as a solution, opting instead for "seek" and "kill." Although the United States invested expertise and resources to build a rehabilitation program in Iraq, as a government, the United States did not espouse the concept of rehabilitation. Building on the success of TF-134 in Iraq, the United States initiated a similar program by Joint Task Force 435 in Parwan (previously Bagram), Afghanistan, during 2010. But, at this point of time, there are more countries that do not believe in rehabilitation than those that embrace and promote it. A number of other countries, such as Israel, do not believe that extremists can be ideologically rehabilitated; so, instead, they spend their resources only on criminals. Unfortunately, it is evident that even if extremists disengage from violence, they still need to be deradicalized. Israel is reluctant to try it, but how else might the hatred and violence of the Middle East end?

To make extremist rehabilitation a global imperative, there must be agreement that rehabilitation is a part of the global solution to solve the problem. The key to establishing a global rehabilitation regime is to build a sufficient number of national rehabilitation programs. A roadmap toward establishing national programs might include:

1. *Exchange of personnel*: Governments worldwide lacked both human expertise and material resources to start ad hoc rehabilitation initiatives and structured rehabilitation programs. One of the most effective methods to build capacity to rehabilitate terrorists is to exchange personnel. Exchange of personnel will lead to information sharing on systems, modes, and best practices of terrorist rehabilitation. Capacity building helps raise new—and improve existing—capabilities of detainee and inmate rehabilitation. Countries with rehabilitation programs can send their specialist staff to support countries keen to build rehabilitation programs. Likewise, countries keen to build rehabilitation programs can learn from countries with rehabilitation programs. Such exchanges also will enable countries with ad hoc programs to build systematic programs, and countries with no programs to initiate programs. Personnel can learn by observing inmate/detainee counseling to management of facilities and operations.

2. *Joint research, publication, education, and training*: Joint research into terrorist mindset, psychology, use of religion, and other areas could pave the way for collaboration in more challenging areas. For terrorist rehabilitation to be successful, all the staff of the program should be oriented toward understanding the necessity and purpose of the program.. For this specialist discipline, clerics, scholars, psychologists, security and intelligence professionals, prison guards, and others servicing the program should be trained. While courses on counseling skills could range from 7 months to 1 year, a course on counterextremism and counterterrorism could range from 1 week to 2 years. Specialist trainers or trainees can be exchanged either to impart or to receive training. When conducting courses,

countries with fully fledged rehabilitation programs could invite staff from countries keen to initiate rehabilitation programs to participate. As the number of specialist trainers is limited, some courses could be jointly conducted. A successful rehabilitation program requires the government, academia, and community to work together. Without well-trained dedicated and motivated staff, a national program cannot succeed.

3. *Transfer of expertise and resources*: Without a vision and a strategic direction, no terrorist rehabilitation program can succeed. For a rehabilitation program to be successful, a long-term commitment of intellectual and material resources is a must. Rehabilitation comes with the notion that a country must gain a greater understanding from others to put into their resources. The program in Egypt died a natural death because the resources were diverted. In contrast, governments like those in Uzbekistan, Singapore, and Saudi Arabia have allocated significant resources, and, thus, the programs have thrived. Although Malaysia, Indonesia, and Yemen have allocated resources, they need to have a full-time dedicated specialized staff focusing exclusively on extremist detainees and inmates to succeed. To make terrorist rehabilitation a global imperative, wherever possible, countries need to share the expertise and resources with countries that lack them. As of 2010, Pakistan, Bangladesh, Thailand, and Philippines expressed an interest to build programs. To build a global regime to rehabilitate extremists, governments with the expertise and resources need to pave the way and create a path for other nations. Every successful program requires a long-term investment of intellectual and other resources.

4. *Sharing of experience*: Every national rehabilitation program is country specific. Saudi Arabia, for instance, supports the detainee to enter mainstream life, and, therefore, would look for wives for the detainees and also buy them cars, homes, give them jobs, and assist to start businesses.* To change the mindset, there is sustained family pressure to transform. Some have made use of the benefits and gone back to violence. Instead of seeking to replicate national models, what would be useful is to draw lessons and adapt them to the specific country conditions. There are many common areas for collaboration—from research into key Islamic concepts misinterpreted by the terrorists to the assessment of progress or nonprogress in rehabilitation.

---

* As of 2011, no females have been invited to participate in the Saudi Arabia terrorist rehabilitation program.

To make terrorist rehabilitation a global imperative, the government needs to move from a cooperative to a collaborative model. While preserving their unique identities, they must be willing to advance common interests. This means collaborating when and where necessary, and actively working toward finding a framework that all can globally utilize and benefit from. With this in mind, the International Advisory Council on Terrorist Rehabilitation (IACTR) was created in September 2010 through the collaboration of the International Center for Political Violence and Terrorism Research in Singapore with Dr. Gunaratna and Maj. Gen. Stone leading the effort. The mandate of the council is to "create awareness and build support for a global regime on terrorist rehabilitation." Being such, IACTR is intended to bring support to an international terrorist rehabilitation regime by bringing necessary elements together. Further, it will help set modalities and provide strategic directions for the community of terrorist rehabilitation practitioners and scholars, as well as serve to provide expert advice to governments on issues related to countering the threats of extremism and on strategies, mechanisms, and activities required to develop, implement, evaluate, and improve holistic rehabilitation programs for terrorist detainees. The council therefore will plan and prepare for an annual international conference on terrorist rehabilitation. This conference should serve as a platform to project to the world the message of rehabilitation. It will be a place where case studies are given, questions are asked, and dialogue is encouraged to improve on global rehabilitation efforts. To make terrorist rehabilitation a global imperative, there must be an agreement that rehabilitation is a critical part of the overall solution to radicalization. The key to establishing this is to build a sufficient number of national rehabilitation programs; the IACTR was designed with this in mind, according to author Gunaratna and Maj. Gen. Stone.

CONCLUSION

Extremist rehabilitation can be seen as a strategic yet holistic program. For rehabilitation to work, community engagement is as important as the seven modes of rehabilitation. The confluence of these two domains must take place to bring about successful rehabilitation. The most crucial partnership is between the government and the community. As communities produce extremists and terrorists, the participation of the community in the fight against extremism is essential. Law enforcement, intelligence, and military forces can help, but, ultimately, the community must be empowered to defeat terrorism. Without community participation, where the *ulema* and other secular leaders take the lead, no program can succeed. There should be synergy where the government works with the community elite to create an environment hostile to the terrorists and unfriendly to extremists.

The Islamic world has yet to play the frontline role in both countering extremism and its vicious by-product terrorism. As religion has been misused and abused, the Muslim world looks up to Saudi Arabia to debunk the terrorist ideology. Yet, Saudi Arabia has yet to do that. What is needed is for the *ulema* in Saudi Arabia to provide a bold mandate, resources, and direction to the rest of the Muslim world. Other strong referral points should be Egypt and Pakistan, where radical movements have emerged and festered. Unless the *ulema* in Muslim-majority countries, such as Indonesia, Bangladesh, Jordan, and Algeria, speak up, a segment of the Muslim community will continue to consider Dr. Ayman al Zawahiri, Abu Bakar Bashir, and Abu Mohamed al Maqdisi as the *ulema*.

In most Muslim-minority governments, the greater challenge rests with government. Muslims have little or no channels to the government. As counterterrorism is within the realm of national security, to successfully target the conceptual terrorist infrastructures, the government has no option but to invite Muslim leaders, elders, and the elite to work together. Governments must take the initiative and create bridges and pathways: by opening doors, inviting participation, and empowering Muslim leaders to make a difference to the national Muslim identity. However, in order for this to occur, governments must take the lead. It will be difficult in the beginning to engage the Muslim community, and, initially, it may only be a handful of genuine Muslim leaders and institutions that step forward. But, with success and time, more volunteers will join, and greater participation will ensue. The Singapore government's approach in building close partnership between its Muslim minority communities in countering terrorism by fostering interracial, interfaith understanding among its various communities in the country is a good model from which to learn.

To instill greater Muslim participation and support, the orientation of the fight should change from a tactical and operational standpoint to a more strategic footing. Rather than enforcement, it will be on an engagement threshold. The very concept of extremist rehabilitation will refocus the attention of the world to the battlefield of the mind, and make persons think strategic and long term. To have universal acceptance of an idea such as terrorist rehabilitation, the understanding of the community of nations (especially the West) is vital. Working toward a United Nations convention making it mandatory for member countries to pass legislation for rehabilitation needs work. Nations that constitute the United Nations need to be convinced. This will require a step-by-step approach of formally and informally educating the government and the intelligentsia, building a significant number of national rehabilitation programs and initiatives, and eventually approaching the United Nations. If the United Nations, a world body, passes a resolution on extremist rehabilitation, more countries will pay attention. And, in response, they are likely to initiate rehabilitation programs that will provide solid tangible results convincing others that rehabilitation works. Similar to countering the financing of terrorism or banning torture, a worldwide resolution to encourage and enforce rehabilitation will be regarded as a humanitarian and important gesture, particularly by the Muslim world. The potential for positive impact cannot be overemphasized.

CHAPTER **14**

Strategy for an Unconquerable Nation

PASSION

I want to leave you with this: To me, it's personally rewarding to see the U.S. forces and coalition forces having a positive impact on a person's life. When I first came here in 2003, I wasn't sure about what we will be able to do with the detainees other than locking them up and provide security. But, it's very rewarding to see after all these years and after all the many recommendations and lessons learned, they were able to make a difference in a person's life by having some rehabilitation opportunities. Will you reach 100 percent of the population? No, never. Because No. 1, not everyone wants to cooperate and be a part of it. And No. 2, we don't have the resources to reach the total population. Our goal was to separate the extremists and the moderates. I think we've done that successfully. And, because of it, moderates take advantage of our education program and our vocational programs and leave here better persons (Col. John Huey, personal interview, January 25, 2010).

Undoubtedly, we are in an unconventional war on terror, and, such a war calls for extraordinary measures. When U.S. forces first arrived in Iraq in 2003, they were ill-prepared for the road ahead. Misconceptions about time restraints and a lack of leadership and personal accountability accounted for many mistakes. Poor choices were made in the classification of detainees, which also contributed to a violent atmosphere ripe for indoctrination. Blemished and shamed, the U.S. military forces and political foreign policy officials nevertheless used the opportunities and challenges in Iraq in order for the United States to grow stronger as a nation and as a world leader. However, with those choices came increased responsibility. We need to ensure that we have set our standards and honed our skills to the level that we, as well as the rest of the world, demand. As a world leader, the United States is on a platform: Every action we take is meticulously examined around the globe. Abu Ghraib was a dark moment in American history. Yet, we would argue that the outcome of the war in Iraq, with the revamped strategy of the victors on detention operations and introduction of rehabilitation, has done wonders on the global war on terror. The undeniable change in atmosphere after the initiation of the rehabilitation programs is proof of the victors' success. Less than 3 months after the introduction of the rehabilitation programs, violence in detention centers decreased by greater than 50 percent. At the same time, intelligence from detainees about other Iraqis—both inside the wire and out—increased by three times the previous amount. There is no doubt that countless American lives have been saved because of the introduction, implementation, and continued evolution of the rehabilitation programs in Iraq. If we leave Iraq with one thing, it should be with our heads held high because we haven't given up the fight against terrorism and, as a world leader, we never should.

THE WRAP-UP

As of January 1, 2009, after the new security agreement between the United States and the Government of Iraq, all military operations were conjoined. So, if an Iraqi coalition operation detained or captured persons, the majority of them went into the Iraqi judicial system. Consequently, the only persons the United States processed as detained or captured in this Iraqi situation in 2009 (240 in total) were at the special request of the Government of Iraq. Even then, it was only done with a detention order and arrest warrant, and with the knowledge that they would be turned back over to Iraq when the complete transfer of authority from the United States to Iraq occurred, according to Lt. Col. Eric Mullai (personal interview, 2010). And, so, with the departure of the last TF-134 commander, Maj. Gen. David Quantock, in March 2010, and the inevitable (if long overdue) turnover of the only remaining theater internment facility (TIF)—Camp Cropper—on July 15, 2010, American history has closed another chapter in Iraq.

Task Force 134 faced many challenges in the implementation of detainee and extremist rehabilitation programs. But, fortunately, due to the pioneering efforts of Maj. Gen. Douglas Stone, the programs persevered and have since spread rapidly through the global community. To make terrorist rehabilitation a global imperative, there must be an agreement that rehabilitation is a critical part of the overall solution to radicalization. The key to establishing this is to build a sufficient number of national rehabilitation programs. In April 2009, Gen. David Petraeus called upon Maj. Gen. Stone to apply his successful experience from Iraq to study the U.S. policy on detaining captives apprehended in Afghanistan. His 700-page report was finished in August 2009, and Maj. Gen. Stone briefed senior officials, including Secretary of State

Hillary Clinton, Richard Holbrook (President Obama's Special Envoy for the region), and General Stanley McChrystal, then-Commander of U.S. forces in Afghanistan. While the report was never made public, the outcome of it established Joint Task Force 435, commanded by Vice Admiral Robert Harward. Task Force 435 altered the direction of the war in Afghanistan with the implementation of detainee rehabilitation programs at Camp Parwan (formerly Bagram). The programs are similar to Iraq's model, but arguably better as they have built on Iraq's successes while customizing the programs to better address the specific needs of the Afghan population. Based on his previous success with Iraq, the appointment of Gen. Petraeus as Commander of U.S. forces in Afghanistan (to replace Gen. McChrystal) on June 29, 2010, will no doubt increase the capacity and direction of the Afghanistan rehabilitation programs.

AMERICAN DREAM

Americans should not underestimate the dream of many foreign nationals to live in the United States. The United States has long been seen (or, in some cases, possibly mistaken) as the land of freedom, opportunity, abundance, and tolerance among foreign nations. According to Salah Al-Hindawy (personal interview, 2010), who was born in Iraq, but has lived in the United States since the late 1980s, "If you ask Iraqis where they wish to go, forget about politics; first thing they're going say is that they want to go to America, just because [of] the way Americans treat them here." In Dr. Angell's experience, this was true for most Iraqis, including detainees and employed local Iraqi nationals alike. Based on the way they were treated in detention during many of the rehabilitation programs, detainees expressed a desire to move to America. Plaguing us with questions, they would enquire about the process, the costs, and whether or not they could bring their families. Likewise, after working in the rehabilitation programs alongside the military and contractors in Iraq, many employed local Iraqi nationals confessed to having the dream of bringing their families to the United States, which they saw as having much better opportunities for their families and for their future. To that end, many of them worked tirelessly through the long painful process of applying for a green card, collecting recommendation letters (at least one from a general is required with the application) while doing their best to prove allegiance and goodwill to the United States. The hard work must have paid off because now several of the local nationals (LNs) who passionately dedicated themselves to reducing the threat of radical extremism through their work in the rehabilitation programs have been awarded green cards and are exuberantly living in the United States.

Meanwhile, the potential impact—of those granted green cards after working the rehabilitation programs—on the American public should be capitalized on. Their enthusiasm and passion for reducing terrorism are contagious; we have no doubt it will overcome any narrow-minded individuals, some of whom are everywhere, who might take a while to comprehend the gold mine of authentic experience that these individuals encapsulate.

LEAP OF FAITH

Undoubtedly, the question Dr. Angell gets asked countless times over and over again is: "How do you know the rehabilitation programs work?" Well, the answer is simple. We don't, because when you are dealing with hearts and minds, it's a leap of faith. You can't read a person's mind, so you have to go by his/her actions. We have plenty of actions to support the hypothesis that the rehabilitation programs work in the successful transformation of destructive ideologies. Besides the significant reduction in violence and increase in intelligence that markedly took place after the initiation of the rehabilitation programs in 2007, we have countless other examples of the impact the programs have made on Iraqi detainees. One of these is an incident that occurred in early 2008 at Camp Bucca. Guards, hearing a commotion, approached a compound to find a group of detainees around a bearded detainee. The detainees had pinned the bearded man up against the fence and proceeded to shave off his beard. When the shocked guards enquired of the detainees what they were doing, they told him, "We are sick of him causing all the trouble in this compound. We are sick of his radical ideas. And we don't want to take it anymore." The newly beardless detainee was accused by the others of preaching radical ideas and trying to hand out stern punishments if they were not followed. Unfortunately for him, the overwhelming majority had lost patience with him and thereby decided to teach him a lesson, according to Maj. Gen. Stone (personal interview, 2009). The first time this happened, the incident swept through the detention centers like a bolt of lightening; everyone was incredulous. But, by the second and third time, well, we just smiled and nodded heads in support.

In other cases, detainees have pleaded to stay longer at the detention center in order to finish education classes. One who was handed his release paperwork a month before he was to take his final fifth-grade examination practically wept as he asked for permission to stay the remainder to earn the certificate. Another detainee begging to stay elaborated: "I won't get this opportunity out there; I cannot afford it." Likewise, family members have been known to implore U.S. soldiers to keep their loved one in detention until vocational and educational training is complete, so that they "will be able to get a job and not be enticed back to bad activities" (D. Mansour, personal interview, November 14, 2010). Letters coming in and out of detention have highlighted such. One letter from a detainee to his sister told her about how he was learning English and implored her to do the same. Another detailed his positive experience in detention during the holy time of Eid [English translation from Arabic]:

> I am writing this letter the second day of Eid after prayer. We had the sermon, then the detainees wished each other well, and we were as one big group. The whole compound, which is over 170 detainees, all sat down together; which is rare and nice. Best of all, it felt as if we were at a wedding dinner all sitting down together; as if we were at a wedding in the countryside. We were served eggs, dates, bread, rice pudding, oranges, and milk by the soldiers. After dinner, all the detainees hugged. It was beautiful. The only thing missing was you. [Detainee ISN: 331239]

Mothers have wept in happiness, expressing the belief that the United States not only changed their sons' thinking, but effectively gave them a second chance through education and vocational training. Many expressed that their time in detention, and the opportunities they got there, not only changed their way of thinking, but changed their lives as well.

There are countless other examples. The artwork created in the creative expressions program exemplifies detainees' hope and desires. They have drawn and painted pictures symbolizing Mother Mary, Jesus, and the prophet Mohammed, sometimes all together, expressing, "We are all brothers." They have drawn pictures of Martin Luther King Jr., Mahatma Gandhi, and the Dalai Lama, calling them their heroes as "messengers of peace." Lessons learned during Islamic Discussion Program (IDP) and civics classes have been taken back to compounds by the participants, who then engage the other detainees in their newfound knowledge. Dr. Angell has passed compounds where there is a detainee with all of his notes and handouts spread out around him, talking to the other detainees about what he learned that week in IDP, outlining and refuting false Qur'anic teachings. Detainees have asked to have combined compounds where both Sunni and Shiite, who are tired of the senseless violence, can live together without fear and in peace. Likewise, released detainees have allegedly moved their families to new communities where all factions are welcome, and the only stipulation is that everyone respects one another. Stories of harmony, of changed lives, and transformations abound around every corner since the rehabilitation programs were introduced and implemented. The programs got detainees excited about release; they got them excited about learning as much as they could so that when they returned to their families, they could do so with dignity and honor. No longer were they the ones without an education or skill, and now they had the certifications to prove it. It was (and is) very empowering.

Then we have individuals like Picasso* and Akeel.* Previously, as a detainee, Picasso* went through all the rehabilitation programs. Evidently, he was so transformed that he made a marked impression up to the rank of generals, including Maj. Gen. Stone, who took it upon himself to personally guarantee him no longer a security threat to American forces. No sooner had he been released than he returned as an Operational Support and Services (OSS)-employed local Iraqi national art teacher to work at the very TIF where he had just been detained, but this time as a civilian. Dr. Angell cannot overemphasize what an impact he made walking back into the detention center that first day. You could feel the hope and jubilation in the air as detainees, faces glowing with pleasure, warmly welcomed back their comrade who was now an employed civilian. Etched into each wide smile was that America keeps its promises, and that release and jobs are possible. It was an incredible moment as she stood back and watched the many hugs and kisses exchanged as Picasso* excitedly told the other detainees about the changes taking place outside. No amount of information operation (IO) campaigns can do what Picasso* was able to do in just 15 minutes. Fifteen minutes talking with him was all it took for every detainee in that compound to decide that he was going to take all the rehabilitation classes he could, and cooperate and actively engage with the military to secure his release. They got a glimpse of what life was now like in Iraq outside detention facilities and they wanted to be a part of it. For days detainees excitedly discussed how nice it would be to live in a society more relaxed, where one could go to the mosque or not, where one could wear jeans or not, where one could be the person whom he most wants to be without fear of reprisal to him or his family, according to Picasso* (personal interview, 2008).

Akeel* spent 2 years at Abu Ghraib before he was transferred to Camp Cropper for another 12 months. Other detainees called him "abu kafir," the father of the infidel, because he practiced the English that he had learned from playing video games, and watching movies with the American guards. Some warned him that he needed to stop engaging with the Americans, but he said he "didn't care." As the rehabilitation programs were starting, he talked to the officers and advised them how to make the programs even more interesting and engaging to the

---

* An asterisk (*) is used throughout this book to protect the security and confidentiality of certain individuals whose lives might be threatened otherwise.

detainees. He collected internment serial numbers (ISNs) of detainees interested in participating in courses. He was so inspired with the concept of the programs that once released in 2007, Akeel* sought a job with OSS as a local Iraqi national social worker. He was offered it and, in 2010, when Dr. Angell visited with him again, he was social worker team lead at Camp Cropper. He confided in her that things are a lot different now in Iraq than they were when the Americans first came, and that detainees are now seeing the differences; not only from the Iraqis teaching the rehabilitation classes, but from family members who come to visitation. He proffered that the rehabilitation programs have had a huge impact on the motivation change in detainees; that they are bridging the gaps between those detained and their brethren outside. When they take the rehabilitation classes, they are learning to understand the changes and embrace newfound freedoms. Many have grown excited to experience what they call "the new life in Iraq" (Akeel,* personal interview, January 26, 2010).

There are too many stories for the available space, but the bottom line is, if you ask us if we think the rehabilitation programs work, Dr. Angell will tell you, "I don't think they work. I know they work. I saw them in action. I saw and experienced the transformation of ideologies and lives because they worked." What is sometimes forgotten in detention operations is that we are dealing with a dynamic population, and, like any of us, these people also have families and emotions. This should not be forgotten because it can help in customizing the best possible rehabilitation program for each population. When Dr. Angell asked Wasan,* (personal interview, 2010) a detained carpenter who was helping to teach in the carpentry vocational program, what his hopes for the future were, his answer was understandable:

> I wish to go back to my family and hope for them to live in peace. When they arrested me, I was in my work clothes. I will go back to my work. I hope they will give me the same job.

For Hamid,* another detainee at Camp Taji, his response could have been given by any one of us. "I just want to hug my children," he said in a personal interview in 2010.

The challenge now is how to deradicalize the most radical of individuals, because, while the majority of our colleagues insist that there are a certain number of individuals who cannot be transformed through rehabilitation programs, we are hesitant to agree. We might venture that perhaps we are just not doing something right for those individuals because every rehabilitation program needs to be customized to some degree. Different detainees will respond better to some stimuli than others. It's just a matter of finding the right combination, then having the time, patience, and guts to see it through. We have not been in the business of rehabilitating detainees and terrorists long enough to say with any amount of certainty that there are a certain number of individuals who cannot be rehabilitated. We are not convinced that we ever will be, not when dealing with the inexact science of hearts and minds.

PERSISTENCE

We are the lions of war who do not scare—we are the soldiers who sleep on the backs of horses and if someone calls for Jihad, ... we will answer that call.

Abu_Ugla, Jihadist Internet user

Ignoring the problem is not going to help. Terrorism is not going to go away without a fight nor can it be won by physical force alone. We are in an ideological war and we need to respond accordingly. In essence, the future of extremist rehabilitation will reflect exactly what we—as a global community—put into it. How much is preventing and eliminating terrorism worth to us? Are we willing to take a risk? To invest in the larger picture? Are we willing to push other countries into compliance through actively seeking international legal support from bodies such as the United Nations? What does it take to push the envelope so far? What do we have to gain from doing it? What are potential repercussions? How much is it going to cost? And, perhaps most importantly, who is willing to join in the fight?

These are all questions that individuals, organizations, and countries might—and should—consider before committing themselves to helping eradicate terrorism through deradicalization and rehabilitation programs. Because once you are committed, you will then be part of an elite body taking a risk. Those of us already involved are quite aware of what we stand to lose, but, we also are well aware of what we stand to gain.

Custodial and community rehabilitation of terrorists and extremists is a new frontier in the fight against terrorism. Abdul Rahman Al-Hadlaq, adviser to the Minister of the Interior in Saudi Arabia, while discussing Saudi Arabia's approach to terrorist rehabilitation, said that "what we are fighting is an ideological war of ideas," and the only way to confront ideology is with alternative ideology. "As a result," he said, "the government is trying to engage with terrorists and would-be terrorists, at every level: in schools, in mosques, and even inside maximum-security prisons" (Durham, 2008). Rehabilitating terrorists and immunizing the community through engagement are two intertwined strategies of meeting a serious and a sustained threat. By engaging the community, mainstream leaders can raise awareness and immunize the community against extremist ideas and beliefs. Otherwise, those radicalized by terrorist and extremist propaganda will advocate, support, and participate in violence. By investing in community engagement upstream, terrorist recruitment can be disrupted. Similarly, by investing in terrorist rehabilitation downstream, terrorist regeneration can be disrupted. Neither of these strategies is perfect, but they offer the best hope for community ownership and participation in the fight against extremism and its vicious by-product: terrorism. There are three principal reasons why we must invest in rehabilitating terrorist detainees and inmates:

1. Unless terrorists in custody change their views, when released they will continue to pose an enduring threat to public safety and security.
2. The terrorists will contribute to regeneration by contaminating the rest of society with their vicious ideas, thus increasing the pool of supporters and sympathizers.
3. The terrorists will form a part of the terrorist iconography, earning the status of hero worthy of respect and emulation by the next generation of terrorist recruits.

There are increasing concerns about radicalization in prisons, and the process of recruitment where the Muslim world is responding faster than the West. To address this and other concerns, all programs should continue to evolve and adapt according to the knowledge of the people who run them, and the response of those who attend. Notably:

- More recruitment and radicalization now happen in the virtual world, while operational planning happens at the local level.
- Each "narrative" that the individual has "accepted" must be addressed.
- All need to address issues of disenfranchisement and marginalization that lead to the formation of grievances.
- Life situations can change behavior.

No program has been in existence long enough to know the long-term impact; however, we can establish a few baselines. If released detainees return to the fight, it's a failure in the process. If they assist in reducing the fight, it's a success in the process. With innocent lives at stake, can we really afford not to take the chance? We have spent billions on trying to counter the terrorist threat, but only at the tip of the iceberg, unwilling to commit to addressing the underlying cause. We are committed to making an effort to have a visible impact. However, if we are serious about addressing terrorism, we have to go much deeper. We have to commit to addressing the root cause; we can no longer afford not to, nor can we afford to continue to permit those with destructive ideologies to continue to radicalize populations. This problem is not going to go away without active involvement on our part. Nobody is born a terrorist. A terrorist is made, and unless we do something about it, terrorists will continue to grow in strength and numbers.

Maj. Gen. Stone was in Iraq for 15 months. He wanted to ensure that the rehabilitation programs were not only up, but that they were running well and effectively before his departure. In the summer of 2008, he returned home to the United States, and is now retired (as of September 2010). He continues to champion detainee and inmate rights. He has traveled the world in order to meet presidential and other government officials and discuss with them the importance of a global regime for detainee and terrorist deradicalization and rehabilitation. His message resounds, as it is not only solid academically, but has proved itself in practical application. He said:

> The magic of what we did is we recognized that violent Islamic engagements have threatened those outside of Islam just as much as they have threatened those inside Islam. We must empower the moderate ulama [learned Islamic Scholar] to engage the violent ulama. Then the war will be managed. But, in the meantime, we need to make sure their war is not our war. We haven't been attacked any more than Islam has been attacked. If you detain Islamic leaders, you need to deradicalize them. Separate them from the population, set the conditions, and then engage. We have to protect our own citizens and economy, no doubt about that. We have to. And we will, but, I don't know if that means ignoring Gitmo and Iraq and Afghanistan ... ignoring deradicalization issues. What I am opposed to is just detaining without engaging in the battlefield of the mind. Everyone can change in detention. But, needs have to be addressed. Without a deradicalization rehabilitation program, individuals become more radical themselves and are effectively creating more enemies. Deradicalization is the *only* way I know that works. Detain—but *not* without deradicalization. It is essential.

References

AFP. (2003, April 1). Ansar al-Islam prepares for suicide attacks. Retrieved from http://www.freerepublic.com/tag/alshafei/index

Agence France-Press. (2008, January 7). Main Sunni group vows no deal with the U.S. Retrieved from http://www.military.com/NewsConten t/0%2C13319%2C159483%2C00.html

Alexander, M. (2008). How to break a terrorist. New York: Simon and Schuster.

Alexander, M. (2009, November 30). I'm still tortured by what I saw in Iraq. *The Washington Post*. Retrieved from http://www.washington-post.com/wp-dyn/content/article/2008/11/28/AR2008112802242. html

American Forces Press Service. (2006, May 8). Terrorist chemical expert killed: Firefighters find explosives. Retrieved from http://www. defense.gov/news/newsarticle.aspx?id=15837

Ashour, O. (2010). The de-radicalization of Jihadists: Transforming armed Islamist movements. London: Routledge.

Associated Press, The. (2006, February 16). Jordan sentences Zarqawi, in absentia, to death in chemical plot. *The New York Times*. Retrieved from http://www.nytimes.com/2006/02/16/international/ middleeast/16amman.html?_r=2&oref=slogin

Associated Press, The. (2009, February 17). Yemen captures al Qaeda commander, a former Guantanamo detainee. *Fox News*. Retrieved from http://www.foxnews.com

Baier, B. (2005, August 10). Terror tape shows attack prepara-tions. *Fox News*. Retrieved from http://www.foxnews.com/ story/0,2933,163633,00.html

Bairdain, E. F. & Bairdain, E. M. (1971). *The final report Psychological Operations Studies–Vietnam*. Pretoria, South Africa: Human Sciences Research Inc.

Barnett, T. P. M. (2008, April). The man between war and peace. *Esquire Magazine*. Retrieved from http://www.esquire.com/features/fox-fallon

BBC News. (2002, August 19). Al Qaeda archive uncovered. Retrieved from http://news.bbc.co.uk

BBC News. (2002, October 28). US diplomat shot dead in Jordan. Retrieved from http://www.bbc.co.uk/

BBC News. (2003). Norway to expel Mullah Krekar. Retrieved from http://www.bbc.co.uk/

BBC News. (2006, June 12). Al Qaeda in Iraq names new head. Retrieved from http://www.bbc.co.uk/

BBC News. (2006, August 15). Guide: Armed groups in Iraq. Retrieved from http://news.bbc.co.uk/2/hi/middle_east/4268904.stm

BBC News. (2006, September 18). Iraq chiefs vow to fight al-Qaeda. Retrieved from http://www.bbc.co.uk/

BBC News. (2008, September 11). No victory in Iraq, says Petraeus. Retrieved from http://news.bbc.co.uk/2/hi/middle_east/7610405.stm

Benjamin, M. (2006, February 16). Salon exclusive: The Abu Ghraib files. Retrieved from http://www.salon.com

Blaydes, L. & Rubin, Lawrence. (2008). Ideological reorientation and counterterrorism: Confronting militant Islam in Egypt. *Terrorism and Political Violence, 20*(4), 461–479.

Borum, R. (2006, December). Radicalization in America: What we are (slowly) learning. Radicalization: An overview and annotated bibliography of open-source literature. Arlington, VA: Homeland Security Institute.

Bradford, L. (2009, May 28). Detainees hone agricultural, art skills. Retrieved from http://www.usfiraq.com/?option=com_content&task=view&id=26752&Itemid=225

Brisard, J.-C. & Martinez, D. (2005). *Zarqawi, The new face of Al-Qaeda.* New York: Other Press.

Bruce, J. (1995, April 1). Arab veterans of the Afghan war. *Jane's Intelligence Review, 7*(4), 175.

CBC/*Insight News TV.* (2008). *From Jihad to rehab* [video]. Available from http://www.pbs.org

CBS News. (2008, October 6). Kurdistan brigades pledges allegiance to Al Qaeda-led group. Retrieved from http://www.cbsnews.com/blogs/2008/10/06/monitor/entry4504531.shtml

Center on Global Counterterrorism Cooperation. (2008, December 4). Project on U.S. global engagement, radicalization/de-radicalization: Lessons for the next U.S. president. Rabat, Morocco.

Central Intelligence Agency (CIA). (2004, July 7). Report on the U.S. intelligence community's prewar intelligence assessments on Iraq. Retrieved from http://www.globalsecurity.org/intell/library/congress/2004_rpt/iraq-wmd-intell_toc.htm

Chiarelli, P. W. & Michaelis, P. R. (2006). Winning the peace: The requirement for full-spectrum operations. *Military Review 3*, July/August.

Chivers, C. J. (2003, April 27). Instruction and methods from Al Qaeda took root in North Iraq. *New York Times.* Retrieved from http://www.nytimes.com

Choike, A. (2006, June 16). MPs get new detainee training center. Retrieved from http://www.military.com/features/0,15240,101516,00.html?ESRC=armynews.RSS

Church, A. T. (2005). Executive summary (U). Retrieved from http://www.defenselink.mil/news/Mar2005/d20050310exe.pdf

CNN News. (2005, March 26). Escape tunnel found at Iraqi prison. Retrieved from http://edition.cnn.com/2005/WORLD/meast/03/25/iraq.tunnel/

CNN Politics (2008, April 23). Petraeus picked to lead central command. Retrieved from http://edition.cnn.com/2008/POLITICS/04/23/petraeus/index.html

Cody, E. (2004). Iraqis put contempt for troops on display. *The Washington Post*, June 12.

Curveball, B. D. (2007). *Spies, lies, and the man behind them: The real reason America went to war in Iraq.* London: Ebury Press.

Cuthbertson, I. M. (2004). Prisons and the education of terrorists. *World Policy Journal*, 15.

Danner, M. (2009). Abu Ghraib: The hidden story. *The New York Times Book Review.* Retrieved from http://www.nybooks.com/articles/17430

Daragahi, B. (2003, February 8). Islamic militants show press the Camp Powell called poison site. Associated Press. Retrieved from http://www.ap.org/

Department of Defense. (2006, September 5). Directive 2310.01E, The Department of Defense Detainee Program. *The Washington Post.* Retrieved from http://www.washingtonpost.com/wpsrv/politics/documents/cheney/dod_directive_2310_01E.pdf

Department of the Army. (1997). AR 190-8 Enemy prisoners of war, retained personnel, civilian internees and other detainees. Retrieved from http://www.army.mil/usapa/epubs/pdf/r190_8.pdf

Department of the Army. (2001). FM 3-19.40 Military police internment/resettlement operations. Retrieved from http://www.uaff.info/fm3_19_40.pdf

Department of the Army and Marine Corps Combat Development Command. (2006). Field Manual 3-24: Counterinsurgency. *Marine Corps Warfighting Publication No. 3-33.5.* Washington, D.C.: Government Printing Office.

Durham, N. (2008, January 14). Can therapy 'cure' terrorism? *CBC News.* Retrieved from http://www.cbc.ca

Fainaru, S. & Shadid, A. (2005). In Iraq jail, resistance goes underground. *The Washington Post.* Retrieved fromhttp://www.washingtonpost.com/wp-dyn/content/article/2005/08/23/AR2005082301525.html

Fay, G. R. & Jones, A. (2004, August). AR 15-6 Investigation of the Abu Ghraib detention facility and 205th military intelligence brigade. Retrieved from http://www.defenselink.mil/news/Aug2004/d20040825fay.pdf

Fink, N. C. & Hearne, E. B. (2008, October). *Beyond terrorism: Deradicalization and disengagement from violent extremism.* Washington, D.C.: International Peace Institute.

Finn, P., Warrick, J., & Tate, J. (2009, August 25). CIA report calls oversight of early interrogations poor. *The Washington Post.* Retrieved from http://www.washingtonpost.com/wp-dyn/content/article/2009/08/24/AR2009082402220.html

Giordono, J. (2007, October 31) Prison camp in Iraq once listed to close now sees major upgrades. *Stars and Stripes.* Retrieved from http://www.stripes.com

Global Security. (2006, March) Umm Qasr. Retrieved from http://www.globalsecurity.org/military/world/iraq/umm-qasr.htm

Gregory, K. (2008, November 5). Ansar al-Islam (Iraq, Islamists/Kurdish separatists), Ansar al-Sunnah. Council on Foreign Relations. Retrieved from http://www.cfr.org

Gulf Times. (2006, June 18). Identity of Zarqawi's successor still a riddle. Retrieved from http://www.gulf-times.com

Gunaratna, R. (2003, February 19). Iraq and Al Qaeda: No evidence of alliance. *International Herald Tribune.* Retrieved from www.iht.com/

Gunaratna, R. (2009, October). [I] The battlefield of the mind: Rehabilitating Muslim terrorists. UNISCI Discussion Papers--Madrid, Spain. Retrieved from www.ucm.es.

Halaby, J. (2004, January 20). Jordanian military prosecutor seeks death penalty for 11 terror suspects. The Associated Press. Retrieved from http://www.ap.org/

Hamm, M. S. (2009). Prison Islam in the age of sacred terror. *British Journal of Criminology, 49, 667–685.*

Hedges, C. (1996). Baghdad's move puts the future of Kurdish safe haven in doubt, *The New York Times*, September 1.

Hisham, I. (1994). *Al-Sirah Al-Nabawiyyah li Ibn Hisham [The Life History of the Prophet by Ibn Hisham].* Beirut: Dar Ihya' Al-Turath Al-Arabiyy.

Homeland Security Institute. (2006, December). *Radicalization: An overview and annotated bibliography of open-source literature.* Arlington, VA.

Horgan, J. (2009). *Walking away from terrorism: Accounts of disengagement from radical and extremist movements.* New York: Routledge, pp. 152–153.

Horgan, J. & Braddock, K. (2010). Rehabilitating the terrorists?: Challenges in assessing the effectiveness of de-radicalization programs. *Terrorism and Political Violence*, 22(2), 267–291.

Human Rights Watch. (2009, May 11). Libya/U.S. investigate death of former CIA prisoner. Retrieved from http://www.hrw.org

International Committee of the Red Cross. (2004, February). *Report of the International Committee of the Red Cross (ICRC) on the treatment by the coalition forces of prisoners of war and other protected persons by the Geneva Conventions in Iraq during arrest, internment and interrogation.* Retrieved from http://cryptome.org/icrc-report.htm

International Crisis Group. (2003, February 7). Radical Islam in Iraqi Kurdistan: The mouse that roared? Middle East Briefing No 4. Retrieved from http://www.crisisgroup.org

Jehl, D. (2005, November 6). Report warned Bush team about intelligence doubts. *The New York Times*. Retrieved from http://www.nytimes.com

Jenkins, B. M. (2006). Unconquerable Nation: Knowing Our Enemy, Strengthening Ourselves. California: RAND Corporation.

Jihadism and Terrorism Threat Monitor, The. (2006, October 12). Jihad groups in Iraq take an oath of allegiance. Retrieved from http://www.memrijttm.org/

Kagan, F. W. & Kagan, K. (2008, March 10). The Patton of counter-insurgency. *The Weekly Standard*, 13(25).

Katzman, K. (2000, June 27). CRS report for Congress: Iraq's opposition movements. Retrieved from http://www.au.af.mil/au/awc/awcgate/crs/98-179.pdf

Kavkaz Center. (2006, October 16). Islamic State of Iraq has been proclaimed. Retrieved from http://www.kavkazcenter.com/eng/content/2006/10/16/5985.shtml

Kazimi, N. (2006, November 20). Al-Muhajir's evil presence. *The New York Sun*. Retrieved from http://www.nysun.com/opinion/al-muhajirs-evil-presence/43815/

Kepel, G. (1985). *Muslim extremism in Egypt: The prophet and the pharaoh*. (J. Rothschild, Trans.) Berkeley: University of California Press.

Koladish, L. & Briere, K. (2010, January 2). New command marks milestone in Iraq. Retrieved from http://www.army.mil/-news/2010/01/02/32437-new-command-marks-milestone-in-iraq/

Lanchin, M. & Mahmoud, M. (2008, February 4). Iraq signs up to Awakening movement. *BBC News*. Retrieved from http://news.bbc.co.uk/2/hi/middle_east/7226974.stm

Lasso, A. (2009). Building and deploying biometrically enabled prison management systems. National Association for Justice Information Systems (NAJIS) Conference, Nashville, TN.

Levin, C. (2005, November 6). [Senator] Levin says newly declassified information indicates Bush administration's use of pre-war intelligence was misleading. Retrieved from http://levin.senate.gov

Linzer, D. & White, J. (2007, March 16). Two senators secretly flew to Cuba for alleged 9/11 mastermind's hearing. *The Washington Post*. Retrieved from http://www.washingtonpost.com/wp-dyn/content/article/2007/03/15/AR2007031500865.html

Mayer, J. (2005, February 14). Outsourcing torture. *The New Yorker*. Retrieved from http://www.newyorker.com

Mazzetti, M. & Cloud, D. (2007, April 27). CIA held [al-]Qaeda leader in secret jail for months. *The New York Times*. Retrieved from www.nytimes.com

McElroy, D. (2003, January 12). Chemical war threat by Iraq's Taliban. *U.K. Telegraph*. Retrieved from http://www.telegraph.co.uk

McGregor, A. (2005, May 5). Ricin fever: Abu Musab al-Zarqawi in the Pankisi Gorge. *Terrorism Monitor, 2*(24). Retrieved from http://www.jamestown.org

McKean, L. & Ransford, C. (2004). Current strategies for reducing recidivism. Retrieved from http://www.Impactresearch.org/documents/recidivismfullreport.pdf

Michaels, J. (2004). Tour provides glimpse of Abu Ghraib. *USA Today*. Retrieved from http://www.usatoday.com/news/world/iraq/2004-05-06-prison-tour_x.htm

Middle East Media Research Institute (MEMRI). (2006, October 6). Sunni Al-Bubaz tribe joins Shura Council of Jihad fighters in Iraq. Retrieved from http://www.memri.org/report/en/0/0/0/0/0/0/1896.htm

Miniter, B. (2004, June 1). The Fallujah brigade. How the marines are pacifying an Iraqi hot spot. *Wall Street Journal*. Retrieved from http://www.opinionjournal.com/columnists/bminiter/?id=110005152

Morgan, D. (2009). Pentagon: 61 ex-Guantanamo inmates return to terrorism. Reuters, January 13.

Moss, M. & Medkhennet, S. (2007). Jailed 2 years, Iraqi tells of abuse by Americans, *International Herald Times*, February 18.

Muir, J. (2002, July 24). 'Al-Qaeda' influence grows in Iraq. *BBC News*. Retrieved from http://news.bbc.co.uk

Murphy, B. (2007, February 24). Blast may hint at growing Sunni conflict. *The Washington Post*. Retrieved from http://www.washingtonpost.com/wp-dyn/content/article/2007/02/24/AR2007022401259.html

Nefa Foundation. (2007, September 14). Audio statement from Abu Omar al-Baghdadi. Retrieved from http://nefafoundation.org/miscellaneous/FeaturedDocs/nefabaghdadi0907.pdf

Nefa Foundation. (2007, October 27–November 1). Islamic Army of Iraq(IAI) selected communiqués. Retrieved from http://www1.nefafoundation.org/miscellaneous/iaidigest1107-1.pdf

Nefa Foundation. (2008, January 4). An interview with Hamas in Iraq. Retrieved from http://www1.nefafoundation.org/miscellaneous/FeaturedDocs/nefahamasiraq0308.pdf

Nefa Foundation. (2008, April 15). Communiqué from "Army of al-Mustafa." Retrieved from http://www.nefafoundation.org/miscellaneous/mustafaarmy0408.pdf

NPR News. (2008, March 18). General Petraeus defines victory in Iraq. Retrieved from http://www.npr.org/templates/story/story.php?storyId=88482985

Oxford English Dictionary. (2002). New York: Oxford University Press, p. 703.

Perry, M. (2008, January 23). US military breaks ranks, Part 1: A salvo at the White House. *Asia Times.* Retrieved from http://www.atimes.com/atimes/Middle_East/JA23Ak02.html

Perry, C. (2009). Ex-inmate recalls days of abuse at Abu Ghraib. *CNN World.* Retrieved from http://edition.cnn.com/2009/WORLD/meast/05/21/iraq.abu.ghraib.inmate

Powell, C. (2003, February 6). Transcript of Powell's U.N. presentation. United Nations News Centre. Retrieved from http://www.un.org.

Priest, D. (2009). Bush's 'war' on terror comes to a sudden end. *The Washington Post,* January 23, A01.

Ram, S. (2003). The enemy of my enemy: The odd link between Ansar al Islam, Iraq and Iran– commentary. The Canadian Center of Strategic Studies. Retrieved from http://www.ciss.ca

Reuters. (2006, November 26). Iraq tribes says it kills dozens of Qaeda fighters. Retrieved from http://www.alertnet.org/thenews/newsdesk/PAR630329.htm

Ricks, T. E. (2009). *The Gamble.* New York: Penguin Press, HC.

Ridolfo, K. (2006, September 29). Iraq: New security initiatives aim to lessen violence. *Radio Free Europe Radio Liberty.* Retrieved from http://www.rferl.org

Ridolfo, K. (2007, May 1). Iraq: Al-Qaeda in Iraq leader struggles with native insurgents. Radio Free Europe Radio Liberty. Retrieved from http://www.rferl.org

Roberts, J. (2006, August 28). Abu Ghraib prison totally empty. *CBS News.* Retrieved from http://www.cbsnews.com/stories/2006/08/28/iraq/main1940091.shtml

Robertson, N. & Boettcher, M. (2002, August 23) Tapes give evidence of Al Qaeda's reach. Retrieved from http://archives.cnn.com/2002/US/08/22/terror.tape.main/index.html

Rubin, A. J. & Cave, D. (2007, December 23). In a force for Iraq calm, seeds of conflict. *The New York Times* Retrieved from http:www.nytimes.com

Rubin, E. (2003, April 3). The battle for Beyara, A year of training for 12 hours of fighting in northern Iraq. Retrieved from http://www.slate.com/id/2081117/

Rumsfeld, D. (2002, January 19). Memorandum for chairman of the Joint Chiefs of Staff. Subject: Status of Taliban and Al Qaeda. Washington, D.C.: Government Printing Office, p. 1.

Sa-ardsorn, P. (2008, August 24). Death-row inmates take up painting to get peace of mind. *The Nation.* Retrieved from http://www.nation-multimedia.com

Saddam a Caring Man–Nurse (2007, January 1). *News24.* Retrieved from http://www.news24.com/Content/World/Archives/IraqiDossier/1072/4b3706153e864a0da1996475f8c7b151/01-01-2007-08-49/Saddam_a_caring_man_-_nurse

Sauret, M. (2008, September 25). Iraq detainees return to society armed with skills, education. Retrieved from http://www.defense.gov/news/newsarticle.aspx?id=51303

Scarborough, R. (2002). U.S. tracked top Al Qaeda planner's visit to Baghdad. *The Washington Times,* October 4.

Schanzer, J. (2004, Winter). Ansar al-Islam: Back in Iraq. *Middle East Quarterly, XI*(1). Retrieved from http://www.meforum.org

Schlesinger, J. R., Brown, H., Fowler, T. K., Homer, C. A., & Blackwell, J. A. Jr. (2004, August). Final report of the independent panel to review DoD detention operations. Retrieved from http://www.defenselink.mil/news/Aug2004/d20040824finalreport.pdf

Scrimshaw, S. (2010, February 25). Thailand: Art for all. *Times Union.* Retrieved from http://blog.timesunion.com/scrimshaw/thailand-art-for-all/359/

Security Service of Kurdistan. (2009). Links between Al-Qaeda and Kurdish Groups. Paper presented at the meeting of the International Centre on Political Violence and Terrorism Research, Singapore, February 19.

Senate Armed Services Committee. (2004, May 19). Abizaid, Sanchez, Miller, Warren on Iraq prisoner abuse (transcript). Retrieved from http://www.scvhistory.com/scvhistory/signal/iraq/sasc051904.htm

Shanker, T. & Farrell, S. (2008, September 15). Gates praises Petraeus on eve of duty transfer. *The New York Times.* Retrieved from http://www.nytimes.com/2008/09/16/world/middleeast/16gates.html?_r=1

Shrader, K. (2007, February 28). Spy chief pushes for action in Pakistan. *The Washington Post.* Retrieved from http://www.washingtonpost.com/wp-dyn/content/article/2007/02/28/AR2007022800270.html

Skelton, R. (2003, March 24). Need for that one final shot was fatal. *The Sydney Morning Herald* Retrieved from http://www.smh.com.au/articles/2003/03/23/1048354478285.html

Soza, S. (2010, February 8). Art of war: Detainee murals at Theatre Internment Facility paint brighter future. Retrieved from http://www.army.mil

Spanner, J. (2008, October 5). David H. Petraeus. *The New York Times*. Retrieved from http://topics.nytimes.com/top/reference/timestopics/people/p/david_h_petraeus/index.html?inline=nyt-per

Stanley, T. (2005). Definition: Kufr-Kaffir-Takfir-Takfiri. Retrieved from http://www.pwhce.org/takfiri.html

Taguba, A. (2004) Article 15-6 Investigation of the 800th Military Police Brigade. Retrieved from http://www.dod.mil/pubs/foi/detainees/taguba/TAGUBA_REPORT_CERTIFICATIONS.pdf

Task Force 134. (2006, March 28). Detainee from Camp Bucca dies. Retrieved from the http://www.mnf-iraq.com/index.php?option=com_content&task=view&id=751&Itemid=21

Thompson, S. (2006, August 18). New facility to help MPs learn detainee handling. Retrieved from http://www.tradoc.army.mil/pao/TNSarchives/August%2006/081806-4.htm

Tom. (2009, February 10). Tom Ricks on the gamble in Iraq [Web log post]. Retrieved from http://www.omnivoracious.com/2009/02/tom-ricks-on-the-gamble-in-iraq.html

Turner, K. (2005, October 26). DIALetter.102605 from Central Intelligence Agency. Retrieved from http://levin.senate.gov/newsroom/supporting/2005/DIAletter.102605.pdf

USA Today. (2004, November 5). The tragic death of Nick Berg. Retrieved from http://www.usatoday.com/news/gallery/2004/nick-berg/flash.htm

United States of America v. Abdul Zahir [a.k.a. Abdul Bari]. (2006, January 20). Retrieved from http://www.defense.gov/news/Jan2006/d20060120zahir.pdf

U.S. Department of Defense. (2007, April 27). Defense Department takes custody of a high-value detainee. No.494-07. Retrieved from http://www.defense.gov

Walker, S. (2006). *Sense and non-sense: About crime and drugs*. Belmont, California: Thompson Higher Education.

Walsh, J. (2006, March 14). The Abu Ghraib files–Introduction. Retrieved from http://www.salon.com

Ware, M. (2003, February 26). Kurdistan: Death in the afternoon. *Time*. Retrieved from http://www.time.com

Washington Times, The. (2007, February 17). Al Qaeda's outrages swing Sunnis to U.S. Retrieved from http://www.washingtontimes.com

White House, The. (2006). The national security strategy. Retrieved from http://georgewbush-whitehouse.archives.gov/nsc/nss/2006/

Wordsworth Concise English Dictionary, The. (1993). London: Wordsworth Editions Limited, p. 838.

Worth, R. F. (2009). Freed by the U.S., Saudi becomes al Qaeda chief. *The New York Times*, , January 23.

Wypijewski, J. (2008, March/April). The final act of Abu Ghraib. Retrieved from   http://www.motherjones.com/politics/2008/03/final-act-abu-ghraib

Zagorin, A. (2007, August 29). The Abu Ghraib cases: Not yet over. *Time*. Retrieved from http://www.time.com

Zamelis, C. (2006). Radical networks in Middle East prisons. *Terrorism Monitor, 4*, p. 7.

Zernike, K. (2004, May 22) Handful of soldiers spoke out, as many kept quiet on abuse. *The New York Times*. Retrieved from http://209.157.64.200/focus/f-news/1140191/posts

Appendix

PHOTOGRAPHS FROM IRAQ

FIGURE A.1   Shiite detainees celebrate a holiday: Camp Bucca, Iraq, 2008. (Photo courtesy of U.S. Department of Defense.)

FIGURE A.2 Shiite detainees celebrate a holiday by creating art and hanging it on their caravan: Camp Bucca, Iraq, 2008. (Photo courtesy of U.S. Department of Defense.)

FIGURE A.3 Sandstorm: Camp Victory, Iraq. (Photo by Sonia Herrera.)

FIGURE A.4 Sandstorm: Camp Bucca, Iraq. (Photo by Sgt. Matthew Sugars.)

FIGURE A.5 The most common way to travel to and from Camp Bucca is by Blackhawk helicopter: Camp Bucca, Iraq, 2008. (Photo by Feras Khatib.)

FIGURE A.6   Soldiers use their creativity in a variety of ways. This illustrates a "Christmas" chair made out of unusable weapons in preparation for transport to the base dining facility where a soldier dressed up like Santa Claus will sit in it as he wishes everyone a Merry Christmas. (Photo by Sonia Herrera.)

FIGURE A.7 A two-star Iraqi correctional officer details how he plans to continue the rehabilitation programs after the U.S. forces withdraw: Camp Cropper, Iraq, 2010. (Photo by Ami Angell.)

FIGURE A.8   The most popular way to fly in and out of Baghdad is in a C-130 airplane: Baghdad, Iraq, 2009. (Photo by Ami Angell.)

FIGURE A.9   Unused, old Iraqi tanks gather dust on Camp Taji, Iraq, 2010. (Photo by Ami Angell.)

FIGURE A.10 Aw Faw Palace, previously one of Saddam Hussein's palaces, but after 2003 used as office space for military operations and official ceremonies: Camp Victory, Iraq. (Photo courtesy of David L. Butler, Jr.)

FIGURE A.11 Inside Aw Faw Palace: Camp Victory, Iraq. (Photo by David L. Butler, Jr.)

FIGURE A.12 One of Saddam Hussein's thrones: inside Aw Faw Palace, Camp Victory, Iraq. (Photo courtesy of Jeffrey Folkertsma.)

FIGURE A.13 Nicknamed "the Flintstone Palace," a castle created by Saddam Hussein for his children and VIP's children, complete with elevators, swimming pools, BBQ areas, and play rooms: Camp Slayer, Iraq, 2009. (Photo by Sonia Herrera.)

FIGURE A.14   Dr. Rohan Gunaratna, Maj. Gen. David Quantock, Dr. Ami Angell: Camp Cropper, Iraq, 2010. (Photo courtesy of Maj. Gen. David Quantock.)

Index